Culture, Crisis and America's War on Terror

Since the infamous events of 9/11, the fear of terrorism and the determination to strike back against it has become a topic of enormous public debate. The 'war on terror' discourse has developed not only through American politics but via other channels including the media, the church, music, novels, films and television, and therefore permeates many aspects of American life. Stuart Croft suggests that the process of this production of knowledge has created a very particular form of common sense which shapes relationships, jokes and even forms of tattoos. Understanding how a social process of crisis can be mapped out and how that process creates assumptions allows policy-making in America's war on terror to be examined from new perspectives. Using international relations approaches together with insights from cultural studies, this book develops a dynamic model of crisis which seeks to understand the war on terror as a cultural phenomenon.

STUART CROFT is Professor of International Relations in the Department of Political Science and International Studies at the University of Birmingham. He is the author of *Security Studies Today* (with Terry Terriff, Lucy James and Patrick Morgan, 1999), *The Enlargement of Europe* (with John Redmond, G. Wyn Rees and Mark Webber, 1999) and *Strategies of Arms Control* (1996).

Culture, Crisis and America's War on Terror

STUART CROFT

CAMBRIDGE
UNIVERSITY PRESS

CAMBRIDGE UNIVERSITY PRESS

Cambridge, New York, Melbourne, Madrid, Cape Town, Singapore, São Paulo

Cambridge University Press
The Edinburgh Building, Cambridge CB2 2RU, UK

Published in the United States of America by Cambridge University Press, New York

www.cambridge.org
Information on this title: www.cambridge.org/9780521687331

First published 2006

Printed in the United Kingdom at the University Press, Cambridge

A catalogue record for this book is available from the British Library

ISBN-13 978-0-521-86799-3 hardback
ISBN-10 0-521-86799-1 hardback
ISBN-13 978-0-521-68733-1 paperback
ISBN-10 0-521-68733-0 paperback

Contents

Figures

Acknowledgements

For a number of years I have been trying to identify symbolic debates in the United States, to understand how the 'war on terror' had permeated so much of everyday life. I wanted to understand the impact of popular culture on America's international relations, and to theorise about the role of crises in generating new and powerful discourses. The result is this book. I travelled across America to conduct the research, covering over 5,000 miles by road, as well as flying to many locations, in fifteen different states, from the coasts to the Midwest. I should like to thank the countless number of 'ordinary' Americans who engaged so willingly in discussions, offering invaluable advice as to what I should look at and where, in novels, films, television programmes and on websites, from those in 'mainstream' book stores to people in evangelical churches. I also wanted to show how important the internet is in creating understandings in contemporary America, and so have spent a good deal of time finding web sources to footnote. I have benefited from discussions with, and been inspired by, a number of people in different disciplinary traditions working on the Economic and Social Research Council's *New Security Challenges* Programme, of which I am currently Director. A number of people have read drafts of the text. I am particularly grateful to Matt MacDonald, Paul Williams, Chris Browning, Anand Menon, Jo Van Every, Brian Rappert, Jane Usherwood, Richard Jackson, Theo Farrell, David Armstrong, Rita Taureck, Jack Holland and Wolf Roepke for their detailed comments and sometimes even encouragement, and to two anonymous reviewers for comments on parts of the text. I should also like to thank Terry Terriff for providing a variety of sources and suggestions while I have been working on this project.

Writing a book can become a rather obsessive activity, crowding out everyday and worthwhile activities. For Sam, it has meant less football, rugby and cricket over the past few years; and so it seems only right to dedicate this book to him.

Introduction

THE juxtaposition of 'terror' and 'culture' is provocative: after all, is terror not the antithesis of culture? Terror represents the brutal, the barbarian, the destructive, and culture is that which represents the highest achievements of humanity. Perhaps. Yet the meaning of terror is constructed; and culture influences opinion and attitudes powerfully at the popular level as well as through 'high' culture. The meaning of terror attacks, and what should be done about them, is produced and reproduced by political elites *and* by the producers of popular culture. Without understanding what has occurred in America at the level of popular culture, its meaning and impact, it is not possible to fully comprehend the American crisis discourse that is the 'war on terror'.

Discourses create and reflect identities, and thus they construct those who are our allies and those who are our enemies. When not in flux, they settle who 'we' are, and who 'they' are; what 'we' stand for, and what 'they' mean to 'us'. They construct the space for 'our' legitimate activity, and the space for the behaviour we will (and will not) tolerate from 'them'. At times 'we' and/or 'they' construct such hostility that violence results, and lives are lost. And both 'we' and 'they' may blame the other, and engage in absolution of responsibility. The creation and expansion of such constructions is mostly played out in and through a crisis, and it is crises that are the engines of radical discursive change. Crises often mark the origins of a particular discourse, and a discourse that emerges with credibility in a crisis – in a sense, that which gives the crisis meaning – will soon take on the hallowed status of 'common sense' amongst those concerned with the issues both raised and threatened by that specific crisis. These dynamics have been played out many times, and in many places, and at present they represent the roles being adopted both by the United States and its enemies in America's 'war on terror'. That 'war' is a social construction, as indeed is that which we call security, the very meaning of which varies according to context, place and time.

This book analyses the discourse that emerged from the impact of the terrorist attacks on the United States on 11 September 2001. America's 'response' to those attacks was not obvious, not 'natural', nor based on some objective standard of 'common sense'. Policy had to be built on a narrative that could be shared amongst those who felt threatened; and that had to be America's government and, importantly, American society as a whole. The construction of that narrative was an elite project: but that elite in contemporary America is not just government, it also exists in many other social institutions, in the media and in popular culture. In an age of immediate and mass communication, that narrative had to be constructed speedily, and it had to contain a logic that credibly responded to the threat now identified: there had to be an action plan that followed logically (and thus had credibility) from its own precepts. And to function, it had to be based on a particular foundational image, which was to be the memorialisation of the events of 11 September 2001. The shock of the crisis led to the construction of a new narrative, which was but one of many possible narratives, and one which led to new policy direction, which subsequently became institutionalised. As Richard Jackson put it, 'Within the confines of this rhetorically constructed reality, or discourse, the "war on terrorism" appears as a rational and reasonable response; more importantly, to many people it feels like the right thing to do.'[1] That new narrative, though, could not of course be completely new; it had its own past, or genealogy – it had to connect with pre-existing narratives in the United States. But it felt new, it seemed like the only solution to the new terrible problems that had to be faced.

Any new policy programme prescribed in and through this new discourse would inevitably be challenged over time. Policy programmes decay in the normal course of debate as issues and attitudes change over time; and new crises are constructed, ones that produce different discourses that take different directions. In short, there is a pattern of social responses to crisis here, and it is that process that will be examined and developed throughout this volume.

For many hundreds of years, discursive practices in England created a distinction between the accepted, 'native', population (the 'we') and

[1] Richard Jackson, *Writing the War on Terrorism* (Manchester: Manchester University Press, 2005), p. 2.

the Jewish, 'outsider', population (the 'they'). Jews were exploiters, moneylenders, parasites upon the indigenous population in the general construction, so perfectly displayed in the portrayal of the character of Shylock in Shakespeare's *The Merchant of Venice*. It was this discursive construction of 'we' and 'they' that set limits to the legitimate and acceptable activity of the Jewish population, and movements in these discursive practices created the policy programme of the expulsion of the Jews from England, enacted in the reign of Edward I, king of England (1272–1307). Shylock, the despised and ridiculed moneylender in *The Merchant of Venice*, sets a trap for Antonio, who represents all the 'we-ness' denied to Shylock, when he needs to borrow money. The trap is set when Shylock offers a horrible deal:

> If you repay me not on such a day,
> In such a place, such sum or sums as are
> Express'd in the condition, let the forfeit
> Be nominated for an equal pound
> Of your fair flesh, to be cut off and taken
> In what part of your body pleaseth me.[2]

The arrangement is readily accepted by Antonio, and the collision course – the emerging crisis – then becomes the core of the play.

Passions run high about *The Merchant of Venice*. When released as a film in 2004, cultural reaction in America was strong.[3] Forrest Hartman, for example, represented the views of many when he deplored 'such a blatantly anti-Semitic work', being very uncomfortable with 'the material, which I find despicable'.[4] He argued that the play's conclusion on ethnic relations 'seems a horrible position to perpetuate in our supposedly enlightened society. Particularly when we find our country engaged in what many enemies see as a religious conflict.'[5] That is, Hartman believed that *The Merchant of Venice* reproduced religious exclusion, the very antithesis of America's commitment in the 'war on terror'. The hostility to the film was such that the director, Michael Radford, felt

[2] William Shakespeare, *The Merchant of Venice*, act I, scene iii.

[3] *William Shakespeare's The Merchant of Venice* was released in 2004 by Sony, directed by Michael Radford (who also wrote the screenplay).

[4] Forrest Hartman, '"Merchant" peddles superb acting, racist themes', *Reno Gazette Journal*, 24 February 2005, at http://www.rgj.com/news/stories/html/2005/02/24/93105.php [last date of access to a website is in square brackets by month and year throughout the book: here 3/2005].

[5] Hartman, 'Merchant'.

it necessary to defend Shakespeare himself from the charge of being anti-Semitic.[6] And the contemporary resonance of the play is such that this is by no means unusual. No less a body than the Royal Shakespeare Company itself addresses the question of 'Shakespeare and race' on its website.[7] Was Shakespeare merely reporting the attitudes of the time, as Radford (and presumably the RSC) maintains? Or was he, in so doing, perpetuating those attitudes, reproducing them from one community to another, and from one generation to the next, the essence of Hartman's critique?

Hartman is clearly persuasive on the point that such cultural reproduction is powerful. Attitudes that are embedded into a variety of popular texts – today that would include novels, films, television and other cultural products – produce and reproduce those views of the world in their readership. Shakespeare's work is, today, the provenance of high culture. But it was not at the time it was written, when Shakespeare spoke to a wide swath of opinion, bridging high and popular culture. Which is why Shylock's most famous speech in the play is so important:

> If you prick us, do we not bleed?
> If you tickle us, do we not laugh?
> If you poison us, do we not die?
> And if you wrong us, shall we not revenge?
> If we are like you in the rest, we will resemble you in that.[8]

The excluded Jew, Shylock is saying, will learn from his treatment at the hands of the Christian; and if Christians right wrongs through revenge, so will the Jew. The behaviour of the majority ('we') would be reproduced by the socially excluded ('they'). So what was it that Shakespeare was reproducing: society's anti-Semitism, or a more tolerant view of inclusion, by illustrating the lessons that the majority teaches the minority? The ambiguity in *The Merchant of Venice* creates argument, but it is debate based on the notion that behaviour patterns can be reproduced through cultural power. Thus, the argument, as exemplified by the positions expressed by Hartman and Radford, is

[6] Michael Radford, 'Shakespeare and the Jews', *Movienet*, 2004, at http://www.movienet.com/wsmerchantofvenice.html [3/2005].
[7] 'Shakespeare and race', RSC Exhibitions, Royal Shakespeare Company, at http://www.rsc.org.uk/picturesandexhibitions/action/viewExhibition?exhibitionid=9&sectionid=3 [4/2005].
[8] *The Merchant of Venice*, act III, scene i.

about *what* is reproduced, rather than the principle of reproduction itself.

Much of the work published in the English language on security issues is developed from a rather different assumption to that uniting Hartman and Radford: that it is possible – and indeed desirable – to be able to identify *objective* threats. After all, security issues are often about the most important issues affecting a state: the continued existence of that state itself. A security crisis arises when there seems no alternative other than the use, or the threat of use, of military force to produce a resolution. And if there might be doubts about intentions, they have often been swept away by the use of devices such as 'worst-case analysis', in which 'they' are so threatening that 'we' simply have no choice other than to assume that 'they' will 'get us' if the opportunity arises. 'We' assume the worst, and plan on that basis.

What, though, if the 'objective' nature of a threat was only the last stage of a process that is much more social in its character? Security, then, would be a constructed good, one that varies across time and space. The emergence of a security crisis would have gone through various social phases, in which 'we' are identified and solidified, 'they' are identified and demonised, and when discourses are fixed, 'their' unreasonable demands upon 'us' are enumerated. The crisis emerges when these interests clash, by which time they have been constructed as 'objective' interests and, in the violence of war, have 'objective' outcomes.

A crisis is therefore itself constructed in and through social interaction. It is given meaning through social processes, through a decisive intervention which gives meaning to the situation and which also provides a route for future policy. That is, there are no objective ontological criteria that a crisis must fulfil to be a crisis: a crisis is one when it permeates discourse, and creates new understandings and, thereby, new policy programmes. Antonio faces a crisis that has real, objective power when he cannot pay his debt, for Shylock then demands the pound of flesh so lightly agreed to earlier. Both are playing social roles: the loyal, trustworthy Christian with whom 'we' are to identify, and the cruel, money-obsessed Jew, who represents 'them'. Those roles have not been constructed in isolation from one another; but instead they were mutually constituted. The groups have identified particular roles for their identities in the interaction of their collective society. So the crisis is a social one; and it is resolved by a decisive intervention, when Portia gives a new interpretation that leads to a new policy programme:

> This bond doth give thee here no jot of blood;
> The words expressly are 'a pound of flesh':
> Take then thy bond, take thou thy pound of flesh;
> But, in the cutting it, if thou dost shed
> One drop of Christian blood, thy lands and goods
> Are, by the laws of Venice, confiscate
> Unto the state of Venice.[9]

'We' have found a resolution to the crisis that frustrates 'them'. But there is more – Portia enunciates the new policy programme that flows from the decisive intervention. Shylock has threatened the life of a Venetian, and custom and law require that he should be punished by losing his wealth, unless of course he converts to being a Christian. And in so doing, 'we' triumph over 'them', because 'they' join with 'us'.

'Crisis' is an oft-used word to describe a large number of situations. Antonio's crisis became one for Shylock through the decisive intervention of Portia, who gave a new understanding to that crisis. This new interpretation, this new discourse, could only work because of pre-existing power balances constructed through the roles that the individuals were to play: Shylock was the outsider, despised by all insiders for being successful in the only legitimate space available to medieval European Jews. And outsiders are always subject to the power to create meaning held by the insiders, new meaning to substantiate the position of the powerful.

Crisis was at the origin of the American state, a sentiment ably expressed in a pamphlet published in 1776 by Thomas Paine, entitled *The American Crisis*.[10] In his State of the Union speech in 1811, President Madison ended 'I can not close this communication without expressing my deep sense of . . . crisis . . .' ahead of the war with Britain that was to see the White House burnt to the ground the following year.[11] Such international crises were to continue for America – the

[9] *Merchant of Venice*, act IV, scene i.

[10] Thomas Paine, *The American Crisis*, 23 December 1776, at http://odur.let.rug.nl/~usa/D/1776-1800/paine/AC/crisis01.htm [4/2005].

[11] President Madisons, 'State of the Union' speech, 5 November 1811, at http://edsitement.neh.gov/lesson_images/lesson572/MadisonStateUnion.pdf [4/2005].

world wars, the crises with the Soviet Union in the cold war. In October 1962, with Soviet missiles on the way to being deployed in Cuba, President Kennedy told the people that his 'Government feels obliged to report this new crisis to you in fullest detail.'[12] But crises were also 'domestic'. In the words of President Lincoln: 'In my opinion, it [pro-slavery agitation] will not cease until a crisis shall have been reached and passed.'[13] American crises were therefore 'domestic' as well as 'international' in their construction. The Great Depression was a crisis; so was the pressure raised by the civil rights movement in the 1960s. By the 1970s, crises could be moral as well as economic and social: President Carter spoke of America's moral and spiritual crisis.[14] And crisis is at the heart of America's contemporary 'culture wars'. For Wayne Baker, one view of the 'crisis of values is the division of society into opposed groups with irreconcilable moral differences. This view is expressed in the popular view that America is engaged in a "culture war" between two opposed moral camps with incompatible views of the American way of life.'[15] Certainly, as will be seen later in this volume, America's 'culture wars' motivate very differing political and cultural judgements. The 'culture wars' have continued since radical groups launched attacks on conservative ways of living in the 1960s; conservative backlashes have been symbolised by the electoral victories of Richard Nixon and Ronald Reagan.[16] In the wake of popular protest against the Iraq War, Bevin Alexander published a popular book of conservative response entitled *How America Got It Right: The US March to Military and Political Supremacy*.[17] Cultural behaviour patterns have

[12] President Kennedy, 'The Cuban Missile Crisis speech', 22 October 1962, at http://www.famousquotes.me.uk/speeches/John_F_Kennedy/2.htm [4/2005].

[13] Abraham Lincoln at Springfield, 17 June 1858, http://www.bartleby.com/251/1001.html [4/2005].

[14] President Carter, 'Energy and the national goals – a crisis of confidence', 15 July 1979, at http://www.americanrhetoric.com/speeches/jimmycartercrisisofconfidence.htm [7/2005].

[15] Wayne Baker, *America's Crisis of Values: Reality and Perception* (Princeton University Press, 2004), pp. 17–63. Baker argues that despite the 'culture wars', there are commonalities: 78% of Americans pray every day, and 96% are 'proud to be American'.

[16] Douglas Kellner, *Media Culture: Cultural Studies, Identity and Politics Between the Modern and the Postmodern* (London: Routledge, 1995), especially pp. 18–19.

[17] Bevin Alexander, *How America Got It Right: The US March to Military and Political Supremacy* (New York: Dutton, 2005).

been politicised by this ongoing cultural struggle between liberal and conservative perspectives, and a variety of issues are thereby politicised. Al Franken's contribution from the liberal perspective was a top-selling book entitled *Lies and the Lying Liars Who Tell Them: A Fair and Balanced Look at the Right.*[18] Bernard Goldberg's high selling book was called *100 People Who Are Screwing Up America* (from the conservative perspective): number 2 in the list was Arthur Salzberger, the publisher of the *New York Times*; unsurprisingly, Michael Moore achieved the number 1 position.[19] Neither Franken nor Goldberg sought to be balanced or fair: neither sought to convince others. As Richard Brookhiser put it in the *New York Times*, the contributions of Franken and Goldberg 'are part of the puppet theater of modern political discourse'.[20]

Crisis has thus shaped who 'we' and 'they' are between Americans and others, and between Americans themselves, and thus 'crisis' plays a constitutive role in American society. The 'war on terror' that has emerged in the United States since the decisive intervention that gave meaning to the events of 9/11 thus has created dividing lines – 'we' and 'they' – that cut across both international and domestic lines. Crises have occurred throughout American history. Each time they have been constructed, and have been given contemporary meaning through the lens of the decisive intervention that came to shape each crisis. A genealogy of any particular crisis would identify alternative understandings of the crisis, and with them alternative policy programmes, but alternatives that have been silenced by the noise of the successful interpretation.[21] Producers of particular decisive interventions will inevitably include political elites, and thus this competition between understandings of a situation is intensely political. But it is not enough to consider political elites alone. Those responsible for the production of a decisive intervention, one capable of shaping a policy programme following the creation of a shared understanding of a particular crisis,

18 Al Franken, *Lies and the Lying Liars Who Tell Them: A Fair and Balanced Look at the Right* (New York: Dutton, 2003).

19 Bernard Goldberg, *100 People Who Are Screwing Up America* (New York: HarperCollins, 2005). Goldberg put Franken at number 37.

20 Richard Brookhiser, '100 people who are screwing up America: who is number one?', *New York Times*, 28 August 2005.

21 In a different context, I have tried to illustrate this by looking at the construction of a new European security framework in the early 1990s: 'The return of architectural debate', *European Security*, 9:3 (Autumn 2000).

have to include the creators of popular culture in a society such as that of contemporary America.

It is one thing to suggest that popular culture reproduces discourse, even that it amplifies it, and quite another that it (co-)produces it. Reproduction takes place in a variety of forms – television, film, media, organised religion – those that transmit particular understanding. The comprehension of 'we' and 'they', and the characteristics that define each, have been played out in many contemporary art forms, and may well spread such understandings more widely and more deeply than official political statements. That which is thought about an issue may affect more people if reproduced in an episode of a popular television programme than in a speech of the President. Which is, of course, why political advisors monitor television and other aspects of contemporary culture with such care.

But what of the claim that popular culture *(co-)produces* discourse? This is to say, in effect, that the political elite and some producers of popular culture are mutually constructed in the contemporary United States. One cannot articulate a political project without impact upon popular culture; popular culture is not comprehensible without considering the political. Not all political discourse is apparent in popular culture (consider, for example, the nuances of taxation policy); not all elements of popular culture are political in a sense understood by the political elite. But the articulation of a particular understanding of crisis, the formation of discourse, occurs both at the level of the political elite and at that of popular culture. Their mutual constitution means that the way in which the crisis of 9/11 came to be understood was produced by both the Bush administration *and* many cultural producers in the United States.

In order to understand this phenomenon – political and cultural dimensions of the production and reproduction of the 'war on terror' discourse in the United States – this volume will seek out the political in the cultural. And manifestations are found in interesting places: humour; tattoos; religion. As the first chapter examines, each impacts upon the policy programme that is the 'war on terror'. By looking broadly for the political, this book seeks to develop an understanding of contemporary security studies through an understanding of the 'war on terror' as discourse. Although the events of 11 September 2001 in the United States were 'real' – real people died, real buildings were destroyed – 'reality' is still constructed in particular ways. Those events happened; but what we take from those events depends upon a process of social interaction. Chapter 2 seeks to situate 9/11 in the context of work on crises. On this view, crises are socially constructed, and competing discourses in a crisis are resolved by the success of one, the 'decisive intervention', which names and creates agreed meaning for the crisis event over the claims of other constructions. That 'decisive intervention' creates an understanding, a meta-narrative, one which 'explains' the event to general satisfaction, and then constructs and reconstructs a variety of practices. The meta-narrative orders experiences and thought according to claims of a universal truth. Chapter 2 therefore establishes the concept of the social construction of crises, and postulates a process. Chapter 3 examines how that meta-narrative – the 'war on terror' – became widely spread throughout the United States. 9/11 constituted an *American* sense of emergency, and a very particular American sense of emergency at that. The decisive intervention, articulated in and through the Bush administration, was able to build on a particular narrative of 9/11, although that was only one of a number of possible narratives. There was, in short, nothing 'inevitable', nothing 'objective' about America's 'response' to 9/11. It all had to be constructed intersubjectively.

One of the central tools was a process of memorialisation of the events of 11 September 2001. In books, on television, in novels, and in many other particular acts, it became social common sense that 9/11 had to be remembered and commemorated. But, of course, embedded within this memorialisation was a particular understanding of what September 11th meant, and that understanding was reproduced further not simply by political decree from the President – although the statements of senior politicians are important – but was produced and reproduced through popular culture, including pop music, blockbuster films and the popular novel. In such ways, a foundational myth was created about America and American-ness, and about friendly others and enemy peoples and ideas, all through meanings attributed to the 'reality' of 9/11.

Political leaders are empowered in times of insecurity. And thus, as a source for understanding the nature of the narrative, to comprehend the essence of the discourse, the statements of the political leadership are vitally important. However, those declarations and actions are insufficient for a full understanding, and so the study of international relations can benefit by engaging with cultural studies. As a distinctive field of academic enquiry, cultural studies was established to oppose the traditional notion that cultural products and objects could be studied objectively, as with the treatment of canonical texts in music and literature (such as, of course, *The Merchant of Venice*). Instead, cultural studies suggests that cultural products cannot be studied separately from the social context of their production and their consumption, and also that cultural production and reproduction are widespread, not simply contained within the (socially defined) parameters of high culture. Thus, legitimate subjects for study include the impact of global market pressures in the creation of chewing gum and its impact on local lives; the spread of the taste for cappuccino, and its role in the construction and reconstruction of identities, as well as the social impact of the coffee industry more generally; and the implications of developments in children's fashion for the construction of identities.[22]

Such matters are generally seen to be outside the purview of political science and international relations. But they should not be. Americans choose from more than one hundred designs for tattoos that commemorate 9/11. A regular search of products for sale on eBay demonstrates the enduring popularity of the memorialisation of 9/11. Children are taught in books the meaning of 9/11; that is, they are taught to understand lessons in particular ways. Novels are written that are based on and through that construction of 9/11. Television programmes are made which do the same. Then there are the 9/11 films. There is also the impact of 9/11 on religious understandings of the world in much of the American Midwest. All of this is political, and has political implications, not least on a government, and on political parties, that seek popular support through elections that are themselves constructed by social understandings of threat, opportunity and common sense.

This book therefore draws on cultural studies in the sense that it

[22] Examples from Michael Redclift, who 'seeks to understand the processes through which livelihoods dependent on the extraction of a primary product . . . were forced to accommodate to major shifts in the world consumer market', http://www.consume.bbk.ac.uk/research/redclift_full.html; Jonathan Morris, who examines 'the nature of local and global cultures of consumption, and the transfers between them, such as the value of "nationality" in brand equity; the role of food and drink in the formation of social identities amongst diaspora communities', http://www.consume.bbk.ac.uk/research/morris.html; see also Antony Wild, *Black Gold: A Dark History of Coffee* (London: Harper Perennial, 2005); and C. Pole at http://www.consume.bbk.ac.uk/research/morris.html [all 4/2005].

seeks the discourse of the 'war on terror' not only in and through political speeches and acts – though these are of course important – but also beyond, in American society more generally. The rational certitude of the neoconservatives may be a key element of American foreign policy after 9/11; but neoconservatism does not exist independently of social context. Chapter 3 therefore searches for the popular reproduction of the 'war on terror' discourse, and illustrates how quickly and deeply the discourse was internalised and reproduced throughout American society from the attacks themselves to the end of 2001. That discourse became the new common sense. In so doing, chapter 3 modifies the crisis process outlined in the previous chapter. By examining in detail the creation of the foundational myth of 9/11, of its production and cultural reproduction throughout American society, an understanding is sought of the ways in which common sense was reconstructed. That lays the basis for chapter 4, in which the institutionalisation of the 'war on terror' as discourse is examined. New institutions and laws were created; the military were refocused onto the new task; the narration of the 'war on terror', following the decisive intervention, continued to be reproduced; and that narration was transmitted globally. That is, having secured an understanding of 9/11, that understanding led to a reconstruction of many different aspects of public policy and of popular culture in the United States, and then the project of spreading that understanding and that commitment to the reconstruction of public policy to states around the world.

Such analyses allow the crisis cycle to be reconstructed again. A decisive intervention produces a narrative that achieves hegemony within the polity that is focused on the crisis. Thus, the 'war on terror' as discourse achieved a hegemonic position within the American debate, and within American society when thinking about identities and the world. When Riley Ray Chiorando looked around in 2005 for those cultural items that were now worth only 99 cents, *Fodor's Pocket: Istanbul 2001* stood out: 'like a dino gene embedded in amber, [it] is a reminder of a time when US citizens actually took vacations to Islamic countries . . . post-Sept. 11, it seems a bit unloved, even radioactive'.[23]

Over time, discourses decay under the weight of internal contradictions and external alternative narratives. If a socially produced crisis

[23] Riley Ray Chiorando, 'The 99-cent archaeologist', *Los Angeles Times Magazine*, 21 August 2005, p. 16.

ensues, the dominant discourse might be overthrown by a new decisive intervention. In the United States, elements of this process occurred alongside the moves towards war in Iraq throughout 2002 and into 2003. As the discourse came under attack (in part for representing a betrayal of the foundational myth) amongst political and cultural figures, and amongst large numbers of people, one would expect that 2003 would have seen the collapse of the discourse into a new socially constructed crisis. Chapter 5 traces this logic, and outlines the means by which the 'war on terror' discourse survived and adapted.

Thus chapter 5 examines the 'sites of resistance' to the meta-narrative. Through protest against war, a new discourse emerged – 'no war for oil' – that animated street demonstrations, pressure groups and popular music. A socially produced crisis developed, but it was not one that led to a new decisive intervention for, as chapter 5 shows, the 'war on terror' discourse had become deeply embedded in a range of social institutions that remained unaffected by the alternative discourse. Following its successful survival in the face of discursive challenge, chapter 6 examines the phenomenon in which the 'discourse strikes back'. Of course, that discourse impacted greatly upon the construction of the presidential election campaign of 2004. But one of the greatest strengths of the 'war on terror' as discourse has been the way in which it has been so widely spread throughout America. Chapter 6 looks not only at how the discourse shaped an election won by President Bush, in which (by American standards) large numbers of people were motivated to come out and vote, but also how that discourse shaped popular culture. Thoughts on who to vote for come from a variety of sources, but an obvious one is a notion of what is common sense, and thus what is right. And common-sense knowledge is transmitted in a number of ways: in television programmes; in films; in newspapers and magazines; on the internet; and in popular fiction. All of these sources merit study, illustrating how strong the discourse remained despite or perhaps even because of the challenges of an alternative discourse.

The conclusion revisits the crisis process, and sets out how the crisis of 9/11 has led to a much broader sense of the social construction of crises, and the longevity of the discourse produced. It also assesses the importance of the fuller sense of culture as a source for understanding the development of political narratives. A crisis cycle is a good way in which to conceive of the legitimation, and subsequent decay, of a discursive project. But it should not be seen in a closed sense; fragments of previous discursive projects exist beyond the lifetime of that project. Thus, genealogy is a crucial part of the construction of meta-narratives. But understanding 9/11 in particular ways silences other readings, and the conclusion also offers thoughts on how that impacts upon the American pursuit of global counter-terrorism.

1 *Disrupting meaning*

September 11th

NEARLY EVERYONE IN THE WHOLE WORLD understands immediately what is meant by the phrase 'September 11th'. Events that began in the morning of that day were to shake the world. 'A building – a symbol of the nation – collapsed in flames in an act of terror . . .'[1] People died in numbers that were initially unknown, in acts of violence that cost some 3,000 civilians their lives on that day and subsequently. Not only the events, but also their source became important, and quickly the actions of those outside the state became a focal point for understanding the day's events. The very democracy of the state itself, and its institutions, were put at risk. And in the shock of it all, the way in which the world was described changed.

The year was 1973; the country Chile. On 9/11 of that year, President Allende's democratically elected government was overthrown by military forces led by General Pinochet, with American political and organisational (though not military) support.[2] La Moneda Palace, the official residence of the President, was attacked from the air by the Chilean air force. On that day and later thousands were killed, or 'disappeared', probably around 3,000, a number equivalent to those who lost their lives in the American 9/11.[3] The democ ratically elected government was overthrown, and the President committed suicide or was murdered; this is a contentious point. As Kenneth Maxwell noted many years later in *Foreign Affairs*: 'Thirty

1 Editorial, *The New York Times*, 11 September 2003.

2 See Peter Kornbluh, *The Pinochet File: A Declassified Dossier on Atrocity and Accountability* (New York: The New Press, 2003), based on some 24,000 declassified US documents.

3 The Chilean Truth and Reconciliation Commission came to a total of 3,197: see http://www.usip.org/library/tc/doc/reports/chile/chile_1993_toc.html [1/2004].

years after its initiation, the coup of 1973 remains deeply etched in collective memory.'[4]

Despite the global impact of the events of 11 September 2001, the phrase '9/11' can still mean different things to different people. To the government of President George W. Bush, the act began a war. To others, the perpetrators of the violence of that day are the 'Magnificent 19'; for Omar Bakhri, 9/11 was 'a cry of *Jihad* against unbelief and oppression' and it was an event worth celebrating as 'the anniversary of the division of the world into two great camps – the camp of faith and the camp of unbelief'.[5] This is not an attempt to create a moral equivalence between the events of 9/11 1973, and 9/11 2001; still less between the Bush administration and al-Qaeda. It is, rather, to ask about meaning. Labelling gives meaning and creates silence. A focus on the American 9/11 carries with it certain understandings: for example, the horror of the murder of people at work; the tragedy of the orphaning of children; and the need to free the world from such threats in the future. Or the meaning could be the revival of 'the obligation of jihad worldwide, as can be seen through the operations in Indonesia, Riyadh, Iraq, Palestine, Afghanistan . . .'[6] And focusing on either or both can silence other 9/11s, such as the Chilean 9/11, or the Irish 9/11. On 11 September 1649, Cromwell perpetrated the massacre of Drogheda, killing 3,000 people. A focus on 9/11 that concerns only New York and Washington, and the field of Pennsylvania, silences the voices of the 6,000 others lost in the Chilean and Irish 9/11s.

Indeed, not only does it do that: it is not even enough to specify the 'American' 9/11. The horror of 11 September 2001 was not even America's first 9/11; that fell 144 years earlier, in 1857. On 11 September 1857, all but the youngest children in a wagon train of 130 emigrants, mostly from Arkansas, were slaughtered. They had been besieged for five days by, they thought, Native Americans. On the morning of 11

[4] Kenneth Maxwell, 'The other 9/11: the United States and Chile, 1973', *Foreign Affairs*, November/December 2003, at http://www.foreignaffairs.org/20031101 fareviewessay82615/kenneth-maxwell/ the-other-9-11-the-united-states-and-chile-1973.html [1/2004].

[5] Omar Bakhri in 'London convention will celebrate 9/11', *Middle East Media Research Institute*, no. 774, 3 September 2004, at http://memri.org/bin/ articles. cgi?Page=subjects&Area=jihad&ID=SP77804 [9/2005].

[6] The website of al-Muhajiroun, the press release concerning their conference entitled 'The magnificent 19', 11 September 2003, at http://www.4law.co.il/ Lea193.htm [1/2004].

September, a Mormon official came into the camp, and suggested that the emigrants leave with him and his soldiers. They did so, the men escorted by a Mormon guard, the women and children in wagons. The Mormon guard executed the men; Mormons dressed as Native Americans attacked and murdered the women and children. The Mountain Meadows massacre saw some 120 men, women and children killed in cold blood: Americans, killed by Americans, in the name of religion.[7]

This is not a book that details the events of what we should now call more precisely 'the second American 9/11', that of 11 September 2001; nor does it seek to reach moral judgements about the claims made of that day. Rather it seeks to understand how that day was given meaning in the United States; how that meaning has been embedded in everyday language and practices; how that meaning has shaped the policies and institutions of the state. It is an examination of the production of meaning in crisis, of the cultural production of a discourse, and of the political and cultural reproduction that followed. Although the book does focus on a particular crisis response – from 2001 – it does so by seeking to problematise so many aspects that have taken on the status of 'common sense' to destabilise certainties; and the beginning of that process has to be remembering that there are other 9/11s. From this point forwards, therefore, in this book the events of 11 September 2001 will be labelled 'the second American 9/11'; and the discourse and policy programme to which it gave rise, the 'war on terror'.

Security and film

In 2004, Disney/Pixar released a film entitled *The Incredibles*, written and directed by Brad Bird.[8] In the first weekend of its release in the United States, it took $70.5 million at the box office.[9] It is a fairly simple plot, designed to entertain the 'family' audience – that is, to work as entertainment for both children and adults, and thus increase

[7] Josiah F. Gibbs, *Mountain Meadows Massacre*, second edition, 1910, reproduced at http://www.utlm.org/onlinebooks/meadowscontents.htm [3/2005] and John Krakauer, *Under the Banner of Heaven* (New York: Anchor Books, 2004), especially pp. 210–29 and 238–42. The memorial to the massacre is at http://asms.k12:ar.us/armem/brondel/ [2/2005].

[8] Disney/Pixar, 2004, directed and written by Brad Bird: http://www.imdb.com/title/tt0317705/ [4/2005].

[9] David Lieberman, 'The Incredibles keeps passion for Pixar alive', *USA Today*, 15 November 2004.

turnover in the way made fashionable and successful by films such as *Shrek*, *Toy Story* and *Finding Nemo*. Mr Incredible is a superhero; or rather, he used to be. Mr Incredible is now known as Bob Parr, and he lives a 'normal' life because lawsuits submitted by those the Incredibles have saved have forced them into hiding. His wife, Helen, was also a superhero – Elastigirl – and their three children – Violet, Dash and Jack-Jack – inevitably also have special powers.

The Incredibles – or, rather, the Parrs – lead a suburban life in the American Midwest, Bob being an insurance claims agent who is unhappy with the amorality of the profession, and yearns for the old days. But Helen has put so much work into building family life that for her this investment has to be protected and developed. Suddenly, unexpectedly, danger returns, and Mr Incredible and the whole family must reveal themselves as superheroes to save many, many innocent lives (to prevent 'genocide' as Fred Topel, in *Action Adventure Movies*, puts it).[10]

Such is the plot line. The film is, as Lawrence Toppman put it in the *Charlotte Observer*, 'really about an America that celebrates the average, that prefers conformist mediocrity to nurturing high achievers'.[11] The enemy figure, Syndrome, has an evil plan, in which eventually he will give everyone superpowers; because when everyone is special, no one is special. It is in part, therefore, a film rejecting liberal visions of equality: David Kelley writing for the Objectivist Center asks 'Who would have thought that an animated film would finally touch a nerve, putting egalitarians on the defensive? That is the achievement of . . . *The Incredibles*, the story of a family of superheroes who struggle against the reign of mediocrity and finally break free to excel.'[12] As Brad Bird – the film's creator – put it, 'On sports day my kids all get a prize; this devalues achievement and the efforts of the kids who have busted a gut to do well.'[13]

10 Fred Topel, 'Q. What did you think of Disney/Pixar's The Incredibles?', at http://actionadventure.about.com/od/theincrediblesmoviefaq/f/aaincredibles11.htm [12/2004].

11 Lawrence Toppman, '"Incredibles" lives up to name', *Charlotte Observer*, 5 November 2004, at http://ae.charlotte.com/entertainment/ui/charlotte/movie.html?id=175785&reviewId=16547&1c [11/2004].

12 David Kelley 'The Incredibles', The Objectivist Center Media Center, at http://www.objectivistcenter.org/mediacenter/articles/dkelley_rff-the-incredibles.asp [12/2004].

13 Brad Bird, quoted in 'Making the Incredibles', Future Movies, at http://www.futuremovies.co.uk/filmmaking.asp?ID=98 [12/2004].

However, there is more to *The Incredibles* than a narrative about the undervaluing of special ability. Are the Parrs not a metaphor for America itself? America used to save the world with its omnipotence during the cold war. This purpose and past glory is expressed in many ways, but undoubtedly one that would resonate with American audiences is the conflict with the enemy figure 'Bomb Voyage', a character complete with French accent and mime make-up and costume. But that was the past and since then, since the victory over criminals / the end of the cold war, the Parrs/America have gone soft. There has been a loss of moral core, symbolised by Bob Parr himself in physical form. Mr Incredible had an amazingly powerful physique; Bob Parr is grotesquely overweight, a metaphor for materialistic America. But there has also been a loss of focus: as Robert Wilonsky explains in the *Dallas Observer*, the Incredibles were superheroes doing real good 'until the government outlawed superheroes when the public turned on them, damning them as nuisances'.[14] That is, America did it to itself; it stopped itself from doing good in the world after the collapse of communism. It accepted that there was no value in exceptionalism. And thus the Parrs, like America, turned inwards in the 1990s; Americans focused – like Helen – on materialism. Like America in the 1990s, the Parrs also ignore questions of right and wrong; as an insurance claims agent, Bob Parr does this for a living (except, just sometimes, he works the system for the 'little guy'). And yes, the undervaluing of special ability also reads as the undervaluing of American exceptionalism in the world.

Of course, this is not the only narrative in the film beyond the text. There are powerful patriarchal narratives throughout the film concerning gender roles. Further, this America is a startlingly white one (only one character is black, Frozone, Mr Incredible's friend who can turn anything into ice: the 'black-people-are-cool' stereotype).[15] Phil Villareal notes the opportunity inherent for 'commentary on societal prejudice, with the superpowers as an analogy for hidden race or sexuality amid an intolerant society. Instead, the screenplay heads for easier,

14 Robert Wilonsky, 'These heroes may be Incredibles, but they're also normal', *Dallas Observer*, 4 November 2004.

15 Brad Bird commented: 'With Frozone, here's a guy who's just absolutely cool all the time . . .' 'Interview with the Incredibles Brad Bird', *Cinema Confidential*, 1 November 2004, at http://www.cinecon.com/news.php?id=0411011 [12/2004].

cheaper laughs . . .'[16] And there are narratives about work and atomisation: in commenting on the film, Ella Taylor, from *LA Weekly*, argued that 'Few nations have been as efficient a builder of giant corporations as the United States, and no other culture has grown as robust a hatred and mistrust – or expressed its hostility more floridly in movies – of those same institutions.'[17] Much of this is played out visually; after all, this is an animation film, giving the film-makers all sorts of opportunities with the technology of computer-generated imagery. But it is deployed most powerfully in the settings. Mr Incredible's great superhero acts are carried out in a set that looks very much like 1950s America; the miserable present being represented as the 1960s (of course, the beginning of the culture wars); but then the action takes place in a 'James Bond' style world, with a musical score to match. These narratives are all recognisable to the general viewing public in contemporary America.

However, for the purposes of this book, it is the security narrative that is of greatest concern. And here we see the Incredibles as the metaphor for America, Mr Incredible's past as the cold war, and the current struggle as that against al-Qaeda. The domestic American setting gives a sense of safety and security, which, when threatened, makes a still stronger impact. Importantly, the film was given a PG certificate. Ken Tucker in *New York Magazine* wrote that 'The reason *The Incredibles* is Pixar's first PG movie is because Bird earned it – by placing a family in peril, he stages urgent, primal emotion as action, asserting that love can defeat enemies like jealousy, vindictiveness, and the whims of a remorseless universe.'[18] Peril emerges after a period of lethargy; and into this could be read a metaphor for 9/11, that is, the second American 9/11. The family – America – realises the folly of amorality and materialism, and commits itself to the fight. But the fight is difficult, because so much adjustment has to be made: to Mr Incredible's body, to Mrs Incredible's sense of materialism, to Violet's introversion. That is, to America's weakened military, consumerist public, and lack of self-confidence about its place in the world.

16 Phil Villareal, 'Conventional "Incredibles" ', *Arizona Star*, at http://www.azstarnet.com/sn/ent_movies/46113.php [12/2004].

17 Ella Taylor, 'The "Incredibles" shrinking man', *AlterNet*, 2 December 2004, at http://www.alternet.org/mediaculture/20657/ [12/2004].

18 Ken Tucker, 'Animate this', *New York Magazine*, at http://www.newyorkmetro.com/nymetro/movies/reviews/10249/ [12/2004].

Rob Vaux writes that 'villainy appears in the form of Buddy Pine (Jason Lee), who was Mr Incredible's biggest fan as a child, but has since transformed his geeky adulation into a tool for globe-imperiling evil'.[19] It is, of course, widely assumed that Osama bin Laden was an American protégé in the 1980s war in Afghanistan, and again the parallel is clear. Buddy/Syndrome is Osama. And as Gary Thompson notes in the *Philadelphia News*, reflecting the different times in which films are made, '*The Incredibles* shows that there are . . . stark differences between Pixar products: *Monsters, Inc.* reassured children that the beasties in their closets were benign. *The Incredibles*, by contrast, stipulates that sometimes, the bad guys really do want to kill you.'[20] Indeed, Mrs Parr/Elastigirl is explicit about this, explaining to her children that the enemy is not like that in the past, not like those in Saturday morning films. This enemy wants to kill, even children. And so she tells Violet – and thus America – that 'there is no room for doubt now'. The film is a rallying call to the struggle against the threat from outside: as Bob Strauss puts it in *UFilm*, the underlying message is 'Eat your creaky hearts out, Team America.'[21]

The film ends with a showdown between the forces of good and evil. Two aspects of this are particularly important. Despite trying to defeat Syndrome/Osama on his own territory, there is in the end no doubt that the final battle will be fought on the territory of the United States itself. And in bringing with him a fiercesome robot, the film-makers indicate that the enemy can have mastery of the most deadly weapons in the world, weapons in different forms threatening mass destruction. Hence, the scenario of weapons of mass destruction in the hands of a terrorist enemy, the professed motivation for American military action in Iraq, is at the very heart of the screenplay for *The Incredibles*, a film released a year after the beginning of that war.

What are the political implications of reading one of the most popular films of the year in this way? It suggests that certain narratives had currency at a particular time in the United States. For all the film-makers'

[19] Rob Vaux, 'The Incredibles', *Flipside*, 11 May 2004, at http://www.flipsidemovies.com/incredibles.html [12/2004].

[20] Gary Thompson, 'Pixar delivers a great movie: "Incredibles" perfect for post-election world', *Philadelphia News*, at http://www.philly.com/mld/dailynews/living/10104936.htm?1c [12/2004].

[21] Bob Strauss, ' "Incredibles" wins with action, heart', *UFilm,* 3 November 2004, at http://u.dailynews.com/Stories/0,1413,211~24684~2511286,00.html [12/2004].

commitment to 'art', the point of *The Incredibles* is to make money. That is, to understand a market, and to speak to it in such a way that it can be exploited. In his review of the film, Gary Thompson argues that 'Although *The Incredibles* was conceived a decade ago, it is unnervingly on point as regards our post 9/11 culture of fear.'[22] That is, *The Incredibles* both exploits this sense of fear, and also reproduces it in novel ways and to new audiences (children, in particular).

Indeed, much of the cultural production in the United States since the second American 9/11 has to be read in terms of the influence of those events on the construction of meaning concerning the world outside America's shores, and also about the construction of threat within. Another particularly good example is *The Last Samurai*.[23] Captain Nathan Algren is a military hero, decorated in the Civil War and in the 'Indian Wars' of the 1870s. Tormented by a sense of guilt at the slaughter of Native Americans, and tired of the politics and bureaucracy of the American state, he is sent to Japan, to assist the Emperor – America's friend – defeat the backward-looking Samurai. As Robert Ebert explains it, 'Japan has been seized with a fever to shake off its medieval ways and copy the West, and the West sees money to be made in the transition. Representatives from the Remington arms company are filling big contracts for weapons, and the US Embassy is a clearinghouse for lucrative trade arrangements.'[24] Algren is captured by the Samurai, learns of the culture and the commitment to values lacking in American life – loyalty, honour, fortitude, sacrifice – and, when he sees the betrayal of those values and the Samurai by the Emperor's advisors, backed by the Americans, he becomes committed to supporting the Samurai cause. And so, at the very moment of the Iraq War, Hollywood produced a film that showed one of their leading actors (Tom Cruise) as an American hero fighting against America's ally; and, once the final battle is over, Cruise goes explicitly against professed American national interests in persuading the Emperor of the value of the Samurai, of the commitment to values lost in America. Inevitably, this reading led to hostility towards the film. It is, therefore, a film about

[22] Thompson, 'Pixar delivers a great movie'.

[23] Director Edward Zwick, writers John Logan, Marshall Herskovitz and Ed Zwick; Warner Bros., 2003.

[24] Roger Ebert's review is from the *Chicago Sun-Times*, 5 December 2003, at http://rogerebert.suntimes.com/apps/pbcs.dll/article?AID=/20031205/REVIEWS/312050302/1023 [12/2004].

contemporary America and the world, not about nineteenth-century Japan, as Mick LaSalle noted. 'Most historical epics are not really about the time they depict but about the era in which they were made', he wrote. 'And so it is today with *The Last Samurai*, an old-fashioned adventure that's really a modern and very emotional lament about the encroachments of technology and the dangers of American hegemony.'[25] Barry Paris missed this entirely when he wrote: 'Its rough equivalent would be leaving the heroic figure of Lord Nelson left to preside over the dead at Gettysburg: moving, to be sure – if geopolitically absurd.'[26]

The political aspect of the film resonated with some critics. Eric Lurio wrote:

> *The Last Samurai* is evil. Why? Ideology. The villains are the heroes and the heroes villains. Screenwriters . . . have created a profoundly reactionary and anti-American tale where ancient oppressors are seen as saintly, and those who favor democracy and liberation awful fiends . . . The sad part is that the film is sooooooo well done that it'll hurt America's international situation by giving aid and comfort to those who long to go back to the days of 1970s Bulgaria.[27]

Or, as Ed Blank put it, 'Although *The Last Samurai* unfolds mostly in 1876, it panders so embarrassingly to trendy notions of politically correct American self-loathing that it would not have hatched in this form until fairly recently.'[28] And we get explicit lines of text in the film that draw the parallel with the war in Iraq. Those uncomfortable with the war were presented in the United States by their opponents as traitors; and the role of traitor (or rather, standing for values instead of blindly supporting the flag) is that ascribed to Captain Algren. The American army colonel, who Algren holds responsible for the slaughter of Native Americans, and who represents the pro-Iraq War community

[25] Mick LaSalle in the *San Francisco Chronicle*, 5 December 2003, at http://www.sfgate.com/cgi-bin/article.cgi?f=/c/a/2003/12/05/DDGNG3FDKI1.DTL [12/2004].

[26] Barry Paris' review was in the *Pittsburgh Post-Gazette*, 5 December 2003, and is at http://www.post-gazette.com/movies/20031205samurai1205fnp3.asp [12/2004].

[27] Eric Lurio, 'The Last Samurai', *Greenwich Village Gazette*, 6:26 (2003), at http:// www.nycny.com/movies/last_samurai/index.html [1/2005].

[28] Ed Blank, *Pittsburgh Tribune-Review*, at http://www.pittsburghlive.com/x/tribune-review/entertainment/movies/reviews/s_168456.html [12/2004].

in all of its one-dimensional presentation, vocalises this when he asks Algren: 'What *is* it about your own people that you hate so much?'[29]

Such narratives clearly demonstrate the nature of discourse in the United States at a particular point of time. Of course, it would be wrong to ascribe a single political motif; there are also ethnic and gender narratives in the film with which many felt uncomfortable.[30] But for the purposes of this book, while *The Incredibles* exhorts public support for the war on terror (for there is no alternative), *The Last Samurai* posits that there are values that are more important than crude nationalism.

Popular culture and security

Film studies are interesting, providing insights into cultures and attitudes in particular periods of time; but can a film such as *The Incredibles*, or *The Last Samurai*, be read in a way that conforms to the construction of contemporary academic political science and international relations? The answer is, almost certainly not, in the conventional sense in which the discipline is constructed in the United States and the United Kingdom. But films can be about sets of issues and readings that are most definitely about the 'political'. That is, there are issues treated as political, which lie outside the normal purview of political science and international relations.

This is not to deny that the academic study of international relations has had its own 'cultural turn'. But that turn has seen culture defined in a very 'thin' sense – to mean, for example, an organisational culture – rather than a 'thick' use of culture, which would look at popular manifestations.[31] In this 'thicker' or 'fuller' sense, culture is defined as

[29] Ty Burr in 'The Last Samurai', *Boston Globe*, at http://www.boston.com/movies/display?display=movie&id=1850 [12/2004].

[30] Bill Gallo commented: 'Stubborn Hollywood phoniness imbues almost all of *The Last Samurai*, right down to Cruise in his fat red beetle suit . . . and, more crucially, the fact that it takes a heroic white soldier from the American heartland to remind the waffling Japanese emperor of his own heritage and, inevitably, to win the heart of the movie's Japanese porcelain doll . . .', *Dallas Observer*, at http://www.dallasobserver.com/issues/2003–12–04/film2.html/1/index.html [1/2005].

[31] For an examination of the use of 'culture' in security studies, see Theo Farrell, 'World culture and military power', *Security Studies*, 14:3 (2005). Jackson uses a 'thin' version of culture, in which political discourse is privileged over others; Jackson, *Writing the War on Terrorism*, pp. 16–18, 126.

'the complex everyday world we all encounter and through which we all move . . . the two most important or general elements of culture may be the ability of human beings to construct and to build, and the ability to use language (understood most broadly, to embrace all forms of sign system)'.[32] It is this 'fuller' sense of culture that this book seeks to begin to draw upon.

Indeed, there are many sources that talk about political issues that lie beyond political science and international relations as an academic discipline. Consider, for example, the comics of *Wonder Woman*. Shortly after the attacks of 11 September 2001, DC Comics released a book-length graphic novel.[33] It had to be over-size to allow the full impact of the artwork, in order to substantiate the claim that comic art can be *Art*. It, of course, also allowed the publishers to make money on the larger scale, pseudo-erotic image of Wonder Woman herself. But the book also contained the discourses of post-second-9/11 America. Wonder Woman's adventure leads her to 'the desert nations', which are overtly Islamic in their imagery, 'where she learns "that rural villages have been emptied, their people forced into use as human shields" '.[34] Mitra Emad substituted 'America' for 'I' in one of Wonder Woman's statements, and the following message emerged:

> America is aware that [her] appearance, by mortal standards, is strange, even unsettling. If America is to be an ambassador of [her] people, tradition dictates that [she] look the part. Sadly, those who judge America on [her] looks alone ignore the causes America champions. Still, when the need arises, America is a warrior.[35]

In the immediate post-second-9/11 American world, such messages were read avidly, and widely endorsed. Continuing this theme, the back-cover blurb can be reread replacing 'Wonder Woman' with 'America':

> America is at an impasse. Despite her lofty goals and ideals for the world beyond Paradise Island, her message of peace, understanding, and fellowship

[32] The quote is from the definition of culture by Andrew Edgar in Andrew Edgar and Peter Sedgwick (eds.), *Cultural Theory: The Key Concepts* (London: Routledge, 1999), p. 102.

[33] Paul Dini, *Wonder Woman: Spirit of Truth*, DC Comics, 1 November 2001.

[34] Mitra C. Emad, 'Reading *Wonder Woman*'s body: mythologies of gender and nation', *Journal of Popular Culture* (2004), available at http://www.d.umn.edu/~memad/ReadingWonderWomanPaperFinal.htm [6/2005].

[35] Ibid.

is rejected because of the way she is perceived. Not every nation is willing to embrace America – despite her actions and best intentions.[36]

The message conflating America and Wonder Woman, in which the misunderstood nevertheless stands up to danger, is an illustration of the ways in which politics influences popular culture, and popular culture influences politics.[37] Indeed, the two are in many ways mutually constituted.

Film studies, gender studies, cultural studies – all of these disciplines, and others, focus on the political. And they draw in sources – film, television, novels, websites – that talk about the political. This book seeks to engage with those sources to understand how discourse in America has been produced and reproduced in terms of developing a metanarrative following the events of 11 September 2001, and how that has structured action. That is, it is the discourse – its production and reproduction in all its cultural forms – that is the central focal point of this text. Politics exists beyond the sphere of the politician.

This is a different approach to traditional political science and international relations, in which the focus would be on the rise and influence of neoconservatism as a political ideology in the United States; on how policy was decided upon; and in relation to the international relations of neoconservative prescriptions. Such analysis is extremely valuable, but it only addresses some of the issues raised. Political life is not just about the detail of ideology and decision, important as these are: it is also about the control of discourse. Agents are of course important in the construction of meaning in a range of events, from gender narratives in *Wonder Woman*, to the 'commonsense' meaning of the second American 9/11. Yet meaning is also intersubjectively constructed. It is perhaps unlikely that Brad Bird thought explicitly about how to link Osama bin Laden and Syndrome in writing *The Incredibles*. Rather, there are structural factors at work. Social practices and institutions are constituted by discourse, and of course are situated within discourse. Thus, a discourse is intersubjectively produced and reproduced, and it is that discourse that produces and

[36] Ibid.
[37] The next *Wonder Woman* book was similarly influenced by the 'war on terror' discourse, even though it was largely a rehash of previously (pre-second 9/11 American) stories. J. M. DeMatteis and Phil Jimenez, *Wonder Woman: Paradise Lost*, DC Comics, 1 February 2002.

organises meaning within a social context. Hence, if the recognition of the new 'reality' in the 'post-9/11' world is to be understood fully, it must be achieved by identifying and deconstructing the meaning of the 'war on terror' as discourse. Not only that, but the 'common sense' that is produced in that discourse must be problematised in order to understand that which counts as knowledge and that which does not; that which constitutes identity with a particular group, and that which constitutes identity against a particular group.

Crisis cycles

Crisis cycles are common forms of understanding complex processes. One early example of a crisis cycle is to be found in the Old Testament. In the Book of Judges, the people of Israel fall into sinful ways; and so God allows them to be defeated, and sent into slavery. Then, the people are sorrowful, and cry out for help, and so God sends a saviour, a judge, who delivers them from evil. Out of gratitude, the people serve God faithfully, and so God rewards them with prosperity. But with prosperity comes a forgetting of the covenant, and so they fall into sinful ways; and from there, defeat and slavery are but a short step. The cycle is important in Judaism, and in theological studies. But this, and other cycles, are important beyond that. Some in America's evangelical community believe that the world itself is engaged in a long cycle, and that it will come to a conclusion with the rise of the Antichrist, Armageddon and the Second Coming. In such an understanding, true believers will experience the Rapture before the destruction of the world: they will be literally lifted to Heaven.

If 'common sense' is to be questioned, one of the elements is to understand that to Europeans, 'familiar America' can be rendered strange. For example, in America the theories of intelligent design and evolution stand in competition with each other: the Book of Genesis versus Darwin. 'The theory of intelligent design (ID) holds that certain features of the universe and of living things are best explained by an intelligent cause rather than an undirected process such as natural selection. ID is thus a scientific disagreement with the core claim of evolutionary theory that the apparent design of living systems is an illusion.'[38]

[38] From the Intelligent Design Network at http://www.intelligentdesignnetwork.org/ [9/2005].

The Discovery Institute, based in Seattle and a strong advocate of ID, has published a bibliography of key scientific texts supporting and developing ID theory.[39] In the state of Kansas, legislators are seeking to ensure that children are taught ID alongside evolution.[40] Kansas is not alone: districts in other states, such as Pennsylvania, Wisconsin, California, Georgia, Oklahoma and Tennessee, are following a similar logic.[41] President Bush said, in the summer of 2005, that children should be taught ID in school.[42] A survey following this put support for teaching ID alongside evolution at 64 per cent.[43]

Such beliefs, and now practices, are deeply engrained in the heartland of America. Organisations such as the Statesmanship Institute and the Center for Christian Statesmanship offer courses to train those looking for elected office in how to follow God's principles in public policy. Patrick Henry College in Virginia has been able to secure 100 places for their evangelical students in the Bush administration. These institutions are, as the *Los Angeles Times* put it, 'Grooming politicians for Christ'.[44] Students are asked to consider how Christianity is viewed in Washington: 'Have you noticed that it's okay to say you're a Christian, just as long as your faith doesn't seep too much into your public life? That's the gap theory in action, but that gap can make your faith worthless. Void. Useless.'[45] Ideas about evangelical Christianity and foreign policy are developed in institutions such as Bob Jones

[39] See http://www.discovery.org/scripts/viewDB/index.php?command=view&id=2640&program=CSC%20-%20Scientific%20Research%20and%20Scholarship%20-%20Science [9/2005].

[40] For documents of the debate in Kansas, see http://www.kansasscience2005.com/ [9/2005].

[41] On Pennsylvania, see Martha Raffaele, 'School board OKs challenges to evolution', MSNBC, 24 November 2004, at http://www.msnbc.msn.com/id/6470259/. On districts in other states, see Anna Badkhen, 'Anti evolution teachings gain foothold in US schools', *San Francisco Chronicle*, 30 November 2004, at http://sfgate.com/cgi-bin/article.cgi?file=/c/a/2004/11/30/MNGVNA3PE11.DTL [both 9/2005].

[42] Peter Baker and Peter Slevin, 'Bush remarks on "Intelligent Design" theory fuel debate', *Washington Post*, 3 August 2005.

[43] Laurie Goodstein, 'Teaching of creationism is endorsed in new survey', *New York Times*, 31 August 2005.

[44] The Center for Christian Statesmanship is at http://www.statesman.org/ [8/2005]. See Stephanie Simon, 'Grooming politicians for Christ', *Los Angeles Times*, 23 August 2005.

[45] From the Statesmanship Institute website at http://si.statesman.org/Default.aspx [9/2005].

University as well as Patrick Henry College.[46] In the annual survey of religious belief in the United States carried out by the Princeton Religion Research Center, some 45 per cent of Americans defined themselves as 'evangelical' or 'born again'.[47] Jerry Falwell claims that this equates to 70 million people. Others estimate this to be as high as 100 million.[48]

Inevitably, evangelical belief carries with it analyses and policy prescriptions concerning America's interaction with the world. One theme is that the values of America and of Europe are different, and the conclusion is that therefore their interests will differ. Research by the Center for the Study of Global Christianity at the Gordon-Conwell Theological Seminary shows that in all west European states and Canada, the proportion of those who 'never' or 'practically never' go to church increased between 1981 and 2001; it has declined in the United States, which has the lowest absolute figures except for Ireland.[49] In a similar vein, George Weigl mused over the 'Europe problem', a 'problem of cultural and civilizational morale', in a book subtitled *Europe, America and Politics without God*.[50] Europe's lack of Christian fibre – shown in its policies towards abortion, contraception and tolerance of radical Islam – marks it as a continent where America is unlikely to find true allies. In contrast, Israel becomes much more important. As former White House speechwriter David Frum put it, 'Many evangelicals identify the return of Jews to Israel as of the imminence of the Second Coming – and see the attacks on Israel as portending the Antichrist.'[51] And particular interpretations of religion create discursive contexts in the United States that are different to those in other parts of the world. The impact of the second

46 See http://www.bju.edu/ and http://www.phc.edu/.

47 See the representations from 1975–2000 at http://www.wheaton.edu/isae/Gallup-Bar-graph.html [7/2005].

48 This would include African-Americans, of whom some 60% define themselves as being evangelical, but whose organisational structures differ from those of white churches in some important ways. See 'Defining evangelism', the Institute for the Study of American Evangelicals at Wheaton College, at http://www.wheaton.edu/isae/defining_evangelicalism.html [7/2005].

49 The database is at http://worldchristiandatabase.org/wcd/and the Center's website is http://www.globalchristianity.org/. These analyses were front page news in *USA Today*. See Noelle Knox, 'Religion takes a back seat in western Europe', *USA Today*, 11 August 2005.

50 George Weigl, *The Cube and the Cathedral: Europe, America and Politics without God* (New York: Basic Books, 2005), p. 6.

51 David Frum, *The Right Man* (London: Weidenfeld & Nicolson, 2003), p. 260.

American 9/11 was read in that different context; the imagery of the memorialisation was heavily religious; and pre-existing faith understandings created policy expectations. Some argued that 'Prophecies show the September 11 terrorist attack very specifically.'[52] In Paul Crouch's *The Shadow of the Apocalypse*, Bible codes show that the second American 9/11 was prophesied in Psalm 23:4 (the text of 'World Trade Center' crosses 'September 11, 2001', 'president', 'George Bush'), Malachi 2:10 ('president' and 'George Bush' on the same line, 'firemen', airplane, 'war', 'knife'), and Malachi 4.2 ('Osama', 'Bin', 'Laden', 'Taliban', 'anthrax').[53]

Such evangelical analyses are not of course a creation of the post-second American 9/11 discourse; rather, they shape meaning. In 1982, the then-American Secretary of Defense, Caspar Weinberger, was asked whether he believed the world was going to end. He replied: 'I have read the Book of Revelation and yes, I believe the world is going to end – by an act of God, I hope – but every day I think that time is running out.'[54] This is an example of premillennialism, a strand of thinking that has come to dominate American evangelical Protestantism. In this worldview, we are living at the end of time, and, as Michael Northcott put it: 'It is an era of growing lawlessness and dreadful wars which threaten to extinguish human life on earth. Only after these events will Christ return to inaugurate a literal "thousand year reign of peace".'[55] This is predicted in the Book of Revelation, but in addition, premillennialists believe in the Rapture, in which true believers will be raised by God from the planet before the Great Tribulation, which therefore will only have to be faced by those of no, or insubstantial belief and those chosen by God to fight Antichrist alongside God. For true believers, the end of time is to be welcomed, for it brings closer the Kingdom of God on earth.

[52] September 2001, Greater Things, at http://www.greaterthings.com/News/911/index.html [5/2004].

[53] Paul Crouch, *The Shadow of the Apocalypse: When All Hell Breaks Loose* (New York: Berkley, 2004), pp. 187–9.

[54] Caspar Weinberger quoted in 'Washington Talk', *New York Times*, 23 August 1982, cited in Robert Scheer, *With Enough Shovels: Reagan, Bush and Nuclear War* (New York: Vintage Books, 1983), preface.

[55] Michael Northcott, *An Angel Directs the Storm: Apocalyptic Religion and American Empire* (London: I. B. Taurus, 2004), p. 44. Revelation 20:4–6 is the passage that speaks of the thousand-year reign.

Premillennialism animates churches, and believers, across the United States. And it can be found not only in churches, but also throughout American popular culture. 'The most recent pop culture manifestation of the Book of Revelation is a series of novels by Tim LaHaye and Jerry Jenkins called *Left Behind* . . .'[56] In the first book, published in 1995, believers begin to disappear; the Rapture has begun. The subsequent eleven books apply the core teachings of the Book of Revelation, as understood by the authors, to the current day. The final book, *Glorious Appearing*, concerns the final reckoning: 'It's been just over seven years since the Rapture and almost exactly seven years since Antichrist's covenant with Israel. Believers look to the heavens for the Glorious Appearing of Christ, as the world stands on the brink of the end of time.'[57] *Glorious Appearing* sold 2 million copies before publication. In the article in *Newsweek* which went alongside the authors' picture on the front cover, we learn that 'the "Left Behind" books have sold more than 62 million copies'.[58] In 2005, a third film in the series was released – *Left Behind: World at War* – for showing in churches rather than in cinemas.[59] Connecting premillennialism still more directly with contemporary events, Grant Jeffrey's *War on Terror: Unfolding Bible Prophecy* (published in January 2002) made bold claims.[60] He showed that the 'war on terror' against Iraq had been prophesied by Jeremiah over 2,500 years previously and gave documented evidence to show that Iraq was behind the attacks of the second American 9/11.[61] Biblical prophecy and premillennialism are deeply rooted in American culture. For example, Fun Trivia.com is a web based company that sells trivia and quiz games ranging, it claims, 'From Harry Potter to

[56] David E. Nantais and Michael Simone, 'Apocalypse when?', *America Magazine: The National Catholic Monthly*, 189:4 (August 2000), at http://www.americamagazine.org/gettext.cfm?articleTypeID=1&textID=3116&issueID=447 [4/2005].

[57] The series has its own website, which also passes opinion on current issues in terms of their biblical potential, see http://www.leftbehind.com/channelbooks.asp?channelID=46 [4/2005].

[58] David Gates, 'Religion: the pop prophets', *Newsweek*, 24 May 2005.

[59] ' "Left Behind" gets the "passion" treatment', *USA Today*, 19 August 2005.

[60] Grant Jeffrey, *War on Terror: Unfolding Bible Prophecy* (New York: Water Brook Press, 2002); Water Brook is the evangelical religious publishing division of Random House, Inc.

[61] Saddam was trying to re-establish the Babylonian Empire, claimed Jeffrey in chapter 6.

Particle Physics . . .'; it also sells eight games based on the Book of Revelation.[62]

Much has been written about the influence of neoconservatism on the administrations of President George W. Bush; perhaps as much if not more needs to be written on the influence of evangelical Christianity itself.[63] David Frum, a former speechwriter for President Bush, opens his account of his time in the White House with his first meeting, and the first words he heard in the White House: 'Missed you at Bible Study.'[64] President Bush had announced 6–8 September 2002 as National Days of Prayer and Remembrance to commemorate the events of 11 September 2001.[65] There is an enormous literature on eschatology (the study of the end of times) in the United States. And enormous interest in how it is being received – many premillennialist websites hold polls to gain a sense of the lay of the theological land.[66] A *Time*/CNN poll in June 2002 indicated that 'more than one-third of Americans say they are paying more attention now to how the news might relate to the end of the world, and have talked about what the Bible has to say on the subject. Fully 59 per cent say they believe the events in Revelation are going to come true, and nearly a quarter think the Bible predicted the Sept. 11 attack.'[67] In a *Newsweek* poll in August 2005, one-third of Americans defined themselves as evangelical in their belief, 80 per cent believed that God created the world in some form (of course, they are not all adherents to the theory of intelligent design), and two-thirds of Americans prayed everyday.[68] Clearly, such foundational beliefs would and do shape discursive practices throughout the country. Paul Crouch wrote of the prophecy in the Book of Revelation that at the Endtimes the world would move towards a cashless

[62] See http://www.funtrivia.com/quizzes/religion/new_testament/revelation.html [4/ 2005].

[63] Bush's Cabinets have been filled with evangelical self-proclaimed Christians, including the President himself, Condoleezza Rice and John Ashcroft.

[64] The words were aimed at Frum's companion: Frum, *Right Man*, p. 1.

[65] Bush said: 'In the aftermath of the attacks, the words of the Psalms brought comfort to many.' Thomas M. Freiling (ed.), *George W. Bush On God and Country* (Washington, DC: Allegiance Press, 2004), p. 47.

[66] For example, According to Prophecy, at http://www.according2prophecy.org/future.html [4/2005].

[67] Nancy Gibbs, 'Apocalypse now', *Time Magazine*, 23 June 2002, at http://www.time.com/time/covers/1101020701/story.html [4/2005].

[68] Jerry Adler, 'Spirituality 2005', *Newsweek*, 29 August/5 September 2005, pp. 48–54.

society.[69] Following a presentation I made at Los Alamos National Laboratory in 1996, I was asked by a member of staff whether Europe was yet fully cashless: bringing forward the expectation that Antichrist would rise in Europe after the abolition of cash. Such views are not only held in the rural Midwest.

Abortion, the teaching of evolution as a theory, homosexuality, political correctness – all have been issues in the cultural life of America that have carried significant political weight. Some argue that 'The homosexual activist movement has long been an integral part of America's pro-abortion movement, and vice-versa.'[70] That is, some fear there is an anti-*Christian* plot. The organisation Christian Parents decries 'UN threats to American liberty'.[71] The Christian Alert Network claims that the UN is about to 'impose' world government, and therefore worries that 'We have a very serious and urgent problem in our country and we need *your* help.'[72] J. Zane Walley writes that 'The clamor to get America out of The UN is direly inadequate. If our country is to regain sovereignty, we must abrogate all international treaties and require that our federal bureaus withdraw from UN pawn agencies.'[73] The conservative radio personality, Hugh Hewitt, a church elder in Orange County, California whose radio programmes are heard over most of America by over 700,000 people a week, sees a fundamental challenge in the attacks of the second American 9/11: 'The attack upon the West and Christianity became undeniable after 9/11 . . .', he argues.[74] None of these are statements by political leaders or scholars. And yet they have real resonance in the cultural and political life of America. The United States, when viewed in these ways, is a very strange society to European eyes.

69 Crouch, *Apocalypse*, pp. 9–11.

70 Robert Knight, 'Planned parenthood to host homosexual bishop at prayer breakfast', Concerned Women For America, 13 April 2005, at http://sepwww.stanford.edu/sep/josman/culture/frissues.html [4/2005].

71 Christian Parents at http://www.christianparents.com/unplan01.html [accessed April 2005].

72 'United Nations poised to impose one world government', Christian Alert (Fall 1999), at http://www.vvm.com/~ctomlin/a87.htm [4/2005].

73 J. Zane Walley, 'A lightning bolt of reality: the UN threat to America', World Newsstand (a Christian organisation based in Missouri), 23 July 2001, at http://www.worldnewsstand.net/NEWS/reality.htm [4/2005].

74 Hugh Hewitt, *In, But Not Of: A Guide to Christian Ambition* (New York: Nelson, 2003), p. 16.

Discourses of security

The use of discourse as an analytical tool can be controversial in the academic study of international relations in the United States, and even to an extent in the United Kingdom. Rival epistemologies can be cast as weapons, and academic identities and categories constructed and reconstructed. Can a study involving discourse even be seen to be legitimate social science? These are important questions; but they are not addressed in this volume. This is not a book in which one theory, approach or methodology is asserted and argued to be better than another. There is no comparative structure to the book, in which a discursive approach is compared to a neorealist one, and perhaps a constructivist or neoliberal one. These are perfectly legitimate academic enquiries. In international relations, over time such enquiries lead to a redrawing of categories, in ways that are important and interesting. But that is not the task of this work. This book will be categorised in particular ways; but that is being left to others. The task of this volume is to suggest that a focus on the cultural can enlighten international relations and security studies. It will ascertain how such a discursive approach might inform an understanding of the policies and actions of the United States government, in the period since the second American 9/11. As a consequence, the study postulates that processes of memorialisation followed the construction of meaning after that second American 9/11, forming a foundational myth. The task is therefore to construct, and reconstruct, a discursive process of crises.

In so doing, the writing draws on a series of parallels from historical experience: the European 'witchcraze' of the Middle Ages; Aztec engagement with Europeans; representations of the Rwandan genocide; the 'shock' of the launch of Sputnik. One reaction to the impact of the second American 9/11 was to resist open debate as 'anti-American': the publication of *Defending Civilization: How Our Universities Are Failing America and What Can Be Done About It* in November 2001 was a perfect example.[75] Published by the American Council of Trustees and Alumni, it was written by Jerry L. Martin, ACTA's president, and by Anne D. Neal, ACTA's executive director.

[75] Jerry L. Martin and Anne D. Neal, *Defending Civilization: How Our Universities Are Failing America and What Can Be Done About It*, ACTA, November 2001, emphasis in the original.

They argued that 'Rarely did professors publicly mention heroism, rarely did they discuss the differences between good and evil, the nature of western political order or the virtue of a free society. Their public messages were short on patriotism and long on self-flagellation. Indeed, the message of much of academe was: *Blame America First*!'

Such powerful claims to uniformity as that by the American Council of Trustees and Alumni could only be legitimized by a uniform reaction to the events of the second American 9/11, and the ability to create one powerful narrative of those events that could be shared by all, a narrative that explained what had happened to whom by whom, and what the necessary steps would be as a consequence. The construction and content of that narrative will be analysed in the next chapters. But its production and reproduction was not the preserve of the government, or of the political elite. The narrative that became the 'common sense' in America was developed and reproduced across popular culture. One example of this was the work of the cartoonists, who in the immediate aftermath of the second American 9/11 produced powerful work of loss and revenge. One shows firemen lifting the Stars and Stripes flag over the rubble of the fallen Twin Towers, in the image so familiar from Iwo Jima in the Second World War, symbolising triumph in adversity. Another shows Uncle Sam, looking deeply sorrowful, carrying a dead fireman from the collapsed building. In one, a man (America) dressed as an exterminator goes down a sewer marked 'terrorism' with the comment: 'Bear with me, this might take some time.' In another, the American eagle is shown sharpening its claws. And yet another shows the Democrat Donkey and the Republican Elephant running together, one saying 'to arms, old buddy' the other replying 'to arms, old chum'.[76] Unity, sorrow and loss, revenge and ultimate victory speak from these and other cartoons drawn in the final third of the year 2001. Such imagery reinforced and reproduced that which had become the dominant reaction to the attacks, therefore helping to portray the policy that flowed subsequently as common sense.

This book draws extensively on material from popular culture, and in some ways seeks therefore to utilise a methodology more familiar to cultural studies than to international relations. A wider range of sources gives a deeper sense of the collective discourse shaped by the

[76] All were produced at the end of 2001: http:/webpages.charter.net/svitale/tribute.html [4/2004].

interventions following the second American 9/11. In the renegotiations of identity and behaviour in the United States, there has still been room for humour, one widely shared throughout American society. The *Orange Peel Gazette* is published in Florida for Polk County and Plant City. It is a free publication, funded by a large amount of advertising. Volume 5, number 8 was published on 19 August 2004, and it was an important issue, being the first after the state suffered major destruction following Hurricane Charley. The first text is on page 2, where the following was produced:

> After his death, Osama bin Laden went to paradise. He was greeted by George Washington, who slapped him across the face and yelled angrily, 'How dare you attack the nation I helped conceive!' Then Patrick Henry punched Osama in the nose and James Madison kicked him in the groin. Bin Laden was subjected to similar beatings from John Randolph, James Monroe, Thomas Jefferson and 66 other early Americans. As he writhed in pain on the ground, an angel appeared. Bin Laden groaned, 'This is not what I was promised!' The angel replied, 'I told you there would be 72 Virginians waiting for you! What did you think I said?'[77]

Again, unity of 'American-ness' – here across time – and the identification of the enemy, and his ultimate defeat (and humiliation) are all clear in this powerful representation of the discourse. This joke could only be constructed as it was if the 'war on terror' discourse had achieved a hegemonic position.

To understand the power and spread of the 'war on terror' as discourse a clear conception of its origin is needed, and the next chapter develops a process for explaining crisis discourse that will be developed throughout the book.

[77] 'Osama in paradise?', *Orange Peel Gazette*, 5:8 (19 August 2004), p. 2.

2 *Deconstructing the second American 9/11*

Introduction

THE EVENTS OF 11 September 2001 were profound: for those families and friends who lost loved ones; for the politics of the United States; and for the way in which global security is spoken of and practised. The Palestinian writer M. Shahid Alam likened the second American 9/11 to 'an eruption, a volcanic eruption that has thrust lava and ashes from our netherworld, the dark netherworld of the Periphery, into the rich and tranquil landscape of America'.[1] The violence that is so much an everyday event in so much of the world, the violence outside, spilled over into the American inside. Three thousand people died at work, or on their way to work. America became embattled. President George W. Bush said:

> September the 11th was a horrible day for our nation, and we must never forget the lessons of September the 11th . . . It's a time that really changed our perspective about the world. See, we never really thought America would be a battlefield. We thought oceans would protect us. That was kind of the conventional wisdom of the time. And therefore, our defenses were aligned that way, our offenses were aligned that way.[2]

The United States began to spend enormous amounts of money on 'homeland defence': the new department was to receive $19.5 billion in 2002, and $37.7 billion in 2003.[3] American defence budgets were

[1] M. Shahid Alam, 'Making sense of our times: is there an Islamic problem?', The Electronic Intifada, 14 October 2004, at http://electronicintifada.net/v2/article3231.shtml [3/2005].

[2] 'Information sharing, Patriot Act, vital to homeland security', speech in Buffalo, 20 April 2004, at http://www.whitehouse.gov/news/releases/2004/04/20040420-2.html [4/2004].

[3] *Securing the Homeland, Strengthening the Nation*, at http://www.whitehouse.gov/homeland/homeland_security_book.html [4/2004].

to rise from some $300 billion in 2000, to $396 billion for 2003; with a projected increase to $470 billion for 2007.[4]

The change in policy practice followed a dramatic change in perception and debate. The world had changed, it was being said, and so policy must change too. As George W. Bush put it, 'For the United States, September the 11th, 2001, cut a deep dividing line in our history – a change of eras as sharp and clear as Pearl Harbor or the first day of the Berlin Blockade.'[5] Secretary of State, Colin Powell, had said in October 2001 that 'Not only is the cold war over, the post-cold war period is also over.'[6] National Security Advisor, Condoleezza Rice, told us that 'The fall of the Berlin Wall and the fall of the World Trade Center were the bookends of a long transition period.'[7] Deputy Secretary of Defense, Richard Armitage, said, in reference to the second American 9/11, 'History starts today.'[8] The White House speech writer, David Frum, remarked that September 11th ended 'America's long vacation from history . . .'.[9] This rhetoric – the emergence of a new age, as clearly defined as the cold war – was replicated in academic journals: Chris Seiple, writing in *Orbis*, argued that 'As in the early cold war, the next five years are likely to establish patterns of global engagement and international relations that will define the next *fifty* years.'[10] The second American 9/11 indeed led to a war in Afghanistan, and inexorably to war and occupation in Iraq. President Bush explained that 'The reason I keep insisting that there was a relationship between Iraq and Saddam and al-Qaeda, is because there was a relationship between Iraq and

[4] Michael O'Hanlon, 'Rumsfeld's defence vision', *Survival*, 44:2 (Summer 2002), pp. 108–11.

[5] George Bush, 23 May 2002, in Thomas M. Freiling (ed.), *George W. Bush on God and Country* (Washington, DC: Allegiance, 2004), p. 242.

[6] Colin Powell, 'Remarks at business event, Shanghai', 18 October 2001, at http://www.state.gov/secretary/rm/2001/5441.htm [7/2004].

[7] Condoleezza Rice, 'A balance of power that favours freedom', *US National Security Strategy: A New Era*, in *US Foreign Policy Agenda: An Electronic Journal of the Department of State*, 7:4 (December 2002), at http://usgovinfo.about.com/gi/dynamic/offsite.htm?site=http://usinfo.state.gov/journals/itps/1202/ijpe/ijpe1202.htm [5/2004].

[8] In Andrew J. Bacevich, *The New American Militarism* (New York: Oxford University Press, 2005), p. 202.

[9] David Frum, *The Right Man* (London: Weidenfeld & Nicolson, 2003), p. 114.

[10] Chris Seiple, 'Homeland security concepts and strategies', *Orbis,* 46:2 (Spring 2002), p. 261; emphasis in the original.

al-Qaeda.'[11] In so doing, the attacks of 11 September 2001 were discursively linked to the regime in Baghdad, legitimising subsequent military intervention. Policy practice was to change in dramatic ways, but through a change in language and ideas. Such discursive practices are archetypical: they seek to create new meaning out of a socially constructed crisis. And that new meaning was to be called the 'war on terror'.

'You can't declare war on a noun . . .' declared Michael Moore, in one of his many interviews about the American 'war on terror'.[12] Moore's film, *Fahrenheit 9/11*, came to symbolise dissatisfaction with the Bush administration and its foreign policy.[13] The title evoked Ray Bradbury's epic novel of censorship and resistance written fifty years earlier, *Fahrenheit 451*, in which the job of the fireman is to burn all books, and the houses in which they are found.[14] After ten years of burning, one particular fireman, Guy Montag, learns that this normality was new, that there was a past without censorship, and that there can be a future without censorship too. That is, the 'common sense' of today was not that of the past, and need not be that of the future – common sense can be contested because it is socially constructed. Moore undoubtedly does not equate himself with the complicity of Montag's past, but he does sympathise with the mission of ending censorship, and the lies, as he sees it, of the Bush administration: that is, with problematising the construction of common sense. Of course, *Fahrenheit 9/11*, unlike *Fahrenheit 451*, was highly controversial, with debates about its accuracy, politics and appropriateness. Michael Moore's own website went to great lengths to 'prove' the 'facts' underlying the film.[15] But this highly politicised, highly personalised debate missed a very important point. American society – both the left and right – had experienced a crisis together on 11 September 2001, one

[11] 'Bush insists Iraq, al-Qaeda had "relationship" ', CNN, 17 June 2004, at http://www.cnn.com/2004/ALLPOLITICS/06/17/Bush.alqaeda/index.html [8/2004].

[12] In Richard Corliss, 'The world according to Michael', *Time Magazine*, 12 July 2004.

[13] The text of the film is at http://www.redlinerants.com/index.php?subaction=showfull&id=1088491633&archive=&start_from=&ucat=1& [7/2004].

[14] Ray Bradbury, *Fahrenheit 451* (New York: Ballantine/Random House, 1991; originally published in 1953, although a shorter version was published in *Galaxy Science Fiction* in 1950).

[15] See http://www.michaelmoore.com/warroom/f911notes/ [8/2004]. Most of the 'facts' are quotes.

that was socially constructed across the whole of American society. This is not to say that it was not 'real'; that 3,000 people did not die. Deepak Chopra might argue that there is no objective reality when he says that 'people grow old and die because they have seen other people grow old and die. Ageing is simply learned behaviour.'[16] But this cuts across empirical evidence, and following the attacks of 11 September 2001, there were 3,000 personal tragedies for the families and friends of those involved, although the meaning attached to that event was social.

The terrible events of the second American 9/11 occurred; but their meaning, and hence the policy reaction, was the product of social interaction, not of some kind of 'normal' or 'commonsense' response. On 11 September 2001, four commercial aircraft were hijacked.[17] By just after 9 o'clock in the morning, two aircraft had been flown into the World Trade Center. By 9.45, the Pentagon had been struck by another aircraft, and some ten minutes later, the South Tower of the World Trade Center collapsed. By 10.15, part of the Pentagon buckled after the impact, and some ten minutes or so later, the fourth aircraft crashed in Pennsylvania. Within minutes, the North Tower of the World Trade Center had also collapsed. Some 3,000 people had died.[18]

The impact on the American psyche was profound. The nature of American interaction with the world had to change. As John Lewis Gaddis put it, 'It was not just the Twin Towers that collapsed on that morning of September 11, 2001: so too did some of our most fundamental assumptions about international, national, and personal security.'[19] The event had to be memorialised as a marker not only of respect, but also as to that which must change.[20] As Strobe Talbott

16 Chopra in Francis Wheen, *How Mumbo-Jumbo Conquered the World* (London: Harper Perennial, 2004), p. 47.

17 These were: American Airlines Flight 11, Boston to Los Angeles; United Airlines Flight 93, Newark to San Francisco; American Airlines Flight 77, Washington to Los Angeles; and United Airlines Flight 175, Boston to Los Angeles.

18 A list is at http://www.cbsnews.com/stories/2002/09/11/60II/main521718.shtm: 'Sept 11 and since' then 'List of victims' [6/2004]. The number of dead has changed as studies investigate the missing and the remains. For example, Phil Hirschkorn, 'New York reduces 9/11 death toll by 40', CNN, 29 October 2003, at http://www.cnn.com/2003/US/Northeast/10/29/wtc.deaths/ [9/2005].

19 John Lewis Gaddis, *Surprise, Security and the American Experience* (Cambridge, MA: Harvard University Press, 2004), p. 80.

20 The WTC was to be replaced by the tallest building in the world; some wanted the land left as a memorial. See http://911digitalarchive.org/ [7/2004].

(a member of the Clinton administration) put it, the second American 9/11 'made Americans more supportive of the new, unilateralist premise of their government's foreign policy. In the course of that single, brilliant, blue-sky morning . . . Americans suddenly saw the world as a more perilous place . . .'[21] So much, in retrospect, seems normal, seems to be common sense. That is what happens through socially constructed crises, in which a new discourse emerges thereafter.

Sadly, events in which around 3,000 people die are not rare. There are, in fact, a significant number of recent examples. In 2003, a heat-wave struck much of Europe. In France, the conditions were particularly severe, and at least 3,000 people died of heat-related causes. In 1998, three huge tidal waves struck the northwest coast of Papua New Guinea; again, at least 3,000 died.[22] There were 3,000 intifada-related deaths in the three years after the violence reignited in Palestine.[23] Amongst India's Islamic population, 3,000 people were killed in the sectarian violence in Gujarat.[24] There is nothing particularly unique in an event in which 3,000 people die except, of course, for those directly concerned in France, Papua New Guinea, Palestine and India. In fact, in global terms, 3,000 is not a very large total. In South Africa alone, some 3,000 people die from HIV/AIDS every month.[25] The American murder rate was hailed in 1997 as being the lowest for thirty years: however, that total still reached 18,209. In 2002, California alone saw nearly 2,000 Americans murdered.[26]

Each of these statistics can be the subject of lengthy argument in its own right, but of course the point is not dependent upon statistical accuracy. Argue with the numbers if you must; and of course the total numbers of deaths do matter greatly to the families and friends of those lost not just in New York and Washington on 11 September 2001, but those lost to HIV/AIDS, to the heatwave, and to political violence around the world. But in political terms, there is no objective power to

21 Strobe Talbott, 'War in Iraq, revolution in America', *International Affairs*, 79:5 (October 2003), p. 1043.

22 See http://www.cnn.com/2003/WORLD/europe/08/14/paris.heatwave/ and http://www.chron.com/content/interactive/voyager/sail/news/98/07/980720png.html [7/2004].

23 '3,000 dead yet peace remains elusive', *Guardian*, 29 September 2003.

24 See http://www.muslimnews.co.uk/news/news.php?sub=753 [7/2004].

25 See '3000 dead every month in South Africa', The Big Story, 1 June 2002, at http://thebigstory.org/lost/lost-aids.html [8/2004].

26 See http://www.cnn.com/US/9901/02/murder.rate/ [7/2004].

these numbers, in which the loss of a particular total of people leads inexorably to a particular political response. That 3,000 people died on 11 September 2001 was not enough, in itself, to explain the emergence of a discourse known as the 'war on terror', one shared on the American left as much as propagated on the American right. Louis Menand, writing in *The New Yorker* twelve months after 11 September 2001, argued that 'The initial response of most cultural and political critics to the attacks of September 11th . . . was: it just proves what I've always said. The attacks were treated as geopolitics for dummies, confirming conclusions that sensible observers had reached long before . . .'[27] Indeed so. But that is the power of a particular discourse at work, in retrospect as well as in prospect; it is not evidence of the absolute power of numbers.

Discourse and the second American 9/11

Discourse affects how we live in fundamental ways. It concerns the manner in which linguistic elements form wholes, structures, that are larger than the sum of their parts. Discourse structures who we are, who we like, who we hate. It shapes how we behave towards 'ourselves', and how we behave towards 'others'. Discourses are related sets of ideas that are expressed in a variety of places by those with social power, and are reproduced by others with power and those without. Discourses organise our minds. Categories are created into which people are then placed. All male 'Mexicans' are irresponsible, all 'Indians' are trustworthy, in D. H. Lawrence's account of *Mornings in Mexico*. 'The Indian, it seems to me, is not naturally dishonest. He is not naturally avaricious, has not even any innate cupidity . . . To the real Mexican, no! He doesn't care . . . He doesn't want to keep anything, not even his wife and children.'[28] Discourse defines the means by which language conveys meaning through the production, distribution and reception of texts on a conscious and unconscious level. That is, discourse 'does not mirror an independent object world but constructs

[27] Louis Menand, 'Faith, hope and clarity: September 11th and the American soul', *New Yorker*, 16 September 2002, at http://www.newyorker.com/critics/atlarge/?020916crat_atlarge [8/2004].

[28] D. H. Lawrence, *Mornings in Mexico* (London: Penguin, 1986, originally published 1927), p. 33.

and constitutes it'.[29] As Henrik Larsen puts it, 'discourses dictate what it is possible to say and not possible to say. Discourses therefore provide the basis on which policy preferences, interests and goals are constructed.'[30] And this it is does intersubjectively through language. As Albert Yee argued, 'Languages and discourses consisting of vocabularies, rules, symbols, narratives, and the like are necessarily public and therefore intersubjectively constituted and accessed.'[31]

Language as discourse is not simply about representing the world; it is concerned with treating it as a form of social action.[32] That is, a focus on how certain things are done by people with words. Particular descriptions become not only important in themselves, but also in terms of constituting an understanding of that which is under discussion. 'Descriptions of the world do not simply represent the output of some underlying reasoning process that ponders the nature of reality; they are instead managed descriptions given in a particular interactional setting.'[33] Focusing on discourse in this way means problematising structures, questioning common sense. As Nietzsche put it, 'The world seems logical to us because we have made it logical.'[34] The analysis is not concerned with the validity of what is said; but rather with understanding what is done through particular accounts. A discursive approach to knowledge claims is not concerned with evaluating between competing claims on the grounds of empirical evidence or logical consistency. Rather, it seeks to understand how constructing language in particular ways leads to particular outcomes. Words, ideas, language matter to the policy world. In academic analyses, 'discourse' can and is used in a variety of different ways. And in this volume, this complex and varied sense of 'discourse' is the one that drives the analysis. 'Discourse' here is to be used in an eclectic fashion, considered in terms of shaping relationships, but also in terms of the impact upon

[29] Chris Barker and Dariusz Galasinski, *Cultural Studies and Discourse Analysis* (London: Sage, 2001), p. 1.

[30] Henrik Larsen, 'British and Danish European policies in the 1990s: a discourse approach', *European Journal of International Relations*, 5 (1999), p. 453.

[31] Albert S. Yee, 'The causal effects of ideas on policies', *International Organization*, 50:1 (Winter 1996), p. 96.

[32] On this see, for example, Jonathan Potter, *Representing Reality* (London: Sage, 1997).

[33] Brian Rappert, *Controlling the Weapons of War* (London: Routledge, forthcoming 2006), p. 35.

[34] Friedrich Nietzsche, *The Will to Power* (New York: Vintage, 1968), p. 283.

psychology. There are multiple ways of thinking about discourse, and in using some of those ways in this book, the intention is to open routes into considering more fully the cultural nature of political interaction.

The discourse that is important for this book, therefore, can be found in a variety of places. Of course, it is produced in the words and statements of government and political leaders, and in their reproduction by major outlets of the media, particular constructions of what is and what is not common sense permeate society. But a *crisis* discourse infuses society in a variety of ways. That is, the sense in which a crisis discourse is truly a social one – one that is shared throughout the body politic, and not just its leadership – can be understood from its cultural representations. Thus, as we shall see, the interpretation of the second American 9/11 that came to discursively dominate was one that was co-produced and reproduced in many different aspects of American cultural life: television programmes, novels, movies, in shopping products, and in other areas. Of particular importance in contemporary America, discourse is produced and reproduced through internet sites and email communication. These different areas have not only seen the reproduction of discourse but also its production, in two senses. First, the discourse of the second American 9/11 did not come from nowhere; but rather from a particular set of understandings about the world that had been as much produced in and by the media, by churchleaders and by television, radio and novelists as by politicians. There was a mutual constitution between the these groups, who form an American elite. Second, in reproducing the meanings of the second American 9/11 subsequent to the event, very little discursive space was allowed for alternatives, or indeed for discursive moves from that post-9/11 mindset. Although bitter, the discursive space between George W. Bush and John Kerry as they fought the 2004 presidential election campaign was, over the meaning of the second American 9/11, very small indeed. As Andrew Bacevich put it, Kerry 'framed his differences with George W. Bush's national security policies in terms of tactics rather than first principles'.[35] That was in no small part a product of the way in which popular cultural representations of self and other in the post-9/11 world had been constructed.

Discourse, therefore, is wider than those words spoken and written by a political elite. It incorporates those relevant words spoken and written in popular culture, authored by this wider elite. And in so doing, dis-

[35] Bacevich, *American Militarism*, p. 15.

course includes images. Images can produce and reproduce discursive understandings. A number of authors have led the way in international relations' thinking about moving beyond the written and the spoken in security discourse. Michael Williams has written of the need to include television images.[36] Lene Hansen has written of the role of silence in security dynamics, and persuasively of the need to 'understand security as a practice which through discursive and bodily acts inscribe particular subjects as threats and being threatened'.[37] Ole Waever has argued that 'it is possible to think about meaning effects in other media than language'.[38] These are all calls in different ways to consider a 'thicker' notion of culture than that most often found in the security studies literature.

That images can produce and reproduce security meaning has been illustrated historically very often. The Mayans marked the power of one city or leader over others in images as well as text. When the city state of Tikal defeated and occupied the city state of Uacactun by the year 377, the event was marked in a stela in the Tikal Ballcourt, the centre of the triumphant city; and the defeated people of Uacactun had an image of their conqueror, Smoking-Frog, raised in the centre of their city, to remind them of their subservience.[39] Ramses II's victory over the Hittites at the Battle of Kadesh in 1275 BC was marked on the Temple of Luxor by images of victory, including one in which the Pharaoh single-handedly charges the enemy, a dramatic image of power designed to intimidate all.[40] Examining representations of meaning in images related to the second American 9/11 shows the power of the discourse.

Figure 2.1 is an image closely associated with the foundational myth. It is of a cross, formed from the steel girders from the World Trade Center, at Ground Zero in New York. The steel cross symbolises not only loss, but also the Christian imagery with which the 'war on terror'

36 Michael C. Williams, 'Words, images, enemies: securitization and international politics', *International Studies Quarterly*, 47 (2003), pp. 511–31.

37 Lene Hansen, 'The little mermaid's silent security dilemma', *Millennium: Journal of International Studies*, 29:2 (2000), p. 304.

38 Ole Waever, 'Securitisation: taking stock of a research programme in security studies', unpublished manuscript, 2003, cited in Rita Taureck's doctoral study, University of Birmingham, 2006.

39 Linda Schele and David Freidel, *A Forest of Kings* (New York: William Morrow, 1990), pp. 130–64, 150 and 146.

40 These form what Richard Jackson calls discursive actions, and in contemporary America he gives examples such as the introduction of armed sky marshals on to commercial aircraft. See Jackson, *Writing the War on Terrorism* (Manchester: Manchester University Press, 2005), pp. 113–14.

Figure 2.1. Ground Zero, New York City, April 2004 (photograph by the author)

is so replete. It is an image that – along with those of airliners crashing into those buildings – has come to dominate the memory of the attacks of 11 September 2001. In contrast, figure 2.2 is of a 'Subway' sandwich shop in Haines City, a small town in Florida, which at the time had been heavily damaged by Hurricane Charley. Despite the destruction all around, the sandwich shop – which stands by a crossroads – proclaims to all driving and passing through its demand to 'Remember 9/11'. An advertising hoarding at an intersection, not sold for commercial use, but rather to market a particular idea, and the policy programme that went along with it. Figure 2.3 is one that evokes the nationalistic demand for unity of purpose in the context of the freedom challenged on 11 September 2001. It stands in the railway yards in the north of Kansas City, overlooking one of the major road routes into and out of the city. Rather like figure 2.2, this is advertising space not used for Coca-Cola or other commercial products, but rather for a policy product. Whereas figure 2.2 is from a small town, this is from a large Midwest city. Figure 2.4 is a simple sign, homemade, put alongside the road in Phoenix, Arizona, expressing the frustration that Osama bin Laden should remain free. Just before this photograph was taken, *USA Today* published a poll showing that the number of Americans who thought that Osama bin Laden would be captured or killed had fallen to 55 per cent, from 78 per cent in September 2001.[41] It illustrates the adoption of the policy programme at a popular level. In similar

[41] Bill Nichols, 'Poll shows fewer Americans expect bin Laden to be caught', *USA Today*, 10 August 2005.

Figure 2.2. Haines City, Florida, September 2004 (photograph by the author)

Figure 2.3. Kansas City, April 2005 (photograph by the author)

vein, figure 2.5 shows the popular imagery found at Shanksville, Pennsylvania, at the crash site of the fourth plane. It is a place where the public have created markers, and much of the memorabilia there is both religious and family oriented in nature. There is a wire fence covered in caps and coats, and flags. And each lost passenger and crew-member has a hand-made angel with their name upon it; here, we see that for Mark Bingham. Finally, figure 2.6 is that of a school in southern California. During the occupation of Iraq, the apolitical space of

Figure 2.4. Phoenix, Arizona, August 2005 (photograph by the author)

an educational establishment was itself occupied to demand solidarity behind the cause, for any questioning of the direction of American policy would be to fail to support those troops standing 'in harm's way'. The 'realities' of America's engagement with the 'war on terror' were in such ways directly communicated to the nation's youth.

These images are all united in a narrative sense – they tell the same story – even though they do not originate from national government. Each image communicates directly with the observer to remind him or her – in their place of pilgrimage to Ground Zero, then further afield wherever they live and work throughout the United States – of the key messages of a country under attack, needing unity of resolve, changing its behaviour, fighting back.

Imagery is important not only physically in terms of reproducing common sense, it is also important virtually. One of the dimensions of

Figure 2.5. Shanksville, Pennsylvania, September 2005 (photograph by the author)

the wars that have followed the second American 9/11 – in Afghanistan, but particularly Iraq – has been the development of 'blogs' (personal web-based logs of events) in which the use of imagery has been very strong. There are images of American soldiers teaching weapon safety to children; of the weapons of the insurgents in Iraq; of the everyday life of soldiers in Iraq.[42] Each image contains a political message related to and shaped by the dominant discourse.

[42] See http://patrickhenry.worldmagblog.com/patrickhenry/archives/011892.html, 11 January 2005; http://rofasix.blogspot.com/2005/05/iraq-through-eyes-of-soldiers.html; and http://www.sgtlizzie.blogspot.com/ [all 6/2005].

Figure 2.6. A school in southern California, September 2005 (photograph by Jane Usherwood)

This is not to say that everything is reducible to language. It is sometimes said that, in response to any analysis that seeks to examine the discursive structures underlying policy, material reality can be underplayed. A tank is, after all, an object that can kill and inflict major damage regardless of what it is called. But that is not the point. Rather, what is also important is the meaning attached to an object, meaning that is constructed intersubjectively. Patrick Wright's outstanding volume, *Tank*, gives many illustrations: that of the 265 war battered tanks presented to those British towns that had raised the most money in war bonds after the First World War; of the tank represented in the stained glass window of a medieval Cambridgeshire church; of the bitter political argument in Prague in 1991 about whether the painting of a T-34 Soviet tank, on display to represent the liberation of the city by the Soviet Army nearly fifty years earlier, could be pink.[43] That is, not the tank of killing and destruction, but the tank representing national pride and reward, the weapon of God, the emblem of liberation, repression or remembrance. Or take something as simple as cod, a fish used to construct a slave economy (salt cod was commercially linked with slaves and molasses in the trade route from Africa, to America, to the Caribbean); and because of the *taste* for the fish during the Second World War, Iceland was able to move 'in one generation from a fifteenth-century colonial society to a modern post-war

[43] Patrick Wright, *Tank* (London: Faber and Faber, 2000), pp. 122, 113, 379–90.

nation'.[44] Or, profoundly for the nature of the modern world, an argument about the meaning of Confucian thought that constrained Chinese imperialism from global reach. At a time when Chinese ships had a capacity four times greater, and half a century earlier, than those of Columbus, and when Chinese fleets may have visited Australia as well as North and South America, imperial Chinese discourse evolved away from expansion of trade and influence towards introspection.[45] It is meaning that is constructed through discourse.

Language impacts upon society as a whole. Ideas and language cannot exist without the other in a social context, and their coming together to create a discourse is reproduced in speech and in text, and in action. The *Malleus Maleficarum* was published in 1486 and was a powerful representation of a new discourse in medieval Europe.[46] The 1480s were a period of bitter argument about witchcraft. Some held to variations of the traditional view that witchcraft was impossible, in that it would indicate that God was not omnipotent. Others made arguments that Christendom was – as Tom Clancy would have put it – in clear and present danger from Satan. As the Pope veered towards the latter, Inquisitors were established; but they found resistance to their use of torture and execution by local church and secular authorities. The *Malleus Maleficarum* was developed as a text that provided the theoretical underpinning for the existence of 'sorcery' (in part one); a record of the practices of sorcery (in part two); and in the third part, instruction as to how the accused should be interrogated (tortured) and punished if convicted (mainly burned to death). The book represented the discursive shift of the period, and became a 'textbook' of practice. It was reprinted some twenty-six times until the final edition, as late as 1669.[47] The discursive shift led to slaughter on a massive scale. In *Witchcraze*, Anne Llewellyn Barstow suggests that before the 1480s, there had been fewer than 500 executions for witchcraft. In the period to the final publication

[44] See Mark Kurlansky, *Cod: A Biography of the Fish that Changed the World* (London: Vintage, 1999), quote from p. 155.

[45] Louis Levathes, *When China Ruled the Seas: The Treasure Fleet of the Dragon Throne, 1405–33* (New York: Oxford University Press, 1997); and Gavin Menzies, *1421: The Year China Discovered America* (New York: William Morrow, Co., 2003).

[46] *The Malleus Maleficarum of Heinrich Kramer and James Sprenger* (New York: Dover Publications, 1971); the text is at http://www.malleusmaleficarum.org/

[47] Practices transferred from the Old World to the New, where they outlived those of the Old World: the Salem witch trials in America did not take place until 1692.

of the *Malleus Maleficarum* in 1669, the total was some 75,000 people, overwhelmingly women.[48] The core element of the *Malleus Maleficarum* was in achieving a discursive shift in which 'witchcraft' was deemed to be an 'exceptional crime', one against which it was legitimate to dispense with regular rules and legal safeguards. Indeed, it was one's religious duty to prosecute the accused with all force necessary.

It is not the argument that the 'war on terror' is comparable with that of the 'witchcraze'; however, during both discursive shifts, legal and ethical boundaries of behaviour towards a newly constructed enemy were to be changed. This can be illustrated by a brief examination of the speech of Attorney General John Ashcroft on 24 September 2001, in presenting the Mobilization Against Terrorism Act to the House Committee on the Judiciary. Ashcroft set out the immediate danger posed, and the need for radical new legislation:

> The danger that darkened the United States of America and the civilized world on September 11 did not pass with the atrocities committed that day. It requires that we provide law enforcement with the tools necessary to identify, dismantle, disrupt and punish terrorist organizations, before they strike again. Terrorism is a clear and present danger to Americans today . . . This new terrorist threat to Americans on our soil is a turning point in America's history . . . The death tolls are too high, the consequences too great. We must prevent first, prosecute second. The fight against terrorism is now the highest priority of the Department of Justice . . . Today, we seek to enlist your [i.e. Congress's] assistance, for we seek new laws against America's enemies, foreign and domestic . . . Every day that passes with outdated statutes and the old rules of engagement is a day that terrorists have a competitive advantage.[49]

On behalf of the administration, Ashcroft made the case that terrorism was an exceptional crime, and that it could be committed by those within the state as well as those outside. Thus, the change in the balance of civil liberties contained in the Patriot Act of 2001, and in other measures, was a logical consequence. They led Timothy Lynch,

[48] Anne Llewellyn Barstow, *Witchcraze: A New History of the European Witch Hunts* (London: Pandora Books, 1995), appendix B in particular. Note that these figures from both before and after the watershed of the 1480s exclude inquisitions for heresy, which were extensive and brutal.

[49] 'Ashcroft outlines proposed changes in anti-terrorism laws', *Global Security*, 24 September 2001, at http://www.globalsecurity.org/military/library/news/2001/09/mil-010924-usia05a.htm [9/2005].

at the libertarian CATO Institute, to conclude that 'The Bush Administration has supported measures that are antithetical to freedom, such as secretive subpoenas, secretive arrests, secretive trials and secretive deportations.'[50] And the suspension of the Geneva Conventions towards those interned in Guantanamo Bay also followed from a position in which terrorism was constructed as an exceptional crime, against which exceptional measures were required. In the Egyptian *Al-Ahram* newspaper, Nyier Abdou concluded that 'The rights of POWs under the Geneva Conventions are considerable, which means it is in the interest of the US to classify them otherwise.'[51]

The discursive shift of contemporary international security which took place after the second American 9/11 has been termed the 'war on terror'. It is a discourse that was developed within one particular political perspective in the United States, but has been reproduced across the American political spectrum and then again in other countries in Europe, the Middle East and South and Central Asia. It has altered understandings and perceptions and, as a consequence, has led to new patterns of behaviour.

In order for this shift to occur, there needs to be a securitising actor, one clearly 'in a position of authority'.[52] It is this discursive act of securitisation that takes politics 'beyond the established rules of the game' which then elevates the issue to that of 'absolute priority'.[53] Discursive structures are practices that constitute and organise social relations.[54] 'Discourse as a framework for analysis', as described by Vivien Schmidt, provides an explanation for dramatic change, such as France's reversal of state *dirigisme* (Mitterrand, 1983), and Britain's

[50] Timothy Lynch, 'Breaking the vicious circle: preserving our liberties while fighting terrorism', *CATO Institute Policy Analysis*, no. 445, 26 June 2002, at http://www.cato.org/pubs/pas/pa443.pdf [9/2005].

[51] Nyier Abdou, 'Winner's Rules', *Al-Ahram*, no. 572, 7–13 February 2002, at http://weekly.ahram.org.eg/2002/572/in11.htm [9/2005].

[52] Ole Waever, 'The EU as a security actor: reflections from a pessimistic constructivist on post-sovereign security actors', in Morten Kelstrup and Michael C. Williams (eds.), *International Relations Theory and the Politics of European Integration* (London: Routledge, 2000), pp. 250–94, quote from p. 253.

[53] Barry Buzan, Ole Waever and Jaap de Wilde, *Security: A New Framework for Analysis* (Boulder, CO, and London: Lynne Rienner, 1997), p. 176.

[54] See, for example, Ernesto Laclau and Chantal Mouffe, *Hegemony and Socialist Strategy: Towards a Democratic Politics* (London: Verso, 2001).

refutation of the post-war consensus in favour of radical neoliberalism (Thatcher, 1979).[55] Policies and outlooks were changed due to a fundamental discursive shift which was initiated by those with social power; and, in turn, that shift, that discourse, was reproduced by others. For Schmidt, discourse 'consists of whatever policy actors say to one another and to the public in their efforts to generate and legitimise a policy programme. As such, discourse encompasses both a set of policy ideas and values and an interactive process of policy construction and communication.'[56] Hence fundamental changes in policy are produced by discursive shifts which create new meaning; and in the security field, they raise an issue to a level that is above that of 'normal' political interaction. Such is the story of the response to the second American 9/11.

It was the socially constructed crisis of 9/11 that created a new discursive project. As Timo Kivimaki said, 'The very fact that we refer to the post-911 order (not . . . 119 order) reveals that it is the *American* sense of *emergency* that motivates the drastic changes in world affairs.'[57] Schmidt argued that a crisis in the policy programme 'may come from outside events which the policy programme cannot solve and the discourse explain or from contradictions within and/or between policy discourse and programme . . .'.[58] The second American 9/11 represented precisely this phenomenon in that it was constructed as an outside event which the policy programme – that is, the then-existing construction of American security policy – could not solve, and was therefore representative of contradictions within that programme, that had left the United States open and vulnerable to terrorist attack. *Time Magazine*'s commentary was that by the summer of 2001, 'many of those in the know – the spooks, the buttoned-down bureaucrats, the law-enforcement professionals in a dozen countries – were almost frantic with worry that a major terrorist attack against American interests was imminent. It wasn't averted because 2001 saw

[55] Vivien Schmidt, *The Futures of European Capitalism* (Oxford: Oxford University Press, 2002); the title of chapter 5.

[56] Schmidt, *Futures*, p. 210. Also Vivien Schmidt, 'Democracy and discourse in an integrating Europe and a globalising world', *European Law Journal*, 6:3 (2001), pp. 277–300.

[57] Timo Kivimaki, 'Changing perspectives on security in Asia and Europe', *EU-Asia One Year after September 11*, pp. 1–2, at www.eias.org/conferences/euasia911/euasia911kivimaki.pdf [8/2004].

[58] Schmidt, *Futures*, p. 225.

a systematic collapse in the ability of Washington's national-security apparatus to handle the terrorist threat.'[59] And if the internal system of security was discredited, so was America's network of international alliances. 'NATO matters less and less . . .', observed the *Wall Street Journal*. 'With the exception of the Brits and Turks, Europeans have been less relevant to waging that war than the Uzbeks and the Kazaks and the Pakistanis.'[60] Thus, an American post-cold-war security order discourse collapsed under the new challenge. Pre-existing narratives about internal security and external alliances suddenly seemed fraught with contradictions and failure. The crisis demanded resolution through a new understanding.

As will be explored later, the second American 9/11 marks that point of discursive reconstruction. The second American 9/11 cannot be judged, objectively, to have been an event of such magnitude (in terms of the loss of human life) that it would inevitably produce a particular reaction; it cannot be seen that a series of calculable events led to some particular response. Narratives were important – historical analogy had real power: 11 September 2001 was constructed in the United States as a narrative in the same vein as the attack on Pearl Harbor (where, in passing, almost the same number of people died as on 11 September 2001).[61] In this, the narrative was strengthened in that one of the big blockbuster films of 2001 was the 'action classic' *Pearl Harbor*.[62] Pearl Harbor – the historical event – was the reference point of several articles published on 12 September in the major American newspapers.[63] And it was a theme common on the American right: 'Immediately after the 9/11 terrorist attack, some people compared

59 Michael C. Elliot, 'Could 9/11 have been prevented?', *Time Online Edition*, 4 August 2002, at http://www.time.com/time/nation/article/0,8599,333835,00.html [9/2004].

60 'Unmighty Europe', *Wall Street Journal*, 5 February 2002, at http://www.wallstreetjournal.com [5/2004].

61 See Adam Clymer, 'A day of terror', *New York Times*, 12 September 2001; Robert Daman, 'We must fight this war', *Washington Post*, 12 September 2001; Stephen Heflin, 'Terrorism introduces new reality', *Dallas Morning News* 13 September 2001, at http://www.cfr.org/pub4096/stephen_e_flynn/terrorism_introduces_new_reality.php [5/2004].

62 Buena Vista / Touchstone Productions, directed by Michael Bay.

63 See, for example, David Von Drehle, 'World war, cold war won. Now the gray war', *Washington Post,* 12 September 2001; Adam Clymer, 'A day of terror; in the capital; in the day's attacks and explosions, official Washington hears the echoes of earlier ones', *New York Times*, 12 September 2001.

that attack to the Japanese surprise attack on Pearl Harbor on 12/7/1941. It now seems that the comparisons might be more appropriate than anyone could have imagined.'[64] And three years later, as the report was published in the United States on the intelligence failures of 2001, *USA Today* reported the story under the headline 'As 9/11 report arrives, remember Pearl Harbor'.[65]

Crises play a political role, advancing one set of ideas over others, and also acting as a means for translating these ideas into common linguistic currency. Some books act powerfully to produce and particularly to reproduce ideas; a good example in 2003 was that of Robert Kagan's *Paradise and Power*.[66] Kagan's argument – that America's Mars was to Europe's Venus – became widely embedded in political debate, a clear point of reference. The terminology was particularly powerful, echoing that of the popular book *Men Are From Mars, Women Are From Venus* and thereby ascribing male values to America, female ones to Europe.[67] Phrases such as 'Europe should do the dishes' in peacekeeping missions followed this highly gendered stereotyping: the title of a speech by the NATO Secretary General was 'Those who do the fighting and those who do the dishes'.[68] This interplay of discourse can have a variety of effects. Robert Kaplan's *Balkan Ghosts* was said, by Richard Holbrooke, then a key figure in the Clinton administration, to have played a key role in convincing that administration not to intervene militarily in Bosnia in the middle 1990s. The administration, it seems, were taken by Kaplan's narration of a conflict based on 'ancient hatreds', thus

[64] Jacob G. Hornberger, '9/11 and Pearl Harbor', commentaries, The Future of Freedom Foundation, May 2002, at http://www.fff.org/comment/com0205l.asp [5/2004].

[65] Editorial, 'As 9/11 report arrives, remember Pearl Harbor', *USA Today*, 21 July 2004.

[66] Robert Kagan, *Paradise and Power: America and Europe in the New World Order* (New York: Random House, 2003).

[67] John Gray, *Men Are From Mars, Women Are From Venus* (New York: HarperCollins 2004: originally published in 1992). On page 9: 'Martians value power, competency, efficiency, and achievement.' And on page 11: 'Venusians have different values. They value love, communication, beauty, and relationships.' This maps on to Kagan's categorisations.

[68] Jaap de Hoop Scheffer, 'Those who do the fighting and those who do the dishes', Munich Security Conference, 7 February 2004, at http://www.paginedidifesa.it/2004/natosg_040207.html [9/2005].

not amenable to resolution brought from 'outside'.[69] Within five years, that narrative had been replaced by one in which the government of Slobodan Milosevic was seen to be taking Europe back to the dictatorships of the 1930s.

The crisis of the second American 9/11 was narrated to advance primarily neoconservative, but also premillennial sets of ideas over others, given that both had achieved a position of discursive prominence in America's political and popular cultural debates in 2001.[70] Andrew Bacevich argues that the second American 9/11 was used to energise a neoconservative plan: 'Osama bin Laden and the events of 9/11 provided the tailor-made opportunity to break free of the fetters restricting the exercise of American power.'[71] Norman Podhoretz, neoconservative guru, wrote enthusiastically and evangelically of the coming war with the terrorists at the end of 2001: 'What I mean is that nothing less than the soul of this country is at stake, and nothing less than an unambiguous victory will save us from yet another disappointment in ourselves . . .'[72]

These are the key aspects of the creation of the 'war on terror' discourse from the socially constructed crisis of the second American 9/11. Colin Hay draws a distinction between, on the one hand, contradiction and failure (in the sense of an accumulation of contradictions), and crisis on the other. 'The crucial point is that a given constellation of contradictions can sustain a multitude of differing and incommensurate conceptions of crisis . . .'[73] He goes on to argue that the success of crisis narratives 'generally resides in their ability to provide a simplified account sufficiently flexible to narrate a great

[69] Robert D. Kaplan, *Balkan Ghosts: A Journey Through History* (New York: Vintage Books, 1994). Holbrooke's comments are in *To End a War* (New York: Modern Library, 1999), p. 22. This is supported by James Gow in *Triumph of the Lack of Will: International Diplomacy and the Yugoslav War* (New York: Columbia University Press, 1997), p. 218.

[70] Michael Northcott, *An Angel Directs the Storm* (London: I. B. Taurus, 2004), pp. 87–8. [71] Bacevich, *American Militarism*, p. 91.

[72] Norman Podhoretz, 'Syria yes, Israel no?', *Weekly Standard*, 12 November 2001, at http://www.weeklystandard.com/check.asp?idArticle=457&r=edhtn [9/2005].

[73] Colin Hay, 'Crisis and political development in post-war Britain', in David Marsh, Jim Buller, Colin Hay, Jim Johnston, Peter Kerr, Stuart McAnulla and Matthew Watson, *Postwar British Politics in Perspective* (Cambridge: Polity Press, 1999), p. 91.

variety of morbid symptoms whilst unambiguously apportioning blame'.[74] Therefore there are no objective levels of contradiction that lead inevitably to a particular narrative of crisis and response: the events of the second American 9/11 did not lead inevitably to the 'war on terror'. 'Crises are constituted in and through narrative.'[75]

The 'war on terror' emerged as the dominant discourse through the crisis of 2001. And this is because of the success in being able to produce a narrative that proved more socially powerful than any other. 'Those who are able to define what the crisis is all about also hold the key to defining the appropriate strategies for resolution.'[76] That the events of 11 September 2001 constituted a crisis is clear. Analysis after analysis reproduced the point; the impact of the event and the reaction to it were played out repeatedly.

> In dozens of exclusive interviews with *ABC News*, Congressional leaders told of chaos on Capitol Hill, Cabinet secretaries described a war council deep in a secret bunker beneath the White House, generals and sergeants told of how they ramped up for a possible nuclear strike, and the President and vice president were said to have ordered US pilots to shoot down any planes threatening the nation's capital.[77]

Indeed, President Bush did execute a classified 'Continuity of Operations' plan, fearing a nuclear attack on the heart of the American federation, and establishing a 'government in waiting' underground.[78] The Secretary of State did not know what had happened: he told reporters that 'Other planes crashed elsewhere in the United States, one crashed near Camp David and the other crashed out in western Pennsylvania', and, of course, no aircraft crashed near to Camp David.[79]

74 Ibid., p. 92.

75 Colin Hay, 'Narrating crisis: the discursive construction of the "winter of discontent" ', *Sociology*, 30:2 (May 1996), p. 254.

76 P. t'Hart, 'Symbols, rituals and power: the lost dimensions of crisis management', *Journal of Contingencies and Crisis Management*, 1 (1993), p. 41, cited in Hay, 'Narrating crisis', p. 255.

77 'Moments of crisis', *ABC News*, at http://abcnews.go.com/onair/DailyNews/sept11_moments_1.html [5/2004].

78 Dennis M. Gormley, 'Enriching expectations: 11 September's lessons for missile defence', *Survival*, 44:2 (Summer 2002), p. 19.

79 Colin Powell, 'Corrected version: press briefing on board plane en route Washington DC', 11 September 2001, at http://www.state.gov/secretary/rm/2001/4863.htm [5/2004].

Officials at the State Department reported that they had been subjected to attack by car bomb.[80] The National Security Advisor had been due to give a speech that day on national security: al-Qaeda and Islamic terrorism were not going to be mentioned.[81] On the following day, the *San Francisco Examiner*, the city's second largest newspaper with a circulation of around 97,000, covered the events under an enlarged title page with the word 'Bastards!'[82]

Analyses constructed the crisis in historical terms: *CBS News* declared that 'No president since Abraham Lincoln had seen such horrific loss of life in a war on American soil. No president since James Madison, nearly 200 years ago, had seen the nation's capital city successfully attacked.'[83] A full sense of the media coverage of the crisis is recreated in the book *September 11, 2001*, which reproduces newspaper front pages from the following day from across the United States.[84] The *New York Times* created a banner under which all news – whether domestic or international, military or on 'homeland security' – was presented, and it was that of '*A Nation Challenged*'. This sense of crisis was reproduced in the academic literature over the course of the following months. Steven Miller declared that 'The terrorist attacks of September 11 will scythe through history, separating a naively complacent past from a frighteningly vulnerable future.'[85] Miller succinctly encapsulated the sense of crisis, and the switch of narratives.

It was strongly in the churches of America that the narration of the second American 9/11 was developed. On the day of the attacks, churches opened for noonday and evening services, and were filled

80 See Davide Dukcevich, 'US under attack: World Trade Center destroyed', Forbes.com, 11 September 2001 at 11.34 EST, at http://www.forbes.com/2001/09/11/0911usattack3.html [9/2005].

81 See 'Undelivered Rice speech scrutinized', CNN.com, 2 April 2004, at http://www.cnn.com/2004/ALLPOLITICS/04/01/rice.speech/ [5/2004].

82 See the report by Steve Johnson, 'San Francisco paper puts visceral reaction on page one', *Chicago Tribune*, 13 September 2001, at http://www.chicagotribune.com/features/chi-0109130346sep13,1,6503847.story?ctrack=2&cset=true [5/2005].

83 'The President's story', *CBS News*, 12 September 2002, at http://www.cbsnews.com/stories/2002/09/11/60II/main521718.shtml [9/2004].

84 The Poynter Institute, *September 11, 2001: A Collection of Newspaper Front Pages Selected by the Poynter Institute* (Kansas City: Andrews McMeel Publishing, 2001).

85 Steven E. Miller, 'The end of unilateralism or unilateralism redux?', *Washington Quarterly*, 25:1 (Winter 2002), p. 15.

with people.[86] At the end of the week, a poll conducted by Pew showed that 69 per cent of Americans were 'praying more' in response to the events of the week.[87] Some felt directly threatened in their faith: Franklin Graham, the son of evangelist Billy Graham, told his audience that Islam was evil and wicked.[88] Jerry Jenkins, co-author of the enormously successful *Left Behind* series, expressed the views of conservative Christian America in an interview in October 2001. 'Many want to know if this is a sign of the end and if Antichrist will soon emerge', Jenkins said. 'Some even ask if Osama Bin Laden could be Antichrist, but of course he cannot. The prophecies are clear that Antichrist will be charismatic, attractive, charming, winsome, and that almost everyone will believe he is not only a wonderful person but perhaps even Jesus reincarnate. I don't think anyone thinks that of Bin Laden.'[89] By November, some 78 per cent of Americans agreed in another Pew poll that the role of religion in American life 'is increasing'.[90] And, of course, the speech that George Bush gave on 14 September concerning the attacks was delivered at the National Cathedral, on the National Day of Prayer and Remembrance. In a critical part of the speech, he called for America to 'rid the world of evil'.[91] One assumes that given the location and the personal beliefs of the President, this was not a loose use of the term 'evil', but one rooted very much in evangelism. As Terry Eagleton put it, 'In the so-called war against terrorism . . . the word "evil" really means: Don't look for a political explanation.'[92]

The crisis permeated through all levels of American society and, as such, had to become the subject of humour. Many 'jokes' were

[86] Mark Wingfield, 'Texas Baptists turn to prayer and Bible as nation mourns', *Baptist Standard*, 17 September 2001, at http://www.baptiststandard.com/2001/9_17/pages/attacks_mourn.html [5/2004].

[87] Pew Research Center, 'American psyche reeling from attacks', 19 September 2001, at http://people-press.org/reports/print.php3?PageID=32 [4/2005].

[88] On *NBC Nightly News*, November 2001, in Bacevich, *American Militarism*, p. 145.

[89] Jerry B. Jenkins interviewed by Deborah Caldwell in 'Nothing more needs to be fulfilled before the coming of Christ', Beliefnet, October 2001, at http://www.beliefnet.com/story/89/story_8910_1.html [4/2005].

[90] See Pew Research Center, 'Post 9/11 attitudes', released 6 December 2001, at http://pewforum.org/publications/surveys/post911poll.pdf [4/2005].

[91] George W. Bush, 'President's remarks at the National Day of Prayer and Remembrance', 14 September 2001, at http://www.whitehouse.gov/news/releases/2001/09/20010914-2.html [9/2005].

[92] Terry Eagleton, *After Theory* (London: Penguin, 2003), p. 141.

constructed, and recycled, in the period from 11 September 2001 to the defeat of the Taliban. The key commentators of television were at the forefront. Jay Leno quipped 'Allied forces have hit all the Taliban military installations and bases. To give you an idea how successful these strikes have been: the Taliban has been telling young men that when they get to heaven, there may not be enough virgins to go around. They were promised 72. Now they are down to 45, but were told, "Your virgins may vary."'[93] One of David Letterman's jokes was: 'It looks like now the military action is taking effect. They think that bin Laden's organization is starting to break down. Today satellite photos actually show the sand fleas are leaving his beard.'[94] As leading popular commentators, Leno and Letterman's use of humour was a means of spreading both the impact of crisis and means of understanding it. Other jokes in circulation in October 2001 included:

Q: How is bin Laden like Fred Flintstone?
A: Both may look out their windows and see Rubble.

Q: What do bin Laden and Hiroshima have in common?
A: Nothing . . . Yet

Q: What does [sic] Osama bin Laden and General Custer have in common?
A: They both want to know where those Tomahawks are coming from![95]

And so on.

These and other jokes began to emerge fairly quickly after 11 September 2001. Of course, there were different styles of humour. Some, as above, were in the format of one-liners. Others, as below, required the use of imagery. But there were also the slightly longer jokes, those that were spread very quickly by email. There were many, but here the focus will be on two to illustrate the genre:

A Canadian, Osama bin Ladin and Uncle Sam are out walking together one day. They come across a lantern and a Genie pops out of it. 'I will give each of you each one wish, that's three wishes total,' says the Genie. The Canadian says, 'I am a farmer, my dad was a farmer, and my son will also farm. I want the land to be forever fertile in Canada.' With a blink of the Genie's eye, 'POOF' the land in Canada was forever made fertile for farming. Osama bin Ladin was amazed, so he said, 'I want a wall around Afganistan [sic], so that

[93] Recorded at Bressler.org; see http://bressler.org/obl_jokes.asp [3/2005].
[94] Ibid. [95] Ibid.

no infidels, Jews or Americans can come into our precious state.' Again, with a blink of the Genie's eye, 'POOF' there was a huge wall around Afganistan [sic]. Uncle Sam (a former civil engineer) asks, 'I'm very curious. Please tell me more about this wall.' The Genie explains, 'Well, it's about 15,000 feet high, 500 feet thick and completely surrounds the country; nothing can get in or out – virtually impenetrable.' Uncle Sam says, 'Fill it with water.'[96]

Of course, what is important about this joke is the focus of this narrative – that Afghanistan itself, and thereby its people – are the enemy, to be destroyed by American ingenuity. Shortly afterwards, as the war began, that narrative changed: the Afghan people were now freedom loving, and in need of liberation by their American friends from extremist dictatorship. This joke is therefore early in the period of settling upon post-second American 9/11 narratives, and indeed it has been dated to, at the latest, 4 October 2001. By ascribing civil engineering expertise to Uncle Sam, America is also 'expert'; an important sub-theme. The joke that follows dates from, at the latest, 6 October. That is, they both would have existed before that, but this is the earliest that a dated record can be found (in the form of a saved and dated email). Such humour is able to spread so quickly because the structure of the joke is familiar in different contexts: one can replace the key protagonists above – Osama bin Laden and Uncle Sam – with any two protagonists; the third actor (the Canadian) is there as a worthy figure – it does not matter where he or she is from.

A second example of this form of joke may be even more familiar, in terms of its structure, than the first:

I have a moral question for you. This is an imaginary situation, but I think it is fun to decide what one would do. The situation: you are in the Middle East, and there is a huge flood in progress. Many homes have been lost, water supplies compromised and structures destroyed. Let's say that you're a photographer and getting still photos for a news service, travelling alone, looking for particularly poignant scenes. You come across Osama Bin Laden, who has been swept away by the floodwaters. He is barely hanging on to a tree limb and is about to go under. You can either put down your camera and save him, or take a Pulitzer Prize-winning photograph of him as he loses his grip on the limb. So, here's the question and think carefully before you answer the question overleaf:

96 http://www.coe.unco.edu/RosemaryHathaway/ENG238/Sept11archive/Jokes/jokes.html [4/2005].

Which lens and shutter speed would you use?[97]

Such 'popular' jokes reproduce meaning, and also reproduce the collective identity (the 'we' that are being threatened) throughout society.

However, humour is not only verbal: pictures will often have at least as deep an impact. As argued earlier, discourse can be found not only in words, but also in imagery. Humour strengthens the way in which a particular issue is understood; humour, often portrayed as a radical force in society, also has the effect of cementing notions of common sense. A collection of 'humorous' images dating from the end of 2001 and early 2002 have been archived on the website Strange Cosmos. Images threaten death: one entitled 'Osama – the next video' shows a skeleton loosely dressed in what might appear to be an Arabic headdress. Other images show Osama bin Laden in a variety of disguises: with Elvis Presley hair in 'Osama bin Elvis – why we can't find him!'; as an action figure, replacing 'GI Joe' with 'Jihad Joe'; hiding inside an Easter rabbit costume in 'Osama bunny'.[98] In such ways, the enemy is identified, ridiculed, humiliated, but still clearly marked as dangerous.

As Bill Ellis has argued, 'Folk culture played a central role in the process of allowing common citizens to react to the anxieties raised by these horrific events.'[99] Folk is sometimes seen alongside the marginal, in opposition to the public, the mainstream, the mass. But what was crucial in the narration of the second American 9/11 was that this story was reproduced by the marginal, the folk, as well as by the mass, the mainstream. Would it have mattered had this not been so? Perhaps it would: at least inasmuch as some space, traditionally reserved for alternative narrations, would have been used for this purpose. But it was not. Instead, on the internet, through Usenet message boards, a different form of humour spread. Ellis' earliest recorded joke was from 14 September 2001: 'Subject: Weather forecast for Kabul. Cloudy, windy, 5,000,000 degrees farenheit.'[100] As above, here Afghans as a people were being constructed as the enemy, a different story to that which dominated the war

[97] Ibid. This joke circulated through email in November 2004, when the character being swept away was George W. Bush. Personal correspondence, October/November 2004. Thanks also to Sally Mallard.

[98] At http://www.strangecosmos.com/content/item/106495.html [4/2005].

[99] Bill Ellis, 'Making the Big Apple crumble: the role of humor in constructing global response to disaster', *New Directions in Folklore: A Publication of Newfolk*, issue 6 (June 2002), at http://www.temple.edu/isllc/newfolk/bigapple/bigapple1.html [3/2005].

[100] Ibid.

in that country from the American perspective just a month later. And, of course, this emphasizes the then-current American expectation that enemies are by nature territorial first, ideological second.

Some humour was to be in a different, more graphic, form; but the narration was still the same. 'What was the last thing going through Mr Jones' head sitting in 90th floor of the WTC? – The 91st floor . . .', which was posted on the internet on 17 September 2001, is in a different mode than earlier examples; it is a joke that revels in shock value. But nevertheless, it underlines the point of the innocent 'we' being under attack.[101] 'Q: Why are police and firemen New York's finest? A: Because now you can run them through a sieve' underlines the tragedy of the loss of the heroes, while seeking a legitimate space for 'bad taste' humour that nevertheless does not challenge the central tenets of the story. A longer example of this form of humour illustrates that point: it is the rewriting of George Bush's speech that he made in reaction to the attacks of 11 September 2001. The rewrite is excerpted here to illustrate the incorporation of the more 'alternative' element of American comedy into the main and emerging 'war on terror' narrative.

To the people responsible for today's tragedy, I say this: Are you f****** kidding me? Are the turbans on your heads wrapped too tight? Have you gone too long without a bath? Do you not know who you are f****** with? Americans are so hungry to kill, that we shoot at each other every day. We will relish that opportunity for new targets for our aggression.

Have you forgotten history? What happened to the last people that started f****** around with us? Remember the little yellow b******* over in Japan? We slapped them all over the Pacific and roasted about 2 million of them in their own back yard. That's what we in America call a big ass barbecue. Ever seen Texas on a map? Ever wonder why it's so big? Because we wanted it that way, Mexico started jacking around with the Alamo and now they cut our lawns.[102]

And so on. As with much alternative humour of this kind in the United States, it is supposed to be 'politically incorrect', but here manages to be so in the voice of another, in this case, the President, and thus is able

101 Ellis, 'Making', appendix A, from the jokes of 17 September 2001, at http://www.temple.edu/isllc/newfolk/bigapple/bigappleappe.html [4/2005].

102 Mitchell R. Robb, 'If I were President George Bush's speech writer', in Ellis, 'Making', at website cited in note 101. Ellis dates this to 14 September 2001. Language edited.

to give voice to the 'true' feelings of the wounded American giant. And in so doing, while gently poking fun at George W. Bush himself, it is a joke that reproduces all the main elements of the meta-narrative then under construction. The joke tells us that Americans cannot be defeated; America is special, and has been throughout its history. But the dividing line on taste was delicate. ABC had produced a national television programme entitled *Politically Incorrect*. On 17 September 2001, host Bill Maher took issue with President Bush's description of the September 11th attackers as cowards: 'We have been the cowards lobbing cruise missiles from 2,000 miles away . . . That's cowardly. Staying in the airplane when it hits the building, say what you want about it, it's not cowardly.'[103] The comments were met with a storm of protest – it went against the narration of al-Qaeda cowardice / American heroism – and ultimately the show was cancelled six months later, an event Maher himself had predicted in the aftermath of the criticism of the 17 September show.[104]

Such a crisis – politically and socially deep, culturally profound in popular terms – demanded a response. But that is the character of all crises: 'crisis refers to a moment of decisive intervention, a moment of thorough-going transformation, a moment of rupture'.[105] It was not just a crisis for the elite; it was one felt throughout society and, as such, was one in which the whole of society would be involved. On 11 September 2001, the window for decisive intervention was short. It was not clear which narrative would be developed at that moment. Did the second American 9/11 represent failure by the American state's security apparatus? Was this the onset of more attacks? Was the government to blame?[106] Should the response be low key, and engaged with conflicts

103 In Mark Armstrong, 'White House politically corrects Maher', 27 September 2001, at http://www.eonline.com/News/Items/0,1,8886,00.html [4/2005].

104 'Bad taste' humour about the September 11th attacks that circulated on message boards was also subject to complaints.

105 Colin Hay, 'Crisis and the structural transformation of the state: interrogating the process of change', *British Journal of Politics and International Relations*,1:3 (October 1999), p. 323. Also, Colin Hay, 'From crisis to catastrophe? The ecological pathologies of the liberal-democratic state form', *Innovation*, 9:4 (1996), especially pp. 423–5; and Hay, 'Narrating crisis', especially pp. 270–3.

106 Two journalists were fired for publishing articles critical of Bush. Mark Tapscott, 'Don't publish unpopular views, then fire authors', *Heritage Foundation Commentary*, 31 October 2001, at http://www.heritage.org/Press/Commentary/ed103101.cfm [6/2004].

abroad, above all the Israel–Palestine dispute? Many different narratives could have come into play. But importantly, 'State power (the ability to impose a new trajectory upon the structures of the state) resides not only in the ability to respond to crises, but to identify, define and constitute the crisis in the first place.'[107] And it was at the heart of the American state that the decisive intervention came to be played out.

However, before examining that decisive intervention, it is worth spending a few moments further considering the discursive context of that American state, that which is deemed by so many to be so familiar, because of the influence of American politics, news and culture across the world. Can we again render strange the familiar that is the United States of America? Indeed so, if this political analysis takes into account the power of religious discourse on much of the country. Evangelical Christianity constructs an understanding of the future for the individual and for the state, and thereby for international relations. This affects popular culture, with one target being *Harry Potter*: as Pastor David J. Meyer puts it, the 'books by J. K. Rowling teach witchcraft!'[108] For many Americans, a key part of their discursive reality is the power of the Rapture 'that time when a trumpet will sound, and our Lord Jesus . . . will descend from heaven with a shout, and we believers who are alive at the time will rise to meet our Lord in the air, our mortal bodies being changed into glorified immortal bodies. This is a literal future event.'[109] The Rapture is therefore an event to be welcomed, and progress towards it can be mapped. 'Satanic rage is increasing – a sure sign that we are at the end of the age.'[110] Whereas the metaphorical doomsday clock of the *Bulletin of the Atomic Scientists* aims to worry the world when its hands move forward to the global disaster that would be midnight, the Rapture clock's logic works in an entirely opposite way.[111] Rapture Ready publishes its Armageddon Clock, which

[107] Hay, 'Narrating crisis', p. 255.

[108] Pastor David J. Meyer, 'Harry Potter: what does God have to say?', Last Trumpet Ministries, at http://www.lasttrumpetministries.org/tracts/tract7.html [4/2005].

[109] Sheila Lewis Busby, 'What does the Bible really say about the timing of the Rapture?', at http://www.lookup.org/ [2/2005].

[110] 'Nearing Midnight', Rapture Ready, 31 January 2005, at http://www.raptureready.com/rap16.html [2/2005].

[111] 'Since its inception in 1947, the Doomsday Clock has signified the level of threat posed by nuclear weapons and other changing factors in international security', http://www.thebulletin.org/doomsday_clock/ [3/2005].

unlike the Doomsday Clock, moves ever forward. Each tick of its second hand . . . brings the world nearer the starting point of what will be man's most horrific war. The Armageddon Clock marks Antichrist's confirming the false peace covenant described in Daniel 9:27. The signing of that covenant will initiate the Tribulation era . . . That great conflict will culminate with the Second Coming of Jesus Christ back to Planet Earth.[112]

Thus, by early 2005, while the Doomsday Clock's time was 17 minutes to midnight, that of the Armageddon Clock was a mere 3 minutes to midnight.

In geopolitics, the major debate is the place of origin of the Antichrist in terms of whether he will rise in Europe, or the Middle East. The most popular view is that the Antichrist will rise in Europe. In the *Left Behind* series, Antichrist is Romanian. 'Daniel chapters 2 and 7 reveal a strong connection between the formation of the European Union and end-times scripture. The possible fulfillment of this scripture began in 1950 when the Roman Empire began to show signs of being revived.'[113] In Rapture Ready's frequently asked questions we learn that 'The EU, however, could be, I'm convinced, the matrix or nucleus out of which that power bloc of Revelation 17:12–13 will evolve.'[114] Following a long explanation of the development of the EU, Alan Franklin concluded: 'Now it awaits just one thing: the supreme ruler who will weld it into the most terrifying institution ever seen on the face of the earth. The Bible calls him Antichrist. Expect his arrival on the scene in the not too distant future.'[115] Jack van Impe agreed: 'Someone recently asked if the European "Superstate" and the coming "New World Order" are signs of Christ's return. The short answer is Yes!'[116] Stephen Castle identified the Antichrist: 'I have said in the past that I believed that Tony Blair is a strong candidate for the next permanent leader of the European Union. Whoever the next leader is,

112 http://www.raptureready.com/rr-armageddon2.html [3/2005].

113 Jennifer Rast, 'Is the EU the revived Roman empire?', Contender Ministries, at http://www.contenderministries.org/prophecy/romanempire.php [3/2005].

114 http://www.raptureready.com/faq/faq428.html [3/2005].

115 Alan Franklin, 'The EU superstate – future base of Antichrist', Moriel Ministries, at http://www.moriel.org/articles/discernment/church_issues/EU_superstate_future_base_of_Antichrist.htm [4/2005].

116 Jack van Impe, 'EU superstate and the new world order', Shalom Jerusalem, at http://www.shalomjerusalem.com/bible/bible17.htm [2/2005].

I believe will be the Antichrist.'[117] Rapture Ready produced a list of candidates for the likely Antichrist, in the format of the FBI 'Most Wanted' posters. In 2005, those named included Silvio Berlusconi, Romano Prodi, Vladimir Putin, Tony Blair, Jacques Chirac, Javiar Solana, Gerhard Schroeder and Pope John Paul II. However, Rapture Ready's list of Antichrist candidates did not only contain Europeans; covering its geopolitical bets, it also included some from the Middle East, including Saddam Hussein ('it's not impossible that another evil leader such as Osama Bin Laden could attempt to save Saddam'), Crown Prince Abdullah, Mohammed Khatami and Bashar Asad.[118] This reflects the geopolitical split between those who see Europe as being the vehicle of Antichrist, and those who see the Middle East as the more likely origin. Frank Caw argues that 'Thus, the Antichrist will *not* come to power by being appointed leader of the European Union. Daniel 8:9 proves that the Antichrist will conquer countries which are located south or east of Lebanon, i.e., his country of origin . . . that means the "three horn countries" which will be conquered by the Antichrist during his initial rise to power most likely will be Israel, Syria and Iraq.'[119] Arthur W. Pink agrees: 'it would seem that the country from which Antichrist will first be manifested is Syria'.[120] However, there are those who see the rise of Antichrist in Iraqi democracy: Joseph Chambers at the Paw Creek Ministries in North Carolina sees the biblical reference to flattery as being part of the democratic world. 'The powers of "flattery" is [sic] nothing but a prophetic word describing a "skilled politician" . . . Much of the geography where Iraq is located will change to make way for the skilled political tricks of the "man of sin" soon to step into the political arena.'[121]

The evangelical Bible community of America is a very complex one, and it is certainly not the case that geopolitical argument is the single

[117] Stephen Castle, 'Skeleton EU Constitution calls for strong president', Calvary Prophecy, 28 October 2002, at http://www.calvaryprophecy.com/q175.html [3/2005]. [118] http://www.raptureready.us/antichrist.htm [3/2005].

[119] Frank L. Caw, 'The ultimate deception', at http://www.frankcaw.com/ [4/2005]. Also Caw, *The Ultimate Deception: New Scriptural Insights on the Final Great Deception by Antichrist* (Bloomington, IN: Authorhouse, December 2001).

[120] Arthur W. Pink, *The Antichrist*, chapter 6: 'The career of the Antichrist', at http://www.gregwolf.com/antichrist/antichrist-awp-6.htm [4/2005].

[121] Joseph R. Chambers, 'Iraq: first steps to democracy', Paw Creek Ministries, at http://www.pawcreek.org/articles/pna/IraqTheFirstStepsToDemocracy.htm [9/2005].

key to understanding it. But it is a large community, and one with believers at the heart of government. Representative Tom DeLay, then House majority whip, told supporters in April 2002 that he was working for God to promote a biblical worldview.[122] And the narration of the events of 11 September 2001 had to work in the context of a complex and diverse set of religious themes that were deeply embedded within American discourse before the events of that day took place. Indeed, the second American 9/11 increased the commitment to faith. Joel Osteen has become one of the most visible evangelical leaders in the 2000s, seen weekly on television by 100 million people, with his Lakewood Church holding some 30,000 people. $10 tickets to see Osteen have sold for $100 on the internet.[123] In an interview in 2005, reflecting upon the rise of his church and his own ministry, he noted that 'Since 9/11, people have turned inwards, towards the church.'[124]

The narration of the second American 9/11

So what were the key elements of the narration of the crisis of 9/11 that paved the way for the development of the 'war on terror' as the dominant discursive structure in the security of the United States? There were four: the construction of an enemy image; the avoidance of blame on any other than the enemy; a definition of core values that were at risk; and a claim to global leadership, that these values were global as well as American, and that the world accepted American leadership in protecting them.

The first of these elements was the (re)construction of an enemy image. The nature of that construction was clearly articulated in a fully formed fashion nine days after the attacks of September 11th. The name of al-Qaeda was spoken by President Bush in his speech to Congress on 20 September 2001: 'The evidence we have gathered all points to a collection of loosely affiliated terrorist organizations known

122 In Paul Krugman, *The Great Unraveling* (New York: W. W. Norton, 2004), p. 274.

123 See Ted Olsen, 'Weblog: $10 Osteen tickets going for $100+', *Christianity Today*, 21 February 2005, at http://www.christianitytoday.com/ct/2005/108/51.0.html [9/2005].

124 Joel Osteen, interview, *BBC 10 O'Clock News*, 25 August 2005, personal observation.

as al-Qaeda.'[125] Subsequent speeches by President Bush made the narrative of the war against al-Qaeda clear:

> . . . the stakes could not be higher. We are the target of enemies who boast they want to kill, kill all Americans, kill all Jews and kill all Christians. We've seen that type of hate before, and the only possible response is to confront it and to defeat it. This new enemy seeks to destroy our freedom and impose its views. We value life; the terrorists ruthlessly destroy it. We value education; the terrorists do not believe women should be educated, or should have health care, or should leave their homes. We value the right to speak our minds; for the terrorists, free expression can be grounds for execution. We respect people of all faiths and welcome the free practice of religion; our enemy wants to dictate how to think and how to worship, even to their fellow Muslims . . . We wage a war to save civilization itself.[126]

A war to save civilisation had been called into existence; against an enemy committed to destroy freedom, kill Americans, Jews and Christians ['Jews and Christians', not 'Christians and Jews'], with a contempt for human life, and a determination to restrict the freedoms of women, free expression and freedom of religion. An absolute enemy had been called into being. And it was an enemy that would have friends in the 'rogue regimes' of the world. Edward Feulner at the Heritage Foundation was arguing for such a link as early as 14 September: 'The President should ask for – and Congress should approve – a formal declaration of war to address terrorism. Not just the attacks of Sept. 11, but the ability of terrorists and their state benefactors to conduct further attacks.'[127]

The second element was an absence: an absence of blame on any within the state. That America had been vulnerable was not the fault of the army or the intelligence services; not even to be blamed on the previous administration, nor even on the person of former President,

[125] President Bush, 'Address to a joint session of Congress and the American people', 20 September 2001, at http://www.whitehouse.gov/news/releases/2001/09/20010920-8.html [2/2004].

[126] The text of President George W. Bush's address to America before representatives of firefighters, law enforcement officers and postal workers in Atlanta, GA, on 8 November 2001, 'My fellow Americans, let's roll', at http://www.september11news.com/PresidentBushAtlanta.htm [6/2004].

[127] Edward J. Feulner, 'Declare War', *Heritage Foundation Commentary*, 14 September 2001, at http://www.heritage.org/Press/Commentary/ed091401.cfm [11/2004].

Bill Clinton.[128] That was perhaps a surprise; and conservative media circles were certainly clear that the failure and impact of the second American 9/11 could directly be blamed on Clinton himself.[129] Others sought to focus on the failings of the intelligence services.[130] Jerry Falwell, the Baptist minister who had founded the Moral Majority, immediately blamed 'liberals'. On 14 September, Falwell said: 'I really believe that the pagans, and the abortionists, and the feminists, and the gays and the lesbians who are actively trying to make that an alternative lifestyle, the ACLU, People For the American Way, all of them who have tried to secularize America. I point the finger in their face and say "you helped this happen".'[131] None of these discursive moves worked; Falwell, for example, felt compelled to apologise for his remarks. These alternative narrations fell, and the rejection of blame within served to allow a 'national unity' behind a newly emerging discourse to develop; it also allowed the focus to remain on the enemy, that which was being constructed to stand in antithesis to the United States, conceived as a value system. Colin Powell was asked on 12 September why the attack was not foreseen. He replied:

> I say that we do have the best intelligence system. We have the best military on the face of the Earth. But as has been demonstrated many times in the past, if you are a determined enemy and if you are prepared to go after soft targets . . . are prepared to do it in ways that are rather different from anything we've seen before, unless we get something that cues us, something that gives us some indication that this kind of asymmetric attack is coming, we are always at risk. We can't defend against every single possibility short of shutting ourselves up into some kind of blockhouse. We're an open society.[132]

128 But there were early signs of intelligence failures: see, for example, James Risen, 'In hindsight, CIA sees flaws that hindered efforts on terror', *New York Times*, 7 October 2001.

129 See on the conservative NewsMax.com: 'Clinton skates on 9/11 responsibility', 10 September 2002, at http://www.newsmax.com/archives/articles/2002/9/9/161758.shtml, and 'How the left caused the 9/11 attacks', 23 April 2002, at http://www.newsmax.com/archives/articles/2002/4/22/175758.shtml [both 12/2004].

130 Seymour M. Hersh, 'What went wrong: the CIA and the failure of American intelligence', *The New Yorker*, 8 October 2001.

131 In 'Falwell apologizes to gays, feminists, lesbians', CNN, 14 September 2001, at http://archives.cnn.com/2001/US/09/14/Falwell.apology/ [4/2005].

132 Colin Powell, 'Interview on CBS Morning News', 12 September 2001, at http://www.state.gov/secretary/rm/2001/4865.htm [7/2004].

Thus, the attacks had been brought about at least in part because America's openness and freedom made it particularly vulnerable. The attacks succeeded because of the liberal country that American was. This absence of blame created a discursive closure. It allowed the focus to remain on the perpetrators – the 'evil' enemy – rather than on US actions and lack of preparations.

Third, the (re)construction of the self focused on the central claims for America's mission, those of freedom and justice. On the very evening of 11 September 2001, President Bush was already articulating a construction that was about a war to defend freedom itself. 'Today, our fellow citizens, our way of life, our very freedom came under attack in a series of deliberate and deadly terrorist acts . . . America was targeted for attack because we're the brightest beacon for freedom and opportunity in the world. And no one will keep that light from shining.'[133] A claim to values, and leadership according to values, was a theme woven through all of the decisive intervention. Colin Powell, speaking to the Organization of American States, told them that 'The United States has stood with you and now you stand with us, partners in resolve as well as in grief. Free peoples committed to the collective defense of our security and of the democratic ideals that we hold so dear.'[134] And in a *Cato Institute Commentary*, we find the following call: 'One consequence of the evil acts of September 11 was to help us all remember what is good about America.'[135]

The final element was the claim to global support and leadership. President Bush immediately declared that, given America's role in the world, attacks were on more than just America. On 12 September 2001, he stated that 'This enemy attacked not just our people, but all freedom-loving people everywhere in the world.'[136] In his speech to a joint session of Congress on 20 September 2001, President Bush declared

133 'The text of President Bush's address Tuesday night, after the attacks on New York and Washington', CNN.com, 11 September 2001, at http://www.cnn.com/2001/US/09/11/bush.speech.text/ [8/2004].

134 Colin Powell, 'Remarks to the Special Session of the Organization of American States', 21 September 2001, at http://www.state.gov/secretary/rm/2001/4997.htm [7/2004].

135 David Boaz, 'Attacks on American values', *Cato Institute Commentary*, 1 October 2001, at http://www.cato.org/dailys/10-01-01.html [7/2004].

136 'Remarks by President Bush in photo opportunity with the National Security Team', 12 September 2001, at http://www.whitehouse.gov/news/releases/2001/09/20010912-4.html [7/2004].

that 'America will never forget the sounds of our National Anthem playing at Buckingham Palace, on the streets of Paris, and at Berlin's Brandenburg Gate. We will not forget South Korean children gathering to pray outside our embassy in Seoul, or the prayers of sympathy offered at a mosque in Cairo. We will not forget moments of silence and days of mourning in Australia and Africa and Latin America.'[137] By 23 September, the nature of American diplomacy was clear. Colin Powell said in 'Meet the Press' that 'we have begun a broad campaign against the perpetrators of this attack, and also against terrorism in general. The campaign has already begun. It has begun with rallying the international communities on our side of this issue, letting nations around the world know that this is a time to choose. You're either for freedom or you're for terrorism.'[138] In such ways, American leadership in and beyond the crisis that America had defined was clearly marked.

In all crisis situations, a meta-narrative of crisis is constructed, which then frames each individual narrative. This process can be seen in other, brutal, examples. The Nazis were responsible for horrendous crimes: the Kristallnacht, Bergen-Belsen, the forced euthanasia of the disabled, including children, all horrors committed in line with a particular understanding of what was right and what was wrong; a particular understanding of common sense. A few lines from the film *Schindler's List* illustrate this, when the Nazi commander Amon Goeth says of further impending slaughter: 'For six centuries, there has been a Jewish Cracow. By this weekend, those six centuries, they're a rumor. They never happened. Today is history.'[139] Each of these events, and the contemporary and *subsequent* expression of them in popular culture, were and are only comprehensible in terms of the Nazi meta-narrative – that of the destruction of European Jewry. As Pat Johnson put it, 'other victim groups were inextricably swept up in the vortex of the Holocaust, but the Final Solution was, first and foremost, aimed at

137 President Bush, 'Address to a joint session of Congress and the American people', 20 September 2001, at http://www.whitehouse.gov/news/releases/2001/09/20010920–8.html [6/2004].

138 Colin Powell, 'Meet the Press', 23 September 2001, at http://www.state.gov/secretary/rm/2001/5012.htm [8/2004].

139 The script is at http://www.un-official.com/The_Daily_Script/slist.doc. This dialogue is raised by Robert S. Leventhal, 'Jean François Lyotard, *The Differend: Phrases in Dispute*', at http://www3.iath.virginia.edu/holocaust/lyotarddiff.html [both 9/2005].

the Jews'.[140] Meta-narrative is not used here in a loose post-modern sense of there being competing fictions. The horror was real. As Richard Evans argues, 'Auschwitz was not a discourse. It trivializes mass murder to see it as a text. The gas chambers were not a piece of rhetoric.'[141] But a series of actions are given meaning, and that collective meaning is provided by a meta-narrative and without an understanding of that, the full brutality of Nazism is incomprehensible.

In a very different sense, a further example is Britain's 'winter of discontent' in 1979. The meta-narrative was one of the country being 'held to ransom' by 'militant' trades unionists, to the fury of the 'average' citizen. Individual narratives (shortage of food in shops, 'the dead left unburied') were given meaning by the meta-narrative over a period of months.[142] But the socially constructed crisis of the second American 9/11 was very unlike this British process of crisis in that it was constructed in hours: in America it was about being subject to attack, being vulnerable, being unable to control events, but of being heroic, resolute. And also, importantly, it was constructed as an event without pre-history: it was shorn of relations between the United States and the Middle East, the rise of radical Islam, the practices of the Saudi regime, the Israel–Palestine question – the second American 9/11 just 'happened'. Secretary of State, Colin Powell, had argued that 'it has nothing to do with Iraqi sanctions, it has nothing to do with our presence in the Persian Gulf. We are there to defend Muslims, to defend Muslims from other Muslims. So our purpose there is noble, [it] is an attack against who we are, our value systems, our belief in the dignity of the individual, our belief in democracy, our belief in the free enterprise system . . .'[143] James Kurth, amongst many academics, talked of 'The war that began with the terrorist attacks of September 11th . . .'[144]

These events, although recent, are also historical. Representing the past, even of only a few years before, is a delicate task. Conventionally,

[140] Pat Johnson, 'The diverse victims of Nazism', *Jewish Independent*, 28 March 2003, at http://www.jewishbulletin.ca/archives/Mar03/archives03Mar28-02.html [9/2005].

[141] Richard Evans, *In Defence of History* (London and New York: Granta Books, 2001), p. 124.

[142] Colin Hay, 'Narrating crisis', pp. 266–8.

[143] Colin Powell, 'Campaign against terrorism', remarks to the House International Relations Committee, 24 October 2001, at http://www.state.gov/secretary/rm/2001/5572.htm [7/2004].

[144] James Kurth, 'The war and the West', *Orbis*, 46:2 (Spring 2002), p. 321.

history is the revealing of *real* events, as they happened: the discovery of truth. But such an objectivist representation of the past is not fully persuasive; history is, rather, a process of identifying competing narratives which frame actions. Such narratives can be identified in a number of ways. To see Art Spiegelman's *Maus* as history is contentious. Spiegelman articulates a conversation between himself and his father about the latter's survival during the Second World War as a Jew in Poland.[145] The format is that of the comic book (the Jews are mice, the Nazis are cats, the Poles are pigs . . .). As Alun Munslow puts it, 'The Spiegelman combination of serious topic and apparently flip form is a potent deconstruction of the concept of history as a formal representation of the past as it really was.'[146] But, of course, *Maus* contains many 'truths'. And it demonstrates the importance of imagery and memorabilia in the creation and reproduction of remembrance, as will be examined later, not least in Spiegelman's own rendering of the second American 9/11.

The sense of shock that was so evident and was reproduced so powerfully in the state with the most discursive power on the planet – politically and thus culturally – is one dimension that separates the crisis of the second American 9/11 from many other political crises. That sense of shock is one well expressed by John Lewis Gaddis, who wrote:

> for most of us most of the time historical and personal experiences don't intersect . . . We can all see the importance of developments like the collapse of the Soviet Union . . . but these developments rarely affect the way we get up in the morning, go to work, fall in love, raise families . . . Less frequently, surprises produce more lasting linkages between the historical and the personal . . . September 11, 2001, before the morning had even ended, attained a similar status in our minds.[147]

Of course, this in many ways represents the luxury of 'everyday' American life that Shahid Alam wrote of in the quote at the beginning of this chapter; and indeed it represents the luxury of life in most of the developed world. 'Development' has created a barrier between the 'historical' and the 'everyday', precisely the opposite of that experienced in much of the developing world. In the global south, the 'historical' and the 'everyday' are deeply intertwined, whether it be due to war and civil unrest, revolution, disease, drought and/or famine. But the

145 Art Spiegelman, *Maus: A Survivor's Tale* (London: Penguin, 1987).
146 Alun Munslow, *The New History* (Harlow: Pearson, 2003), p. 142.
147 Gaddis, *Surprise, Security*, pp. 1–2.

absence of 'history' due to affluence is precisely one of the reasons why the discursive conditions for a socially constructed crisis around the second American 9/11 were so propitious.

The second American 9/11 – crisis and discourse

The events of the second American 9/11 had to be given meaning, and that meaning had to be constructed in terms of a meta-narrative; and given the nature of that second American 9/11, that meta-narrative had to be developed at extraordinary speed – in a matter of hours and days. Inevitably, such a new meta-narrative had to be developed using ideas and insights gained previously – as Thomas Risse explained, 'ideas do not float freely'.[148] There are no sets of objective ideational realities, simply waiting to be discovered. As Terry Eagleton put it, ideas and cultures are 'not really free-floating. Which is not to say that . . . [they are] firmly anchored either. That would be just the flipside of the same misleading metaphor.'[149] Ideas come in and through social and political discourse; crises are the mechanism for the legitimisation of some ideas, and the delegitimisation of others. But of course there was no complete system of ideas to be selected, off the shelf as it were, as the second plane hit the World Trade Center. There was a period of casting around for meaning, illustrated by the engagement by the American government of Hollywood writers to help in 'thinking the unthinkable'.[150] According to Walter Clemens, 'Within weeks of 9/11, the brains behind *MacGyver*, *Die Hard*, *Delta Force One*, *Missing in Action*, *Fight Club* and *The Rocketeer* were lending their imaginations to the war on terror . . . Would the competition prompt al-Qaeda to consult with Bollywood or studios in Tehran?'[151] Yet the period of casting around was remarkably short in comparison to other crises; and the change brought about can best be understood as periods of 'punctuated evolution'.[152]

[148] Thomas Risse, 'Ideas do not float freely: transnational coalitions, domestic structure and the end of the cold war', *International Organization*, 48:2 (Spring 1994), pp. 185–214. [149] Eagleton, *After Theory*, p. 57.

[150] Through the University of Southern California's Institute of Creative Technology. See James Der Derian, '9/11: before, after and between', in Craig Calhoun, Paul Price and Ashley Timmer (eds.), *Understanding September 11* (New York: New Press, 2002).

[151] Walter C. Clemens, *Bushed!* (New York: Oakland, 2004), p. 123.

[152] Hay, 'Crisis and political development', especially pp. 100–2.

A useful way of developing a theory of crisis can be developed by drawing on sets of thinking in British political science concerning so-called 'neo-evolutionary theory'.[153] Neo-evolutionary thinking emphasises chance rather than determinism, randomness over fatalism, open-endedness over linearity, qualitative thresholds over gradualness, and ascribes a crucial role for human agency. The key is a move in focus from what is likely to occur, to what is not: thus, neo-evolutionary thinking is about what is unlikely, about potentialities and limits, not about grand laws and unilinear direction.[154] Neo-evolutionary theory is not an attempt to equate social evolution with biological evolution; it is not an attempt to posit teleological principles for social change; it is not a reworking of the use of evolution in structural–functionalist work, such as that of Talcott Parsons in the 1960s and early 1970s.[155] It is an attempt to move beyond the use of 'evolution' as a metaphor for change.

Evolutionary thinking or theorising in the social sciences has, according to Peter Kerr, rightly had a great deal of criticism. He argues that 'Whereas in the natural sciences, "evolution" is recognised as a contingent process based upon certain "chance" or "random" factors, in social science the term has most often been used to infer certain types of historical "logic" and "pattern".'[156] He suggests that as a consequence, evolutionary theorising has often assumed a unilinear path to progress, based upon functionalist explanation, with laws of structural determination and an underplaying of the role of human agency. Evolution in the social sciences has thus, oddly, seemed to have much in common with Intelligent Design. But as George Modelski and

[153] See Peter Kerr, 'Saved from extinction: evolutionary theorising, politics, and the state', *British Journal of Politics and International Relations*, 4:2 (June 2002), pp. 330–58.

[154] Kerr's approach is contested. Some argue that social evolution cannot be separated from biological, and the neo-evolutionary theory misunderstands biological evolution. See Oliver Curry, 'Get real: evolution as metaphor and mechanism', *British Journal of Politics and International Relations*, 5:1 (2003), pp. 112–17. Others suggest that there is a close tie between neo-evolutionary theory and functionalism; Adrian Kay, 'Evolution in political science', *British Journal of Politics and International Relations*, 5:1 (2003), pp. 102–9. The editors of the special issue of *International Studies Quarterly*, 40:3 (September 1996), 'Evolutionary Paradigms in the Social Sciences', George Modelski and Kazimierz Poznanski, frame the volume in terms of the 'shift from mechanics to biology – that is, a shift in metaparadigms . . .', p. 316. In the same special issue, Ann Florini draws explicitly on gene theory to examine the evolution of norms in international relations: 'The evolution of international norms', pp. 363–90.

[155] See Kerr, 'Saved', pp. 332–3. [156] Ibid., p. 332.

Kazimierz Poznanski put it, evolutionary theory 'does not lead to "laws of history" proclaiming developmental sequences familiar in, and rejected by, social sciences . . .'.[157]

Kerr argues that neo-evolutionary reasoning has a number of central elements, of which three are of particular importance.[158] First, that such reasoning must focus on a dynamic and process account of change. That is, variables are viewed as being in motion, and the purpose is to examine those processes that generate that movement. We cannot consider the period of time since the second American 9/11 to be static. Second, a neo-evolutionary perspective views change in terms of probables rather than as deterministic – that is, examining the relationship between 'path-dependent' changes and those that are contingent. Once a particular trajectory has developed, the environment will demonstrate a 'selective' bias in favour of certain outcomes. In this way, a policy programme is developed. Third, neo-evolutionary theory exhibits a concern with viewing change as both path-dependent and contingent, a constant contest between innovation and reinforcement. These are not binary opposites but are rather conceived as mutually constituted; and there must be, in Kerr's words, 'a continuing and dialectic relationship between both institutions and agents and processes of selection and adaption'.[159] Through adaptive learning, agents learn how to deal with environmental constraints, and can affect that environment not only to achieve policy change, but also to bring about an evolution in the ideational dimension. Discursive patterns can adapt in the light of challenge, important in the 'war on terror' in the light of discursive challenge over the Iraq War. Kerr's key issues are therefore motion, then, once a discursive contest is underway, selectivity, and, in the context of the mutual constitution of the path-dependent and the contingent, adaptivity.

International relations ought to be a discipline that is very interested in neo-evolutionary approaches. After all, the American–European traditions of international relations have been troubled by the 'failure' to account for, or predict, the end of the cold war.[160] Neo-evolutionary

157 Modelski and Poznanski, 'Evolutionary paradigms', p. 324.
158 Kerr, 'Saved', pp. 334–9, has four elements; two are here conflated.
159 Ibid., p. 337.
160 One of the most celebrated articles was John Lewis Gaddis, 'International relations theory and the end of the cold war', *International Security*, 17 (Winter 1992/3), pp. 3–58.

thinking allows scope for the identification of 'signals, signposts and symptoms that could have pointed to the end of that historical era'.[161] Neo-evolutionary theorists are concerned by the same central dilemma as Vivien Schmidt: how to explain dramatic change, such as occurred in France in 1983, and in Britain after 1979. Schmidt herself seeks to make a distinction between 'evolutionary' (maintaining policy objectives while altering policy instruments as, she argues, with the 1997 Blair government), and 'revolutionary' (where, as with Thatcher's 1979 government, objectives as well as instruments change). In a similar vein to Hay, Schmidt suggests that political, social and/or economic crisis creates the challenge, which could lead to revolutionary change in the discourse, evolutionary change, or no change if the policy programme is sufficiently 'supple'.

It is therefore possible to posit an approach which suggests that crises are pivotal points in understanding the development of policy. 'Crisis is the moment in which the unity of the state is discursively renegotiated and, potentially, reachieved and in which a new strategic trajectory is imposed upon the institutions that now (re-)comprise it.'[162] A crisis is discursively constituted, represents a point of rupture, and is subject to a variety of narratives that constitute the decisive intervention, of which one is successful in constituting a new strategic trajectory. Crisis is thus a process. The nature of the contestation of narratives is shaped by selectivity and adaptivity. Once that strategic trajectory is established, it leads to a period of stability, during which time, contradictions emerge and develop, which will come to constitute, discursively, the next crisis. 'In such periods of political settlement and comparative tranquillity, the unity of the state resides primarily in the fact that the legacy of its former crises set the parameters within which the agencies and institutions that give effect to state power must operate.'[163]

In this, periods of accelerated reform are followed by phases of consolidation and relative stasis. That which is being reformed is a 'policy paradigm', or 'ideational package', and it limits legitimate responses to a particular issue. Thus, in Hay's analysis, the post-war policy package was 'Keynesianism', it was established by accelerated reform in the

[161] James N. Rosenau, 'Signals, signposts and symptoms: interpreting change and anomalies in world politics', *European Journal of International Relations*, 1:1 (March 1995), p. 115. Rosenau did not talk explicitly about neo-evolutionary approaches.

[162] Hay, 'Crisis and the structural transformation', p. 337.

[163] Ibid., p. 332.

1940s (punctuated evolution) and then followed by consolidation and relative stasis in which certain policy prescriptions (for example those later adopted under the Thatcher administrations) were deemed illegitimate, with a series of interventions to overcome contradictions which ultimately failed (under a 'ripening of contradictions') creating a socially constructed crisis, in which competing crisis narratives engaged, and Thatcherism emerged.[164]

This process can be represented as in figure 2.7. The crisis period represented at the top of the diagram is the moment of drama, in which the focus of attention is not just on what has brought this about, but on the discursive competition between narratives. Once that is complete, a new strategic trajectory is framed by that newly dominant discourse that has named and explained the crisis, and, in so doing, has constructed a discourse of danger. This hegemonic discourse then leads to institutional restructuring, as certain modes of behaviour are deemed no longer appropriate, and are replaced by the concepts and practices of the new discourse. It is here that an 'institutionalisation of securitisation' spoken of by Buzan, Waever and de Wilde takes place.[165] This then leads to a period of stabilisation, as those practices become embedded, only to lead to the growth of contradictions in the process, which grow and develop, until an event is seen to be catalytic in bringing together those contradictions. It is that event that enables the meta-narrative to be challenged, and which then leads into a subsequent crisis.

By thinking about developing this social crisis process in the context of the experience of the second American 9/11, a process can be articulated that could be of use in understanding other social crises. After all, as Peter Katzenstein put it, high-profile events in world politics 'provide students of international relations and comparative politics with the closest thing to a natural experiment. The terrorists' attacks

[164] Other neo-evolutionist approaches to understanding change in British politics include: Peter John, 'Ideas and interests: agendas and implementation: an evolutionary explanation of policy change in British local government finance', *British Journal of Politics and International Relations*, 1:1 (1999), pp. 39–62; Peter John, 'The uses and abuses of evolutionary theory in political science', *British Journal of Politics and International Relations*, 2:1 (2000), pp. 89–94; Peter Kerr, *Post-War British Politics: From Conflict to Consensus* (London: Routledge, 2001); and Hugh Ward, 'The possibility of an evolutionary explanation of the state's role in modes of regulation', in J. Stanyer and G. Stoker (eds.), *Contemporary Political Studies*, vol. 1 (Exeter: Political Studies Association, 1997).

[165] Buzan et al., *Security*, pp. 27–9.

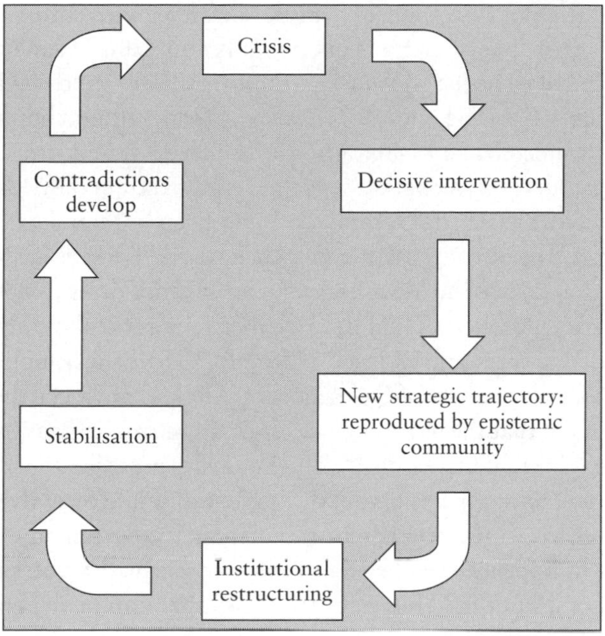

Source: Developed from figure 3, in Hay, 'Crisis and the structural transformation', p. 339.

Figure 2.7. The social crisis process

on the United States on 11 September 2001 are no exception.'[166] Understanding the specific case of the second American 9/11 can lead to a wider and more general understanding of the nature of socially constructed crises.

Conclusions

One of the few 'rules' of international relations is surely that should an invader cross the boundary of another polity, bent on bringing that nation under its rule, it will be met by resistance, not welcomed into the capital city. But, actually, that is not always so. To take a third example from the late medieval period, if the discourse creates different

[166] Peter Katzenstein, 'Same war – different views: Germany, Japan and counter-terrorism', *International Organization*, 57:4 (Fall 2003), p. 731.

meaning, the policy responses will be different. Hernan Cortes led a small group of Spanish fighters into what is now Central America. They fought the tribes of the Maya. And then they were welcomed into the capital city of the Mexica (or Aztecs), Tenochtitlan, because their leader, Montezuma, and his advisors believed that Cortes was the returning god, Quetzalcoatl. It was the year 1-Reed in the Mexican calendar, the year in which Quetzalcoatl had been born and, in a cyclical calendar, it was also the year in which he died. 1-Reed, in the *Codex Chimalpopoca*, was always a bad year for kings. Cortes came from the east, where Quetzalcoatl had disappeared on a raft of serpents. When they landed, Cortes and his men wore black, for it was Good Friday; yet black was the colour of Quetzalcoatl. All this convinced the Mexica establishment that the narrative was one of a returning deity, albeit one that would bring destruction.[167] The Spanish, or rather, the Castilians, saw in the Mexica aspects of the Moors that they had recently defeated, which had led to the construction of 'Spain': their temples were like mosques in appearance; their clothing was deemed to be similar. As Hugh Thomas put it, 'This memory of another conquered civilisation pervaded Spanish confidence, in the improbable circumstances of being in Tenochtitlan.'[168] Here was a real conflict, and a clash of civilisations, constructed through clashing discourses.

The discursive structures of the early and late fifteenth century, and the early sixteenth, shaped lives and practices in fundamental, life-changing, ways. Why would a nation choose not to expand its trade and territory, if it had the means? The question flies in the face of common sense, given the long history of European (and other) imperialism. But early fourteenth-century China did eschew expansion which, discursively, was not valued. Why would societies create enemies within, to brutalise and kill? Surely that flies in the face of common sense, for it would weaken the state, and undermine the economy. But the contestations of narratives in late fifteenth-century Europe led precisely to a level of conflict against a newly constructed enemy in the witchcraze. And surely it flies in the face of common sense for a leadership to invite an invader into the capital city? But this is exactly what happened in Tenochtitlan in the early sixteenth century. As a result of these different narratives, hundreds of thousands of

[167] Hugh Thomas, *The Conquest of Mexico* (London: Hutchinson, 1993), pp. 184–5; 40–4. [168] Ibid., p. 293.

people died, the world was configured by European worldviews, not Chinese, fear and terror were spread throughout continental Europe (and, subsequently, the Americas), and a culture of great sophistication was destroyed.

In a similar way, the construction of the meta-narrative of the second American 9/11 has had enormous effects on practice. The discursive shifts that took place in the few months after 11 September 2001 created a new 'common sense', one shared across the American political spectrum and throughout society. That common sense would be reproduced in many cultural forms which would affect Americans' understanding of the world in which they lived. And within this new meta-narrative was contained all the key elements of a good story: identification of the good and the bad, the character's 'state of knowledge', with a clear way forward. As Sanjoy Bannerjee puts it, 'Statements by international actors that describe events, situations and histories inevitably take the form of narratives.'[169] The 'war on terror', that which emerged as the meta-narrative after the attacks, constructed an image of a third world war dominating international relations for a long time: not a vision of potential global conflagration, as had been imagined during the cold war, but one in which there was no choice other than to take the fight to the enemy. As Lawrence Freedman put it a few months after the attacks, an 'alternative third world war' was being 'constructed as an armed struggle underway for high political stakes and with global ramifications . . . In such circumstances, active engagement and even military intervention in Third World conflicts ceases to be a matter of choice and becomes a strategic imperative.'[170] The 'war on terror' had been constructed and its meaning transmitted to all in American society. Now it had to be implemented.

[169] Sanjoy Bannerjee, 'Narratives and interaction: a constitutive theory of interaction and the case of the All-India Muslim League', *European Journal of International Relations*, 4:2 (June 1998), p. 193.

[170] Lawrence Freedman, 'The Third World War?', *Survival*, 43:4 (Winter 2001), p. 64.

3 *The decisive intervention*

Introduction

In 1994, some 800,000 people were killed in a matter of days in a conflict between Hutus and Tutsis in Rwanda. Tutsis and Hutus were brutalised and killed by other Hutus, in an outbreak of government-sanctioned ethnic hatred based – it seemed – on ancient hatreds. In was an event that shocked the world. 'Stereotypes identify the Tutsi as "pastoralists" and the Hutu as "agriculturalists", the Tutsi as "patrons" and the Hutu as "clients", or the Tutsi as "rulers" and the Hutu as "ruled".'[1] Those stereotypes came from a foundational myth, created by German and Belgian imperialists, who had not actually found culturally and geographically distinct Hutu and Tutsi polities in their reading of the relations, but rather had found a great deal of interaction between all the peoples. When there had been conflict, it was mostly between Tutsi groups. The Hutu/Tutsi distinction varied according to the kingdom in which the people lived, but all families could move from one designation to another over time. This complexity and fluidity was formalised and racialised under colonial occupation with the production of ethnic identity cards and the privileging of one group over another on the grounds that they were 'more white'. The principle of the identity card continued into the independence era, and so it was easy for the Tutsis to be identified in the early 1990s.[2] The foundational myth of ancient hatreds in Rwanda (and neighbouring Burundi and eastern Congo) has not been borne out by an examination of the historical record. 'Far from being the product of ancient and immutable "tribal" distinctions, however, they [the hostilities] are based above all in political rivalries and experiences of current

[1] Africa Policy Information Center, 'Talking about tribe', 1997, at http://www.africaaction.org/bp/ethall.htm [9/2005].

[2] Human Rights Watch, 'Leave none to tell the story: genocide in Rwanda', 1999, at http://www.hrw.org/reports/1999/rwanda/ [9/2005].

generations.'[3] The film *Hotel Rwanda* tells the story of how Paul Rusesabagina, a hotel manager, took in over a thousand Tutsis and saved their lives during the genocide. The real Paul Rusesabagina explained that there are no differences between Hutus and Tutsis – his parents were mixed and he, a Hutu, had married a Tutsi. As to the roots of the conflict, though, he said, 'There are many problems in Rwanda. First of all there is the fear of the other.'[4] Such is the power of a foundational myth in the construction of an other and, sometimes, in pursuit of its destruction.

The tragic events of 11 September 2001 did not lead inexorably to a particular response and set of policies. Rather, the events were socially constructed to give particular meaning, and those events were spoken of in terms that created a foundational myth. In this emerging meta-narrative, the United States had been attacked 'out of the blue'. This undeserved attack had not been the product of American policy or behaviour; rather, it was an attack on the essence of America: freedom and justice. As Scott McConnell noted in a carefully written piece days after the attack, the overwhelming view in America was:

> We are the victims of unfathomable hatred from radical Arabs or Muslims, people who just hate freedom. 'Freedom and democracy are under attack', is how the President put it. Others point more broadly to an implacable Islamic hatred of the West, a hatred that knows no reason. They, the Arabs, or Islamic fundamentalists, hate us for 'who we are' – or as one pundit asserted on *Geraldo*, they hate us because of our 'separation of church and state'. They are, it would seem, born that way. Few in the American political class question these bromides.[5]

This, to McConnell, was entirely unpersuasive. He argued that at least a contributory factor was American policy towards the Middle East. But at this point in the emerging discourse, at the end of 2001, such alternative constructions failed to find popular favour and, indeed, were constructed as unpatriotic.

[3] Africa Policy Information Center. Also the finding of the Human Rights Watch Report, 1999.

[4] 'Interview with Paul Rusesabagina', *Out Now*, 13 February 2005, at http://www.outnow.ch/specials/2005/HotelRwanda/interview-Rusesabagina.E/ [9/2005].

[5] Scott McConnell, 'Why they hate us', *New York Press*, 14: 38 (19–25 September 2001) at http://www.nypress.com/14/38/taki/conformist.cfm [9/2005].

The foundational myth of the second American 9/11 was based not only on the 'attack from the blue', but was also constructed around American heroism in response: the response of the firefighters in the World Trade Center, and of the passengers and crew of Flight 93. This heroic response was a licence for the government to fight back; not to do so would have been to let the heroes down. And, because the American response was to be inclusive, Islamic-Americans who had been involved in the rescue efforts in New York and Washington as firefighters and police officers were in particular chosen to be lauded in public.[6]

In order to understand the process by which the meta-narrative of the 'war on terror' began a process of institutionalisation, this chapter first examines the discursive context of the attacks of September 11th. The attacks were to be seen in terms of 'the day that changed America'; as a pivotal moment in history. It is this reaction from political leaders and media commentators, from the political left and right, that was to be so well embedded in popular culture that it constructed the context for the decisive political intervention in the development of the institutions that came to comprise the 'war on terror'.

The foundational myth of the second American 9/11

The new 'truth' was that 11 September 2001 was the 'day that changed America'. That became the preferred interpretation, a construction created in the period immediately after the attacks. It was, thereby, an event transported into the everyday life of all Americans, not just those who lived or worked in New York and Washington. This sort of attack could happen to you or your family, on your way to work, in the South or the Midwest or anywhere in your state, was the very clear message. A special commemoration was held on 11 December 2001; in his comments President Bush said that 'We remember the perfect blueness of the sky that Tuesday morning. We remember the children travelling without their mothers when their planes were hijacked. We remember the cruelty of the murderers and the pain and anguish of the murdered. Every one of the innocents who died on September the 11th was the most important person on earth to somebody. Every death

[6] There were five such officers; see http://usinfo.org/usia/usinfo.state.gov/usa/islam/a020102.htm [9/2004].

extinguished a world.'[7] This was not simply a political reaction limited to those in the White House and on Capitol Hill; the construction of this foundational myth was a wider cultural phenomenon. That wider cultural impact is vital in understanding the power of the new meta-narrative. This was particularly evident in the major media outlets, each of which played with variations on the 'day that changed America' theme.[8] But it was a phenomenon felt throughout society. The President's speech on 20 September took place during an exhibition ice hockey match between the Philadelphia Flyers and the New York Rangers. Between the second and third periods, the President's speech was shown; when it was switched off, the fans objected: the President's speech was shown in full and the match abandoned.[9]

What developed in the six or seven months after September 11th was a *process* of remembrance. It was through these acts and processes of remembrance that the foundational myth became solidified in the national discourse. They were created in a variety of media, particularly, of course, on the websites of the news organisations. But other acts of remembrance were to be found in the plethora of books published after the attacks, such as Camilo José Vergara's *The Twin Towers Remembered*; Peter Skinner's *World Trade Center*; and *Sometime Lofty Towers: A Photographic Memorial of the World Trade Center* by Jake Rajs and Robert Hutchinson.[10] Indeed, there is an extraordinary range of books of photographs of the events of the second American 9/11, published in the weeks and months after the

7 George W. Bush, 'President: World will always remember September 11', 11 December 2001, at http://www.whitehouse.gov/news/releases/2001/12/20011211-1.html [6/2004].

8 For example, it is the strapline to the CBS materials on the events – see http://www.cbsnews.com/sections/september11/main500249.shtml. Fox News has a slight variation – 'the day America changed', http://www.foxnews.com/story/0,2933,61465,00.html [both 6/2004]. For analysis, see M. Shahid Alam, 'A day that changed America', *Counterpunch*, 17 December 2002, at http://www.counterpunch.org/alam1217.html [9/2004].

9 See 'Out of Respect', *CNN Sports Illustrated*, 20 September 2001, at http://sportsillustrated.cnn.com/hockey/nhl/news/2001/09/20/flyers_president_ap/ [9/2005].

10 Camilo José Vergara, *The Twin Towers Remembered* (Princeton Architectural Press, December 2001); Peter Skinner, *World Trade Center* (New York: Metro Books, 1 April 2002); Jake Rajs and Robert Hutchinson, *Sometime Lofty Towers: A Photographic Memorial of the World Trade Center* (New York: Browntrout, October 2001).

event, and bought in large numbers.[11] Then there are the books of personal remembrance of those who were there; again, what is astonishing is the range of volumes available.[12] *Life Magazine* produced a special issue and a book, entitled *One Nation*: important, of course, in that part of the narrative that was constructed concerned the 'oneness' of America in such a time of challenge.[13]

Artists in all media sought to find ways to mark the events. Irving Boker's *Helmet Resurrection* was a painting of a New York Fire Department helmet, upside down, with flowers growing in it. R. David Mattiza's sculpture *9/11 Eagle The Day America Cried* was a bust of an eagle, with 'September 11' around its collar. Lorenzo Green's collage *May God Forever Bless* was of the Twin Towers, President Bush, the Statue of Liberty, the Capitol Building, all being wrapped in the Stars and Stripes by citizens, watched by firefighters.[14]

Poems, too, were written to commemorate the terrible events and widely shared, often through the internet. One example is that by Amalthea Celebras, entitled 'Lady Liberty Cried':

> Another bright September day
> Another sun-filled sky
> She stands her ground with endless pride
> As planes above her fly
>
> She looks upon her children
> Her loved ones dear to heart
> As they go through their normal chores
> Some only just to start

[11] See, for example, Michael Feldschuh, *The September 11 Photo Project* (New York: Regan Books, 16 April 2002); Magnum Photographers, *New York September 11* (New York: powerHouse Books, 16 November 2001); Howell Raines, Jenny Scott and Gloria Emerson, *Portraits: 9/11/01: The Collected 'Portraits of Grief' from the New York Times* (New York: Times Books, 1 May 2002).

[12] For example, David Halbertam, *Firehouse* (New York: Hyperion Books, 1 May 2002); Dennis Smith, *Report from Ground Zero* (New York: Penguin Putnam, 18 March 2002); and Richard Picciotto and Daniel Paisner, *Last Man Down: A New York City Firechief and the Collapse of the World Trade Center* (New York: Berkley Publishing Group, 20 April 2002).

[13] The editors of Life Magazine, *One Nation: America Remembers September 11, 2001* (New York: Little Brown, 6 December 2001).

[14] These, and other artworks, were shown at the President George H. Bush Library from the autumn of 2002 to January 2003, and are shown on the George H. Bush Presidential Library website at http://bushlibrary.tamu.edu/pastexhibits/remember9_11.php [8/2005].

But soon the peace was shattered
As men so filled with hate
Soon turned their rage to senseless acts
To meet their horrid fate

First one and then another hit
Impossible to seem
Two other impacts hit elsewhere
As in a horrid dream

Tho' some did fight the evil
As heroes they had died
And as the proud twins met their fall
The Lady Liberty cried[15]

Note the common themes here: surprise attack; its undeserved nature; the shock; the heroism. And, of course, there are many other examples of work of this nature.[16]

It became possible to buy all sorts of memorabilia, such as a framed picture of the firefighters raising the US flag; a 9/11 lighter; an 'FBI World Trade Center 9-11 Commemorative' lapel badge; 9/11 remembrance candles; a 'counted cross stitch America United 9/11 kit'; a 9–11 'remembrance [teddy] bear'; a motorcycle helmet, with a picture of the Twin Towers and 'Never forget 9-11' printed; a 9/11 glass plate; 'Heroes of 2001' US postage stamps in collectors' kits.[17] It is possible to buy romanticised pictures of loss, such as an image of the lost flights going to heaven, or of a firefighter's statue.[18] A regular search of the internet auction site eBay reveals the popularity of these items. They, and other emblems, marked the attack as special and worthy of commemoration, and they sold in large numbers. Samuel Huntington has

[15] This poem, and others, can be found on a website dedicated to '9-11: united in courage and grief', at http://www.journeyofhearts.org/jofh/kirstimd/911_poems.htm#Event [9/2003].

[16] See also the e-book of poems written after the second American 9/11, produced in Dawn Richerson, *911: Poems in the Wake of a National Tragedy* (New York: Autumn Zephyr Press, October 2001). There are many other collections of poems on websites: see, for example, http://lindleyonline.com/sept11/poems.htm and http://www.geocities.com/britiz/9112.html [5 and 6/2004].

[17] All available for purchase on eBay August/September 2004: http://www.ebay.com/

[18] From those on sale at Webshots. There are at least 18 second American 9/11 images from which to choose. See http://community.webshots.com/album/48741494bCuvWj [4/2005].

noted that 'In early October [2001], 80 per cent of Americans said they were displaying the flag . . . Wal-Mart reportedly sold 116,000 flags on September 11 and 250,000 the next day . . .'[19]

In addition, there was an outpouring of musical commemorations of the events, including Bumblefoot's *9.11* and Pat McManus' *9-11 Stand Tall America*. An excerpt from the latter gives a good sense of the popular discourse on these events, focusing on the shock, the undeserved nature of the attack, the inclusive nature of the response and, of course, the clarity of the view that in the new war, the heroism of those Americans involved on September 11th would be the bedrock of America's inevitable victory.

> Oh 9-11, the day that innocence lost
> 9-11, is this what freedom cost?
> Well you can't kill freedom
> And you can't kill hope!
> Although innocence has been tarnished,
> We're gonna stand up and cope! . . .
> Cause, he may be your brother New York, New York
> And she may be your sister in Washington DC
> And they may be your family in Pennsylvania
> America, America, America!
> America, red, brown, black and white!
> America, we'll fight the good fight!
> America, where people live free
> America, yes it's home to you, it's home to me!
> We Shall Overcome
> Despite all our differences, united we are one
> We Shall Overcome
> Christian, Jew or Muslim, many faiths, it's the love that makes us one!! . . .[20]

Then there are other forms of commemoration created in the period after the attacks. One such example is the Todd M. Beamer Foundation, created in memory of one of those who fought the hijack-

[19] Samuel Huntington, *Who Are We? America's Great Debate* (London: Simon & Schuster, 2004), p. 3.

[20] Bumblefoot, *9.11*, Hermit, November 2001; Pat McManus, *9-11 Stand Tall America*, December 2001. Lyrics from http://www.rockinprevention.org/songs.htm [6/2004]. Also Various Artists, *America: A Tribute to Heroes* (Interscope Records, December 2001).

ers on Flight 93, focusing on helping traumatised children.[21] And then there are the videos, again produced in large numbers, reliving the events of the day, and again popular on eBay.[22] And websites, commemorating the impact of the day; major news stations specialised in them, CNN's under the subtitle 'A 21st century day of infamy'.[23] What is remarkable is that all of the materials cited here were launched in the critical six months of the decisive intervention after the second American 9/11.

There was another, equally if not more potent symbol of the foundational myth: calling upon God. The idea of engaging 10 per cent of Americans to pray for the President was one that emerged from the contested and bitter presidential election of 2000; but it was the impact of the second American 9/11 that brought it to the forefront. On 12 September 2001, a determination to launch the Presidential Prayer Team was taken, and it formally began on 18 September. Tens of thousands of Americans joined every day. By 30 November, the Presidential Prayer Team was top of the religious website charts in America, in terms of website hits.[24] By 15 December, one million Americans had signed up: this represented an average of over 10,000 Americans a day joining since its launch. By February, at the National Prayer Breakfast, the President was able to say to his audience:

> Since we met last year, millions of Americans have been led to prayer. They have prayed for comfort in time of grief; for understanding in a time of anger; for protection in a time of uncertainty. Many, including me, have been on bended knee. The prayers of this nation are a part of the good that has come from the evil of September the 11th, more good than we could ever have predicted.[25]

Prayer was part of the decisive intervention.

[21] See http://www.beamerfoundation.org/ [8/2004].

[22] For example, Ben Cartwright, director, *Remember September 11th*, DVD/VHS, 1 February 2002; and *America, 911 – We will never forget*, DVD, 4 December 2001.

[23] See http://www.cnn.com/SPECIALS/2001/trade.center/day.section.html [4/2005]. The 'day of infamy' reference is a connection to Pearl Harbor, described as such by President Roosevelt.

[24] 'The history of the Presidential Prayer Team', at http://www.presidentialprayerteam.org/history.php [4/2005].

[25] George W. Bush, 'President's remarks at National Prayer Breakfast', 7 February 2002, at http://www.whitehouse.gov/news/releases/2002/02/20020207-1.html [9/2005].

This process of institutionalisation was about creating a shared meaning, and acts of remembrance were being reproduced for the next generation.[26] These constructions are being taught to successive generations of American children.[27] One example of the process was seeking essays from children around the United States on their response to the events of 11 September 2001. These were then published, under the title *From the Mouths of Babes*.[28] The promotional material explains that 'The book is a collection of the best of over 2,000 essays from kids across the country – ages 4–18 – regarding the tragedies. It is warm, funny, poignant, tragic, touching, evocative and pure writing. The children's perspectives will touch anyone's heart and show how American kids really are thinking about all that has happened.'[29] But, of course, this is not one-way traffic – communication from children to adults; it also has the effect of creating a narrative for children to understand. Books were written by adults specifically to explain the second American 9/11 to children.[30] That narrative was also to be found in subsequent publications for children including, for example, the *The World Almanac for Kids 2003* (published August 2002), which begins with a section on the second American 9/11 entitled 'Remembering Tragedy and Response'.[31] On television, although not referring to the second American 9/11 directly, four editions of *Sesame Street* were spe-

[26] 'Institutionalisation' refers to the channelling of behaviour into one direction as opposed to others that are possible, although the strength of this impulse will vary. See John Gerard Ruggie, *Constructing the World Polity* (London: Routledge, 1998), p. 2.

[27] See materials provided by *Scholastic News*, 'America's leading news source for kids'. Their second American 9/11 materials are under the heading 'the day that changed America': http://teacher.scholastic.com/scholasticnews/indepth/911/. Children's reactions are in a March 2002 website: http://www.thinkquest.org/library/site_sum.html?tname=CR0211220&url=CR0211220/ [both 7/2004].

[28] Wendy Keller, *From the Mouths of Babes: Children Talk about the Day the World Changed* (Sophia Publishing, 1 January 2002). [29] Ibid., cover.

[30] See Jill C. Wheeler, *September 11 2001: A Day that Changed America* (Edina, MN: Abdo Publishing Company, 1 January 2002). Wheeler's book is part of a series of twelve volumes published by Abdo, focusing on the 'war on terror'. The series, according to Abdo, 'provides accurate, age-appropriate information, puts events in proper perspective, and offers reassurance that democracies are doing what is necessary to make the world safe'. See http://www.abdopub.com/c/@nwUJAlAujm7sQ/Pages/product.html?nocache@6+record@P224 [7/2004].

[31] *The World Almanac for Kids 2003* (New York: World Almanac Publishers, 3 August 2002).

cially commissioned to deal with September 11th issues: 'with firefighters and fire safety; understanding and relating to others who may be different from you; and strategies for coping with loss and grief'.[32]

Creating shared meaning requires a variety of cultural productions, so that the meaning penetrates to all parts of society. A meaning that relies solely upon the production of a new opera to share a particular interpretation will have limited social impact. But the memorialisation of the second American 9/11 worked across different aspects of cultural production: books, popular music, television, educational materials, collectibles, and that potent cultural symbol, the tattoo. In the aftermath of the event, demand grew for tattoos that would represent the shock of that day, that would be in themselves acts of remembrance. Petula Dvorak reported in the *Washington Post* in August 2002 that 'Tattoo parlors across the nation were flooded with requests for patriotic tattoos shortly after the terrorist attacks last year.'[33] And in the years that followed, the range of choice that developed was astonishing. Some of the representation was obvious: a tattoo, for example, of a New York firefighter, with head bowed, or one with head raised, a hose in hand pointed towards the carnage. Another representational motif in the tattoos has been the Twin Towers themselves, or the Statue of Liberty. An eagle crying, angels with '9/11' motifs, Stars and Stripes with '9/11' motifs, a ribbon . . . all were developed as tattoos. Karen Hudson, tattoo journalist for *About*, had identified over 100 different designs representing for so many a personal physical memorialisation of the second American 9/11 by the end of 2004.[34] Other tattoos were more forceful: one, an armful of bullets; another, a 'fallen crusader'.[35]

Television, too, played an important part; and not just in the frequent replaying of pictures of the event, and the frequent discussions that took place on the talk shows. Change occurred in meaning which

[32] John P. Murray, 'Your children's neighborhood', *Bearings*, at http://www.poppolitics.com/articles/printerfriendly/2002-09-20-childrenstv.shtml [4/2005].

[33] Petula Dvorak, 'Far more than skin deep', *Washington Post*, 24 August 2002. See also Tar Godvin, 'Tattoos become personal memorials to Sept. 11 and lost loved ones', *Boston Globe*, September 2002, at http://www.boston.com/news/packages/sept11/anniversary/wire_stories/0911_memorial_tattoos.htm [9/2005].

[34] Karen Hudson, '9-11 memorial tattoos', at http://tattoo.about.com/cs/tatart/l/blgal911.htm [12/2004].

[35] See Tattoo Now at http://www.tattoonow.com/Tattoos/Patriotic_tattoos/ [9/2005].

affected many different aspects of programme making. As Immanuel Wallerstein recalled, an episode of *Law and Order* in November 2001 about 'environmental activists' saw their actions frequently labelled as 'terrorism'; as Wallerstein commented, 'By any definition of terrorist, it is a stretch to use the term in this case. But no matter! It was so used, and it will continue to be so used.'[36] Wheeler Winston Dixon's edited volume *Film and Television after 9/11* traced the impact on other aspects of popular culture and, amongst other points, argued that film writers returned to narratives of conflict in 2002, reflecting the new discourse of an America challenged.[37]

For many in the United States, the key to understanding the human condition is through a deep and creative religion. And, inevitably, the second American 9/11 would be constructed in that light. For the evangelical analysts at Cutting Edge, who believe in the power of biblical prophecy, 'An incredible occult signature of eleven [11] undergirds this attack on the Twin Towers and the Pentagon, proof positive that the Illuminati is behind this event! Satan is orchestrating this entire event from his perch above!'[38] Others looked directly to the Bible for a prediction of the events of the second American 9/11, and found them. Greater Things, based in Utah, found that the 'New Testament Dictionary includes the following phrases on page 911: "unawares; hewn in rock; community of free people, disorganized crowd or multitude; a rich, commercial city; the Muslims destroyed the city, and today it is a heap of ruins". The name "Laoden", a variation spelling of Laden, inserts alphabetically on p. 911 with the above phrases.'[39] *Christians United Press* proclaimed the miracle of the Bible that had been left undamaged in the wreckage of the Pentagon after the attack.[40]

36 Immanuel Wallerstein, 'America and the world: the Twin Towers as metaphor', *Social Science Research Council, After September 11th*, at http://www.ssrc.org/sept11/essays/wallerstein_text_only.htm [3/2005].

37 Wheeler Winston Dixon (ed.), *Film and Television after 9/11* (Carbondale, IL: Southern Illinois University Press, 2004).

38 'Massive terrorism against American cities! Is this the beginning of the terrors planned to accompany World War III?', at http://www.cuttingedge.org/news/n1533.cfm [4/2005].

39 Greater Things, '911 (Sept. 11) in alphabetics – prophecy of day of distress', at http://www.greaterthings.com/News/911/alphabetics.htm [4/2005].

40 'The Bible found unharmed in the middle of the destruction of the Pentagon', *Christians United Press*, 2:10 (October 2001), report written on 14 September 2001, at http://www.angelfire.com/al2/Pray/newsletter_archive/October2001/page1.html [4/2005].

Thus, for some, the decisive intervention that followed the crisis of the second American 9/11 had to be comprehensible through an evangelical lens. But they faced one central challenge. Perhaps inevitably, some questioned how God could have let such a terrible attack happen: where was God on 11 September 2001? The evangelicals found Him; He was saving as many as possible, according to a prayer published soon after the events: there were only 266 people on the four planes, that held a capacity of 1,000; only 20,000 were in the World Trade Center, when there could have been 50,000; and the Towers held up long enough for two-thirds to escape.[41] God thereby showed His mercy in so many ways. These interpretations were spread amongst church communities throughout the country, and found a ready audience. Large numbers of Americans had turned to church to pray on the evening of 11 September in impromptu services, many fearing that America was being punished for turning away from God.[42] They understood the new meta-narrative through – in evangelical communities – a pre-existing premillennialist discourse. In sum, for many millions of Americans, the second American 9/11 was also a religious event.

The events of the second American 9/11 therefore impacted culturally throughout the United States: on music, poetry, publishing, videos, children's books, collectibles, television, and on religion. The involvement of American popular culture cannot be overestimated. And this all helped the reproduction of a particular narrative, itself the product of a particular decisive intervention. But for this impact to be as broad and as immediate as it was, there needed to be some core acts of remembrance of the foundational moment of this new understanding of this world.

Remembrance has a vital role to play, therefore, in the construction of a new meta-narrative. 'In the aftermath of war or catastrophe', wrote Jenny Edkins, 'comes the reckoning . . . If it is a war that has been won, commemoration endorses those in power . . . Private grief is overlaid by national mourning and blunted – or eased – by stories of service and duty.'[43] Work on remembrance has been fully connected to its impact in

41 See http://www.angelrays.com/Cards/moon/9/11.html [3/2005]. Also at http://www.swapmeetdave.com/United/Where.htm [4/2005].

42 See LaTonya Taylor, 'Shaken Christians turn to prayer', *Christianity Today* (2001), at http://ctlibrary.com/8306 [3/2005].

43 Jenny Edkins, *Trauma and the Memory of Politics* (Cambridge: Cambridge University Press, 2003), p. 1.

the aftermath of war; but the second American 9/11 was different. Yet that which Edkins describes was precisely the situation with the remembrance frenzy that emerged after 11 September 2001. Heroes were identified amongst the firefighters of New York City, who struggled to save life in the inferno of the Twin Towers, many of whom died in that struggle; and amongst the passengers of Flight 93, who fought and overwhelmed their hijackers. The heroism of these people was transferred to the nation, understood as being manifestations of a heroic *America*.

Theo Farrell argued that 'collective memory is the product of individuals and groups who come together in the act of remembrance'.[44] And so it has been with the second American 9/11. The moment was one of sorrow, loss, shock and tragedy; of unjustness, brutality, violation. All of this became part of, and has continued to be a part of, the meaning of the second American 9/11, that which has been memorialised, that which can now be understood through the meta-narrative of the 'war on terror'.

This was the area in which the decisive intervention operated. All of the aspects examined here were *created* in a relatively short period of time, from 11 September 2001 until the early part of 2002. This is the period of the decisive intervention, spoken of in theoretical terms above. It is the time when meaning, a meta-narrative, is created, developed, spread and reproduced. The meta-narrative covers coffee tables throughout the United States, structures op-ed pieces in serious newspapers, is enshrined in many acts of remembrance, has physical presence on people's bodies, is music on the radio and programmes on television, and is taught to the nation's children. That is, a political project was developed in this period that constructed the crisis in particular ways. That construction did not develop separately from the cultural reaction to the second American 9/11; how could it have done so? It was not the product of purely rationally calculating political actors in Washington. Rather, there was a mutual constitution of the cultural and the political, with the political able to create a narrative in this context that was able to compete successfully against any other possible narratives.

This is not to say that there were no key political actors in this process, because, of course, there were, as is emphasised in neo-evolutionary theory and as will become increasingly clear in successive pages. Those political actors were able to create a decisive intervention in the context

[44] See Theo Farrell, 'Memory, imagination and war', *History*, 87:285 (2002), pp. 61–73.

of a socially constructed crisis that had to be controlled and shaped. That decisive intervention then had to be reproduced and thereby spread by the American epistemic security community, those with the social power accorded to a network of knowledge-based experts with an authoritative claim to policy-relevant knowledge. While Peter Haas coined the term to refer to the international level, others – notably Craig Thomas – have applied the concept to groups within the United States.[45] That epistemic community has reached into those who are involved in wider cultural production. The development of the decisive intervention has to be followed by a successful reproduction of that new narrative in the epistemic community for it to take hold. The epistemic community plays a broader role in reinforcing 'commonsense' assumptions dominant in the discourse. In the context of the emergence of Thatcherite discourse in the UK, Kerr argues persuasively:

> Throughout the literature on the postwar period the intellectual establishment has provided a ringing endorsement of the basic historical narrative of the New Right, abandoning previous assumptions about the adversarial nature of the [British] political system in favour of the idea of a social-democratic consensus. Certainly the aim of most authors has not been to endorse Thatcherism, but that is not the point . . .[46]

It is a function of a policy paradigm to operate in such a fashion; that it be reinforced by an epistemic community. Thus, in the main, the epistemic community surrounding American security policy would reproduce and reinforce the narrative that emerged after the second American 9/11. The following section examines the nature of the decisive intervention.

The decisive intervention: from September 11th to the 'axis of evil'

One of the earliest aspects of the decisive intervention that created the new meta-narrative concerned the naming of the crisis. The description of the attacks and loss of life in New York, Washington and Pennsylvania on 11 September 2001 has become uniformly known as

45 Craig W. Thomas, 'Public management as interagency cooperation: testing epistemic community theory at the domestic level', *Journal of Public Administration Research and Theory*, 7:2 (1997), pp. 221–46.

46 Kerr, *Postwar British Politics*, p. 212.

9/11 or September 11. But this was not what it was known as in the immediate aftermath of the attack. Then, the representation was different: not *9/11*, but *911* – that is, nine-one-one.[47] This subtle shift is of course full of meaning; dialling 911 in the United States is to call the emergency services. To name the event as 911, therefore, was to issue a call for emergency help. 911 is not a reference to be found in the statements of the administration in the first few months after the attacks; rather, the event is named as 'September 11th'.[48] In this way the 'cry for help' meaning of the original terminology of '911' is lost, as the representation becomes that of a tragic moment in time with which America was able to cope without outside assistance.

In retrospect, the creation of the second American 9/11 meta-narrative was perhaps made easier by the lack of a clear foreign policy framework created by the Bush administration in its first eight months in power. That is, no obvious changes in direction were called for that specifically targeted decisions by the Bush administration, as opposed to those of the American government more generally over a longer period of time.[49] Just before September 11th, *Time Magazine* ran a series of articles questioning the ability of the administration to define a direction in foreign policy.[50] Perhaps this was surprising; after all, most of the leading figures of the administration had long experience of foreign policy issues: Dick Cheney, the Vice President; Donald Rumsfeld, the Secretary of Defense; Colin Powell, the Secretary of State; Condoleezza Rice, the National Security Advisor; and at the next tier, although very importantly, the figure of Paul Wolfowitz, the Deputy Secretary of Defense. Partly this was due to the argument over the result of the presidential election, and the consequent slow

47 Many of the electronic references to 911 or 9.11 have been lost as websites have been updated. But see the 911 Digital Archive, at http://911digitalarchive.org/; the Independent Television Service, at http://www.itvs.org/9.11/dsl/; and PBS, at http://www.pbs.org/newshour/extra/features/after911/ [all 6/2004].

48 For example, Donald Rumsfeld, 'Farewell ceremony in honor of outgoing Chairman of the Joint Chiefs of Staff General Hugh Shelton', 1 October 2001, at http://www.defenselink.mil/speeches/2001/s20011001-secdef.html [7/2004].

49 David Frum argues that by the summer of 2001, 'George Bush was on his way to a not very successful presidency', *The Right Man* (London: Weidenfeld & Nicolson, 2003), pp. 272–4.

50 See Johanna McGeary, 'Is he the odd man out?', *Time*, 2 September 2001; Johanna McGeary, 'Odd man out' and Massimo Calabresi, 'The charm of face time', *Time*, 10 September 2001.

confirmation of officials by Congress. Partly it was due to the administration's commitment to move decisively on the domestic agenda. Partly it was due to a commitment to 'policy reviews' in the international sphere.[51] Fundamentally, it was because of a struggle of ideas within the administration.

Subsequent to all the events of the year 2001, it became fashionable to discuss the Bush administration as a 'neoconservative' one; or perhaps one in which 'neoconservatism' and 'multilateralism' were in conflict. Neoconservatism, unlike the 'realism' so often identified in American foreign policy circles, has been explicitly normative. One of the most important of its thinkers, Irving Kristol, has suggested that 'A larger nation has more extensive interests. And large nations, whose identity is ideological, like the Soviet Union of yesteryear and the United States of today, inevitably have ideological interests in addition to more material concerns.'[52] America has not stood up against challenges to its ideas and interests sufficiently in the past, and that has encouraged further challenges. As William Kristol put it at the beginning of the Iraq War, 'America was attacked a little over a year and a half ago. This assault was the product of two decades of American weakness . . . we came to be seen as a "weak horse".'[53] Neoconservatives have held that democracies tend to be supportive of the United States, and it is therefore in the interests of America to spread democracy, if necessary by force. This 'liberation' agenda has to be built upon the rocks of existing democratic alliances, and here the American–Israeli connection comes to the fore.[54] But all democracies should be valued.[55]

51 See Harvey Sicherman, 'Finding a foreign policy', *Orbis*, 46: 2 (Spring 2002), pp. 215–27.

52 Irving Kristol, 'The neoconservative persuasion', *Weekly Standard*, 25 August 2003.

53 William Kristol, 'September 11, 2001 – April 9, 2003: the era of American weakness and doubt in response to terrorism is over', *Weekly Standard*, 28 April 2003, at http://www.weeklystandard.com/content/public/articles/000/000/002/564ueebn.asp [9/2005].

54 On support for Israel, see Fred Barnes, 'The terrorism loophole', *Weekly Standard*, 20 March 2002, at http://www.weeklystandard.com/content/public/articles/000/000/001/032rpuwy.asp [9/2005], which compares bin Laden and Arafat.

55 Leon Aron, 'Poor democracies – instead of condescension they deserve our support', *The Weekly Standard*, 16 July 2001, at http://www.weeklystandard.com/content/public/articles/000/000/000/343qhgwm.asp [9/2005].

Neoconservatism has itself undergone a series of intellectual changes from the late 1960s, and is in any case centrally about the nature of American politics, economics and society, rather than the world. The key ideational discomfort for the Bush administration in the period up to the crisis of the second American 9/11 was with 'realism'. 'Neoconservatism' has been a means through which the administration could reduce the constraints of the 'realist' tradition with which many believed the administration had seemed committed. It had been a tenet of faith that members of the incoming administration were 'realists'. Michael Mazarr had listed those declarations of commitment to 'realism' by Bush, Rice and Rumsfeld.[56] But that is insufficient to understand the nature of the Bush administration's foreign policy. The period before the second American 9/11 was one in which the creation of a meta-narrative for American foreign policy was found wanting. Contradictions in the framework of American foreign policy abounded. Melvyn Leffler argued that 'The history of American foreign relations is not about the struggle between power and ideals, as it is so often portrayed, but about their intermingling. America's ideals have always encapsulated its interests.'[57] Quite so. But the material and the ideational are mutually constituted and expressed through discourse; and it was a new discourse that was given life on September 11th. Thus, for the administration, a particular reading of the second American 9/11 created the possibility of producing a meta-narrative, one that they had been unable to find beforehand; and it created a new context for 'realist' and 'neoconservative' to work together. It would be 'realist' in calling for the use of power to face the new objective threat. It would be 'neoconservative' in seeking to ascribe norms to the new conflict, and in thereby looking for ways to advance American 'ideological' interests, in Afghanistan, Iraq and many other parts of the world. A particular reading would give a purpose and an ideological unity. The critical phase for the decisive intervention was that from the events of September 11th through to President Bush's State of the Union speech declaring the existence of an 'axis of evil' the following January. Developments do not cease, of course, after that event. However, the key point is that by that stage, the strategic trajectory of US security policy had been (re)set.

[56] Michael J. Mazarr, 'George W. Bush, idealist', *International Affairs*, 79:3 (May 2003), pp. 503–4.

[57] Melvyn P. Leffler, '9/11 and the past and future of American foreign policy', *International Affairs*, 79:5 (October 2003), p. 1050.

It has been argued earlier that the narration of the second American 9/11 had four key elements. The first element was the construction of an enemy image. At 9.30 am on the morning of 11 September, when the President spoke about the attacks on the World Trade Center, he said that the federal government would 'conduct a full-scale investigation to hunt down and to find those folks who committed this act'.[58] 'Those folks': this was not a description that was to survive the process that followed. Al-Qaeda was named in the days after September 11th as the perpetrator, and then a process of ascribing (evil) motivation proceeded. There was only that one acceptable interpretation. Russell Berman argues that 'The critics' alternative to a forceful defense necessarily involves coming to some accommodation with the rogue states or the terrorists, despite their proven propensity for violence and deceit. Indeed, many political leaders and large parts of the international public have demonstrated a clear preference for appeasement over any confrontation.'[59] This is a classic speech act: the naming of one perspective as legitimate, reasonable, common sense, and all others as weak, foolish and underhand. Failure to share the meta-narrative of the 'war on terror' is equated with appeasement; that vile crime of sacrificing others to avoid confrontation is equated with the Nazi evil. In the new discourse, al-Qaeda was constructed as a total enemy: one committed to destroy 'freedom' and kill all 'Americans and like minded'. But al-Qaeda was not alone: the other part of the target set were 'state sponsors of terrorism'. Secretary of State Colin Powell made the link specific in October 2001. Speaking of North Korea, he said 'I think perhaps the events of the 11th of September have caused them [the North Koreans] to slow down their decision process. As you know, they are on a list of states that sponsor terrorism . . .'[60]

The second element of the narration of '9/11' was the absence of blame within. The second American 9/11 was not the fault of Americans, whether of the intelligence services, or of the Clinton administration. Not even the *Clinton* administration, so loathed

[58] George W. Bush, 'Remarks by the President after two planes crash into the World Trade Center', Florida, 11 September 2001, at http://www.whitehouse.gov/news/releases/2001/09/20010911.html [9/2005].

[59] Russell A. Berman, 'The psychology of appeasement', *The Hoover Digest*, 3 (Summer 2004), at http://www.hooverdigest.org/043/berman.html [9/2004].

[60] Colin Powell, 'Press briefing aboard aircraft en route to Shanghai', 17 October 2001, at http://www.state.gov/secretary/rm/2001/5427.htm [5/2004].

amongst the Republicans.[61] Subsequently, this element began to break down; but this occurred *after* the military intervention in Iraq. In the period between September 11th and the 'axis of evil' speech, no hint of blame is to be found as the decisive intervention developed. And this was an important discursive move: if al-Qaeda was to be constructed as the antithesis of the values and nature of America, then there was also a process of (re)constructing America, which necessarily meant creating a discursively coherent whole. And, of course, this was to be achieved not only by the administration, but also by the Democrats, only too eager to share in this new endeavour.

The third element logically followed: the (re)construction of America required the naming of core American values: here to be those of 'freedom' and 'justice'. Donald Rumsfeld argued that 'We are a free people. That's what we as a people are. And terrorism tries to deny that freedom.'[62] Thus, America had no choice in its response, because its enemies attacked its very essence. Failure to accept this 'common sense' meant complicity with an absolute, anti-American enemy. As Andrew Bacevich has argued, the claim that America was attacked because of the freedom at its core allowed President Bush to affirm American innocence in the attack, and to relieve the administration of any need to reassess America's global impact.[63] The decisive intervention stipulated that Americans had to engage in the struggle to protect freedom and justice, and this required an international, rather than purely a national, struggle. To fail to engage in that struggle would be to betray the essence of American society. Freedom and justice are, in this narration, universal values, that need to be protected internationally – that is, in Afghanistan and subsequently Iraq as much as in New York.

The fourth element also logically followed from the one before. If there is to be an international struggle to protect values against an absolute enemy, it would be a struggle that the United States would lead with allies; and the world would recognise and value that

61 When the adminstration began, Harvey Sicherman argues the main policy was 'Bush the Anti-Clinton' in 'Finding a foreign policy', *Washington Quarterly*, 46:2 (Spring 2002), pp. 216–18.

62 'Secretary Rumsfeld interview with CBS Early Show', 18 September 2001, at http://www.defenselink.mil/transcripts/2001/t09182001_t0918bg.html [7/2004].

63 Andrew J. Bacevich, *American Empire* (Cambridge, MA: Harvard University Press), 2002, pp. 231–2.

American leadership. Bush asserted on 1 October 2001 'that we're strong and united in the cause of freedom not only here in America, but all around the world'.[64] He later argued that 'Overseas, our diplomatic efforts are strong. Nations all across the globe have bound with the United States to send a clear message that we'll fight terrorism wherever it may exist . . . [world leaders] . . . said, we stand with America. We stand with America in our noble goal of finding the evildoers and bringing them to justice.'[65]

This newly emerging meta-narrative developed from the sense of shock, of vulnerability, of helplessness, of confusion, of needing help – all of which were part of the immediate sense in America on 11 September 2001 itself. There had been no understanding of what was occurring, whether in government, media, or public as the attacks were actually happening: there was no template that could be readily deployed. Meaning had to be ascribed; and that meaning was created over hours and days.

One aspect of this was to build on the example of heroism, and to develop the idea of a people who had been tested. Being 'tested': this was very clearly an idea drawn from Christian experience. Bush brought this together in his reactions to the events: on 16 September 2001, he said:

> Today, millions of Americans mourned and prayed, and tomorrow we go back to work. Today, people from all walks of life gave thanks for the heroes; they mourn the dead; they ask for God's good graces on the families who mourn, and tomorrow the good people of America go back to their shops, their fields, American factories, and go back to work . . . We're a nation of resolve.[66]

As Vice President Cheney said in New York the following month:

> Your firefighters and police, rescue and recovery workers have responded with true heroism, and the entire nation has been deeply moved by the images of men and women working beyond the point of exhaustion, of

64 'President: We're making progress', 1 October 2001, at http://www.whitehouse.gov/news/releases/2001/10/20011001-6.html [7/2004].

65 President Bush, 'Economy an important part of homeland defense', 24 October 2001, at http://www.whitehouse.gov/news/releases/2001/10/20011024-2.html [7/2004].

66 George W. Bush, 'Remarks by President upon arrival', 16 September 2001, at http://www.whitehouse.gov/news/releases/2001/09/20010916-2.html [7/2004].

parish communities throughout the city and New Yorkers of all faith stepping forward to offer any help that is needed.[67]

The heroism of the few and of the ordinary spoke to the need for heroism from the nation. And in this, Cheney's comment on New Yorkers 'of all faith' was important.

A second aspect of the decisive intervention was to (re)construct an idea of equality of treatment of all Americans. Significant work was undertaken in the aftermath of September 11th to avoid the belief of an 'enemy within', an idea that Muslim (or specifically, Arab) Americans were a threat. After all, as Attorney General John Ashcroft had noted on 25 October, 'The attacks of September 11 were acts of terrorism against America orchestrated and carried out by individuals living within our borders. Today's terrorists enjoy the benefits of our free society even as they commit themselves to our destruction. They live in our communities – plotting, planning and waiting to kill Americans again.'[68] But these people were not to be thought of in any sense as *Americans* (whether they be 'failed' Americans, or 'treacherous' Americans) but rather as enemies taking advantage of the nature of America. Nor indeed were they to be seen as 'right-thinking' people, an enemy with whom some accommodation could be reached. The enemy was, in a biblical sense, 'evil'; and evil cannot be accommodated, it can only be destroyed. For David Frum, in the speech that the President gave in the National Cathedral, 'Bush was identifying Osama bin Laden and his gang as literally satanic.'[69] In speaking of an axis of 'evil' in January 2002, the President had again used this imagery. As Bob Woodward put it, 'It was almost as if Saddam was an agent of the Devil.'[70] Evil also confuses people (Antichrist, for example, will lead some to believe that he is Christ returned). The impact of al-Qaeda's attack could be to confuse some Americans, to set neighbour against neighbour. Thus national unity was also almost a religious duty.

[67] 'Vice President Cheney delivers Alfred E. Smith Memorial Foundation Dinner', 18 October, 2001, at http://www.whitehouse.gov/vicepresident/news-speeches/speeches/vp20011018.html [8/2004].

[68] Attorney General John Ashcroft, 'Remarks prepared for the US Mayors' Conference', 25 October 2001, at http://www.usdoj.gov/ag/speeches/2001/agcrisisremarks10_25.htm [9/2004].

[69] Frum, *Right Man*, p. 140.

[70] Bob Woodward, *Plan of Attack* (London: Simon & Schuster, 2004), p. 87.

George Bush illustrated and developed these themes in a number of key speeches that began to set out the nature of the decisive intervention. He said, on 17 September:

> the American people were appalled and outraged at last Tuesday's attacks. And so were Muslims all across the world. Both Americans and Muslim friends and citizens, tax-paying citizens, and Muslims in nations were just appalled and could not believe what we saw on our TV screen . . . The face of terror is not the true faith of Islam. That's not what Islam is all about. Islam is peace. These terrorists . . . represent evil and war.[71]

Warming to these themes, on 26 September, President Bush remarked:

> I also want to assure my fellow Americans that when you pledge allegiance to the flag, with your hand on your heart, you pledge just as hard to the flag as I do; that the outpouring of support for our country has come from all corners of the country, including many members of the Muslim faith. And for that I am grateful.[72]

And Vice President Cheney, on 23 October, added that 'The world understands that we do not fight a religion. Ours is not a campaign against the Muslim faith . . . this is a fight to save the civilized world and values common to the West, to Asia and to Islam. This is a struggle against evil, against an enemy that rejoices in the murder of innocent, unsuspecting human beings.'[73] Not only would al-Qaeda fail to divide America from Muslim Americans, they were not to be allowed to divide America from Islamic state allies, for this also would be to allow evil to prevail.

So the narration of the response to the second American 9/11 constructed by the decisive intervention built upon stories of heroism, and developed inclusivity, both for Americans and with Islamic groups internationally. This led easily into the third element of the decisive intervention: ascribing the values of humanity to the

71 'Islam is peace, says President', remarks by the President at the Islamic Center, Washington, DC, 17 September 2001, at http://www.whitehouse.gov/news/releases/2001/09/20010917-11.html [6/2004].

72 'President meets with Muslim leaders', 26 September 2001, at http://www.whitehouse.gov/news/releases/2001/09/20010926-8.html [6/2004].

73 'The Vice President receives the International Republican Institute's 2001 Freedom Award', 23 October 2001, at http://www.whitehouse.gov/vicepresident/news-speeches/speeches/vp20011023.html [8/2004].

American side in this confrontation. The internal aspect of this was vitally important: Americans had to be reminded of, and be united behind, a bipartisan set of ideas around liberty and freedom. Less than twelve months after a hugely bitter presidential election campaign, one resolved as much in the courts as in the ballot box, this was an important discursive move. Even in the pages of the Heritage Foundation – an organisation that associates itself very strongly with the right – the new unity was valued: a unity of Republican and Democrat, of policy-maker and media. Lee Edwards was one who celebrated this: 'Democratic leaders Joseph Lieberman, Richard Gephardt and Hillary Clinton showed wisdom as they pledged support for a president whose legitimacy they had questioned . . . Now, as in crises past, faith and freedom will produce a stronger America. It's no longer a "red" and "blue" nation. It's red, white and blue. May it be so forever.'[74] Edwards' reference to faith as a binding force was illuminating in the call to unity; but there was also the secular value of progress. In October 2001 the Vice President told his audience of Republican governors, his own team as it were, that 'The advance of human freedom now depends on us.'[75]

This discourse was a common refrain: Look, for example, at the words of the defeated presidential candidate, Al Gore, in a speech that he gave on 29 September 2001, a month earlier:

> Part of our historic mission in the world is not only to demonstrate that freedom unlocks a potential that doesn't get unlocked in any other system. But the other mission that we have is to show that people who came from different lands – generations ago or as immigrants – can in this land of the free and home of the brave not only get along but enrich one another with diversity . . .[76]

Gore here brought together the themes of both freedom and inclusivity. He also paid tribute to heroism, talking of: 'the example of those who died in the inferno. They showed courage. They reached out to

[74] Lee Edwards, 'A red, white and blue nation', *Heritage Foundation Commentary*, 18 September 2001, at http://www.heritage.org/Press/Commentary/ed091801b.cfm [8/2004].

[75] 'Vice President Cheney delivers remarks to the Republican Governors Association', 25 October 2001, at http://www.whitehouse.gov/vicepresident/news-speeches/speeches/vp20011025.html [9/2004].

[76] Al Gore, 'Keynote address to the Iowa State Democratic Party's 2001 Jefferson-Jackson Day dinner', 29 September 2001, at http://www.algore04.com/news/gnn/EpEyAuulAAfQiPjHLV.shtml [9/2004].

one another and demonstrated altruism.'[77] In the defeated candidate, as in the victorious White House, a common strategic trajectory was being fashioned. No matter that Gore's team believed that their candidate had been deprived of the White House unjustly; nor that Gore had been a part of – for the Republicans – the hated Clinton White House. A new 'common sense' had been called into being that spoke across political divides. And so all could support an initiative to reproduce these ideas amongst the nation's students, with the development of the 'Lessons of Liberty' project.[78]

There was yet one further aspect to the decisive intervention. Holding to a view that the United States embodied global values that were under attack from a total enemy, the discourse called for pursuit of the terrorists. And in this, there was no alternative. Colin Powell argued that 'war has been declared upon us by the al-Qaida organization, and we have no choice but to fight that war with the kind of campaign that the President has put together'.[79] As Secretary of Defense Rumsfeld put it on 16 September, 'there is no choice other than to root out terrorists wherever they are across this globe'.[80] In another interview on the same day, he argued that 'We have to wage a war, and it has to be taken to them, where they are. And it will be a broadly based sustained effort, not in a matter of days and weeks but over years.'[81]

It was not just the terrorists that had to be fought, however. The move from searching for a transnational organisation (al-Qaeda) to pursuing 'rogue states' was an *immediate* one: it was inherent in the decisive intervention. On 6 October 2001, George Bush said: 'The United States is presenting a clear choice to every nation: Stand with the civilized world, or stand with the terrorists. And for those nations that stand with the terrorists, there will be a heavy price. America is

[77] Ibid.

[78] 'The "Lessons of Liberty" initiative is an opportunity for American students to learn more about our country and its values, as well as the people that have been called upon to defend its freedom.' http://www1.va.gov/Veteranedu/page.cfm?pg=5 [6/2004].

[79] Colin Powell, 'Interview on CBS' Face the Nation', 21 October 2004, at http://www.state.gov/secretary/rm/2001/5469.htm [7/2004].

[80] 'Secretary Rumsfeld media availability in Washington', 16 September 2001, at http://www.defenselink.mil/transcripts/2001/t09162001_t0916ma.html [7/2004].

[81] 'Secretary Rumsfeld interview for ABC News This Week', 16 September 2001, at http://www.defenselink.mil/transcripts/2001/t09162001_t0916sd.html [5/2006].

determined to oppose the state sponsors of terror.'[82] Here is the final act of the decisive intervention: to construct a global enemy list beyond the total enemy that was al-Qaeda. Donald Rumsfeld had earlier argued, on 16 September, that 'the reality is that the best defense against terrorism is an offense. That is to say, taking the battle to the terrorist organizations and particularly to the countries across this globe that have for a period of years been tolerating, facilitating, financing and making possible the activities of those terrorists.'[83] On 26 November 2001, Bush made the point very starkly. 'If anybody harbors a terrorist, they're a terrorist. If they fund a terrorist, they're a terrorist. If they house terrorists, they're terrorists . . . If they develop weapons of mass destruction that will be used to terrorize nations, they will be held accountable.'[84] In response to this statement, Bush was directly asked if in saying this he had broadened the definition of terrorism. Bush replied, 'Have I expanded the definition? . . . I've always had that definition, as far as I'm concerned.'[85] And one can see why that would seem to be a reasonable response. Here is a very revealing section from remarks Bush made on 19 September: 'I think there's some interesting opportunities to shake terrorism loose from sponsor states.'[86] Indeed, even at this early stage of the decisive intervention, the possibilities for changing international security were being foreshadowed in the President's words:

> Let me say that, in terms of foreign policy and in terms of the world, this horrible strategy has provided us with an interesting opportunity. One of the opportunities is in the Middle East. I'm pleased with the fact that Chairman Arafat and Prime Minister Sharon have taken positive steps toward bringing peace to the region. I think we have an opportunity to refashion the thinking between Pakistan and India.[87]

The decisive intervention, then, was not only about fighting the new enemy, but was also about looking to exploit 'opportunities'. On the

[82] 'Radio address of the President to the nation', 6 October 2001, at http://www.whitehouse.gov/news/releases/2001/10/20011006.html [6/2004].

[83] 'Secretary Rumsfeld interview with Fox News Sunday', 16 September 2001, at http://www.defenselink.mil/transcripts/2001/t09162001_t0916ts.html [7/2004].

[84] In Elisabeth Bumiller, 'Next target in terror war: Bush says it could be Iraq', *New York Times*, 27 November 2001.

[85] Ibid.

[86] 'Remarks by the President at photo opportunity with House and Senate leadership', 19 September 2001, at http://www.whitehouse.gov/news/releases/2001/09/20010919-8.html [6/2004].

[87] Ibid.

very day of the attacks, Senator Carl Levin – a *Democrat* – had argued that 'Our intense focus on recovery and helping the injured and the families of those who were killed is matched only by our determination to prevent more attacks and matched only by our unity to track down, root out and relentlessly pursue terrorists, *states that support them* and harbor them.'[88]

Democrats and Republicans, therefore, shared the responsibility – though unequally – for the decisive intervention that occurred in the aftermath of the attacks of September 11th. This intervention built upon a narrative of heroism and resilience, developed inclusivity, named values that America embodied, but that were global in appeal (most importantly, that were not rooted in a particular faith), and created a mutually constitutive relationship between terrorists and state sponsors.

This new meta-narrative became the 'war on terror': produced by the epistemic community on security matters in the United States – not only policy-makers, but also by the media, think tanks and academics. Binary opposites abound: Antony Blinken argued that 'The war of ideas will help determine whether the new century, like its predecessor, is an American century. The United States brings powerful weapons to the battlefield: freedom, opportunity, and tolerance. The nation's enemies can counter only with repression, regression, and fanaticism.'[89] Other voices were seen as dissenters or radicals: common sense has been defined. And, of course, these discursive acts led directly to policy initiatives.

There were a series of immediate actions to the establishment of the new strategic trajectory. On 13 September, a vast increase in spending was announced: within days, an increase of $20 billion was authorised, and spending not just on the military.[90] The following day, a call-up of 50,000 reservists for homeland defence was issued.[91] On 30 September,

[88] Senator Carl Levin (D-Michigan) in 'DoD news briefing on Pentagon attack', 11 September 2001, at http://www.defenselink.mil/transcripts/2001/t09112001_ t0911sd.html [5/2004]. Emphasis added.

[89] Antony J. Blinken, 'Winning the war of ideas', *Washington Quarterly*, 25:2 (Spring 2002), p. 113.

[90] See 'DoD news briefing – Deputy Secretary Wolfowitz', 13 September 2001, at http://www.defenselink.mil/transcripts/2001/t09132001_t0913dsd.html [7/2004].

[91] See 'Deputy Secretary Wolfowitz interview with PBS News Hour', 14 September 2001, at http://www.defenselink.mil/transcripts/2001/t09162001_t0914pbs.html [8/2004].

the Quadrennial Defense Review was launched, a document recast by the events of the second American 9/11, and one given greater prominence by those events.[92] On the evening of 7 October, the first air strikes were launched against Kabul. In early October, the new Office of Homeland Security was established, and its first director, Governor Tom Ridge, appointed.[93] The FBI launched a website with leading terrorist suspects identified on it.[94] By the middle of October, 750 'terror suspects and material witnesses' were being questioned in custody throughout the United States.[95] At the end of October, the USA Patriot Act was passed, 'an essential step in defeating terrorism, while protecting the constitutional rights of all Americans'.[96] It allowed for enhanced powers in the fight against terrorism, including the tapping of telephones, the interception of emails, and the ability to investigate bank accounts. On 1 November, American carpet bombing of Taliban and al-Qaeda forces in northern Afghanistan began, and the last city under Taliban control fell in early December. In mid-November, a high-profile Airline Security Bill was passed in Congress.[97]

On 18 September, the first of a series of letters containing anthrax was discovered. Over the next few weeks, letters were sent to news media outlets and to two members of Congress; five people died. Inevitably, some saw this as the work of al-Qaeda; the template had been created by the decisive intervention, and could now be applied. Richard Butler, the former weapons inspector, argued that terrorist organisations would not be able to manufacture anthrax, and would have to have it supplied by a state: Iraq being the most likely.[98] The *Wall Street Journal* decided more forcibly in October

[92] See http://www.comw.org/qdr/qdr2001.pdf [8/2004]. For analysis, Michael O'Hanlon, 'Rumsfeld's defense vision', *Survival*, 44: 2 (Summer 2002), pp. 103–17.

[93] 'President establishes office of Homeland Security', 8 October 2001, at http://www.whitehouse.gov/news/releases [6/2004].

[94] See http://www.fbi.gov/mostwant/terrorists/fugitives.htm [8/2004].

[95] 'President outlines war effort', 17 October 2001, at http://www.whitehouse.gov/news/releases/2001/10/20011017-15.html [6/2004].

[96] 'President signs anti-terrorism bill', 26 October 2001, at http://www.whitehouse.gov/news/releases/2001/10/20011026-5.html [6/2004].

[97] 'Air security bill flies through Congress', at http://abcnews.go.com/sections/business/DailyNews/airsecurity_congress011116.html [8/2004].

[98] In 'Ex-UN weapons inspector: possible Iraq-anthrax link', *CNN Health*, 15 October 2001, at http://archives.cnn.com/2001/HEALTH/conditions/10/15/anthrax.butler/ [9/2005].

that al-Qaeda was likely to be responsible, and that it was probably supplied with the anthrax by Iraq.[99] In fact, both Butler and the *Wall Street Journal* were reflecting the administration's own analysis, and much work was undertaken by the government to try to find a link between the anthrax and Iraq.[100] In the first few months of 2002, more and more was written and said to connect al-Qaeda with those anthrax attacks. The *New York Times* and *CBS News* ran stories along these lines, in particular suggesting that the September 11th hijackers' interest in crop spraying aircraft could have been about securing a means of delivering the anthrax to large numbers of people.[101] Richard Muller held that the plan had been 'to murder thousands of people'.[102] Subsequently, the type of anthrax made it clear that it had originated not in Central Asia, let alone Iraq, but came from America's own biological weapons defence programme.[103]

A new meta-narrative had been established, and this had led to a series of actions that had not been at the forefront of the political agenda prior to 11 September 2001 in a serious or coherent fashion. It created new understandings, a new template to be placed over events. In many ways, the summation of this period of the decisive intervention was reached in January 2002, with the President's State of the Union address. This crucial speech was designed to mark a new phase, from developing policy to implementing it. The President said that 'In four short months, our nation has comforted the victims, begun to rebuild New York and the Pentagon, rallied a great coalition, captured, arrested, and rid the world of thousands of terrorists, destroyed Afghanistan's terrorist training camps, saved a people from starvation, and freed a country from brutal

[99] 'The anthrax source', *Wall Street Journal*, editorial page, 15 October 2001, at http://www.opinionjournal.com/editorial/feature.html?id=95001324 [9/2005].

[100] David J. Broad and William Johnston, 'US inquiry tried, but failed, to link Iraq with anthrax attack', *New York Times*, 22 December 2001.

[101] See 'An al-Qaeda–anthrax link?', *CBS News*, 23 March 2002, at http://www.cbsnews.com/stories/2002/03/23/attack/main504460.shtml [9/2005].

[102] Richard A. Muller, 'Al-Qaeda's anthrax', *Technology Review*, 16 April 2002, at http://cache.technologyreview.com/articles/02/04/wo_muller041602.asp?p=1 [9/2005].

[103] See Barbara Hatch Rosenberg, 'Anthrax attacks pushed open an ominous door', *Los Angeles Times*, 22 September 2002, at http://www.fas.org/bwc/news/anthraxreport.htm [9/2005].

oppression.'[104] There were five key claims made by President Bush in the course of this address:

1. The United States was designated to be at the head of an international campaign to save freedom: 'As long as training camps operate, so long as nations harbor terrorists, freedom is at risk. And America and our allies must not, and will not, allow it.'
2. The evidence from the war in Afghanistan was that the nature of the terrorist threat was greater than had been thought; not only was there a risk of suicide attacks, now that had been compounded by the fear that terrorists might use weapons of mass destruction: 'We must prevent the terrorists and regimes who seek chemical, biological or nuclear weapons from threatening the United States and the world.'
3. Not only did the threat come from al-Qaeda, but from a series of other likeminded terrorists: 'A terrorist underworld – including groups like Hamas, Hezbollah, Islamic Jihad, Jaish-i-Mohammed – operates in remote jungles and deserts, and hides in the centers of large cities.'
4. The United States would take to itself the right to intervene even without the support of other states: 'Some governments will be timid in the face of terror. And make no mistake about it: If they do not act, America will.'
5. Finally, the United States had to 'prevent regimes that sponsor terror from threatening America or our friends and allies with weapons of mass destruction . . . States like these [North Korea, Iran and Iraq were named], and their terrorist allies, constitute an axis of evil, arming to threaten the peace of the world. By seeking weapons of mass destruction, these regimes pose a grave and growing danger. They could provide these arms to terrorists, giving them the means to match their hatred. They could attack our allies or attempt to blackmail the United States. In any of these cases, the price of indifference would be catastrophic.'[105]

These five points encapsulated the reorientation of American policy under the new meta-narrative. In many ways, the speech marked the end of the phase of constructing the decisive intervention. But how does this connect to the crisis framework?

[104] 'President delivers State of the Union address', 29 January 2002, at http://www.whitehouse.gov/news/releases/2002/01/20020129-11.html [6/2004].
[105] Ibid.

Revisiting the crisis framework

In chapter 2, a framework was developed for understanding the crisis cycle (represented in figure 2.7). Following the analysis of the discursive constructions after the attacks of 11 September 2001, this can now be applied to the case of the second American 9/11. That crisis has been understood through the decisive intervention that followed the event: the two are mutually constituted.

It is of course possible to imagine alternative narratives to that constructed by the decisive intervention: not an infinite number, because there was a pre-existing discursive context for the social construction of the second American 9/11, but still a substantial number of other stories that might have come to the fore. None of these alternative narratives seems persuasive now, for it seems to be common sense that things turned out as they did. Such is the power of a successful, and hence decisive, intervention: it is not simply a question of 'letting the facts speak for themselves'.[106] But for the purposes of illustration, here are five conceivable alternative constructions.

The first alternative narrative could have been one in which there was an attack on the United States by Saudi Arabian revolutionaries. This view was one very much in the mind of many neoconservative commentators. One reading given by David Wurmser in the *Weekly Standard* spoke of the close connection between al Qaeda and the Saudi establishment.[107] Michael Ledeen was particularly concerned about the 'poison' of Wahhabism, and the danger it posed to America.[108] David Frum reported that at the end of 2001, 'Americans were learning just how up-to-the-eyeballs went Saudi complicity with terror in Afghanistan and the West Bank.'[109] Had this narrative emerged from the second American 9/11, it would have led to a revisiting of the close Saudi–American relationship.

A second alternative was a narrative in which the attacks were

[106] Richard Jackson, *Writing the War on Terrorism* (Manchester: Manchester University Press, 2005), p. 58.

[107] David Wurmser, 'The Saudi connection: Osama bin Laden's a lot closer to the Saudi royal family than you think', *Weekly Standard*, 29 October 2001, at http://www.weeklystandard.com/Content/Public/Articles/000/000/000/393rwyib.asp [9/2005].

[108] Michael Ledeen, *The War Against the Terror Masters* (New York: St Martin's Press, 2002), pp. 196–209.

[109] Frum, *Right Man*, p. 257.

constructed in terms of the abject failure of the American state to understand the new security issues, and to prepare accordingly. That is, an America let down by Americans (whether it be 'big government', 'big business', or the Clinton administration). On the political right, such an alternative narrative had supporters. 'The History Channel will one day air a new episode of "History's Blunders", in which historians will compare the massive intelligence failure preceding the terror attacks against New York and Washington not only with Pearl Harbor, but also with Hitler's disastrous attack on the Soviet Union in 1941 . . .', wrote Ariel Cohen. 'The roots of this calamity lie in institutional sclerosis and bureaucratic ossification.'[110]

A third alternative narrative could have been one in which America was betrayed by its own 'fifth column'. That is, a narrative in which certain identities ('Muslim', 'Arab') were deemed to be ones that could not be changed in the American 'melting-pot'. This would presumably have led to a policy programme that, amongst other elements, would have included internment, a policy subsequently advocated by Michelle Malkin in her highly popular book, *In Defense of Internment*.[111]

A fourth alternative narrative could have been one in which the attack was seen overwhelmingly as being a criminal act, the behaviour of a group that engaged in drug running, money laundering, and all sorts of other acts from *criminal*, rather than political, motivation. That would not have led to a 'war on terror', but a series of police actions. And a fifth possibility could have been a narrative of a crime against humanity, with the number of people from different countries the key defining aspect (more than 80 countries lost citizens in the attacks), rather than it being one of the 'day that changed *America*'. That would have led to an international response, perhaps through the United Nations.[112]

None of these alternatives came to the fore. Rather, the 'war on terror' was conjured from the 'facts' of the second American 9/11. The

[110] Ariel Cohen, 'Intelligence disaster, bureaucratic sclerosis', *Heritage Foundation Commentary*, 16 September 2001, at http://www.heritage.org/Press/Commentary/ed091601.cfm [6/2004].

[111] Michelle Malkin, *In Defense of Internment: The Case for Racial Profiling in World War II and the War on Terror* (Washington, DC: Regnery, 2004), See her website at http://michellemalkin.com/

[112] This was indeed proposed: see Morton H. Halperin, 'Dodging security', *American Prospect*, 20 September 2001, at http://www.cfr.org/pub4055/morton_h_halperin/dodging_security.php [6/2004].

rhetoric of heroism, of a people tested, was the basis for that decisive intervention. Indeed, it contained a clear teleology: an America tested would always be an America ultimately victorious. And the decisive intervention was also one in which the essence of America was respoken, restated: one of unity rather than division (whether that division be religious, ethnic, or party political), and one based on a claim to universal values. America as the embodiment of the human cry for freedom. An America that had to defend freedom around the world against the new total enemy. An America that could legitimately intervene militarily to this end, and one that would be supported by other states. An America that had to defeat not only al-Qaeda, but its partner organisations, and the states that supported them. As Charles Boyd put it on 12 September, 'This nation symbolizes freedom, strength, tolerance and democratic principles dedicated to both liberty and peace. To the tyrants, the despots, the closed societies, there are no alterations to our policies, no gestures we can make, no words we can say that will convince those determined to continue their hate.'[113]

But what next? The crisis process established earlier would suggest that there would be a period of stabilisation, followed by one in which contradictions would occur, leading to another socially constructed crisis, which would produce another decisive intervention. The crisis process, as developed from September 11th through to the early part of 2002, can be represented as in figure 3.1, with those elements in italics representing the stages covered in the development of the discourse in this book so far.

Conclusions

The meta-narrative of the 'war on terror' became the new common sense. Crucially, that common sense was created by Democrats, as well as by the Republican administration. In so doing, the Democrats solidified a discursive shift and legitimised a meta-narrative that was not their own, in a similar way to that of New Labour in Britain, which had strengthened the neoliberal agenda. As Colin Hay has put it, 'by seeking to gauge such preferences as a means of repackaging and representing them as its own, Labour merely served further to establish them as the new "common sense" in a way that the Conservatives

[113] Charles G. Boyd, 'Vulnerable to hate', *Washington Post*, 12 September 2001.

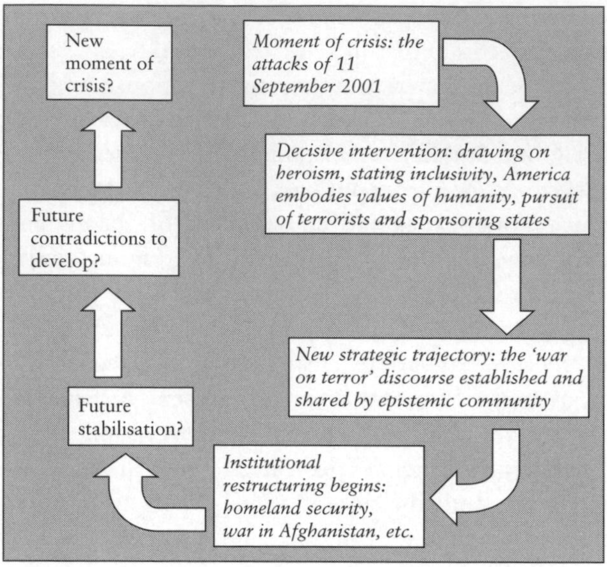

Figure 3.1 The crisis process of the second American 9/11

could never have done on their own'.[114] That is, by accepting, endorsing and contributing to the new meta-narrative, the Democrats entrenched the 'commonsense' view that surrounded a series of political propositions that were not inevitable. In a very wide-ranging speech at Georgetown University on 7 November 2001, former President, Bill Clinton, said:

> as a citizen I support the efforts of President Bush, the national security team, and our allies in fighting the current terrorist threat. I believe we all should. The terrorists who struck the World Trade Center and the Pentagon believed they were attacking the two most important symbols of American materialism and power . . . The people who died represent, in my view, not only the best of America, but the best of the world that I worked hard for eight years to build.[115]

Not only was Clinton endorsing the 'war on terror' and ascribing heroism to America itself, but with the words *that I worked hard for*

[114] Colin Hay, *The Political Economy of New Labour* (Manchester: Manchester University Press, 1999), p. 66.

[115] 'Remarks as delivered by President William Jefferson Clinton', Georgetown University, 7 November 2001, at http://www.georgetown.edu/admin/publicaffairs/protocol_events/events/clinton_glf110701.htm [9/2004].

eight years to build he directly connected his administration to the new war. True, in that speech Clinton did speak to a wider agenda; but that wider agenda was premised upon a defeat of the terrorists. The meta-narrative was unchallenged and, indeed, endorsed.

The acts of remembrance add up to the commemoration of a foundational myth. The events of September 11th were constructed in particular ways and forwarded particular interests. All pre-history was no longer important. The Harvard professor, and former Clinton official, Ashton Carter argued that 'On 11 September 2001, the post-cold war security bubble finally burst.'[116] Stephen Walt asserted that September 11th 'triggered the most rapid and dramatic change in the history of US foreign policy'.[117] And America was cast into this new world; it had no choice. Donald Rumsfeld, reflecting on the debate about civilian deaths in the war in Afghanistan, commented that 'We did not start this war. So understand, responsibility for every single casualty in this war, whether they're innocent Afghans or innocent Americans, rests at the feet of the al-Qaeda and the Taliban.'[118]

This newly constructed enemy was a total enemy, inherently evil, one that could not be reasoned with, and therefore the new common sense held that it had to be destroyed. That common sense was spread beyond America's borders. Even a French critic of American policy in the age of the 'war on terror' – one who felt that it demonstrated America's weakness – felt the need to show contempt for the September 11th terrorists: Emmanuel Todd described them as 'mentally disturbed'.[119] And any comment that was not completely condemnatory of the new enemy was, itself, subject to widespread condemnation. Steve Hanke wrote: 'writer Susan Sontag found it within herself to admire the twisted suicidal thinking that animated the hijackers. She wrote in the *New Yorker* that "whatever may be said about the perpetrators of Tuesday's slaughter, they were not cowards." What an accolade.'[120]

116 Ashton B. Carter, 'The architecture of government in the face of terrorism', *International Security*, 26:3 (Winter 2001/2), p. 5.

117 Stephen M. Walt, 'Beyond bin Laden: reshaping US foreign policy', *International Security*, 26:3 (Winter 2001/2), pp. 56–78.

118 Donald Rumsfeld, 'DoD news briefing', 4 December 2001, at http://www.defenselink.mil/transcripts/2001/t12042001_t1204sd.html [7/2004].

119 Emmanuel Todd, *After the Empire*, translated by C. Jon Delogu (New York: Columbia University Press, 2003), p. 3.

120 Steve H. Hanke 'Barbarians at the Gate', *Cato Institute Commentary*, 16 October 2001, at http://www.cato.org/dailys/10-16-01.html [7/2004].

A policy programme, for Vivien Schmidt, contains four elements: an ability to identify a problem; to specify the applicability of the policy programme to that problem; coherence; and an advantageous relationship over alternatives. The policy programme following the second American 9/11, that of the 'war on terror', had all of these characteristics. The 'war on terror' identified a problem – that of the threat of al-Qaeda and similar terrorist organisations, and their 'state sponsors', to the United States and to freedom. This 'evil' group posed a fundamental threat to America, Americans and American values. The policy programme was directly applicable to a problem so constructed: protect America, Americans and American values at home by creating the institution of homeland security, and the Patriot Act, and by speaking of the 'melting pot' of cultures in the United States, of inclusivity; and abroad by attacking the perpetrators in Afghanistan, and by creating a new alliance of like-minded states based on values, those 'with' America rather than 'with' the terrorists. And it had coherence; the meta-narrative tied together all of the elements – from the Patriot Act to the 'liberation' of Kabul – into one coherent whole, that could easily be grasped and whose core ideas were readily reproduced. Finally, the policy programme of the 'war on terror' achieved a relationship with other possible policy programmes of complete dominance: that there was 'no alternative' to conducting the 'war on terror', which had achieved the status of 'common sense' with the support of Democrats, of academic analysts, of media commentary and reporting, and through imagery.

Michael Williams has argued persuasively that 'political communication is increasingly bound with images and in which televisual communication is an essential element of communicative action'.[121] The imagery of the second American 9/11 was tied carefully and powerfully to the 'war on terror' meta-narrative, or policy programme. The television pictures of the burning Twin Towers, and the horror of seeing human beings leaping from those Towers to their certain deaths, solidified the foundation. The words of songs and poems, and the memorabilia of the events of September 11th all worked to support the

[121] Michael C. Williams, 'Words, images, enemies: securitization and international politics', *International Studies Quarterly*, 47:4 (2003), pp. 511–31, quote p. 524.

foundational myth, that of a new age, a new challenge, a new America, created on and by 11 September 2001. Malise Ruthven drew on the imagery of those events to create a similarity to the impact of a previous 'clash' with 'Islam', in which replicas of an engraving of the 'heroic' death of General Gordon on the steps of government house in Khartoum were to be found in large numbers of British homes in the late nineteenth century, mobilising political investment in securing a military victory over the Sudanese, finally achieved thirteen years later by General Kitchener.[122] The spread of acts of remembrance, the buy-in of the mass media, and the embedding of the 'war on terror' ideas in popular culture, all created a contemporary political mobilisation in the United States.

Neo-evolutionary thought creates a framework for thinking about a crisis process. One key aspect of neo-evolutionary thought is the proposition that there is motion in that which is under study. The ideas and policies brought about by the new strategic trajectory continued to develop. Although the reaction to September 11th produced something new, it also drew on existing impulses. Andrew Bacevich, for example, argued that 'if anything, al-Qaeda's attack on the American homeland eased constraints that during the previous decade had inhibited US officials in their pursuit of greater openness (and expanded American hegemony)'.[123] Neo-evolutionary thinking is concerned with that which went before; otherwise motion lacks any basis for understanding. The second aspect of neo-evolutionary thought – selectivity has been examined above. The 'war on terror' was the selected narrative, and other narratives were not seriously explored. The third proposition is that there is adaptivity; and, again, over the next few chapters, the means by which the 'war on terror' was adapted will become even more apparent.

The new meta-narrative had one other important aspect; it produced a vision of a terrorist threat externally and internally; homeland and national security were to be deeply interconnected. When US claims of successful actions in the period from 11 September to the end of the calendar year were reported in the State Department publication

[122] Malise Ruthven, 'The eleventh of September and the Sudanese mahdiya in the context of Ibn Khaldun's theory of Islamic history', *International Affairs*, 78:2 (April 2002), pp. 339–40.

[123] Bacevich, *American Empire*, p. 227.

Patterns of Terrorism, that interconnection was made clear. In that period, the US had secured many achievements, amongst which were that:

- 150 countries had agreed to freeze terrorist assets, 100 of which reported actions to the UN under security council resolution 1373;
- Terrorist assets worth $34 million had been blocked in the US, $33 million by other countries;
- 136 countries had offered military assistance to the US, 14 other states had deployed in Afghanistan, 55 other states had augmented US efforts;
- US forces had been involved in counter-terror activities in Afghanistan, Philippines, Georgia and Yemen.[124]

The enemy was not only 'out there'; it was also 'amongst us'. It was a perspective that was apparently to be justified in 2002, as a series of arrests of 'American al-Qaeda' suspects were made in the United States.

This chapter has examined a relatively short period of contemporary history; from the middle of September 2001 to early January 2002. It was in this period that the first phases of the crisis process, outlined above, came into effect. This concerned the battle of narratives for how the crisis should be understood, the consequent emergence of a meta-narrative (the 'war on terror'), and its subsequent institutionalisation. This meta-narrative had developed from the foundational myth in which an enemy image was constructed, the avoidance of blame on institutions and individuals within America was achieved, values as signs of American identity and worth were raised, and global leadership of the 'good' against the 'evil' asserted. The crisis process suggests that through institutionalisation, stabilisation occurs, prior to the onset of contradictions and, at some point, a new socially constructed crisis. The witchcraze of the fifteenth century had led to the construction of a new enemy, and agreement that there was an exceptional crime that had to be defeated by exceptional means. Although the means, of course, are not comparable, the 'war on terror' discourse followed a similar pattern. American bombing in Afghanistan had, according to an American critic, led to over 3,000 civilian deaths (the same number, possibly even higher, that died on 11 September

[124] Francis X. Taylor, Ambassador, Coordinator for Counter-terrorism in *Patterns of Terrorism 2001* (Washington, DC: US Department of State, May 2002), p. vi.

2001).[125] This equated to over forty deaths every day during the main phase of the conflict. Despite the use of carpet bombing in Afghanistan and these civilians' deaths, there was still a major discursive distinction to be drawn between the practice – not just the motivations – of the United States and al-Qaeda. America's way of war was normatively superior to that of its enemies, according to Audrey Kurth Cronin: 'The terrorist threat is a brute use of force, more understandable in a medieval context than in post-modern society.'[126] Discourse was shaping understanding and practice in real and measurable ways. The reconstruction of American and global security throughout 2002 is the next key element of the analysis.

[125] See Marc W. Herold, 'Civilian victims of United States' aerial bombing in Afghanistan', at http://www.cursor.org/stories/civilian_deaths.htm [9/2005]. Human Rights Watch declared a figure of 1800 civilian deaths. See Peter Ford, 'Surveys pointing to high civilian death toll in Iraq', *Christian Science Monitor*, 22 May 2003.

[126] Audrey Kurth Cronin, 'Rethinking sovereignty: American strategy in the age of terrorism', *Survival*, 44:2 (Summer 2002), p. 119.

4 *The institutionalisation and stabilisation of the policy programme*

Introduction

By early 2002, a foundational myth had been constructed out of the crisis of the second American 9/11, and a decisive intervention had been articulated – one that achieved its fullest expression in the President's State of the Union address in January. In this new understanding, America had not suffered a one-off disaster on 11 September 2001, the act of criminals; rather, the collective understanding was that the attacks of that day were an illustration of the ongoing threat in a long-term war. As President Bush declared in a speech in January 2002:

> I say terrorist attack because we're still under attack. They still want to come after us. These are evil people that are relentless in their desire to hurt those who love freedom. And since we're the bastion of freedom, the beacon of freedom, we're their target. And we're going to respond, and we're going to deal with it by working together.[1]

The discourse of the 'war on terror' that underlined this statement was uncontested in mainstream political and cultural life in the United States. The 'war on terror' as a policy programme was well underway.

A crisis is understood in specific ways through a decisive intervention that leads to the construction of a meta-narrative, which frames a policy programme that is institutionalised in the discourse and practices of state policy and, in the case of the contemporary United States, in popular culture. An obvious parallel to the experience and construction of the second American 9/11 is that of the attack on Pearl Harbor sixty years earlier. A far better parallel would be the launch of the Soviet space rocket Sputnik in 1957, *The Shock of the Century* as

[1] George W. Bush 'President announces substantial increase in homeland security budget', 24 January 2002, at http://www.whitehouse.gov/news/releases/2002/01/20020124-1.html [8/2004].

Paul Dickson labelled it.[2] The crisis in the United States following the Soviet launch of the world's first missile was political and cultural, and was felt throughout the country, as American families would stand outside at night, looking for a light flying overhead. The event presaged fears of nuclear attack. It led the Eisenhower administration to generate a greater interest in, and resourcing of, education in science and mathematics. It led to the creation of NASA.[3] But it also created a discourse that in part went beyond the control of government; the opposition began to develop the idea of a 'missile gap' in America's preparedness and – although there was no real empirical evidence – this demonstration of an overly confident Republican administration was played against the party at the next presidential election, won by the Democrat, John F. Kennedy.

That the launch of Sputnik was a socially constructed crisis is far less apparent decades later than it was at the time. But the impact is clearly marked in contemporary accounts; that the launch of Sputnik was a crisis for the United States is now an official historical 'fact', revealed in NASA's official history.

> The launch of *Sputnik 1* had a 'Pearl Harbor' effect on American public opinion. It was a shock, introducing the average citizen to the space age in a crisis setting. The event created an illusion of a technological gap and provided the impetus for increased spending for aerospace endeavors, technical and scientific educational programs, and the chartering of new federal agencies to manage air and space research and development.[4]

It is also a part of the history of flight as recalled in the materials produced to support the 'Centenary of Flight' celebrations in the United States in 2003. 'As news of the Soviet accomplishment quickly spread by radio and television reports,' the Centennial material explains, 'untold millions climbed onto rooftops, ventured into city parks, or ambled out to dark backyards, all scanning the heavens for a brief glimpse of a rapidly moving star. It was a communal experience that

[2] Paul Dickson, *Sputnik: The Shock of the Century* (New York: Walker & Co, 2001).

[3] In July 1958, Congress passed the National Aeronautics and Space Act. For text, see http://www.hq.nasa.gov/office/pao/History/spaceact.html [9/2004].

[4] See Roger D. Launius, 'Sputnik and the origins of the space age', on NASA's website at http://www.hq.nasa.gov/office/pao/History/sputnik/sputorig.html [9/2004].

would later become known simply as "Sputnik Night".'[5] Even the portrayal of the impact of the shock on everyday life has parallels. Earlier in this volume, some quotations were excerpted from John Lewis Gaddis' book on the second American 9/11, recalling where he was and what he was doing on that September morning. Similarly, in *Sputnik*, Dickson talks of recalling 'exactly where I was when I heard about Sputnik's launch. I was eighteen years old, a college freshman at Wesleyan University . . . A friend stopped me in the middle of campus to say that he had heard about it on the radio. Instinctively, we both looked up.'[6]

Thus, the early parallels between the Sputnik crisis and that of the second American 9/11 are interesting. Both were events that were constructed socially following a decisive intervention that led to particular discourses that were embedded socially far beyond the political leadership. For Sputnik, it was that of the 'space race'. Both discourses were shared across society, and were articulated by the opposition Democrats as much as by the Republican administration. For the second American 9/11, it is that of the 'war on terror'. Both led to an institutionalisation of that new discourse in a policy programme.

Throughout 2002, the 'war on terror' led to new approaches to the way policy was thought about, spoken of, and enacted. There were four main dimensions to this. First, terrorism was raised to the number one security priority, and a new organisation was created to reflect and embed that priority, the Department of Homeland Defense. New laws were introduced, and practices adopted that sought to make America less vulnerable to attack in terms of access and information. Second, the defence budget was raised and the military reconstructed to conduct the 'war on terror' externally. Third, the political and popular narration of the 'war on terror' developed, which reflected and contributed to the development of the discourse of the 'war on terror' in which American heroism was pitted against the enemy's evil and cowardice. And fourth, the 'war on terror' was extended around the world, in the construction of new threats discursively connected to the second American 9/11, in the generation of new allies, and in the recasting of particular conflicts and tensions. Of course, none of this was new to

5 'Sputnik and the crisis that followed', at http://www.centennialofflight.gov/essay/SPACEFLIGHT/Sputnik/SP16.htm [9/2004].

6 Dickson, *Sputnik*, p. 2.

2002. The decisive intervention following the crisis of September 11th had presaged all of this, and indeed key decisions – over the creation of the Department of Homeland Defense, the passing of the Patriot Act, and the expansion of the military budget, as well as the war in Afghanistan – were all of late 2001. But what was key thereafter was the process of institutionalisation. This chapter will examine each of these dimensions of the institutionalisation of the 'war on terror'.

Terror: the new organisational priority

One of the first acts of institutionalisation was the creation of the Department of Homeland Security, and the appointment of Governor Tom Ridge as its first Secretary. In January 2002, President Bush announced an increase in the 'homeland security' budget to $38 billion.[7] In setting out the case, President Bush had repeatedly sought to explain the need for greater focus and unity in the face of the new global challenge. He explained in June 2002 that 'Right now, as many as a hundred different government agencies have some responsibilities for homeland security, and no one has final accountability.'[8] In response, the President created a cabinet-level department, 'to unite essential agencies that must work more closely together: Among them, the Coast Guard, the Border Patrol, the Customs Service, Immigration officials, the Transportation Security Administration, and the Federal Emergency Management Agency. Employees of this new agency will come to work every morning knowing their most important job is to protect their fellow citizens . . .'[9] The new department was charged with four responsibilities: to 'control our borders and prevent terrorists and explosives from entering our country'; to 'work with state and local authorities to respond quickly and effectively to emergencies'; to 'bring together our best scientists to develop technologies that detect biological, chemical, and nuclear weapons, and to discover the drugs and treatments to best protect our citizens'; and finally, to 'review intelligence and law enforcement information from all agencies of government, and produce a single daily picture of threats against our

[7] 'President announces . . .', 24 January 2002.
[8] George W. Bush, 'Remarks by the President to the nation', 6 June 2002, at http://www.whitehouse.gov/news/releases/2002/06/20020606-8.html [8/2004].
[9] Ibid.

homeland. Analysts will be responsible for imagining the worst, and planning to counter it.'[10] Contained within these aims was a clearly articulated sense that the country was at war, and at war with an enemy that would be prepared to use weapons of mass destruction, and against which the country had to operate on the basis of worst-case analysis.

Thus, in creating the new department, the President sought to underscore the new nature of the international environment, equating this new organisational reality in importance to the time of the creation of the cold war. The President drew upon historical analogy:

> During his presidency, Harry Truman recognized that our nation's fragmented defenses had to be reorganized to win the cold war. He proposed uniting our military forces under a single Department of Defense, and creating the National Security Council to bring together defense, intelligence, and diplomacy. Truman's reforms are still helping us to fight terror abroad, and now we need similar dramatic reforms to secure our people at home.[11]

Finally, the President reinforced the magnitude of the task. 'History has called our nation into action. History has placed a great challenge before us: Will America – with our unique position and power – blink in the face of terror, or will we lead to a freer, more civilized world? There's only one answer: This great country will lead the world to safety, security, peace and freedom.'[12] And here other key elements of the decisive intervention – a nation challenged, with no pre-history to the conflict, and a task that required America to exercise global leadership – were powerfully reproduced.

The Department of Homeland Security has done much to make the 'war on terror' a part of everyday life in the United States, in particular, through the use of a colour-coded security warning system.[13] There is nothing new in the use of such a system, which is the bedrock of most militaries. What was new, however, was the public use of the system to warn about attacks on civilian populations. The system has five levels: Severe, High, Elevated, Guarded and Low, each with its own representative colour. The Advisory System varies across the United States, according to assessments of greatest local vulnerability.

[10] Ibid. [11] Ibid. [12] Ibid.

[13] The Advisory System was introduced in March 2002: see http://www. whitehouse.gov/news/releases/2002/03/20020312-1.html [9/2004].

This Advisory System is designed to give information to various authorities. At each stage of alert, there are agreed protective measures to be put into operation, not only at governmental level, but also in businesses and in schools, and in a variety of other institutions. This is so even at the lowest state of alert (Low), where members of the public should ensure that they have an updated household disaster plan and supplies kit. Organisations should ensure that prearranged protective measures are exercised, and that there is a full training regime. That is, life is not 'normal' in the home or the workplace even at the lowest level of alert; danger is ever-present. If the alert is two stages higher (Elevated), all should be increasing vigilance, and talking through with co-workers, schools and neighbours how to respond to an attack. At the highest level (Severe) non-critical facilities would be closed, and citizens should prepare shelters, or evacuate, if instructed to do so. The new nature of the post-second American 9/11 world is thereby conveyed to citizens in their home and in their workplace as part of everyday life. *Elevated* contains with it the full sense of the threat to everyday life of weapons of mass destruction.

But for this new reality to fully impact upon the population, the impact on home life had to be the most profound. How should the citizen react in an emergency in his or her own home? The Federal Emergency Management Agency (FEMA) produced a revised booklet in September 2002 (*Are You Ready?*) to give clear advice.[14] The booklet begins with the following statement by Joe M. Allbaugh, the director of FEMA. 'We live in a different world than we did before September 11, 2001. We are more aware of our vulnerabilities, more appreciative of our freedoms and more understanding that we have a personal responsibility for the safety of our families, our neighbors and our nation.'[15]

The United States faces many natural threats – hurricanes, tornadoes, earthquakes, floods and the like – epitomised by the destruction wrought upon New Orleans in August 2005 by Hurricane Katrina. Information on how to react to these, along with providing assistance in crises, is the key role for FEMA. It also discusses the danger of household fire and chemical risks, amongst other threats. *Are you Ready?*,

[14] Federal Emergency Management Agency, *Are you Ready? A Guide to Citizen Preparedness*, FEMA Publication H-34, September 2002, at http://www.fema.gov/areyouready/ [15] Ibid., p. i.

though, also includes a section on terrorism. Citizens are advised to 'Assemble a disaster supplies kit at home and learn first aid. Separate the supplies you would take if you had to evacuate quickly, and put them in a backpack or container, *ready to go*.'[16] If you are in a building that is attacked, and 'If you are trapped in debris':

- Do not light a match.
- Do not move about or kick up dust. Cover your mouth with a handkerchief or clothing.
- Rhythmically tap on a pipe or wall so that rescuers can hear where you are. Use a whistle if one is available. Shout only as a last resort when you hear sounds and think someone will hear you – shouting can cause a person to inhale dangerous amounts of dust.[17]

To prepare for the threat of a chemical or biological attack, FEMA recommends that citizens prepare the following: 'Plastic for doors, windows and vents for the room in which you will shelter in place – this should be an internal room where you can block out air that may contain hazardous chemical or biological agents. To save critical time during an emergency, sheeting should be *pre-measured* and cut for each opening.'[18] Across the country, Americans have used their weekends to prepare emergency packages, and to defend their homes against terrorist attack, as FEMA recommends.

Finally, FEMA provided information on what to do in case of a nuclear attack. Explanation was provided that, in all likelihood, this would be a 'suitcase bomb', a 'dirty bomb', and one in which 'The strength of such a weapon would be in the range of the bombs used during World War II.'[19] It was here that FEMA made the crucial discursive link between al-Qaeda and 'rogue' states real to the citizenry of the United States: 'some terrorists have been supported by nations that have nuclear weapons programs'.[20]

By adding material on the nature of preparations in the face of terrorism to information on how to prepare for natural and other potential disasters, several important discursive moves were made. The first was to underline the importance of the terrorist threat. Natural disasters occur every year in the United States. By linking terrorism to these, the threat was made to seem real and immediate, and likely. Second, in

[16] Ibid., p. 84, emphasis added. [17] Ibid., p. 86.
[18] Ibid., p. 88, emphasis added. [19] Ibid., p. 90. [20] Ibid., p. 90.

providing information on how to react, the terrorist threat was offered as a part of everyday living. And third, the connection between al-Qaeda, all terrorist groups and 'rogue' states was powerfully reproduced, a connection present from the time of the decisive intervention, while being one particular aspect of the implementation of the policy programme that was to grow in importance across the year.

American investment in homeland security was immense and widely spread. There was to be greater spending on border security – an extra $5 billion committed to airports and border security.[21] For the State Department, of these monies, $643 million was to be allocated in the FY03 budget request for the Machine Readable Visa Fee-Funded Border Security Program (to provide the technology, personnel and support needed to carry out consular and border security functions). A further $104 million was requested for anti-terrorism and domestic security initiatives and activities funded through Diplomatic and Consular Programs. Some $2.1 million was for protection of USAID domestic facilities.[22]

In law and new policy, the key aspect of this organisational refocus was domestic. The Victims of Terrorism Tax Relief Act was passed, aimed at providing tax relief to families of those killed in the attacks on September 11th, the anthrax attacks after September 11th, and the Oklahoma City bombing.[23] By December 2002, President Bush was able to announce that the US has stockpiled enough smallpox vaccine to inoculate the entire country.[24] Increased spending was announced in February 2002 for hospitals to improve ability to respond to bioterror attack ($1.6 billion); and $2.4 billion for research on treatments.[25] One impact of the second American 9/11 was that new buildings were not

[21] George W. Bush, 'President promises secure and open borders in El Paso', 21 March 2002, at http://www.whitehouse.gov/news/releases/2002/03/20020321-7.html [8/2004].

[22] Colin L. Powell, 'FY2003 homeland security budget request and FY2002 supplemental', Testimony before the Senate Appropriations Committee, 30 April 2002, at http://www.state.gov/secretary/rm/2002/9869.htm [9/2004].

[23] See http://www.whitehouse.gov/news/releases/2002/01/20020123-20.html [9/2004].

[24] George W. Bush, 'President delivers remarks on smallpox', 13 December 2002, at http://www.whitehouse.gov/news/releases/2002/12/20021213-7.html [8/2004].

[25] George W. Bush, 'President increases funding for bioterrorism by 319 per cent', 5 February 2002, at http://www.whitehouse.gov/news/releases/2002/02/20020205-4.html [8/2004].

being constructed, as loans could not be secured because of demands for insurance against terrorist attacks that could not be met financially. The President complained that 'Over $10 billion of construction projects are not going forward because people can't get the proper insurance because of *what the terrorists did to America*.'[26] So the Republican administration stepped in to introduce legislation.[27] The Justice Department refocused its work on the terrorist threat: Attorney General John Ashcroft, in introducing the Department of Justice's budget request for 2003, stated that: 'The first and overriding priority of this budget supports the top priority of the department: to protect America against acts of terrorism and to bring terrorists to justice.'[28] The FBI expanded its Most Wanted list to include an FBI Most Wanted Terrorist list that citizens at home and abroad were asked to consult.[29] Citizens were also encouraged to purchase 'Patriot Bonds', an investment that sought to allow 'Americans one more way to express their support for our Nation's anti-terrorism efforts'.[30] The bonds 'earn 90 percent of 5-year Treasury securities yields. The current rate in effect through April 2002 is 4.07 percent. The bonds sell as half face value and are available in denominations of $50, $75, $100, $200, $500, $1,000, $5,000 and $10,000.'[31]

The Patriot Act was the most high profile of a series of new legal codes enacted.[32] Some feared for the impact upon the freedoms enjoyed by Americans. Sandra Silberstein argued that 'new dangers became possible only with the context of a popularly accepted Bush presidency', a popularity, of course, that had been in many ways a product of the decisive intervention.[33] The Responsible Cooperators Program encouraged non-Americans to give information on terrorist issues to

[26] George W. Bush, 'President focuses on economy and war on terrorism in Kentucky speech', 5 September 2002, at http://www.whitehouse.gov/news/releases/2002/09/20020905-4.html [8/2004], emphasis added.

[27] See 'Terrorism insurance needed now', 19 June 2002, at http://www.whitehouse.gov/news/releases/2002/06/20020619-6.html [9/2004].

[28] Attorney General John Ashcroft, 'CJS Testimony', US Senate Committee on Appropriations, 26 February 2002, at http://appropriations.senate.gov/releases/record.cfm?id=181386 [10/2004].

[29] Updated: at http://www.fbi.gov/mostwant/terrorists/fugitives.htm.

[30] See http://www.publicdebt.treas.gov/sav/savpatriotbond.htm [10/2004].

[31] See http://www.ustreas.gov/press/releases/po854.htm [10/2004].

[32] At http://www.epic.org/privacy/terrorism/hr3162.html [9/2005].

[33] Sandra Silberstein, *War of Words: Language, Politics and 9/11* (London: Routledge, 2002), pp. 39–40.

American authorities. The reward for information would be, potentially, citizenship. As John Ashcroft put it, 'If the information that you provide is reliable and useful, we will help you obtain a visa to reside in the United States and ultimately become a United States citizen.'[34] In July 2002, the Terrorism Information and Prevention System was introduced, a logical next step in which American citizens were encouraged to provide information on potential terrorist activity. The Freedom Promotion Act of 2002 focused on resourcing the State Department to expand its public diplomacy.[35] And in February 2003, the White House published the *National Strategy for Combating Terrorism*, of which more later.[36] There were still yet more ways in which the new organisational priority affected the life of the country. A whole series of new legislation was passed on the designation of September 11th as 'Patriot Day', on bank reauthorisation, on visa reform, intelligence, bioterrorism, and on aviation.[37] New security measures were announced for the railways, and for trucks, which included the advice 'Discuss the fact that any employee could pose a security risk.'[38]

In addition, a whole series of new organisations and websites grew up. An excellent example was www.DefendAmerica.gov created by the Department of Defense, although looking as if it was something separate and independent. It was launched in October 2001, but gained in popularity throughout 2002. Of course, it produced coverage of all statements by the Secretary of Defense, and other senior leaders. There was a photo gallery, a database of military equipment, and a 'Backgrounder' section giving information about the 'war on terror' and its various locations. However, it also created 'human interest': a feature

[34] 'Transcript, Attorney General Ashcroft announces Responsible Cooperators Program November 29, 2001', Avalon Project, Yale Law School, at http://www.yale.edu/lawweb/avalon/sept_11/doj_brief027.htm [9/2005].

[35] See Sheldon Rampton and John Stauber, *Weapons of Mass Deception: The Uses of Propaganda in Bush's War on Iraq* (New York: Jeremy P. Tarcher, 2003), pp. 9–15.

[36] At http://www.whitehouse.gov/news/releases/2003/02/counter_terrorism/counter_terrorism_strategy.pdf.

[37] A useful summary can be found at http://thomas.loc.gov/home/terrorleg.htm [9/2004].

[38] On the former, see http://www.dot.gov/affairs/dot4502.htm; on the latter, http://www.fmcsa.dot.gov/Aboutus/testimonies/SSV_Talk_Pts_Update.htm [both 9/2004].

called 'Americans working together' showed how all could cooperate to defeat the enemy, emphasising the point of collective American identity; a daily feature entitled 'We remember their sacrifice' covered each person killed on September 11th to show that ordinary people had become heroes; and during May 2002, a section was entitled 'America's thank you note', where citizens were encouraged to sign their comments about the valour of the armed forces.[39]

A whole series of other non-official organisations developed. Voices of September 11th was established in October 2001, initially to share information, later to provide support, and then to act as an advocacy group. The Coalition of 9/11 Families brought together various family groups of victims and survivors, seeking a voice in memorials.[40] After two successful fund-raising efforts on motorcycles, the 9/11 Ride Foundation was set up in 2003, to fund college scholarships for family members of firefighters, police and emergency services.[41] By the summer of 2005, a Yahoo search of 'September 11th attacks' organisations produced a list of twenty-four bodies in its Directory.

The policy programme that followed from the 'war on terror' discourse therefore affected political, legal, economic and social aspects of life in the United States. Importantly, it affected the everyday life of America. Detention of immigrants, the designation of some US citizens as 'enemy combatants' without rights to counsel, closed deportation hearings, all enhanced the sense of threat, but also of collective purpose.[42] And that sense of threat was deepened by a series of arrests over the course of 2002 of alleged al-Qaeda 'sleeper cells' in the United States itself. In July, American citizens were told that al-Qaeda suspects were being followed by the authorities in particular American cities. CNN reported the story in the following way: 'Groups of suspected al-Qaeda operatives are being closely watched by the FBI in some of America's biggest cities, including Seattle, Chicago, Atlanta and Detroit . . . The sources would say only that the number of suspected

39 www.DefendAmerica.gov.

40 http://www.coalitionof911families.org/

41 http://www.americas911foundation.org/

42 Thomas Carothers argues that 'The Justice Department's harsh approach sent a powerful negative signal around the world, emboldening governments as diverse as those of Belarus, Cuba and India to curtail domestic liberties, supposedly in aid of their own struggles against terrorism.' 'Promoting Democracy and Fighting Terror', *Foreign Affairs*, January/February 2003, p. 91.

operatives was fewer than 100.'[43] Immediately following this, an arrest was made in Detroit.[44] Over the next few months, more arrests were made, in cities such as Seattle, Buffalo and Portland.[45] Al-Qaeda was portrayed as a highly professional organisation, capable of infiltrating all levels of American society, a theme taken up in television series, as we shall see later. All of this illustrated the depth of the threat, the importance of the refocusing of national priorities, and the success of the new policy programme.

Such fast change led to fears. Andrew Cohen for CBS worried:

> Already armed before the attack on America with the immense power of the state, over the past 12 months the White House, the Justice Department and prosecutors around the country have zealously pushed up against – and in some ways beyond – well-established legal boundaries to put people in jail, to keep them there, and to avoid explaining why for as long as possible.[46]

These dilemmas were illustrated by the case of Jose Padilla. Accused of being a terrorist determined to detonate a 'dirty bomb' on an American city, Padilla was – in the words of *Time Magazine* – an incarnation of 'the sum of our fears': an American citizen, working for al-Qaeda, planning to use a weapon of mass destruction in America.[47] Padilla was arrested at Chicago's O'Hare airport, yet was not charged with terrorist offences, but rather labelled a 'material witness' in the ongoing investigation into terrorism. That enabled Padilla's rights under the Fifth and Sixth Amendments to be bypassed.[48] Padilla was detained in

43 Kelli Arena, 'FBI tracking al-Qaeda suspects in US: looking for the most unexpected places for the enemy', 12 July 2002, at http://archives.cnn.com/2002/US/07/11/fbi.alqaeda/ [9/2004].

44 'Al Qaeda suspect held in Detroit', *BBC News*, 20 July 2002, at http://news.bbc.co.uk/1/hi/world/americas/2140364.stm [10/2004].

45 See 'Seattle man accused of aiding al-Qaeda', 29 August 2002, CNN, at http://archives.cnn.com/2002/LAW/08/29/ujaama.indictment/; 'US probes terror ties of Buffalo suspects', 18 September 2002, CNN, at http://archives.cnn.com/2002/LAW/09/15/buffalo.terror.arrests/; and 'Three of six accused terrorists appear in court', 5 October 2002, CNN, at http://archives.cnn.com/2002/US/West/10/04/oregon.fbi.alqaeda/ [all 10/2004].

46 Andrew Cohen, 'The legal war on terror', *CBS News*, 6 September 2002, at http://www.cbsnews.com/stories/2002/09/05/september11/main520977.shtml [10/2004].

47 Tony Karon, 'Person of the Week: Jose Padilla', *Time*, 14 June 2002, at http://www.time.com/time/pow/article/0,8599,262269,00.html [9/2002].

48 Walter C. Clemens, *Bushed!* (New York: Outland Books, 2004), p. 178.

a federal prison in New York, declared an 'enemy combatant', and then imprisoned at a military site in Charleston, South Carolina.[49] A year later, a number of organisations made a legal challenge on behalf of Padilla or, perhaps more accurately, on behalf of the rights of Americans. One such organisation was the right-of-centre CATO Institute, for whom Robert Levy explained: 'Essentially, on orders of the executive branch, anyone could wind up imprisoned by the military with no way to assert his innocence.'[50]

In cases such as these, senior Democrat voices were not heard in opposition. Democrat voters seemed quite taken by the idea that for terrorist suspects, detention was preferable to trial.[51] Over a year later, Democratic candidates for the presidency avoided any mention of the Padilla case.[52] That there would be al-Qaeda sleeper cells containing more 'Padillas' was taken as read, by Democrats as well as Republicans. In an article for the *Washington Monthly* in September 2002, General Wesley Clark (soon to be a candidate for the Democratic nomination for President) wrote in a matter of fact way of the reality of those sleeper cells.[53] Clark called in that article for a realignment of America's defence policies to be more closely involved with allies. But although the new policy programme was to see a recalibration of the US defence posture, it was more concerned with investment and reorientation to fight against the new enemies than with closer interaction with allies.

[49] 'Feds defend incarceration of "dirty bomb" suspect', CNN Law Center, 27 June 2002, at http://archives.cnn.com/2002/LAW/06/27/dirty.bomb.suspect/ [9/2002].

[50] Robert A. Levy, 'Jose Padilla: no charges and no trial, just jail', CATO Institute, 21 August 2003, at http://www.cato.org/dailys/08-21-03.html [9/2005].

[51] See the ABC poll of June 2002 in which 46% of Democrats supported detention over trial, and 51% trial over detention, although if a trial would 'jeopardise' security, that figure of 46% rose to 58%. See 'Poll: terror threat is not overstated', *ABC News*, 17 June 2002, at http://abcnews.go.com/sections/us/DailyNews/terrorthreat_poll020617.html [9/2005].

[52] With the limited exception of John Edwards – see Nat Hentoff, 'Bush's vanished prisoner', *Village Voice*, 10 October 2003, at http://www.villagevoice.com/news/0342,hentoff,47753,6.html [9/2005]. On Edwards, see his brief exchange with Wolf Blitzer on CNN, 16 November 2003 (Edwards supported Padilla's right to a lawyer) at 'Civil liberties and the presidential candidates', The Century Foundation, at http://www.tcf.org/Publications/HomelandSecurity/candidatetracking.pdf [9/2005].

[53] Wesley Clark, 'An army of one?', *Washington Monthly*, September 2002, at http://www.washingtonmonthly.com/features/2001/0209.clark.html [9/2004].

Recalibrating the defence posture, and naming the Iraqi enemy

The implications of the policy programme for defence were profound. First, the new terrorist enemy, already under attack in Afghanistan, had to be pursued further. Second, in order to achieve this, defence forces required transformation and major investment. Third, the link between terror and rogue regimes – present from the moment of the decisive intervention around September 11th – became deepened. And fourth, that link was made specific in the naming of Iraq as the new locus of threat.

The policy programme had already been speedily implemented with regards to the military in the aftermath of the decisive intervention with the military operation in Afghanistan.[54] But that was never meant to be the end of the military option. As Donald Rumsfeld argued in March 2002:

> We've captured or killed many hundreds of Taliban and al-Qaeda forces and a number of their senior leaders . . . US objectives going forward are very simple, and that is that there be no sanctuary, that there be no safe haven . . . The task is to pursue and run to ground terrorist networks across Afghanistan and across the globe. It's to train and equip forces in friendly countries that are facing terrorist threats, such as we're doing in the Philippines and in Yemen. It's to help them eliminate the possibility of their countries becoming sanctuaries for terrorists.[55]

Afghan / Taliban / al-Qaeda / foreign fighter casualties were indeed high; those of the United States relatively low. But nevertheless, the American casualties began to grow, though slowly, throughout 2002: 12 military related deaths in 2001 in Operation Enduring Freedom was a total exceeded the following year, when 47 deaths were recorded.[56] There were some concerns amongst journalists that the Afghan operation could not easily be brought to a conclusion, that it would end up as 'another Vietnam'. Such perspectives were clearly not part of the

[54] On the campaign in Afghanistan, see Michael O'Hanlon, 'A flawed masterpiece', *Foreign Affairs*, May–June 2002, pp. 47–63.

[55] Donald Rumsfeld, 'DoD news briefing: Secretary Rumsfeld and General Franks', 6 March 2002, at http://www.defenselink.mil/transcripts/2002/t03062002_t0306sd.html [7/2004].

[56] The *Washington Post* keeps a record of American fatalities by date, offering information on each death. See http://www.washingtonpost.com/wp-srv/world/casualties/facesofthefallen_freedom.htm.

policy programme, and had to be resolved before they became full-blown contradictions. General Tommy Franks, the Commander of US Central Command, drew upon sporting analogies in commenting in March 2002 that 'I think that what we looked at in Indochina was an "away game". I think what we're looking at in the global war on terrorism is something entirely different.'[57]

Franks was reflecting an important element in the discourse and in the policy programme: the meta-narrative of the 'war on terror' brought together not just the fight against terrorism in Afghanistan (that is, against both the Taliban and al-Qaeda); it connected this with the domestic search for 'sleeper cells', and with other 'theatres' of operation. For it was said that the phenomenon of jihadism had been allowed to grow, and to spread at alarming speed. Paul Wolfowitz told an American television audience in March 2002 that 'With 20/20 hindsight, I think we can see that if we'd taken more seriously the threat from al-Qaeda in Afghanistan five years ago, we might have prevented September 11th.'[58] Wolfowitz managed to make the point while continuing – using the 20/20 hindsight imagery – to avoid blame on others within the United States. Thus, a military success in Afghanistan was not sufficient; victory there would not defeat jihadism, a force that now had global spread located in sixty nations, as the President and others often repeated.[59]

In order to defeat this new enemy, the policy programme stipulated that America's military forces would need transformation and investment. [60] It was, after all, to be a long-term struggle, with exceptionally high stakes. In December 2001, following the successful campaign to

[57] General Tommy Franks, 'General Franks briefs at the Pentagon', 29 March 2002, at http://www.defenselink.mil/transcripts/2002/t03292002_t329fran.html [8/2004].

[58] Paul Wolfowitz, 'Deputy Secretary Wolfowitz interview with CNN Novak and Shields', 16 March 2002, at http://www.defenselink.mil/transcripts/2002/t03162002_t0316dsd.html [9/2004].

[59] For example, see George W. Bush, 'President Bush delivers graduation speech at West Point', 1 June 2002, at http://www.whitehouse.gov/news/releases/2002/06/20020601-3.html [9/2004].

[60] See Donald Rumsfeld, 'Secretary Rumsfeld speaks on "21st century transformation" of US armed forces (transcript of remarks and question and answer period)', 31 January 2002, at http://www.dod.mil/speeches/2002/s20020131-secdef.html [8/2004].

oust the Taliban, President Bush had introduced the National Defense Authorization Act for Fiscal Year 2002 by saying:

> The Act authorizes the funding necessary to defend the United States and its interests around the globe. In particular, it provides the resources needed to continue the war against global terrorism, accelerate programs for defense against biological or chemical attacks, pursue an effective missile defense, properly support members of the Armed Forces and their families, and begin to transform our Armed Forces to meet the military requirements of the 21st century.[61]

The key actor in this aspect of the policy programme was Donald Rumsfeld, as Secretary of Defense. In an essay for *Foreign Affairs*, he explained that 'Our challenge in the twenty-first century is to defend our cities, friends, allies, and deployed forces – as well as our space assets and computer networks – from new forms of attack, while projecting force over long distances to fight new adversaries.'[62] Investment and transformation was an aspect of the policy programme that was fully endorsed by all sides of the political spectrum. Indeed, to the extent to which there was criticism from outside government during 2002, it was from those who wanted the policy programme to be more fully implemented, more quickly. In an op-ed article in the *New York Times* in May 2002, Nicholas Kristof praised the Afghan campaign as a 'triumph', but criticised the administration for refusing

> to send a small number of troops for a security force to sustain peace in Afghanistan, and thus the entire investment of lives and effort could be lost. Is there any explanation other than inertia to account for the United States' maintaining 47,000 troops in Japan, despite the lack of any threat there except perhaps from extraterrestrials, yet refusing to provide a few thousand troops to keep the swamp drained in Afghanistan?[63]

That this war was to involve a whole series of different theatres of conflict was seen simply to be the new common sense.

[61] George W. Bush, 'President signs Defense Authorization Act', 28 December 2001, at http://www.whitehouse.gov/news/releases/2001/12/20011228-4.html [8/2004].

[62] Donald Rumsfeld, 'Transforming the military', *Foreign Affairs*, May/June 2002, p. 27.

[63] Nicholas D. Kristof, 'The war on terror flounders', *New York Times*, 10 May 2002.

The new war was to be long term, therefore, and expensive. In introducing the budget in February 2002, President Bush opened his speech with a call to arms:

To the Congress of the United States: Americans will never forget the murderous events of September 11, 2001. They are for us what Pearl Harbor was to an earlier generation of Americans: a terrible wrong and a call to action. With courage, unity, and purpose, we met the challenges of 2001. The budget for 2003 recognizes the new realities confronting our nation, and funds the war against terrorism and the defense of our homeland.[64]

He continued, proudly, to announce that 'The 2003 Budget requests the biggest increase in defense spending in 20 years, to pay the cost of war and the price of transforming our cold war military into a new 21st Century fighting force.'[65] Donald Rumsfeld argued:

$379 billion is a great deal of money. But consider: the New York City comptroller's office has estimated the local economic cost of the September 11th attacks on the city alone will add up to about $100 billion over the next three years. *Money* magazine estimates of the cost of September 11th to the US economy at about $170 billion last year – and some estimates range as high as $250 billion a year in lost productivity, sales, jobs, and airline revenue, media and advertising, and costlier insurance for homes and businesses.[66]

This construction was of course based on the assumption that another attack of massive proportions was inevitable were the United States not to make the necessary investments in defence. Thus, not only did the renewed defence spending make political sense in terms of defending the nation, it also made *economic* sense, in pure cost–benefit terms. Because, as Paul Wolfowitz put it, 'What happened on September 11th, terrible though it was, is but a pale shadow of what will happen if terrorists use weapons of massive destruction.'[67] And he amplified the point:

[64] George W. Bush, 'The budget message of the President', 4 February 2002, at http://www.whitehouse.gov/news/releases/2002/02/20020204.html [8/2004].

[65] Ibid.

[66] Donald Rumsfeld, 'Fiscal Year 2003 defense budget testimony – Senate Armed Services Committee', 5 February 2002, at http://www.dod.mil/speeches/2002/s20020205-secdef4.html [9/2004].

[67] Paul Wolfowitz, 'Munich Conference on European Security Policy', 2 February 2002, at http://www.dod.mil/speeches/2002/s20020202-depsecdef1.html [7/2004].

I think what leads to a very, very dangerous place is the mixture of weapons of mass destruction in the hands of terrorists who, as they demonstrated on September 11th, don't even care about their own lives, much less the lives of other people. We now, after September 11th, have a graphic, clear understanding of what commercial airliners can do. We can't wait until we have a graphic, clear understanding of what biological weapons or nuclear weapons can do before we do something about breaking that connection.[68]

The President's '21st century fighting force' would be called upon to face innumerable enemies, because there was a clear connection in the discourse between those involved in jihadist movements, and those states that comprised the 'axis of evil', as set out by the President in the 2002 State of the Union address. In signing the Public Heath Security and Bioterrorism Bill, President Bush made the connection: 'Terrorist groups seek biological weapons; we know some rogue states already have them.'[69] The US State Department's *Patterns of Terrorism 2001* in May 2002 went beyond the 'axis of evil', noting seven countries allegedly involved in the state sponsorship of terror, with evidence cited: Cuba, Libya, Iran, Iraq, North Korea, Sudan and Syria.[70] The problem was a global one. Donald Rumsfeld argued that the problem was:

that there has been a proliferation of weapons of mass destruction. And the terrorist networks have close linkages with terrorist states, the states that are on the worldwide known terrorist list – Iraq, Iran, Libya, Syria, North Korea, one or two others . . . In just facing the facts, we have to recognize that terrorist networks have relationships with terrorist states that have weapons of mass destruction, and that they inevitably are going to get their hands on them, and they would not hesitate one minute in using them. That's the world we live in.[71]

68 Paul Wolfowitz, 'Interview with Fox News on Sunday', 17 February 2002, at http://www.defenselink.mil/transcripts/2002/t02172002_t0217dsd.html [9/2004].

69 George W. Bush, 'President signs Public Health Security and Bioterrorism Bill', 12 June 2002, at http://www.whitehouse.gov/news/releases/2002/06/20020612-1.html [9/2004].

70 'Overview of state sponsored terrorism', *Patterns of Terrorism 2001*, US Department of State, May 2002.

71 Donald Rumsfeld, 'Transcript of testimony at Defense Subcommittee of Senate Appropriations Committee', 21 May 2002, at http://www.dod.mil/speeches/2002/s20020521-secdef.html [9/2004].

It was, therefore, simply common sense to recognise the objective reality of a link between rogue states, weapons of mass destruction and terrorists.

A key moment in the articulation of this central aspect of the policy programme came in a speech delivered by President Bush at West Point in June 2002:

> The gravest danger to freedom lies at the perilous crossroads of radicalism and technology. When the spread of chemical and biological and nuclear weapons, along with ballistic missile technology – when that occurs, even weak states and small groups could attain a catastrophic power to strike great nations. Our enemies have declared this very intention, and have been caught seeking these terrible weapons. They want the capability to blackmail us, or to harm us, or to harm our friends – and we will oppose them with all our power.[72]

Paul Wolfowitz had made the same point in May, with reference to the State of the Union address.

> What the President said about all three of those countries, and Iraq was clearly one of them, is that they represent danger to the United States because they're hostile, because they have or are developing weapons of mass destruction, and because they have a record of supporting terrorism, and that that is not a danger we can afford to live with indefinitely. That we can't wait until there's a 9-11 with a nuclear weapon or a biological or chemical weapon to then go and find the perpetrator.[73]

Wolfowitz had made the link between the generic point – that rogue states supported terrorist movements – to the specific threat: Iraq. The President, in his West Point speech, had drawn the conclusions for the policy programme inherent in the discourse: previous security strategies were inappropriate in the new, post-second American 9/11 age. 'Deterrence – the promise of massive retaliation against nations – means nothing against shadowy terrorist networks with no nation or citizens to defend. Containment is not possible when unbalanced dictators with weapons of mass destruction can deliver those weapons

[72] George W. Bush, 'President Bush delivers graduation speech at West Point', 1 June 2002, at http://www.whitehouse.gov/news/releases/2002/06/20020601-3.html [5/2006].

[73] Paul Wolfowitz, 'Deputy Secretary Wolfowitz at Brookings Harvard Forum', 15 May 2002, at http://www.defenselink.mil/transcripts/2002/t05162002_t0515npc.html [10/2004].

on missiles or secretly provide them to terrorist allies.' [74] It was such language that lay behind the *National Security Strategy*, published in September, which stipulated that in order to 'forestall or prevent hostile acts by our adversaries, the United States will, if necessary, act pre-emptively . . . The purpose of our actions will always be to eliminate a specific threat to the US or our allies and friends . . .'[75]

The decisive intervention had produced a discourse in which international terrorism and rogue states were interconnected, and into that mix had come the worst-case analysis which said that this nexus of 'evil' would eventually develop weapons of mass destruction capable of being launched against the United States. At the United Nations, the President had said that 'In cells and camps, terrorists are plotting further destruction, and building new bases for their war against civilization. And our greatest fear is that terrorists will find a shortcut to their mad ambitions when an outlaw regime supplies them with the technologies to kill on a massive scale.'[76] The principle of defeating rogue states and terrorist networks together had been established, along with the determination to do so earlier rather than later. 'And if an emboldened regime were to supply these weapons to terrorist allies, then the attacks of September the 11th would be a prelude to far greater horrors.'[77] And the most immediate of these threats was posed by Iraq: as Condoleezza Rice expressed it, 'We are on notice. The danger from Saddam Hussein's arsenal is far more clear than anything we could have foreseen prior to September 11th. And history will judge harshly any leader or nation that saw this dark cloud and sat by in complacency or indecision.'[78] As the President put it, 'the Iraqi regime is a threat of unique urgency'.[79] Colin Powell concluded that 'We now

[74] Bush, 'West Point'.

[75] Chapter 5. 'Prevent our enemies from threatening us, our allies, and our friends with weapons of mass destruction', *The National Security Strategy of the United States of America*, September 2002, at www.whitehouse.gov/nsc/nss.html [8/2004]. For analysis, see Robert S. Litwak, 'The new calculus of pre-emption', *Survival* 44:4 (Winter 2002/3), pp. 53–80.

[76] George W. Bush, 'President's remarks at the United Nation's General Assembly', 12 September 2002, http://www.whitehouse.gov/news/releases/2002/09/20020912-1.html [8/2004]. [77] Ibid.

[78] Condoleezza Rice, Wriston Lecture, 1 October 2002, at http://www.whitehouse.gov/news/releases/2002/10/20021001-6.html [8/2004].

[79] George W. Bush, 'President, House Leadership agree on Iraq resolution', 2 October 2002, at http://www.whitehouse.gov/news/releases/2002/10/20021002-7.html [7/2004].

see that a proven menace like Saddam Hussein in possession of weapons of mass destruction could empower a few terrorists with those weapons to threaten millions of innocent people.'[80] Hence, for George Bush, 'That's why Americans must understand that when a tyrant like Saddam Hussein possesses weapons of mass destruction, it not only threatens the neighborhood in which he lives, it not only threatens the region, it can threaten the United States of America . . . The battlefield has changed. We are in a new kind of war, and we've got to recognize that.'[81]

The administration's connection between the perpetrators of the second American 9/11 and those of a future attack on the United States with weapons of mass destruction ran through rogue states, and in particular through Iraq. As the President put it, 'we have every reason to believe he [Saddam Hussein] will use them [weapons of mass destruction] again. Iraq has longstanding ties to terrorist groups, which are capable of and willing to deliver weapons of mass death.'[82] But this claim could only be made because it was consistent with the policy programme; consistent with the discourse that had been introduced through the decisive intervention. The al-Qaeda–Iraq connection had been made in the first days after 11 September 2001. Laurie Mylroie for the American Enterprise Institute had written, on 13 September 2001, that 'Whether Osama bin Laden was involved in Tuesday's terrorist assault remains to be seen. Yet if that proves to be so, it is extremely unlikely that he acted on his own. It is far more likely that he operated in conjunction with a state – the state with which the US remains at war, namely Iraq.'[83]

[80] Colin Powell, 'The administration's position with regard to Iraq', testimony to the Senate Foreign Relations Committee, 26 September 2002, at http://www.state.gov/secretary/rm/2002/13765.htm [9/2004].

[81] George W. Bush, 'President Bush, Prime Minister Blair discuss keeping the peace', 7 September 2002, at http://www.whitehouse.gov/news/releases/2002/09/20020907-2.html [8/2004].

[82] George W. Bush, 'President: Iraq regime danger to America is "grave and growing"', 5 October 2002, at http://www.whitehouse.gov/news/releases/2002/10/20021005.html [8/2004].

[83] Laurie Mylroie, 'The Iraqi connection', *American Enterprise Institute News and Commentary*, Thursday, 13 September 2001, at http://www.aei.org/news/newsID.13140/news_detail.asp [5/2004]. See also Patrick Clawson, 'Why Saddam is ripe for a fall', *Washington Post*, 1 January 2002; Ken Adelman, 'Cakewalk in Iraq', *Washington Post*, 13 February 2002; and James M.Woolsey, 'Should the United States go to war with Iraq?', *CATO Institute Forum*, 13 December 2001, video at http://www.cato.org/events/011213pf.html [6/2004].

In February 2002, Paul Wolfowitz, in speaking about the 'problem' of Iraq, made a clear connection to terrorism when he said that 'To say that the answer is stop talking about it, don't call an evil an evil, we'll just keep sweeping it under the rug the way we've swept terrorism under the rug for 10 or 20 years, that's not an answer.'[84]

Not only had the connection between al-Qaeda and Iraq been made early in the decisive intervention; soon afterwards, neoconservatives sought to increase the pace of 'the revolutionary war against the tyrants'.[85] William Kristol asked how the 'war on terror' was going in October 2001. He answered: 'The administration's plan is shaped by three (self-imposed) constraints: No ground troops in Afghanistan; No confrontation with Iraq; No alarm at home. The result? No evident progress so far.'[86] Michael Ledeen wrote in 2002 that 'In March it already seemed to me that we had waited too long to take the battle to the Terror Masters in Baghdad, Tehran, Damascus and Riyadh, and we had still not acted in June.'[87] America's neoconservative shock troops were running ahead of the consensus, trying to sharpen the 'war on terror' still further.

As the approach to war intensified, so did the repetition of the connections between the second American 9/11, weapons of mass destruction, Iraq and future attacks: Iraq 'has given shelter and support to terrorism, and practices terror against its own people. The entire world has witnessed Iraq's eleven-year history of defiance, deception and bad faith. We also must never forget the most vivid events of recent history. On September the 11th, 2001, America felt its vulnerability – even to threats that gather on the other side of the earth.'[88] In February 2003, the President was even more specific: 'Senior members of Iraqi intelligence and al-Qaeda have met at least eight times since the early 1990s.'[89] And the chorus was joined throughout the administration. Colin Powell explained at the United Nations that 'The United States

[84] Wolfowitz, 'Stakeout outside Fox News studio', 17 February 2002.

[85] Michael Ledeen, *The War Against the Terror Masters* (New York: St Martin's Press, 2002), p. 233.

[86] William Kristol, 'The wrong strategy', *Washington Post*, 30 October 2001, at http://www.weeklystandard.com/Content/Public/Articles/000/000/000/432jflzz.asp [9/2005].

[87] Ledeen, *Terror Masters*, p. 223.

[88] George W. Bush, 'President Bush outlines Iraqi threat', 7 October 2002, at http://www.whitehouse.gov/news/releases/2002/10/20021007-8.html [8/2004].

[89] George W. Bush, 'President's radio address', 8 February 2003, at http://www.whitehouse.gov/news/releases/2003/02/20030208.html [8/2004].

will not and cannot run that risk to the American people. Leaving Saddam Hussein in possession of weapons of mass destruction for a few more months or years is not an option, not in a post-September 11th world.'[90] He amplified this at the UN the following week:

> if we find a post-9/11 nexus between Iraq and terrorist organizations that are looking for just such weapons – and I would submit and will provide more evidence that such connections are now emerging and we can establish that they exist – we cannot wait for one of these terrible weapons to show up in one of our cities and wonder where it came from after it's been detonated by al-Qaida or somebody else. This is the time to go after this source of this kind of weaponry.[91]

Condoleezza Rice repeated the connections explicitly in an article about Iraq's 'lies' published in the *New York Times*.[92]

The connection between terror and rogue states – a core element of the policy programme – was now embedded in policy. It was particularly well expressed in the CIA's *National Strategy for Combating Terrorism*. The relationship was seen to be pyramidal, as shown in figure 4.1. To understand how to define when the 'war on terror' had been successfully concluded, the CIA also illustrated that the endstate was not an end to terror globally, but an end to what it defined as 'global terror'; see figure 4.2. It is very important, therefore, not only to see the attack on Iraq as a core element of the policy programme, though it certainly was that. It was part of the logic of the discourse, and had been inherent from the moment of the decisive intervention. But the attack on Iraq was also a staging post, not a final battle, in the 'war on terror'; though Iraq did play an urgent and immediate role in forestalling the next attack on America. 'In Iraq, a dictator is building and hiding weapons that could enable him to dominate the Middle East and intimidate the civilized world – and we will not allow it. This same tyrant has close ties to terrorist organizations, and could supply them with the terrible means to strike this country – and America will

[90] Colin Powell, 'US Secretary of State addresses the UN Security Council', 5 February 2003, at http://www.whitehouse.gov/news/releases/2003/02/20030205-1.html#18 [9/2004].

[91] Colin Powell, 'Remarks to the United Nations' Security Council', 14 February 2003, at http://www.state.gov/secretary/rm/2003/17763.htm [9/2004].

[92] Condoleezza Rice, 'Why we know Iraq is lying', *New York Times*, 23 January 2003.

Source: *National Strategy for Combating Terrorism*, February 2003, figure 1, p. 6, at http://www.cia.gov/terrorism/publications/Counter_Terrorism_Strategy.pdf [6/2004]

Figure 4.1. The CIA's structure of terror

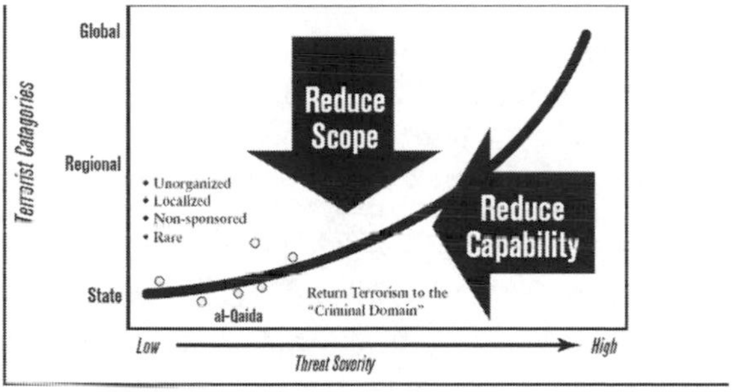

Source: *National Strategy for Combating Terrorism*, February 2003, section of figure 3, p.13 [spelling mistake in original]

Figure 4.2 The CIA's 'war on terror' endpoint

not permit it.'[93] How could America permit it, if the discourse was one in which a series of conflations were made: between the attackers of September 11th and the whole of international terrorism; between international terrorism and rogue states; between rogue states and Iraq; and between international terrorism and attacks with weapons of mass destruction? The weight of the 'war on terror' discourse was on the responsibility on America to act. This is what Colin Powell was reflecting when he said that 'The US seeks Iraq's peaceful disarmament.

[93] George W. Bush, 'President discusses Iraq', 26 February 2003, at http://www.whitehouse.gov/news/releases/2003/02/20030226-11.html [8/2004].

But we will not shrink from war if that is the only way to rid Iraq of its weapons of mass destruction.'[94]

As 2002 progressed, as war in Iraq loomed, voices began to be raised in opposition to these conflations, as will be seen later: dissonance within the discourse began. In response, President Bush's 2003 State of the Union address was different in tone to that of 2002. It discussed tax relief, health care, energy security, compassion before the 'war on terror'. But the speech was of course shaped by the need to move the policy programme forward.

> Evidence from intelligence sources, secret communications, and statements by people now in custody reveal that Saddam Hussein aids and protects terrorists, including members of al-Qaeda . . . Before September the 11th, many in the world believed that Saddam Hussein could be contained. But chemical agents, lethal viruses and shadowy terrorist networks are not easily contained. Imagine those 19 hijackers with other weapons and other plans – this time armed by Saddam Hussein. It would take one vial, one canister, one crate slipped into this country to bring a day of horror like none we have ever known. We will do everything in our power to make sure that that day never comes.[95]

In the official response to the speech by the Democrats, Governor Gary Locke of Washington State criticised the administration on the economy, on job losses and on health care. Yet on the issue of terrorism he said that 'the war against terror is not over. Al-Qaeda still targets Americans . . . Make no mistake: Saddam Hussein is a ruthless tyrant, and he must give up his weapons of mass destruction. We support the President in the course he has followed so far . . .'[96] The nuanced differences were not challenges to the administration; more gentle suggestions of emphasis. But as will be seen in the next chapter, outside the formal institutions of state and society, a powerful alternative discourse, opposing the war in Iraq, was under construction.

The war in Iraq was, therefore, a core part of the policy programme deriving from the discourse that emerged following the decisive

[94] Colin Powell, 'US Policy on Iraq – we will not shrink from war', op-ed, *Wall Street Journal*, 3 February 2003, at http://www.state.gov/secretary/rm/2003/17163.htm [9/2004].

[95] George W. Bush, 'President delivers "State of the Union" ', 28 January 2003, at http://www.whitehouse.gov/news/releases/2003/01/20030128-19.html [8/2004].

[96] Governor Gary Locke, 'Democrats' response to the 2003 State of the Union address', at http://www.cnn.com/2003/ALLPOLITICS/01/28/dems.transcript/ [10/2004].

intervention. It was not a conflict 'chosen' at a later date, for sets of reasons beyond those contained within the logic of the 'war on terror' discourse. It was a project contained within the nature of the decisive intervention, as was the need to produce a democratic and reformed Iraq subsequent to the war, one that would conform to the values said to be underlying the 'war on terror'.[97] Edward Rhodes was one of those who said that this could be easily expressed when he wrote in spring 2003, 'Stripped to its essentials, what the Bush administration envisions is an informal American empire.'[98] And this was inherent in the decisive intervention of September 2001. Fourteen months later, the Bush administration had created a fund of $29 million for a US-Middle East Partnership Initiative that in part was aimed at supporting democracy in the region.[99] As the State Department's Policy Planning Director, Richard Haass, put it, 'US policy will be more actively engaged in supporting democratic trends in the Muslim world than ever before.'[100] Perhaps these tendencies were best observed and articulated by some of those outside the administration, who were seeking to push the logic of the 'war on terror' discourse to its end point. For example, Michael Ledeen, a key author at the American Enterprise Institute, argued:

> Now that we are set to have our great debate on the war against terrorism, it seems it will be the wrong debate. By all indications, the discussion will be about using our irresistible military might against a single country in order to bring down its leader. We should instead be talking about using all our political, moral and military genius to support a vast democratic revolution to liberate all the peoples of the Middle East from tyranny. That is our real mission, the essence of the war in which we are engaged, and the proper subject of our national debate. Saddam Hussein is a terrible evil, and President Bush is entirely right in vowing to end his reign of terror. But this is not just a war against Iraq, it is a war against terrorist organizations and against the regimes that foster, support, arm, train, indoctrinate and

97 See, for example, J. Harding, R. Wolfe and J. Blitz, 'US will rebuild Iraq as a democracy, says Rice', *Financial Times*, 23 September 2002.

98 Edward Rhodes, 'The imperial logic of Bush's liberal agenda', *Survival* 45:1 (Spring 2003), p. 143.

99 See Philip H. Gordon, 'Bush's Middle East vision', *Survival* 45:1 (Spring 2003), pp. 160–1.

100 Richard N. Haass, 'Towards greater democracy in the Muslim world', speech to the Council on Foreign Relations, 4 December 2002, at http://www.cfr.org/pub5283/richard_n_haass/towards_greater_democracy_in_the_muslim_world.php [9/2004].

command the terrorist legions who are clamoring for our destruction. There are four such regimes: in Iran, Iraq, Syria and Saudi Arabia.[101]

Others were equally explicit about the logic of the task at hand; as Sebastian Mallaby put it, 'The logic of neoimperialism is too compelling for the Bush administration to resist. The chaos in the world is too threatening to ignore, and existing methods for dealing with that chaos have been tried and found wanting.'[102] The attack by those nineteen hijackers had, it seemed, exposed a conspiracy against the United States that could only be eradicated by librating the whole Middle East from tyranny. The previous policy programme had failed: long live the new policy programme.

When the war in Iraq began, more than thirty-five nations were involved in giving support.[103] Of course, other countries were opposed to the operation, but the degree of support, and the nature of the debate, illustrated how the 'war on terror' had been expanded around the world, a discourse understood by all, and shared by many. Yet few, if any, were committed to the ongoing conflict as articulated by Ledeen. That was to prove an important contradiction in the policy programme.

The policy programme set in train by the decisive intervention had led to a restructuring of the organisation of the American state and of Americans' lives, a recalibration of the military and an extension of the use of force. For this process to continue, the power of the discourse had to be furthered, as the discursive structures of the decisive intervention continued to be embedded culturally and politically. It is this continued narration of the 'war on terror' according to these principles that is the next focus for this chapter.

The narration of the 'war on terror'

The 'war on terror' was deeply embedded in public understanding of the world in 2002 and early 2003. A simple search for topics covered

[101] Michael A. Ledeen, 'The war on terror won't end in Baghdad', *American Enterprise Institute News and Commentary*, 4 September 2002, at http://www.aei.org/news/newsID.14216/news_detail.asp [9/2004].

[102] Sebastian Mallaby, 'The reluctant imperialist: terrorism, failed states and the case for American Empire', *Foreign Affairs*, March–April 2002, p. 6.

[103] George W. Bush, 'President Bush addresses the nation', 19 March 2003, at http://www.whitehouse.gov/news/releases/2003/03/20030319-17.html [8/2004].

in one of the most popular newspapers in the United States, *USA Today*, reveals that the paper covered 2,668 stories related to terrorism in this fifteen-month period; on average, almost six stories per day.[104] The 'war on terror' also became a part of religious life. The Catholic Church in the United States made response to terrorism a key theme in its annual anti-violence campaign in January 2002.[105] And meanwhile, in popular literature, Tom Clancy published *Cutting Edge*, a struggle for information in Africa with terrorists and rogue states, while he was writing his next novel, entitled *The Teeth of the Tiger*, published in August 2003, in which Americans pursue Islamic terrorists who have teamed up with Colombian drug smugglers and bombed American shopping malls.[106]

The narration of the second American 9/11, it has been argued earlier in this volume, had four central elements. The first was an articulation of self and other: the heroic, resilient American self and the absolute evil of the enemy. The second concerned inclusivity, an attempt to create a sense of identity with all Americans at home, and with all non-terrorist Muslims abroad. The third focused on American claims to exceptionalism; that the United States embodied the best values, and was a beacon for the world. The fourth was a claim to global leadership in pursuit of those values and interests. The policy programme focused fully on the last point but, importantly, the period from the 2002 State of the Union address through to the outbreak of the war in Iraq saw great efforts to continue the embedding of the first three, not just by political leaders, but more widely in society as well.

Through this period, American heroism was contrasted with al-Qaeda cowardice. President Bush reflected that 'September the 11th was a day of great horror and great heroism.'[107] He also spoke several

[104] Statistic generated by accessing the newspaper's website (http://www.usatoday.com/) then going to archives, and generating topics on terrorism in a stipulated time period [7/2004].

[105] See 'Terrorism response noted in annual Stand against Violence', US Catholic Bishops, 3 January 2002, at http://www.usccb.org/comm/archives/2002/02-006.htm [9/2004].

[106] Tom Clancy, *Cutting Edge* (with Jerome Preisler and Martin Greenberg) (New York: Berkley Publishing Group, November 2002); and *The Teeth of the Tiger* (New York: G. P. Putnam's Sons, 2003).

[107] George W. Bush, 'President honors fallen peace officers at memorial service', 15 May 2002, at http://www.whitehouse.gov/news/releases/2002/05/20020515-2.html [8/2004].

times of a particular story. 'One of the most poignant stories I remember is when some going into the danger wrote their Social Security numbers on their arms. It reminds all of us about how dangerous the job is, and about how some are willing to sacrifice for others . . . We saw people drive an airplane into the ground to save others.'[108] Governor Tom Ridge declared that 'The nine months since the terrorist attacks have been a great time to be an American, in spite of the horror and the tragedy associated with the attacks. We have learned so much about what this country and its people are all about.'[109]

This heroism and the tragedy of the day continued to be institutionalised. A website was launched in March 2002 for Flight 93. The 'In Memoriam' section pointedly notes that 'The list above only contains the names of the *heroes* of Flight 93 and does *not* include the 4 terrorists.'[110] One year on, poems continued to be written. One example was 'Let Freedom Ring', by Mary Niederlander, published on the Library Support Staff website.[111]

> Was it real
> Those images . . . smoke and dust . . .
> How could it have happened here
> Would our wounds ever heal
> Does it seem strange that we still feel
> One Year Later
> We're still angry, we wonder
> Can remembering go on to [sic] long
> Can we keep our faith and stay strong
> We still feel shock and face our fears
> We are a Nation resolved to
> Fight our foes and stand tall
> Our pride we wear, we shed the tears

[108] George W. Bush, 'President announces substantial increase in Homeland Security Budget', 24 January 2002, at http://www.whitehouse.gov/news/releases/2002/01/20020124-1.html. For another example, see George W. Bush, 'President Bush delivers commencement address at Ohio State University', 14 June 2002, at http://www.whitehouse.gov/news/releases/2002/06/20020614-1.html [both 8/2004].

[109] Governor Tom Ridge, 'Remarks by Homeland Security Director Tom Ridge to the National Association of Broadcasters Education Foundation 2002 Service to America Summit', 10 June 2002, at http://www.whitehouse.gov/news/releases/2002/06/20020610-7.html [9/2004].

[110] Emphasis in the original. See http://www.flt93memorial.org/ [7/2004].

[111] See http://www.librarysupportstaff.com/sept11resrch.html [8/2004].

I won't ever forget, that fateful day
For the souls lost, and the survivors too
And for those whose lives were changed some way.
God has shed his Grace on Thee and Me
America – truly the land of the
Brave, the Remarkable, and the Free.
It all is real.

The construction of the American self in terms of heroism and resilience, marked with acts of remembrance, also contained the identification of the characteristics of the al-Qaeda other. And here, American heroism was strongly contrasted with terrorist cowardice. For President Bush: 'we've also got to get used to the fact that we're fighting an enemy that's willing to send youngsters to their suicide, to the death by suicide, and they themselves hide in a cave'.[112] The description of the al-Qaeda base as being in 'a cave' was discursively important. It implied primitivism, the undeveloped, the opposite of advanced, American, lifestyle. On another occasion, the President spoke of 'the old days [when] you count the number of tanks you destroy, or the number of airplanes you destroy, and say we're making progress. These folks don't have tanks. They don't have airplanes. They hide in caves. They send youngsters to their suicidal death. That's the kind of people fighting.'[113] In doing so, al-Qaeda therefore stood for anti-progress. Paul Wolfowitz spoke of the terrorists' desire to take the 'Muslim world, at least, and maybe a large part of the rest of the world, back to the Middle Ages'.[114]

A second dimension of the discourse that continued to be emphasised was that of inclusivity. There were three dimensions to this. The first focused on inclusivity within the United States' population. The President spoke powerfully to this theme:

[112] George W. Bush, 'President discusses Homeland Security Department', 7 June 2002, at http://www.whitehouse.gov/news/releases/2002/06/20020607-4.html [8/2004].

[113] George W. Bush, 'President Bush pushes for Homeland Security Bill', 28 September 2002, at http://www.whitehouse.gov/news/releases/2002/09/20020928-2.html [8/2004].

[114] Jim Garamone, 'Wolfowitz says war on terror is choice between future, Middle Ages', 29 May 2002, at http://www.dod.mil/news/May2002/n05292002_200205295.html [9/2004]. But the Islamic world was one of great learning and civilisation during Europe's 'Middle Ages'.

It's important for our fellow Americans to understand that Americans of Muslim faith share the same grief that we all share from what happened to our country; that they're just as proud of America as I am proud of America; that they love our country as much as I love our country. They share my profound belief that no American should be judged by appearance, by ethnic background, or by religious faith . . . Bigotry is not a part of our soul. It's not going to be a part of our future. Sure, there may be some, but that's not the American way . . . In order for us to reject the evil done to America on September the 11th, we must reject bigotry in all its forms.[115]

Related to this was a global inclusivity, in which Muslims could be alongside America in the 'war on terror'. As Colin Powell put it on MTV:

we also want to say to Muslims around the world our campaign against terrorism is not against anybody who is of the Muslim faith; it's against those individuals who are terrorists, who kill innocent people. When you look at where the armed forces of the United States have fought in recent years, we went to Afghanistan to protect Muslims; we went to Kuwait to protect Muslims and give Kuwait back to the Kuwaiti Government. And when you look at what we did in Kosovo, we went to Kosovo to protect Albanian Muslims . . . We are a respecter of all faiths.[116]

In the State Department's *Patterns of Terrorism*, Ambassador Francis X. Taylor wrote of the need to 'emphasize that the war on terrorism is not a war against Islam, and to underscore that terrorists are not martyrs but cowards and criminals'.[117] And a further aspect was a political inclusivity; that Democrats should also be a part of the 'war on terror'. For example, in a speech about increasing funds for anti-bioterrorism measures in Pennsylvania the President said:

I also want to thank two members of the United States Congress who are here, one Democrat, Mike Doyle; one Republican, Melissa Hart. The reason I bring them up with their party affiliations is there is no difference, as far as I can tell,

[115] George W. Bush, 'President Bush holds roundtable with Arab- and Muslim-American leaders', 10 September 2002, at http://www.whitehouse.gov/news/releases/2002/09/20020910-7.html [10/2004].

[116] Colin Powell on 'Be Heard: an MTV global discussion', 14 February 2002, at http://www.state.gov/secretary/rm/2002/8038.htm [9/2004].

[117] Francis X. Taylor, Ambassador, Coordinator for Counter-terrorism, in *Patterns of Terrorism 2001*, US Department of State, May 2002, p. vi.

in Washington, DC about love for country. You don't have to be a Republican to love the country, or a Democrat to love the country; we all love our country.[118]

As Donald Rumsfeld put it, when asked by NBC if the 'war on terror' would play a role in the midterm elections, 'I don't think it is a political issue at all.'[119]

A third aspect focused on American exceptionalism. The President made efforts to articulate this particularly clearly in his Independence Day message in 2002:

Unlike any other country, America came into the world with a message for mankind – that all are created equal, and all are meant to be free. There is no American race; there's only an American creed . . . Watching the events of that day, no American felt this was an attack on others, it was an attack on all of us, on each and every one of us. Every ethnic background is known and respected here in America. Every religious belief is practiced and protected here. Yet, in a moment we discovered again that we're a single people.[120]

And it was this mission that was to underpin America's leadership of the 'war on terror'. For Colin Powell:

Today, as America stands against terrorism with countries all around the world, we also reaffirm what our nation has stood for since its earliest days: for human rights, for democracy and for the rule of law. The worldwide promotion of human rights is in keeping with America's most deeply held values. It is also strongly in our interests. Freedom fights terrorism, instability and conflict.[121]

Ten days later, Powell amplified the point:

We have all got to work together to take this message to the rest of the world, a message that focuses on increasing respect for human rights and ethnic tolerance; a message that talks to the whole world about the rule of

118 George W. Bush, 'President increases funding for bioterrorism by 319 per cent', 5 February 2002, at http://www.whitehouse.gov/news/releases/2002/02/20020205 4.html [8/2004].

119 Donald H. Rumsfeld, 'Interview with NBC Meet the Press', 20 January 2002, at http://www.defenselink.mil/transcripts/2002/t01202002_t0120sd.html [9/2004].

120 George W. Bush, 'President honors veterans at West Virginia Fourth of July celebration', 4 July 2002, at http://www.whitehouse.gov/news/releases/2002/07/20020704-3.html [8/2004].

121 Colin Powell 'Briefing on release of country reports on human rights for 2001', 4 March 2002, at http://www.state.gov/secretary/rm/2002/8635.htm [9/2004].

> law and good governance, that successful societies of the 21st century must rest on the rule of law, for there is recourse to law for all the citizens and for all who might want to invest in that country and help that country move into a world of prosperity and out of the world of poverty; a message of open markets; a message of free trade, growth-generating trade, the kind of trade that allows undeveloped countries to begin the march up the ladder of prosperity; a message of stability and peace, moving away from age old conflicts and ethnic and religious and other kinds of intolerance that lead to the slaughters that we see on our television sets too often.[122]

The decisive intervention did not create the desire for global leadership, the fourth element. Exceptionalism was widely assumed in America, and it was that which came powerfully through in the decisive intervention that produced the claim to that leadership. This claim to exceptionalism and to global leadership was deeply engrained in the 'war on terror' discourse. President Bush spoke of the

> great divide in our time – not between religions or cultures, but between civilization and barbarism . . . Our war against terror is not a war against one terrorist leader or one terrorist group. Terrorism is a movement, an ideology that respects no boundary of nationality or decency. The terrorists despise creative societies and individual choice – and thus they bear a special hatred for America . . . We've seen their kind before. The terrorists are the heirs to fascism. They have the same will to power, the same disdain for the individual, the same mad global ambitions.[123]

The connection to an evil of the past, and a defeated one at that, provided a core spine for the continued power of the decisive intervention.

Thus, the narration of the self and terrorist other, of the claim to inclusivity and exceptionalism continued throughout 2002 and the early months of 2003. The fourth aspect was a claim to global leadership. Enacting this proved to be a core element of the policy programme, as will be developed in the next section.

122 Colin Powell, 'Remarks at National Council for Foreign Visitors', 14 March 2002, at http://www.state.gov/secretary/rm/2002/8778.htm [9/2004].

123 George W. Bush, 'President: We're fighting to win – and we will win', 7 December 2001, at http://www.whitehouse.gov/news/releases/2001/12/20011207.html [8/2004].

Expanding the 'war on terror' around the world

The development of the 'war on terror' discourse in the United States led to a particular policy programme, one that was to be implemented over the following years. One of the important elements of the discourse was the claim to American exceptionalism, and American leadership. The United States was a unique target for al-Qaeda, because it embodied freedom in ways that other countries sought or feared. America had to be a beacon for other states, and it had to lead and protect them in this new dread world.[124] The administration, so often accused of being unconcerned with allies, was actually redefining who were allies (those who supported the 'war on terror'), and what that meant (accepting American leadership explicitly). But the need to work in an international context, to exercise leadership, was a key part of the 'war on terror' discourse. As President Bush said with pride on the sixth month anniversary of the second American 9/11, 'September the 11th was not the beginning of global terror, but it was the beginning of the world's concerted response. History will know that day not only as a day of tragedy, but as a day of decision – when the civilized world was stirred to anger and to action . . . A mighty coalition of civilized nations is now defending our common security.'[125]

Thus, the policy programme also had to contain within it a determination to gather allies in this new struggle. And this was a task undertaken with fervour. Traditional allies were lauded: in a visit by British Prime Minister, Tony Blair, President Bush declared that 'America has no better ally in our war against terrorism than Great Britain.' With Israel, too: following a meeting with Ariel Sharon, the President reported that 'We just had an extensive discussion, first about our mutual desire to rid the world of terror. I assured him that our nation is just beginning in a great objective, which is to eliminate those terrorist organizations of global reach.' The Mexicans were thanked 'for their steady and strong resolve in their efforts to join us in our fight against terror'. And praise was heaped upon the Egyptians: 'Today, the strategic partnership between our countries

[124] That sense is well expressed in the title of Michael E. Brown (ed.), *Grave New World* (Washington, DC: Georgetown University Press, 2003).

[125] George W. Bush, 'President thanks world coalition for anti-terrorism efforts', 11 March 2002, at http://www.whitehouse.gov/news/releases/2002/03/20020311-1.html [8/2004].

is more important than ever, as we confront the threat of global terror. And I want to thank the President for his steadfast support in our war against terror.' The Russians, as well: 'Our nations will continue to cooperate closely in the war against global terror.' Meetings were held to symbolise joint resolve in new global struggle, and the reward for leaders was to be praised by the President. Such declarations occurred with the Peruvians, the El Salvadorians, with the Poles, the Colombians, the Australians and, amongst many others, the Moroccans.[126]

The purpose of this activity, though, was not just to strengthen and reorientate existing relationships, vitally important as that was. It was also to create and orientate new relationships, with states for whom friendship with the United States had not always been an easy choice. President Bush was explicit about the task at hand. He had already constructed a 'with us or against us' dichotomy; now he imbued this with values that were thought to appeal to all. He appealed to 'the civilized world' which 'must take seriously the growing threat of terror on a catastrophic scale. We've got to prevent the spread of weapons of mass destruction, because there is no margin for error and there is no

[126] For references, see, respectively: George W. Bush, 'Radio address by the President to the nation', 6 April 2002, at http://www.whitehouse.gov/news/releases/2002/04/20020406.html; 'President Bush, Prime Minister Sharon discuss Middle East', 7 February 2002, at http://www.whitehouse.gov/news/releases/2002/02/20020207-15.html; 'President promises secure and open borders in El Paso', 21 March 2002, at http://www.whitehouse.gov/news/releases/2002/03/20020321-7.html; 'President Bush welcomes President Mubarak to the White House', 5 March 2002, at http://www.whitehouse.gov/news/releases/2002/03/20020305-18.html; 'President Bush, Russian President Putin sign nuclear arms treaty', 24 May 2002, at http://www.whitehouse.gov/news/releases/2002/05/20020524-10.html; 'President Bush met President Toledo', 23 March 2002, at http://www.whitehouse.gov/news/releases/2002/03/20020323-13.html; 'President Bush met President Flores', 24 March 2002, at http://www.whitehouse.gov/news/releases/2002/03/20020324-2.html; 'President Bush, President Kwasnieski hold joint press conference', 17 July 2002, at http://www.whitehouse.gov/news/releases/2002/07/20020717-3.html; 'President Bush, Colombia President Uribe, discuss terrorism', 25 September 2002, at http://www.whitehouse.gov/news/releases/2002/09/20020925-1.html; 'Secretary Rumsfeld joint media availability with Australian Defence Minister', 10 January 2002 at http://www.defenselink.mil/transcripts/2002/t01102002_t0110aus.html; and 'President Bush and His Majesty King Mohammed VI of Morocco', 23 April 2002, at http://www.whitehouse.gov/news/releases/2002/04/20020423-7.html [all 8/2004].

chance to learn from any mistake.'[127] The choice being offered was one in which a state could be part of deliberations set by the United States according to the discursive principles structured by the decisive intervention, or be condemned to being defined as one of 'the most dangerous regimes'.

In this context, American policies towards South Asia were recalibrated. President Bush 'urged President Musharraf to do everything he could to crackdown on the terrorist network that had bombed the Indian Parliament . . . Terror is terror, and the fact that the Pakistani President is after terrorists is a good sign.'[128] Pakistan, America's traditional ally, was to come under intense American pressure not only to cooperate with American forces over Afghanistan, but also to prevent Kashmiri-based terrorism. To reorientate Pakistani policy – the country had, of course, been one of the very few to recognise the Taliban government – would be a key prize in the 'war on terror'. The President was to welcome 'President Musharraf's firm decision to stand against terrorism and extremism and his commitment to the principle that no person or organization will be allowed to indulge in terrorism as a means to further its cause'.[129] In a meeting with President Musharraf at the White House, he said that 'President Musharraf is a leader with great courage, and his nation is a key partner in the global coalition against terror.'[130]

Perhaps particularly evident in regard to creating new relationships was that with Yemen, a state that had opposed the resolution leading to Operation Desert Storm and the Gulf War of 1991 at the United Nations Security Council. In 2000, the *USS Cole* had been attacked by 'terrorists' from the Yemeni coast.[131] But the Yemenis were now lauded after a visit by Vice President Cheney to Sana'a, the Yemeni capital.

[127] George W. Bush, 'President calls for quick passage of Defense Bill', 15 March, 2002, at http://www.whitehouse.gov/news/releases/2002/03/20020315.html [8/2004].

[128] 'President discusses foreign policy for the year ahead', 31 December 2001, at http://www.whitehouse.gov/news/releases/2001/12/20011231.html [8/2004].

[129] Statement by Press Secretary, 'President welcomes Pakistan's commitment to fight terrorism', 12 January 2002, at http://www.whitehouse.gov/news/releases/2002/01/20020112-2.html [8/2004].

[130] George W. Bush 'US–Pakistan affirm commitment against terrorism', 13 February 2002, at http://www.whitehouse.gov/news/releases/2002/02/20020213-3.html [8/2004].

[131] See William Branigin, '2 sentenced to die for USS Cole attack', *Washington Post*, 30 September 2004.

The Pentagon spokesperson, Victoria Clarke, noted that the Yemenis wanted to work with America, and that 'They want assistance in fighting the terrorism in their own back yard.'[132] They were rewarded with an official visit to Washington, to be told by Colin Powell that 'our bilateral relationship . . . is strong, and I had the opportunity to once again thank the Foreign Minister, and through him to thank President Salih and the people of Yemen for all the help and support they have provided to us in the campaign against terrorism. We have a fine military-to-military level of cooperation taking place right now with US personnel assisting as best they can.'[133] A further example of the ways in which the policy programme required a recalibration of relations was China. President Jiang Zemin, following a meeting with President Bush, emphasised the new focus in relations: 'President Bush and I have also had an in-depth discussion on the international fight against terrorism. We have agreed to step up consultation and cooperation on the basis of reciprocity and mutual benefit, and to beef up the bilateral mid- and long-term mechanism for counter-terrorism exchanges and cooperation.'[134]

These new relationships were not just diplomatically important; they were seen to be important directly in terms of fighting the 'war on terror'. As Rear Admiral John Stufflebeem, deputy director for operations, put it, 'there are also operations that are occurring around the rest of the world, not all of which is visible to us'.[135] Such operations required local intelligence, involvement and cooperation. In February 2002, Donald Rumsfeld reflected:

> After September 11th, many countries assembled to fight terrorism. Many dozens of countries have contributed in a variety of ways, all-important: military, diplomatic, economic, and financial. Some have helped openly,

[132] Cited in Linda D. Kozaryn, 'Yemen: a US partner in the war on terror', 17 May 2002, at http://www.dod.mil/news/May2002/n05172002_200205172.html [9/2004].

[133] Colin L. Powell, 'Remarks with Yemeni Minister Abu Bakr al-Qurbi following meeting', 29 May 2002, at http://www.state.gov/secretary/rm/2002/10563.htm [9/2004].

[134] President Jiang Zemin, 'President Bush meets with Chinese President Jiang Zemin', 21 February 2002, at http://www.whitehouse.gov/news/releases/2002/02/20020221-7.html [8/2004].

[135] Rear Adm. John D. Stufflebeem, 'DoD news briefing', 7 January 2002, at http://www.defenselink.mil/transcripts/2002/t01072002_t0107asd.html [9/2004].

others have helped less openly. Many leaders courageously spoke out against terrorists. Many nations have provided troops, materiel, humanitarian aid, information, overflight and basing privileges. The United States has been joined by not just its traditional allies in the struggle against terror, but by many countries that are not normally part of such alliances.[136]

He continued '12 countries have contributed more than 2,800 personnel to ground operations in the campaign. Eight countries contributed more than 1,500 people to air operations. Eight countries contributed more than 13,000 people to naval operations, and some eight countries contributed 350-plus people to civil operations in Afghanistan.'[137] In June 2002, the President gave a sense of the scale of this activity:

Tonight over 60,000 American troops are deployed around the world in the war against terror – more than 7,000 in Afghanistan; others in the Philippines, Yemen, and the Republic of Georgia, to train local forces . . . Our coalition is strong. More than 90 nations have arrested or detained over 2,400 terrorists and their supporters. More than 180 countries have offered or are providing assistance in the war on terrorism.[138]

The latter was a particularly important claim: it said that the whole world stood with America in the 'war on terror', against the few isolated terrorist states.

However, working with the new allies, on the new alliance, also required the naming of those outside the new American led alliance in the 'war on terror'. Most clearly, this had happened in the State of the Union address, and in subsequent statements identifying rogue states. But there was one other target still to be named – the Palestinian Authority. In April 2002, President Bush declared:

Since September the 11th, I've delivered this message: everyone must choose; you're either with the civilized world, or you're with the terrorists . . . The Chairman of the Palestinian Authority has not consistently opposed or confronted terrorists. At Oslo and elsewhere, Chairman Arafat

[136] Donald Rumsfeld, 'DoD news briefing', 26 February 2002, at http://www.dod.mil/transcripts/2002/t02262002 t0226sd.html [9/2004]. [137] Ibid.

[138] George W. Bush, 'Remarks by the President to the nation', 6 June 2002, at http://www.whitehouse.gov/news/releases/2002/06/20020606-8.html [8/2004].

renounced terror as an instrument of his cause, and he agreed to control it. He's not done so.[139]

In June, the President said 'I call on the Palestinian people to elect new leaders, leaders not compromised by terror.'[140] The 'war on terror' would be deployed to pressurise the Palestinian Authority not only to intensify its police actions, but also to influence the nature of the Palestinians' leadership.

The policy programme therefore required the reconstruction of existing relations with allies, the development of new relations with other states, naming those who would not cooperate appropriately, and the gathering of efforts to deny opportunities to terror in military, political and diplomatic terms. But that could not be all, for it would leave two gaps. The first was in those areas in which 'failed states' operated, which in terms of the 'war on terror' discourse had to be addressed. Failed or failing states couldn't be allies or enemies, but could be a 'breeding ground for terror'. Paul Wolfowitz worried about 'where the Indonesian government is extremely weak in parts of Sulawesi and the Malukus . . . in the case of Sulawesi the concern is, there isn't enough military there to protect the local population or to create the kinds of conditions that keep terrorists out'.[141] In order to address this, a $5 billion fund was set up to alleviate poverty. President Bush said that 'Poverty doesn't cause terrorism. Being poor doesn't make you a murderer. Most of the plotters of September 11th were raised in comfort. Yet persistent poverty and oppression can lead to hopelessness and despair. And when governments fail to meet the most basic needs of their people, these failed states can become havens for terror.'[142] This meant connecting the opportunities provided to terrorists in particular

[139] George W. Bush, 'President to send Secretary Powell to the Middle East', 4 April 2002, at http://www.whitehouse.gov/news/releases/2002/04/20020404-1.html [8/2004].

[140] George W. Bush, 'President Bush calls for new Palestinian leadership', 24 June 2002, at http://www.whitehouse.gov/news/releases/2002/06/20020624-3.html [8/2004].

[141] Deputy Secretary Wolfowitz interview with the *New York Times*, 7 January 2002, at http://www.defenselink.mil/transcripts/2002/t01132002_t0107dsd.html [9/2004].

[142] George W. Bush, 'President proposes $5 billion plan to help developing nations', 14 March 2002, at http://www.whitehouse.gov/news/releases/2002/03/20020314-7.html [8/2004].

parts of the world with poverty. As National Security Advisor, Condoleezza Rice, stated, 'You literally cannot understand what you read in the newspapers these days, without understanding that there is an ongoing struggle for human freedom *and* human dignity. This struggle is central to the world's efforts to confront terror and tyranny and poverty and disease.'[143] This was an important plank in the policy programme, though one often ignored in the focus on Iraq.

The second potential gap was at the ideological level. The policy programme required a commitment to fight against terror, not Islam. (Of course, there had been problems on this front: the initial designation of the war in Afghanistan as 'Operation Infinite Justice' had angered some Muslims, as had the use of the term 'crusade' against terror.) Paul Wolfowitz had said that 'To win the war against terrorism and help shape a more peaceful world, we must speak to the hundreds of millions of moderate and tolerant people in the Muslim world, regardless of where they live, who aspire to enjoy the blessings of freedom and democracy and free enterprise . . .'[144] Such 'western' values were also deemed to be global, to stand in contrast with the narrow and brutal values of al-Qaeda. But of course, as will be examined later, this fell foul of concern about American motives in Iraq, setting up a key contradiction within the policy programme.

Conclusion

Throughout 2002, from the State of the Union speech, to the outbreak of the war in Iraq in March 2003, the discourse of the 'war on terror', as constructed by the decisive intervention to the shock of the second American 9/11, became an implementable and implemented policy programme. Many aspects of American public life came to be seen through the prism of the 'war on terror' discourse. America's military was to be heavily engaged in conflicts in Afghanistan, Georgia, the Philippines, Yemen and ultimately Iraq, while itself being 'transformed'. Throughout, the key concepts behind the discourse were re-emphasised, and the policy programme was given renewed energy by this re-emphasis. The 'war on

143 'Remarks by National Security Advisor Condoleezza Rice at the Karamah Iftaar', 4 December 2002, at http://www.whitehouse.gov/news/releases/2002/12/20021204-17.html [9/2004]. Emphasis added.

144 Jim Garamone, 'Wolfowitz stresses global terror threat to Asia', 1 June 2002, at http://www.dod.mil/news/Jun2002/n06012002_200206011.html [9/2004].

terror' discourse was globalised, transmitted to traditional allies and new allies, as the meaning of alliance itself was reconstructed.

What does this mean for the concept of crisis being developed in this book? The conceptualisation of crisis developed in chapter 2 was modified in chapter 3 to take account of the detail of the case of the social construction of the second American 9/11. In this chapter, the examination of the implementation of the policy programme developed following the decisive intervention leads to the illustration of crisis shown in figure 4.3. The boxes in capital letters illustrate the immediate issues of the crisis of the second American 9/11, and the decisive intervention that constructed it in particular ways; that is, the subject matter of chapter 2. The boxes in italics illustrate the way in which that decisive intervention led to a new strategic direction, and the initial steps towards restructuring priorities; that is, the material of chapter 3. The box in bold therefore illustrates the implementation of the policy programme devised through the development of the new strategic trajectory; that is, the subject matter of this fourth chapter.

The shock of Sputnik similarly produced a decisive intervention to construct the meaning of the event, and to produce a new policy programme. That policy programme became embedded institutionally in the United States and, amongst many other developments, it connected to previously undreamed-of arsenals of nuclear weapons with increasing accuracy, and it became symbolised by the landing of Apollo 9 on the moon some twelve years later. But although there was a policy programme following the construction of Sputnik that changed America in particular ways, the construction of the problem – that is, the decisive intervention itself – was quickly challenged. The 1960 presidential election was one of the closest ever, in terms of the popular vote.[145] That election was won by John F. Kennedy in part because he claimed that Sputnik illustrated the Soviet advantage over the United States, and he alleged that there was a missile gap. Over forty years later, there were again voices outside the policy programme, this time particularly as the war in Iraq became increasingly likely. The growing opposition to the policy programme, and indeed to the 'war on terror' discourse, is the focus of chapter 5, on sites of resistance. But, at this point, it is

[145] Kennedy secured 34,227,096, 49.7% of the votes overall to Nixon's 34,107,646 votes, 49.5%. However, in the Electoral College, Kennedy won easily, by 303 votes to 219.

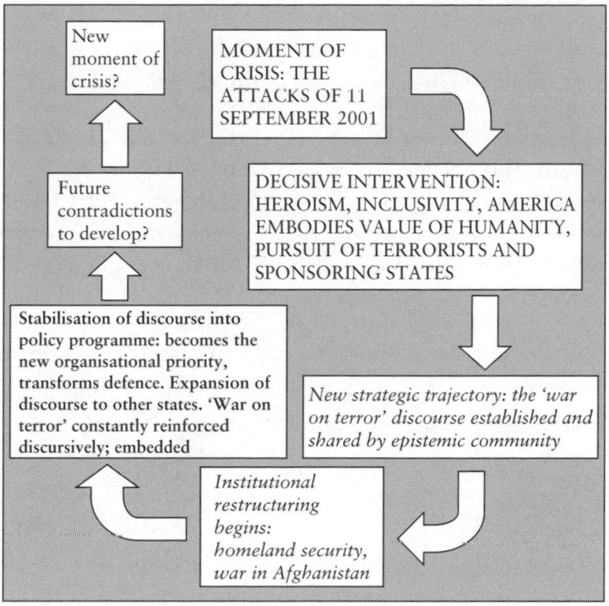

Figure 4.3. The crisis process and policy programme

important to emphasise that to the extent to which there was opposition from within the institutions of the American state, it was just to one aspect of the policy programme: Iraq. Even when speaking against extending the conflict to Iraq in September 2002, for example, Al Gore emphasised:

> I don't think we should allow anything to diminish our focus on the necessity for avenging the 3,000 Americans who were murdered and dismantling that network of terrorists that we know were responsible for it . . . The fact that we don't know where they are, should not cause us to focus instead on some other enemy whose location might be easier to identify.[146]

Note the use of the concept of 'avenging' the attack – with clearly biblical undertones of legitimate violence. But Gore, and the Democratic Party, were not engaged in an attack on the policy programme per se. Millions were opposed to the policy programme, and as the next

[146] Al Gore, speech in San Francisco, 23 September 2002, cited in 'Gore joins Bush's Iraq critics', *BBC News Online*, 24 September 2002, at http://news.bbc.co.uk/1/hi/world/americas/2277698.stm [9/2004].

chapter argues, they developed an alternative discourse. But it was one that was not to penetrate the institutions of the American state.

The State Department's *Patterns of Terrorism* publication claimed:

> Despite the horrific events of September 11, the number of international terrorist attacks in 2001 declined to 346, down from 426 the previous year. One hundred seventy-eight of the attacks were bombings against a multinational oil pipeline in Colombia – constituting 51 percent of the year's total number of attacks. In the year 2000, there were 152 pipeline bombings in Colombia, which accounted for 40 percent of the total.[147]

In short, one conclusion could have been that terror was declining, not least because it was not clear how terrorism in Colombia was in any sense 'global'. But that was not a comprehensible analysis from within the 'war on terror' discourse. Single-year figures were not of great importance in a long-term war. The threat of sleepers and of terrorists acquiring weapons of mass destruction were to the fore. The 'al-Qaeda' attack on Bali in September 2002, in which over 200 people died, reinforced the power of the 'war on terror' discourse, regardless of numbers of terrorist attacks. As George Bush was quick to state, 'I think we have to assume it is al-Qaeda . . .',[148] and therefore part of the global 'war on terror', not part of local conflicts.

The Bali bombing was taken to illustrate the global reach of al-Qaeda, to demonstrate the common sense of the 'war on terror' discourse, and thereby of its policy programme. But a new discourse was under construction – that of 'no war for oil' – which saw the world in radically different ways, and one that saw the 'war on terror' as a cynical justification for seizing resources. The next chapter examines the rise of this discourse, how it led to the socially constructed crisis over the Iraq War, and hence the means by which the 'war on terror' was discursively challenged.

147 'September 11 and review of terrorism 2001', *Patterns of Terrorism 2001*, US Department of State, May 2002.

148 Quoted in 'Tourists flee Bali after bombings', CNN, 14 October 2002, at http://archives.cnn.com/2002/WORLD/asiapcf/southeast/10/14/bali.bombings/ [9/2004].

5 Acts of resistance to the 'war on terror'

Introduction

The crisis process developed in this book suggests that at, some point, the dominant discourse becomes the subject of contradictions, and that the culmination of those contradictions lies in another socially constructed crisis. The way in which the war in Iraq came about, and the way in which it was conducted, led to enormous opposition. Was this the beginning of the onset of contradictions to the 'war on terror' discourse?

A collection of essays written by Pierre Bourdieu was published in 2000 under the title *Acts of Resistance: Against the New Myths of Our Time*.[1] The contributions were written before the second American 9/11; their target was neoliberal economics and its discursive consequences. However, one essay – 'The train driver's remark' – was written in the aftermath of a bomb attack on a train, when the driver had refused to condemn French-Algerians or Muslims, and instead, according to Bourdieu, had said straightforwardly: they are 'people like us'. He wrote:

> This exceptional remark provided the proof that it is possible to resist the violence that is exerted daily, with a clear conscience, on television, on the radio and in the newspapers, through verbal reflexes, stereotyped images and conventional words, and the effect of habituation that it produces, imperceptibly raising, throughout the whole population, the threshold of tolerance of racist insults and contempt, reducing critical defences against pre-logical thought and verbal confusion (between Islam and Islamicism, between Muslim and Islamicist, or between Islamicist and terrorist, for example), insidiously reinforcing all the habits of thought and behaviour inherited from more than a century of colonialism and colonial struggles.[2]

1 Pierre Bourdieu, *Acts of Resistance: Against the New Myths of Our Time*, translated by Richard Nice (Cambridge: Polity Press, 2000).

2 Bourdieu, 'The train driver's remark', originally published in *Alternatives algériennes*, November 1995; in *Acts of Resistance*, pp. 27–8.

Although written in 1995, and targeted at developments in French discursive practices over terrorism, this spoke powerfully to the intellectual drivers of those who believed that there were powerful contradictions in the 'war on terror' discourse: that eliminating terror and weapons of mass destruction in Iraq was really about controlling oil; that far from being a warrior for freedom, America was really concerned with the money that can be made from war.

This sense was articulated by many in America, and expressed in a forum called Refuse and Resist!, a website dedicated to overturning the new directions in American politics. The organisers had held a rally to resist the 'new normalcy' in December 2001, to protest against the '1100 people, mainly Arabs and Muslims, [who] have been rounded up by the FBI and INS and kept in detention, many on the basis of secret evidence or no evidence at all and without any contact with a lawyer'.[3] This rally was an 'act of resistance', a process that began in 2001, but one that was to gather momentum throughout 2002 and into 2003, when a series of enormous, mass demonstrations against the approaching war in Iraq were held. The 'infringement' of civil liberties was seen as part of a process of preparing America for war. Refuse and Resist!, in their founding statement, rejected the dominant discourse's emphasis on inclusivity, and explained that 'There can be no commonality of purpose, healing of divisions, or coming together as one nation behind this new course. To acquiesce further in silence is to be complicit . . . There must be massive resistance.'[4] Would 'massive resistance' lead to a new socially constructed crisis, where the contradictions in the hegemonic discourse of the 'war on terror' would be exposed, and its discursive principles overthrown?

This chapter will examine the onset of contradictions by looking first at the development of the 'war on terror' policy programme to move towards the attack on Iraq. It then examines the nature of the opposition to that 'war on terror' being extended to Iraq. It will then look at the ways in which the 'war on terror' discourse itself was restructured in the face of that opposition. The opposition was

[3] 'Resist the New Normalcy!' 1 December 2001, at http://www.refuseandresist.org/newresistance/112701laforum.html [7/2005].

[4] The founding statement is on the 'Acts of resistance' page of Refuse and Resist!, at http://www.refuseandresist.org/newresistance/index.html [7/2005].

constructed as being outside the discourse and, in that way, as being beyond common sense. The third section examines the way in which the key institutions of American society were involved in a co-production of the 'war on terror' discourse, and how they continued to delegitimise any alternatives. The fourth section illustrates the way in which the 'war on terror' discourse had become part of popular culture and, therefore, how in novels, music, popular television and so on that discourse was powerfully reproduced. Although there were widespread acts of resistance to the dominant discourse, as chapter 6 will show, this only led to the 'war on terror' strengthening its position discursively.

Iraq and the 'war on terror'

The move to war in Iraq was very much part of the policy programme contained within the decisive intervention. In 2002, *CBS News* revealed a story that 'barely five hours after American Airlines Flight 77 plowed into the Pentagon, Defense Secretary Donald H. Rumsfeld was telling his aides to come up with plans for striking Iraq . . . according to notes taken by aides who were with Rumsfeld in the National Military Command Center on Sept. 11 . . .'.[5] According to Bob Woodward in *Plan of Attack*, a book based on extensive interviews with members of the Bush administration, on 16 September Bush indicated to National Security Advisor Condoleezza Rice that while the Afghanistan operation would be first, he was also determined to do something about Saddam Hussein. 'We won't do Iraq now', Woodward quotes the President as saying to Rice, 'we're putting Iraq off. But eventually we'll have to return to that question.'[6] There was widespread support for the idea that the 'war on terror' involved conflict with Iraq. Senator Joseph Lieberman, vice presidential candidate for the Democrats in 2000, argued in October 2001 that the war in Afghanistan should be extended to Iraq, in what he described as a 'phase two' of operations. Lieberman said 'As long as Saddam is there, Iraq is not just going to be a thorn in our side, but a threat to our

[5] David Martin, 'Plans for Iraq attack began on 9/11', *CBS News*, 4 September 2002, at http://www.cbsnews.com/stories/2002/09/04/september11/main520830.shtml [5/2005].

[6] Bob Woodward, *Plan of Attack* (New York: Simon and Schuster, 2004), p. 26.

lives . . .'[7] He was not alone amongst Democrats taking this line. Attacking Iraq – or at least 'widening the focus of the war' after the conflict in Afghanistan – was, in the autumn of 2001, supported by Democrats such as Senator John Kerry, Senator Joseph Biden and Senator Robert Torricelli.[8] Democrat Representative, Gary Ackerman, had opened his testimony to the House of Representatives International Relations Subcommittee in October 2001 with the words: 'In the wake of the September 11th terrorist attacks, I think it's important that we as a nation not lose sight of those states that in the past have wanted to do us harm. Indeed, in the case of Iraq, we have a state that clearly intends to do us harm in the future as well.'[9] That Iraq was part of the 'war on terror' was simply common sense.

Thus, President Bush's 'axis of evil' State of the Union speech in January 2002 did not form from ideas freely floating. It was firmly rooted in the decisive intervention, in the construction of the 'war on terror' discourse.[10] In that speech, Bush had particularly spoken about the problem of Iraq:

> Iraq continues to flaunt its hostility toward America and to support terror. The Iraqi regime has plotted to develop anthrax, and nerve gas, and nuclear weapons for over a decade. This is a regime that has already used poison gas to murder thousands of its own citizens – leaving the bodies of mothers huddled over their dead children. This is a regime that agreed to international inspections – then kicked out the inspectors. This is a regime that has something to hide from the civilized world.[11]

But there was complexity to the idea that the 'war on terror' was precisely that: a war on those constructed as terrorists, not simply the

[7] Cited in Chuck Noe, 'Lieberman urges Bush to oust Saddam', 17 October 2001, *MaxNews*, at http://www.newsmax.com/archives/articles/2001/10/16/200751.shtml [6/2004].

[8] See, 'Opportunist Dems call for war on Iraq', *Village Voice*, 23 November 2001, at http://www.hartford-hwp.com/archives/45/203.html [6/2004].

[9] See, 'Hearing of the House International Relations Committee Subcommittee on the Middle East and South Asia', 4 October 2001, at http://www.iraqwatch.org/government/US/HearingsPreparedstatements/HIRC-hrg-10-4-01.htm [6/2004].

[10] David Frum claims authorship: see *The Right Man* (London: Weidenfeld & Nicolson, 2003), pp. 224–45.

[11] George W. Bush, 'President delivers State of the Union address', 29 January 2002, at http://www.whitehouse.gov/news/releases/2002/01/20020129-11.html [6/2005].

enemy named as responsible for the second American 9/11. In the spring and summer of 2002, therefore, care was taken to specify the problem – the linkage of weapons of mass destruction to terrorist ambitions. The problem was actually one much broader than the specific issue of Iraq. In a speech in March 2002, the President had said 'that we will not let the most dangerous regimes in the world team up with killers and, therefore, hold this great nation hostage. Whatever it takes to defend the liberty of America, this administration will do.'[12] This was an attempt to develop the policy programme into a more general war on terror, in which the conflict in Afghanistan, and any conflict in Iraq, would be mere campaigns. This was pure neoconservatism: the revolutionary war for democracy, as Michael Ledeen had put it. It was not some sort of opportunism: it was embedded into the discourse of the 'war on terror', and originated with the decisive intervention.

However, phase two (if Afghanistan was phase one) had to focus on Iraq, and so the regime's specific threat potential was emphasised. George Tenet, the director of the CIA, made specific connection between the new triad: the Iraqi regime / weapons of mass destruction / terrorism.

> As I said earlier, we continue to watch Iraq's involvement in terrorist activities. Baghdad has a long history of supporting terrorism, altering its targets to reflect changing priorities and goals. It has also had contacts with al-Qa'ida. Their ties may be limited by divergent ideologies, but the two sides' mutual antipathy toward the United States and the Saudi royal family suggests that tactical cooperation between them is possible . . . Iraq continues to build and expand an infrastructure capable of producing WMD. Baghdad is expanding its civilian chemical industry in ways that could be diverted quickly to CW production.[13]

Tenet was called on as the authoritative expert, to reveal 'facts' about Iraqi behaviour that could not be contested. The 'expert' has a special position in debate, having a particular knowledge denied to others. The President built on these 'objective' truths, and laid out the case for

12 George W. Bush, 'President calls for quick passage of Defense Bill', 15 March 2002, at http://www.whitehouse.gov/news/releases/2002/03/20020315.html [6/2005].

13 George Tenet, testimony to the Senate Armed Services Committee, 19 March 2002, at http://www.iraqwatch.org/government/US/CIA/cia-tenet-031902.htm [6/2005].

bringing about change in Iraq with increasing frequency throughout 2002. By September, he was direct:

> We've also got a big chore to make sure the world's worst leaders never threaten, blackmail or harm America with the world's worst weapons. I went to the United Nations the other day. I did so because I wanted to make the case against a mad man . . . who hates America; a man who loves to link up with al-Qaeda; a man who is a true threat to America, to Israel, to anybody in the neighborhood.[14]

And there was the case for war, exposed in all of its dimensions – 'chore', 'threat', 'world's worst weapons', 'mad', 'hates America', 'al-Qaeda', 'Israel'. The solution – regime change – was already official American policy. President Clinton and both Houses of Congress had passed the Iraq Liberation Act in 1998, which called for the overthrow of Saddam and the development of democracy.[15] In October 2002, Congress passed the Joint Resolution to Authorize the Use of United States Armed Forces Against Iraq.[16] And regime change would bring freedom. As the President explained in his speech to the United Nations, 'Liberty for the Iraqi people is a great moral cause, and a great strategic goal. The people of Iraq deserve it; the security of all nations requires it . . .'[17]

The organs of the state were brought to bear in making the case. One example was a glossy brochure entitled *Iraq: From Fear to Freedom* which simply asserted that 'In the time since the September 11 attacks in the United States, intelligence reports have confirmed that al-Qaeda terrorists escaping from Afghanistan are now present in Iraq.'[18] Intelligence reports were again presented as objective fact. And as the construction of the 'war on terror' discourse involved Democrats as

[14] George W. Bush, 'President Bush pushes for Homeland Security Bill', Phoenix, Arizona, 28 September 2002, at http://www.whitehouse.gov/news/releases/2002/09/20020928-2.html [6/2005].

[15] The Act is at http://news.findlaw.com/hdocs/docs/iraq/libact103198.pdf [1/2004].

[16] Reproduced at http://www.yourcongress.com/ViewArticle.asp?article_id=2686 [6/2005].

[17] George W. Bush, 'Remarks by the President in address to the United Nations General Assembly', 12 September 2002, at http://www.whitehouse.gov/news/releases/2002/09/print/20020912-1.html [6/2005].

[18] *Iraq: From Fear to Freedom*, US Department of State International Informational Program, Winter 2002–3, at http://usinfo.state.gov/products/pubs/iraq/iraq.pdf [6/2005].

well as Republicans, so the spreading of the policy programme involved the media as well as the government. In September 2002, Vice President Cheney was interviewed on the television programme *Meet the Press* to make the case for war (if Iraq didn't back down). 'But come back to 9/11 again', he said, 'and one of the real concerns about Saddam Hussein, as well, is his biological weapons capability; the fact that he may, at some point, try to use smallpox, anthrax, plague, some other kind of biological agent against other nations, possibly including even the United States.'[19] Many protested that the Vice President had exaggerated the link between the second American 9/11 – a terrorist attack by al-Qaeda – and the power and interests of the Iraqi state.[20] But discursively the point linking Iraq and the events of 11 September 2001 had been made. *Meet the Press* ended with another powerful reminder: the interviewer, Tim Russert of *NBC News*, finished with these remarks: 'As we leave, we remember the 3,025 who gave their lives on September 11, 2001. Many had sons and daughters born after their own death. One hundred and four babies born since 9/11. They will never know their fathers. May these children always remember the strength, the hope, the faith, the love, their parents, dads and moms, gave us all.'[21] Clearly the viewer was to draw the conclusion that 'something must be done' about Iraq to avoid another '9/11'. But this was not the only example of the media reproducing the 'war on terror' message about Iraq. Judith Miller, the Pulitzer Prize-winning journalist for the *New York Times*, went to prison in 2005 for refusing to name her sources.[22] But in the run-up to the Iraq War, she ran a series of stories that were deeply embedded with the 'war on terror' discourse. For example, on 14 September, one headline ran 'Lab suggests Qaeda planned to build arms', although no such evidence subsequently emerged.[23] Other high-

19 'Transcript of interview with Vice-President Dick Cheney on *Meet the Press*, 8 September 2002', NBC, at http://www.mtholyoke.edu/acad/intrel/bush/meet.htm [6/2005].

20 Anne E. Kornblut and Bryan Bender, 'Cheney link of Iraq, 9/11 challenged', *Boston Globe*, 16 September 2002, at http://www.boston.com/news/nation/articles/2003/09/16/cheney_link_of_iraq_911_challenged/ [6/2005].

21 *Meet the Press*, 8 September 2002.

22 'Reporter jailed for refusal to name leak source', MSNBC, 7 July 2005, at http://www.msnbc.msn.com/id/8417075/ [9/2005]; and Jerry Markon 'N. Va. jail's "unassuming" celebrity', *Washington Post*, 4 August 2005.

23 Judith Miller, 'Lab suggests Qaeda planned to build arms', *New York Times*, 14 September 2002.

lights included: 'Pentagon shifts anthrax vaccine to civilian uses'; 'Qaeda's new links increase threats from far-flung sites'; 'Qaeda leader in US custody provokes alert'.[24] Her work later in the year did much to connect Iraq with weapons of mass destruction.[25] Particular highlights in this field included: 'CIA hunts Iraq link to Soviet smallpox'; 'Chemical weapons – Iraq said to try buy antidote against nerve gas'; and 'The Iraqis – US says Hussein intensifies quest for A bomb parts'.[26] Miller's secret source was revealed to be the Vice President's Chief of Staff, 'Scooter' Libby.[27] But the reproduction of the 'war on terror' discourse in the media ran still further. On 12 December 2002, a front-page heading in the *Washington Post* declared that 'US suspects Al Qaeda got nerve agent from Iraqis'.[28] The media linked al-Qaeda, Iraq and weapons of mass destruction frequently and powerfully.

The acts of resistance

The case for disarming and democratising Iraq, by war if necessary, lay deep within the discursive structure of the 'war on terror'; as such, it was part of the policy programme of the government, and part of the understanding of the world reproduced by much of the media. Yet this held no resonance for many thousands around the world. The opposition to the war was widespread, and dramatic in its appearance, for images were a very important part of the campaign. In October 2002, protestors demonstrated in Madrid and Zaragoza, and on 26 October,

[24] All in the *New York Times*: James Dao with Judith Miller, 'Pentagon shifts anthrax vaccine to civilian uses', 29 June 2002; David Johnston, Don Van Natta Jr and Judith Miller, 'Qaeda's new links increase threats from far-flung sites', 16 June 2002; Judith Miller and Philip Shenon, 'Qaeda leader in US custody provokes alert', 20 April 2002.

[25] For analysis of Miller's reporting, see Franklin Foer, 'The source of the trouble', *New York Metro*, 7 June 2004, at http://newyorkmetro.com/nymetro/news/media/features/9226/ [7/2004].

[26] All in the *New York Times*: Judith Miller, 'CIA hunts Iraq link to Soviet smallpox', 3 December 2002; Judith Miller, 'Chemical weapons – Iraq said to try buy antidote against nerve gas', 12 November 2002; Michael R. Gordon and Judith Miller, 'The Iraqis – US says Hussein intensifies quest for A bomb parts', 8 September 2002.

[27] Libby's indictment at http://www.usdoj.gov/usao/iln/osc/documents/libby_ indictment_28102005.pdf [11/2005].

[28] Barton Gellman, 'US suspects Al Qaeda got nerve agent from Iraqis', *Washington Post*, 12 December 2002.

in Washington, DC, where up to 40,000 people attended the rally against the approaching war.[29] The following month there were demonstrations in Manila, Sydney and Pakistan and on 9 November, up to half a million people (estimates vary wildly) demonstrated in Florence at the European Social Forum. The Forum issued an agreed statement, which began 'To all citizens of Europe; Together we can stop this war!'[30] In London on 2 December, thousands dressed in 'bloody' bandages, protesting against the imminent loss of innocent life, while later in the month a demonstration was organised at the Fairford air force base, a 'launchpad for war'.[31] In Seattle, hundreds of pupils walked out of school to demonstrate against the war.[32] In Oakland, California, demonstrators displayed cardboard coffins, under the slogan 'Iraqi children are not collateral damage'. Protestors gathered in California after the arrest of those from specific countries in the Middle East who had been asked to 'register' at the Immigration and Naturalization Service.[33]

However, it was in the early part of 2003 that the popular protests gathered their greatest momentum. In early January, demonstrators at a rally in Los Angeles held aloft banners entitled 'Don't Cut Medicare for Bombs and Missiles' and, very powerfully, a white board splattered with red saying 'Human blood: $1.09 a gallon', graphically underlining the claim that this was a war for oil.[34] That rally was a precursor for much larger ones the following week. On 18 January, major rallies took place in Tokyo, Moscow, Paris, London, Dublin, Montreal, Ottawa, Toronto, Cologne, Bonn, Gothenburg, Florence, Oslo, Rotterdam, Istanbul and Cairo, amongst other cities. Opposition groups such as Not In Our Name (NION) and Act Now to Stop War and End Racism (ANSWER) organised rallies in Washington, DC, and

29 See the website 'Global protests against the war on Iraq', at http://www.nationmaster.com/encyclopedia/Global-protests-against-war-on-Iraq#January_16.2C_2002 [6/2005].

30 At http://www.2002.fse-esf.org/article.php3?id_article=327 [6/2005].

31 See the images at http://www.stopwar.org.uk/gallery.asp?year=02 [6/2005].

32 J. J. Jensen, 'Several hundred Seattle students march against war', *Seattle Times*, 6 December 2002.

33 See Megan Garvey, Martha Groves and Henry Weinstein, 'Hundreds are detained after visits to INS thousands protest arrests of Mideast boys and men who complied with order to register', *Los Angeles Times*, 19 December 2002.

34 See Erika Hayasaki, 'Thousands rally against war in Iraq, push peace: as more troops are deployed, protesters gather in downtown LA to denounce action', *Los Angeles Times*, 12 January 2003.

in San Francisco which drew large crowds.[35] In San Francisco, protestors taped dollar bills across their mouths.[36] Some saw in this a major political moment: 'The mass anti-capitalist movement is dovetailing with an anti-war mood which in the next period can turn into an overtly socialist movement in which the forces of socialism and Marxism will grow.'[37] Most, however, were focused on the issue at hand: demonstrating so forcibly that the war in Iraq would be averted.

The opposition to the war was a focus of great argument. One of the core elements of the discourse was the American claim to global leadership in the fight for freedom. That those opposed to the next stage in the policy programme – the 'disarming' of Iraq – could match that claim with one of their own to global commitment was very powerful. The arguments that this generated were very bitter indeed. One example was the exchange between the musician and activist Miles Solay, representing NION, and Bill O'Reilly, the presenter on *Fox News*, on prime-time television:

O'REILLY: . . . Unless I'm wrong, Saddam Hussein invaded Kuwait, took over a sovereign country and we rescued that country. You see that as [America] perpetrating violence?

SOLAY: Well, then, let me ask you this, what do you have to say about when Secretary of Defense Donald Rumsfeld met with Saddam Hussein in 1984 as . . .

O'REILLY: What do I have to say about it? I don't care about it. It's not germane or relevant to what we're talking about.

SOLAY: Well, that was when Saddam Hussein gassed the Kurds and Iranian troops in the Iran–Iraq war.

O'REILLY: What do I have to say about the war of 1812? It doesn't matter . . . You're basically saying that we shook our heads at the terrible scenes of carnage, even as we recalled similar scenes. You're comparing 9/11 – all right? – the World Trade Center and the Pentagon, to Baghdad and Panama City. That's obscene. That is so, so offensive to clear-thinking Americans. Don't you have any clue how offensive that is?

. . .

[35] See NION's report of the protests at http://www.notinourname.net/reports/sf_18jan03.html [6/2005]. The organisation ran newspaper adverts, including one in the *New York Times*, in September 2002. For the text, and the list of 'celebrities' who endorsed it, see http://www.nion.us/NION.HTM [7/2005].

[36] Imagery at http://www.bohemianmasquerade.com/peace/peace.html [6/2005].

[37] Committee for a Workers International, 'US empire's war for oil', 12 February 2003, at http://www.marxist.net/war/w2frame.htm?antiwar.htm [6/2005].

SOLAY: What I'm saying about the Not In Our Name statement of conscience, is it's not that it's un-American, it's a statement that's standing with the people of the world. We're not granting privilege to people . . .

O'REILLY: You can say you're standing with the people of the world, but if they believe this, you're standing with the pinheads of the world who don't know anything.[38]

Fox was renowned for its robust position on the 'war on terror'. But there was no denying its popularity. O'Reilly's programme was seen regularly in over 3 million households, predominantly conservative in their disposition, and who on average watched Fox for longer than, for example, the CNN audience. By April, Fox was attracting more viewers for its breakfast programme than CBS, who had traditionally been third amongst the major broadcasters at this time of day.[39] The aggressive, pro-war on terror line of the network, exemplified by presenters such as O'Reilly, was having a major and positive impact on the network's profitability. And the subsequent war in Iraq was a key part of the competition in New York between the tabloid *Daily News* and *New York Post* for sales.[40] There was profit to be made in the 'war on terror'.

The protest developed globally, much aided by the use of the internet. Internet sites were developed and, along with email and message boards, it was easy to find out what the protestors thought and where they would meet, all from a personal computer in the home or the office. The protestors, through utilising and developing internet activism, were able to mobilise and educate very large numbers of people. To focus this into direct political protest, an international day of demonstration was arranged, 15 February. Millions protested against the impending war, in perhaps 600 cities around the world. The *Guinness Book of Records* declared the Italian demonstration in Rome, which attracted some 3 million, to be the 'largest anti-war rally'.[41] More than a million demonstrated in Barcelona and in

[38] Fox News Network, 'The O'Reilly factor', 27 January 2003, at http://www.notinourname.net/media/fox_news_oreilly_jan03.html [6/2005].

[39] See Tim Cuprisin, 'Fox News scores big win in war ratings', 13 April 2003, http://www.jsonline.com/enter/tvradio/apr03/133295.asp [6/2005].

[40] See Jacques Steinberg, 'War stokes fire between city tabloids', *New York Times*, 29 March 2003.

[41] See http://www.guinnessworldrecords.com/ under, 'Modern Society', then, 'War and Weapons' [6/2005].

London. Hundreds of thousands demonstrated in New York, Chicago, Los Angeles and, the following day, in San Francisco, as well as in other parts of the United States. In total, it was estimated that between 6 and 10 million had protested globally.[42]

This was a very powerful challenge to the 'war on terror' discourse. Iraq was supposed to have been involved in the second American 9/11; and thus to prevent a third American 9/11, potentially with weapons of mass destruction, Iraq had to be disarmed. This was supposed to be 'common sense'. But it was not received by all as such. There was supposed to be a global alliance, led by the United States, in the fight against terror; the demonstrations seemed to show that this was not welcomed in those very states that were most supportive of the United States at governmental level: Italy, Spain, the United Kingdom, Australia. The contradictions in the 'war on terror' discourse were manifest to those protesting.

Opponents of the war sought to build on this success with another global day of protest, scheduled for 15 March. Again, there were protest marches in a very large number of cities; and again, those protests were largest in Italy and Spain. However, the turnout was much less than the month before; estimates of the crowd in Washington, DC, for example, being only around 20,000–25,000.[43] The war itself began on 20 March.

Following the outbreak of war, other actions developed to maintain the process of creating contradictions with the dominant 'war on terror' discourse. The Washington, DC, based Institute for Policy Studies was one of many educational establishments around the world that organised a 'teach in', in a deliberate attempt to echo popular resistance to the Vietnam War some forty years earlier.[44] Another was held at Columbia University.[45] A third was held in April at Georgia

[42] See BBC, 'Millions join global anti-war protests' *BBC News*, 17 February 2003, at http://news.bbc.co.uk/1/hi/world/europe/2765215.stm [2/2003]. There is a tale setting out estimated attendances at NationMaster.com's *Encyclopedia* at http://www.nationmaster.com/encyclopedia/Global-protests-against-war-on-Iraq #January_16.2C_2002 [2–7/2005].

[43] Assessment of the Associated Press, cited in NationMaster.com's *Encyclopedia*.

[44] Institute for Policy Studies, 'National teach in on Iraq', at George Washington University, 24 March 2003, at http://www.ips-dc.org/iraq/teach-in/index.htm [6/2005].

[45] See Gary Sick, 'Teach in, Iraq, etc.', Middle East news, Campus Watch, at http://www.campus-watch.org/article/id/612 [6/2005].

Tech.[46] The protest may have gone from the streets into the classroom, but this was all part of the process of generating new meaning.

The challenges of the alternative narrative was powerfully communicated culturally. Above all, this was a task undertaken through pop music. John Mellencamp's 'Washington' articulated the 'no war for oil' themes:

> And he wants to fight with many
> And he says it's not for oil
> He sent out the National Guard
> To police the world
> From Baghdad to Washington
>
> What is the thought process
> To take a human's life
> What would be the reason
> To think that this is right
> From heaven to Washington
> From Jesus Christ to Washington[47]

Mellencamp managed to mix together the themes of war for oil, an imperial America, the immorality of war, and the influence of evangelism on the administration in a few short lines. In a similar vein, REM wrote a song entitled 'Last Straw', which began with this verse:

> As I raise my head to broadcast my objection
> As your latest triumph draws the final straw
> Who died and lifted you up to perfection?
> And what silenced me is written into law.[48]

In this, the triumphalism and the ruthlessness of the administration – both in terms of the approaching war and in stifling dissent through the USA Patriot Act – were clearly articulated, as again was the influence of evangelism. The Beastie Boys song, 'In a World Gone Mad', released in March 2003, articulated powerfully the 'no war for oil' message. They focused more on profit than God as motivation when they sang:

> First the 'War On Terror' now war on Iraq
> We're reaching a point where we can't turn back

46 Link to the audio record at http://www.isye.gatech.edu/~tg/teach-in/ [6/2005].
47 http://www.inlyrics.com/lyrics/J/John%20Mellencamp/154880.html [7/2005].
48 http://www.lyrics007.com/R.E.M.%20Lyrics/Last%20Straw%20Lyrics.html [7/2005].

Let's lose the guns and let's lose the bombs
And stop the corporate contributions that their [sic] built upon
Well I'll be sleeping on your speeches 'til I start to snore
'Cause I won't carry guns for an oil war[49]

In 'Self-Evident', Ani DiFranco sang of the second American 9/11 and its use by the administration as an excuse to wage war around the world. After a verse on the attacks themselves, she continues:

so fierce and ingenious
a poetic specter so far gone
that every jackass newscaster was struck
dumb and stumbling
over 'oh my god' and 'this is unbelievable' and on and on
and i'll tell you what, while we're at it
you can keep the pentagon
keep the propaganda
keep each and every tv
that's been trying to convince me
to participate
in some prep school punk's plan to perpetuate retribution . . .[50]

Lenny Kravitz wrote the song 'We Want Peace', performed with a number of musicians from the Arab world. 'There won't be peace if we don't try', sang Kravitz.[51] That track and others, such as 'March of Death' by Zack de la Rocha and DJ Shadow, however, were designed for distribution via the internet; they were not likely to attract air time on mainstream radio and television stations.[52] A new website was started for this purpose – www.protest-records.com – which illustrated the point: its home page image was of a ribbon in red, white and blue with the words 'Support Subversion' written on it. It was hardly designed to play to the mainstream in the United States.

However, in contrast to these 'street' and 'subversive' songs and methods of distribution stood the contribution of Madonna. Her single 'American Life' contained lyrics that were not those of war and peace, still less those of 'no war for oil', but were about the American dream

49 http://www.sing365.com/music/lyric.nsf/In-A-World-Gone-Mad-lyrics-Beastie-Boys/8F4A37F3DF9AD8A948256CF00005B084 [9/2005].
50 http://www.peace-not-war.org/Music/AniDiFranco/ [9/2005].
51 http://www.lennykravitz.com/rockthevote/index_popup.asp [7/2005].
52 http://www.zackdelarocha.com/ [9/2005].

of fame and success, and how they can lead to emptiness. Nevertheless, the song was produced with a video that contained strong images: of explosions and aircraft dropping bombs; of children's faces; of Madonna herself in uniform, in front of the Stars and Stripes. The video, though, was not to be shown, but was instead withdrawn by the artist, who said that 'It was filmed before the war started, and I do not believe it is appropriate to air it at this time.'[53] Fear of being seen as anti-war during the fighting would not, presumably, have helped sales. And this rather demonstrates the power of the 'war on terror' discourse, and its connection to the war in Iraq, in American society.

In similar vein, the country group the Dixie Chicks – Grammy winners, singers of the National Anthem at the Super Bowl – provoked controversy when one member of the group, Natalie Maines, said to an anti-war crowd in London on 10 March 2003 that she was ashamed that the President was from Texas, her home state. While this got a cheer in London, it caused outrage in the United States. Apologies on 12 and 14 March did not help. Clear Channel Communications, owners of some 1,200 radio stations, and 30 television stations, banned the playing of their records. In a scene that would have been familiar to Montag, the firefighter in *Fahrenheit 451*, piles of Dixie Chick records were collected and destroyed by a bulldozer in Louisiana on 'Dixie Chicks Destruction Day'.[54] Clear Channel Communications had similarly banned some tracks after 11 September 2001, because they might be 'inappropriate' to the public mood. Reportedly, unacceptable songs included Louis Armstrong's 'What a Wonderful World' and John Lennon's 'Imagine'.[55]

[53] http://www.cs.rpi.edu/~kennyz/madonna_lyrics/american_life.html#americanlife. Images of the video are at http://www.thememoryhole.org/arts/american-life.htm. Report by Lia Haberman, 'Madonna's antiwar anthem', 11 February 2003, at http://www.eonline.com/News/Items/0,1,11265,00.html. On the video's withdrawal, see, 'Madonna yanks controversial, "American life" video', *MTV News*, 31 March 2003, at http://www.mtv.com/news/articles/1470876/20030331/madonna.jhtml?headlines=true [all websites 7/2005].

[54] Paul Krugman, *The Great Unraveling: Losing our Way in the New Century* (New York: W. W. Norton, 2004), pp. 290–1. On 'Destruction Day' see 'The Dixie Chicks get criticized for "un-American" Remark', File Room, at http://www.thefileroom.org/html/647.html [9/2005].

[55] From Wikipedia; see http://en.wikipedia.org/wiki/List_of_songs_deemed_inappropriate_by_Clear_Channel_following_the_September_11%2C_2001_attacks [9/2005].

To communicate the message, humour was at the core of the 'no war for oil' discourse in the United States. Activists competed with each other to produce the most amusing one liner. Examples include: 'How did our oil get under their sand?'; 'The only thing we have to fear is Bush himself'; 'Read between the pipelines'; and 'It's the oil, stupid.'[56] More controversially, 'UN Secretary General Kofi Annan says he can think of no reason to attack Iraq right now. I can think of five off the top of my head: Shell, Exxon, Mobil, Texaco and BP.'[57] This joke was later to enter the mainstream when retold on television by Jay Leno.

What was important here was not just the mechanisms of protest, but its discursive impact. Many different groups came together in the global protests: communists, trade unionists, pro-Palestinian groups, various organisations claiming 'Islamic' natures, as well as peace activists. They had different motives, different means of campaigning. However, together, across these different factions and across different countries, an alternative narrative to that on the 'war on terror' had been constructed through the middle and end of 2002 that connected the disparate groups, and the protests were means of communicating that alternative narrative to a global audience. Early 2003 was truly a time of a clash of meta-narratives.

For the protestors, the key narrative was not the 'war on terror' but 'no war for oil'. Central to this was a challenge to the foundational myth of 9/11, articulated by giving prominence to groups such as September 11th Families For Peaceful Tomorrows. This was a grouping of those who had lost family members in the attacks of 11 September 2001, but who were prepared to campaign against the war in Iraq. They legitimised protest, made it acceptable in America to argue for a different narrative, safe in the knowledge that a new narrative was not being built on the American deaths of that day. Some of those families had travelled to Iraq in January 2003, to publicise their view that a war would be wrong.[58] Visible in Baghdad, their presence

[56] From *Political Humor* at http://politics.faxtoons.com/jokes/antiwarslogans.php [6/2005]. Among others, the references were to Roosevelt's phrase 'all we have to fear is fear itself'; George Bush senior's 'read my lips' in the 1988 presidential election campaign; and 'it's the economy stupid', the line created for Bill Clinton in his presidential campaign against George Bush.

[57] Cosmic Iguana site at http://www.cosmiciguana.com/archives/2003/04/more_ iraq_jokes.html [6/2005].

[58] See 'September 11th families for peaceful tomorrows', at http://www.witherspoonsociety.org/02-12/9_11_families.htm [6/2005].

in the crowd in New York, protesting against the war on 15 February, was even more powerful.[59] One of the most dramatic examples was in a confrontation on *Fox News* between Bill O'Reilly and Jeremy Glick, who was speaking against war in Iraq as a member of a family who had lost loved ones in the attacks of 11 September 2001:

O'REILLY: I don't want to – I don't want to debate world politics with you.
GLICK: Well, why not? This is about politics!
O'REILLY: Because, number one: I don't really care what you think.
GLICK: Well, okay.
O'REILLY: You're . . . your're . . . you're . . . uh . . . I want . . . I want –
GLICK: But you do care, because ... the reason why you care is –
O'REILLY: No I don't.
GLICK: – you evoke 9-11 –
O'REILLY: Here's why I care –
GLICK: – to rationalize –
O'REILLY: Here's why I care –
GLICK: Let me finish. You evoke 9-11 to rationalize everything from domestic plunder to imperialist aggression worldwide. You evoke, you evoke sympathy –
O'REILLY: Okay, that's a bunch –
GLICK: – with the 9-11 families –
O'REILLY: That's a bunch of crap. I've done more for the 9-11 families by their own admission – I've done more for them than you will ever *hope* to do.[60]

September 11th Families For Peaceful Tomorrows was important in making it possible to speak about alternative narratives; but those alternatives still had to be built. 'No war for oil' was the core of the protest.

That the war was about controlling oil was axiomatic to the discourse. As Brendan O'Neill put it, ' "It's all about oil." Those four words are often used to denounce the planned attack on Iraq. For many in the anti-war movement, the idea that the "Bushies" plan to invade the Gulf to get their greasy hands on more oil has become an article of faith, an unquestionable truth repeated like a mantra.'[61] It was a line that the great liberal

[59] See 'New Yorkers join anti-war protests', *BBC News*, 15 February 2003, at http://news.bbc.co.uk/1/hi/world/americas/2766917.stm [6/2005].

[60] At http://www.rotten.com/library/bio/entertainers/pundits/bill-oreilly/ [6/2005].

[61] Brendan O'Neill, 'Being antiwar isn't about the oil', *Christian Science Monitor*, 23 January 2003, at http://www.csmonitor.com/2003/0123/p09s02-coop.html [6/2005].

intellectuals of American culture articulated fully. Gore Vidal argued that 'The true motivations are that the government is in the hands of oil and gas people . . . To invent a war means that you've become a wartime president, and you can suspend much if not all of the Bill of Rights . . . Having more or less conquered Afghanistan we want to conquer Iraq, all with incredible powers for the junta in Washington.'[62] Noam Chomsky described the context of the approaching war as follows:

> Iraq has the second largest oil reserves in the world. It has always been likely that sooner or later, the US would try to restore this enormous prize to western control, meaning now US control, denying privileged access to others. But those considerations have held for years. 9-11 offered new opportunities to pursue these goals under the pretext of a "war on terror" – thin pretexts, but probably sufficient for propaganda purposes.[63]

Bob Herbert, the *New York Times* columnist and former NBC presenter, argued that 'The war against Iraq has become one of the clearest examples ever of the influence of the military-industrial complex . . .'[64] Barbra Streisand – in her activist guise – faxed Democrat Dick Gephardt a reminder to attack the vested interests in the administration: 'How can we ignore the obvious influence on the Bush Administration of such special interests as the oil industry, the chemical companies, the logging industry, the defense contractors, the mining industry, and the automobile industry, just to name a few? Many of these industries, run by big Republican donors and insiders, clearly have much to gain if we go to war against Iraq.'[65] Ralph Nader, the consumer rights activist, environmentalist and presidential candidate, was vocal in developing the 'no war for oil' discourse.[66] 'Despite well-known ties to Big Oil, Bush administration officials have managed

[62] Gore Vidal 'Dreaming war: blood for oil and the Cheney-Bush junta', an interview in *USA Today*, 4 February 2003.

[63] Michael Albert, 'Interview with Noam Chomsky about US war plans', *Znet*, 29 August 2002, at http://www.zmag.org/content/showarticle.cfm?SectionID =15&ItemID=2422 [6/2005].

[64] Bob Herbert, 'Spoils of war', *Liberty Mulch*, 10 April 2003, at http://www.libertymulch.org/articles/030410_herbert_bob.html [6/2005].

[65] The fax is reproduced at http://www.drudgereportarchives.com/data/2002/10/01/20021001_025934_strei1.htm [6/2005].

[66] His 2004 presidential election site is http://www.votenader.org/issues/index.php?cid=17 [7/2005]. Nader won 97,000 votes in Florida in the 2000 election, one decided by Bush's victory in that state by 537 votes.

to keep a straight face as they insist that the drive to war against Iraq is motivated only by an effort to eliminate weapons of mass destruction and establish democracy . . .', he stated. 'It is not credible that there would be such a strong push for war if there were no oil in Iraq. Oil is power and this is in significant measure a struggle over that power.'[67] This legitimised demonstrations against gas/petrol stations in the United States as part of the campaign against the war; local stations were outposts of the corporate energy giants that were directly responsible for the Iraq war, in the 'no war for oil' discourse.[68]

That the war was about oil was a key foundational belief for many of those who sought a new policy programme from the emerging socially constructed crisis of the war in Iraq. Lew Rockwell had made the link in February 2002, just five months after the attacks of 11 September 2001.

> To what lengths will the Bush administration, which everyone knows is the muscle end of the domestic oil industry, go to pursue its desire for more production? To war, perhaps? Plenty of dissidents out there doubt that the overthrow of the Taliban and the war on terror generally are about justice for terrorists and security for the Americans. Rather, like the War on Iraq before it, this war is really about securing the profits of American oil companies doing business internationally.[69]

Eight months after Rockwell, Maria Elena Martinez and Joshua Karliner wrote for the campaigning organisation CorpWatch:

> we seem to be perched at the edge of an abyss from which we risk spiraling into a never-ending cycle of war, terrorism, and the evisceration of our democratic rights. Why is Washington risking a morass that might plague the nation and the world for the foreseeable future? There are no simple or complete answers. But one thing is patently obvious. It's a three-letter word: OIL.[70]

67 Statement by Ralph Nader, 4 February 2003, at http://www.nader.org/releases/020403.html [6/2005].

68 Many organised by No War for Oil – see press release at http://targetoil.com/article.php?id=43 [6/2005]. Also see Brian Keogh, 'Anti war activists target gas stations', *Chicago Tribune*, 5 February 2003.

69 Llewellyn Rockwell, 'War for oil?', 27 February 2002, at http://www.lewrockwell.com/rockwell/warforoil.html [9/2004].

70 Maria Elena Martinez and Joshua Karliner, 'Iraq and the axis of oil', 23 October 2002, at http://corpwatch.org/article.php?id=4508 [6/2005].

Some saw personal motivations in this for the Bush family, while others saw it as part of a wider imperialist urge.[71] No what matter the origin, though, of the urge to war – its target was acquisition of the oil reserves of Iraq. Of course, a policy programme followed from this in the 'no war for oil' discourse: 'But while Exxon and Unocal drool at the prospect of how they can best divie up the loot from what may later be known as History's greatest armed robbery, it's time the rest of us pause to think outside the box.'[72] That meant putting different values to the fore: peace, cooperation and the environment.

A second element of the 'no war for oil' discourse focused on the loss of life inherent in any war for oil in Iraq. In response to President Bush's speech in the moment immediately before the beginning of the war, Leslie Cagan, co-chair of the New York based organisation United for Peace and Justice, declared:

> Of course, the President did not explain what unleashing the most powerful and deadly armed force in human history will mean to the children of Iraq. He did not speak of the hundreds of thousands of innocent people the UN estimates will die in this attack. He did not speak of the ways the Iraqi people will suffer, or the potential dangers to the young US servicemen and women already in the region. He did not mention the devastation and horror of war or its impact on our own lives here at home.[73]

Indeed, the moral revulsion at the loss of life in any war – civilians in the aftermath, as much as civilians and military during the conflict – was a powerful element in the argument. In September 2002, Representative Cynthia McKinney wrote that 'This war, like all wars, will be brutal and will leave many American and Iraqi families

[71] One example was John Le Carré: 'George W. Bush, 1978–84: senior executive, Arbusto Energy/Bush Exploration, an oil company; 1986–90: senior executive of the Harken oil company. Dick Cheney, 1995–2000: chief executive of the Halliburton oil company. Condoleezza Rice, 1991–2000: senior executive with the Chevron oil company, which named an oil tanker after her. And so on.' In 'The United States of America has gone mad', *The Times*, 15 January 2003.

[72] Stuart H. Rodman, 'Iraqi oil not enough for US: last days of America', *Culture Change*, 20 (Winter 2002/3), at http://www.culturechange.org/issue20/Last%20days%20of%20America.htm [6/2005].

[73] Leslie Cagan on 18 March 2003, at http://www.unitedforpeace.org/article.php?id=1404 [6/2005].

mourning the loss of their children.'[74] She went on to talk about oil, but put human loss first. In that same month, Peace Action published a pamphlet concerned with arguments to prevent the war in Iraq that did not mention oil, but instead focused entirely on civilian deaths.[75] Stephen Cleghorn, who had helped found the organisation Military Families Speak Out, articulated the fear of the loss of American loved ones in war, as well as the killing of Iraqis, in a speech in February 2003.[76] How could such mass killing be contemplated? As Greenpeace political advisor Steve Sawyer put it, capturing the essence of the protestors' anger, 'If people wanted the world to be ruled by the cowboy with the biggest guns, the UN wouldn't have been created in the first place . . .'[77] And the policy programme that followed from this was also clear: work with others through the United Nations to reinsert inspectors into Iraq, while committing to work to eliminate all weapons of mass destruction, no matter who owned them.

The 'no war for oil' discourse therefore had established some of the principles for taking advantage of the socially constructed crisis over the impending war in Iraq. It was able to attack the 'war on terror' at its roots: speaking for a community – the families who lost loved ones on September 11th – when evidence to the contrary could be presented. And it was able to construct core critiques – that it was a war for oil, and that large numbers of Iraqis, and Americans, would be killed – while articulating it powerfully ('no blood for oil') verbally and in images, and in mobilising a large number of supporters. There was a policy programme contained within the discourse, focusing on the United Nations, international cooperation and the environment. The 'no war for oil' discourse was taken very seriously by many who saw it as fundamentally threatening and, therefore, as fundamentally misguided. Charles Kohlhaas, for example, wrote that 'Nothing demonstrates the political and moral bankruptcy of the American liberal left

[74] Representative Cynthia McKinney (D – Georgia), 'Another oil war', *CounterPunch*, 23 September 2002, at http://www.counterpunch.org/mckinney0922.html [6/2005].

[75] See 'Stop an Attack on Iraq', Peace Action, September 2002, at http://www.peace-action.org/home/iraq/stopattack.pdf [7/2005].

[76] Stephen Cleghorn, 'On the wings of a lie', Military Families Speak Out, at http://www.mfso.org/ under 'Speeches' [6/2005].

[77] Cited in 'Greenpeace calls on UN members to unite for peace', Greenpeace, 12 March 2003, at http://www.greenpeace.org/usa/press/releases/greenpeace-calls-on-u-n-membe [6/2005].

more clearly than the current attempt to portray military action against Iraq as "for the oil".'[78] That is, 'no war for oil' lacked common sense; but common sense was only comprehensible from inside the logic of the 'war on terror' discourse. And so serious was the discursive challenge to the 'war on terror' that it became the subject of ridicule: 'We're actually lucky that Cheney never owned a Major League baseball team and that Iraq doesn't have any talented, young players or we'd probably be treated to the "war for baseball" theory by the anti-war left.'[79] Ridicule is a particularly effective tactic for reproducing that which is common sense, and that which is not.

The 'no war for oil' discourse failed. It was unable to take advantage of the national and international crisis over the construction of war in Iraq; it was unable to overthrow the 'war on terror'. To understand why that was so, it is important to focus on the role of key institutions, those that remained committed to an understanding of the world structured through the 'war on terror' discourse, and it is that focus that will be the subject of the next section.

Surviving the crisis: the role of the key institutions

What this protest amounted to was the creation of a socially constructed crisis, an attempt to replace the policy programme, and hence the 'war on terror' as understood in that discourse, by alternatives. The 'war on terror' had held that Iraq was part of the terror networks, and that it had to be disarmed and changed. The policy programme that led to war in Iraq was inherent in the 'war on terror' discourse. Thus, the challenge of the protestors, in seeking to give alternative meaning and hence an alternative policy programme, was a fundamental political and discursive challenge.

At one level, the challenge had succeeded; it created a wider discourse of suspicion about outcomes as well as motives. As Jay Leno put it, 'Now there are reports from Baghdad that officials are taking bribes for favors, giving jobs to their relatives, taking money under the table

[78] Charles A. Kohlhaas, 'War in Iraq: not a "war for oil"', *In the National Interest*, 2:9 (5 March 2003), at http://www.inthenationalinterest.com/Articles/Vol2Issue9/vol2issue9kohlhaas.html [6/2005].

[79] John Hawkins 'Debunking the war for oil theory', *Right Wing News*, undated (though in the period of the winter 2002/3), http://www.rightwingnews.com/john/warforoil.php [6/2005].

from contractors. You know what this means? The war is less than a week old, and already they have an American-style democracy.' And David Letterman quipped, 'And now the really difficult part: We have to rebuild Iraq into a strong and independent nation that will one day hate the United States.'[80]

But that challenge failed: at least, it failed in the sense that it did not overturn the policy programme, nor did it see the collapse of the 'war on terror' discourse. There were a variety of reasons for this, that will be examined in the course of this section. Fundamentally, powerful institutions continued to propagate the 'war on terror', and did not allow space to be used by the 'no war for oil' discourse. Those powerful institutions comprised: the government; the news media; the political opposition; experts in think tanks; and the evangelical Christian movement.

Of course, central to this was the role of government. Particularly in time of war, or the approach thereof, there is a powerful discursive pull to national unity. In the aftermath of the second American 9/11, that demand was widely heeded. Even in response to actions – such as the passing of the USA Patriot Act – that some feared contradicted American claims to liberty, the pull of unity prevailed. Both the totalising effect of the 'war on terror' and the need for national unity were powerfully articulated by Attorney General John Ashcroft in December 2001, in his testimony to the Senate Judiciary Committee.

> To those who pit Americans against immigrants, citizens against non citizens, to those who scare peace-loving people with phantoms of lost liberty, my message is this: Your tactics only aid terrorists for they erode our national unity and diminish our resolve . . . They give ammunition to America's enemies and pause to America's friends. They encourage people of good will to remain silent in the face of evil.[81]

Given that the President had presented a dichotomy – you are either with us or against us – Ashcroft had easily painted any dissent to government policy as pro-terrorist.

[80] Both from *Political Humor*, at http://politicalhumor.about.com/library/blibliraqwarjokes.htm [6/2005].

[81] Testimony, at 'Ashcroft: critics of new terror measures undermine effort', CNN.com, 7 December 2001, at http://archives.cnn.com/2001/US/12/06/inv.ashcroft.hearing/ [7/2005].

Cracks began to appear in that national unity throughout 2002. In March, Democrats asked for clarity on where the 'war on terror' was going. In response, Democrat Senate Majority Leader, Thomas A. Daschle, was ferociously criticised by his opposite number, the Republican Senate Minority Leader, Trent Lott, for undermining national unity: 'How dare Senator Daschle criticize President Bush while we are fighting our war on terrorism, especially when we have troops in the field? He should not be trying to divide our country while we are united', he said.[82] The theme was taken up in parts of the media. Andrew Sullivan, for example, senior editor at *The New Republic* and essayist for *Time,* has also made a reputation for widely read political 'blogging'. In his March 2002 entry, he argued:

> Now, it's official. I don't think it's an accident that the Democrats have launched an attack on the war's direction the day it becomes clear that the recession, even if it existed in the first place, is now history . . . Daschle figures he has no choice but to risk everything to undermine the war in order to gain some political traction against the President . . . Get the picture? The anti-war left is back with a vengeance. And the battle to protect this country has only just begun.[83]

Note the ferocity of the attacks, when Daschle was merely asking about the nature of the strategy, not even critiquing it. In May 2002, reports broke that the White House had received a warning before the attacks of 11 September 2001 had occurred.[84] This produced, of course, a sense that the government had not done all that it might have; and that it had hidden the truth. Some went further, accusing the government of 'knowing much' and 'doing little'.[85] This challenge to the dominant narrative – of a blameless and united America leading a world coalition – was met with a series of warnings from government (aided by elements of the media) that pursuit of this line

[82] Cited in Helen Dewar, 'Lott calls Daschle divisive', *Washington Post*, 1 March 2002.

[83] Andrew Sullivan, 'The Daily Dish', 1 March 2002, at http://andrewsullivan.com/index.php?dish_inc=archives/2002_02_24_dish_archive.html#10254195 [7/2005].

[84] See, for example, Dan Eggen and Bill Miller, 'Bush was told of hijacking dangers', *Washington Post,* 16 May 2002.

[85] See for example, James Ridgeway, 'Knowing much, Bush did little to protect America', *The Village Voice*, 16 May 2002, at http://www.villagevoice.com/news/0221,ridgeway3,34937,6.html [6/2005].

would damage the 'national interest'. Vice President Cheney warned that the Democrats 'need to be very cautious not to seek political advantage by making incendiary suggestions . . .'.[86] Cheney was warning the Democrats to stay with the government, to be loyal and silent. But the issue of what the administration knew in early September 2001 was an important one: a CBS poll showed that a majority of Americans thought that the administration did have information prior to 11 September concerning those attacks (by 50 to 33 per cent), and a smaller majority thought that the President himself had knowledge of those impending attacks (by 43 to 41 per cent).[87]

On CNN's *Crossfire* programme, one of the hosts – Robert Novak – underlined the 'common sense' that the Democrats were lacking by asking questions of the administration. In a question to Senator Durbin, he stated: 'amid the bleating by your leaders, Dick Gephardt and Tom Daschle, about when the President knew what he knew and the stupid question that our introduction asked, could the President connect the dots, there was a voice of Democratic sanity today . . .'[88] He went on to play a clip from Senator Bob Graham, introduced as the chair of the Senate Intelligence Committee (to give added authority) who had dismissed the criticisms of the White House. In all of this, the Democrat's leadership had launched no alternative to the 'war on terror', even though the political heat that was generated might have suggested otherwise.

The media played a significant role as bastions of the 'war on terror' discourse. As the United Nations met to discuss the second resolution, the *New York Post* front cover picture showed the Security Council with the headline: 'UN meets: weasels to hear new Iraq evidence'.[89]

86 Cited in Dana Milbank and Mike Allen, 'An image of invincibility is shaken', *Washington Post*, 17 May 2002.

87 See 'Polls – what did the President know?', *CBS News*, 21 May 2002, at http://www.cbsnews.com/stories/2002/05/21/opinion/polls/main509702.shtml [7/2005].

88 'Who knew what in the Bush administration about a terrorist attack prior to September 11?; Republicans accuse Democrats of playing politics', *CNN Crossfire*, 16 May 2002, at http://transcripts.cnn.com/TRANSCRIPTS/0205/16/cf.00.html [7/2005].

89 See the image in Marcia Marie Larson, 'La vérité derrière le cliché', Spring 2005, at http://international.tamu.edu/eunotes/Spring_2005/marcia-paper-cliche.doc [7/2005].

Those not supporting the move to war – the French, Germans, Russians – were 'weasels', an odd agricultural term for a newspaper in a metropolis such as New York, but one that conveyed the sense of weakness and untrustworthiness. There has been much controversy about the role of Fox News in the coverage of the Iraq war, and in its aftermath. Certainly, Fox glorified in a robust attitude. It was not the case that Fox represents the mainstream in coverage; nor that it achieved majority support from the television viewing general public in the United States. But Fox's news coverage was important in terms of influence, particularly as each of the major networks' evening newscasts had been declining in the ratings over a number of years.[90] However, the absolute number of viewers was not the point. Fox was able to create a wider discursive space for the 'war on terror' by going further, and more strongly, than the administration thought it could. Fox and the administration were close: 'Roger Ailes, the network's chairman, has been advising the Bush administration.'[91] One particular aspect of this was Fox's continued assertions that weapons of mass destruction *had* been found in Iraq, or were about to be used; a clear attempt to drown out the counter perspective of 'no war for oil'. There were a number of examples:

- 19 March: *The Fox Report* anchor Shepard Smith reported that the Iraqis planned to use napalm and other chemical agents against coalition forces.
- 23 March: a number of reports on the channel asserted that a 100-acre facility discovered by coalition forces at An Najaf was a chemical weapons plant.
- 28 March: a *Fox Breaking News* flash reported that the coalition had observed Iraqi soldiers moving large drums which, it asserted, contained chemical agents.
- 7 April: Fox reported that American forces near Baghdad had discovered twenty medium-range missiles containing sarin and mustard gas.

[90] From 14 million viewers for CBS in 1970 down to 5 million by 2004–5; CBS' decline had been the steepest. But over this period, the total number of viewers for all three channels had halved, from some 33 million to around 18 million. Figures from Nielsen Media Research in Peter Johnson, 'The last of the iconic anchors', *USA Today*, 9 August 2005.

[91] Krugman, *Great Unraveling*, p. 281.

- 10 April: a Fox *Breaking News* report was issued of the discovery of weapons-grade plutonium at Al-Tuwaitha. On the same day, Fox reported that a mobile bioweapons lab had been found.[92]

Fox were able to create a position of power within the discourse, one which, according to CNN's high-profile reporter Christine Amanpour, structured reporting of the subsequent war. 'I think the press was muzzled, and I think the press self-muzzled. I'm sorry to say, but certainly television and, perhaps, to a certain extent, my station was intimidated by the administration and its foot soldiers at *Fox News*. And it did, in fact, put a climate of fear and self-censorship, in my view, in terms of the kind of broadcast work we did.'[93] The massive February 2003 protests were reported on *Fox News* as the 'usual protestors' or as 'serial protestors'; to keep up, CNN's website ran the headline 'Antiwar rallies delight Iraq'.[94]

By the time that the war broke out, many were concerned that the media had become too tightly connected with the 'war on terror' discourse. *USA Today* ran a series of excerpts from newspapers and magazines all around the country on 21 March 2003 – the first day after the war began. The common theme was concern that the media would not report the war 'accurately'.[95] Michael Wolff argued that 'the press is overexcited . . . It has converted itself, willy-nilly, into a wartime press corps.'[96]

The discourse had penetrated deeply into the institutions of the media. This was not to say that there were no counter-voices, for there were, as seen above, and many of them articulated aspects of the 'no war for oil' discourse. But they were largely drowned by those who demanded uniformity in the face of the national emergency, that was now to be fought in a second country half a world away from the

[92] This is a combination of the author's observations, supplemented with other records from web blogs – in particular, Dale Steinreich, 'Fibbing it up at Fox', at http://www.lewrockwell.com/orig/steinreich8.html and also at http://www.fbbn.com/cgi-bin/viewnews.cgi?category=18&id=1073891294 [5/2005].

[93] Cited in Peter Johnson, 'Amanpour: CNN practiced self-censorship', *USA Today*, 14 September 2003.

[94] Cited Krugman, *Great Unraveling*, p. 288. The CNN headline was later updated to 'Iraqi government praises rallies'; see http://www.cnn.com/2003/WORLD/meast/02/16/sprj.irq.protests/ [9/2005].

[95] 'A lot is at stake for the media', *USA Today*, 21 March 2003.

[96] Michael Wolff, 'Behind the lines', *New York Metro*, 31 March 2003, at http://www.newyorkmetro.com/nymetro/news/culture/features/n_8525/ [7/2005].

nation. Michael Kelly, for example, in *The Atlantic Monthly*, constructed a case in which all those who were not fully supportive of the war in Iraq were dangerous, and to be ridiculed.[97]

That the media had a powerful impact can be seen in a series of public opinion polls. Some 46 per cent of Americans sampled in a poll in March 2002 supported a ground war against Iraq.[98] By the summer, 86 per cent agreed that a nuclear-armed Iraq would be a 'critical threat' to the United States.[99] Ari Berman noted that 'In a Jan. 7 [2003] Knight Ridder/Princeton Research poll, 44% of respondents said they thought "most" or "some" of the Sept. 11, 2001, hijackers were Iraqi citizens.'[100] Of course, the correct answer to the survey question was 'none', which was given by only 17 per cent of respondents. Iraq had been constructed as a threat to the United States. A poll in December 2002 produced the following response:

'If Iraq has or if it were to obtain nuclear weapons, do you believe Iraq would attempt to use them against the United States?'[101]

Yes	*No*	*Not sure*
73%	17%	10%

An Iraq armed with weapons of mass destruction was seen to be a threat to America by three-quarters of its population; nearly half of America thought that Iraq had been implicated in the second American 9/11, while a third did not know, and would be tempted to look for authoritative statements, not least in the media. The protests over 'no

[97] Michael Kelly, 'What now? Developments, encouraging and otherwise', *The Atlantic Monthly*, March 2003, at http://www.theatlantic.com/doc/prem/200303/kelly [7/2005].

[98] Some 50% were against. CNN/*USA Today*/Gallup poll, 22–4 March 2002, http://www.pollingreport.com/iraq8.htm [7/2005].

[99] A Chicago Council on Foreign Relations poll; cited in 'Conflict with Iraq', *Americans and the World*, at http://www.americans-world.org/digest/regional_issues/Conflict_Iraq/weapons_MassDest.cfm [7/2005].

[100] Ari Berman, 'Poll suggests media failure in pre-war coverage', *Editor and Publisher*, 26 March 2003, at http://www.editorandpublisher.com/eandp/news/article_display.jsp?vnu_content_id=1848576 [7/2005]. The question asked was: 'As far as you know, how many of the September 11th terrorist hijackers were Iraqi citizens: most of them, some of them, just one, or none?': most 21%; some 23%; just one 6%; none 17%; don't know 33%. See Knight Ridder, 'Poll conducted by Princeton Survey Research Associates', 3–6 January 2003, at http://www.pollingreport.com/iraq8.htm [7/2005].

[101] FOX News/Opinion Dynamics Poll, 3–4 December 2002, at http://www.pollingreport.com/iraq8.htm [7/2005].

war for oil' were therefore seen broadly as futile by Americans. In a snap poll taken after the 15 February demonstrations, CNN attracted 230,000 voters in the United States, 63 per cent of whom believed that the protests would make no difference in the decisions to go to war.[102]

The 'war on terror' discourse was able to survive the socially constructed crisis of going to war in Iraq, and was able to continue with the policy programme despite the challenge of the alternative 'no war for oil' discourse, due to its articulation in government and in much of the media. It is true that there were high-profile supporters for the 'no war for oil' campaign amongst 'celebrities', and it is true that some journalists – such as ABC's Peter Jennings – were singled out for criticism for being anti-war.[103] However, the opinion polls showed the power of the persuasiveness of the 'war on terror' discourse throughout American society.

Yet for the grip of the discourse to be so strong, it also had to be represented in other institutions; and, indeed, it was. The Democrats, as already seen in this chapter, were tempted to find political advantage from *within* the 'war on terror' discourse, and many spoke powerfully to this theme in the United States Congress. Congressman Dick Gephardt, for example, felt able – and felt it necessary – to declare in response to an administration draft resolution for Congress to authorise the use of force against Iraq, that 'I share the administration's goals in dealing with Iraq and its weapons of mass destruction.'[104] Senator Dianne Feinstein argued in October 2002 that 'While the distance between the United States and Iraq is great, Saddam Hussein's ability to use his chemical and biological weapons against us is not constrained by geography – it can be accomplished in a number of different ways – which is what makes this threat so real and persuasive.'[105] Indeed, Democrats lined up to demonstrate their 'reasonableness', to

[102] 'Cities jammed in worldwide protests over war in Iraq', CNN.com, 17 February 2003, at http://www.cnn.com/2003/US/02/15/sprj.irq.protests.main/ [6/2005].

[103] See, for example, 'World News Tonight with Peter Jennings: 20 years of liberal bias', Media Research Center, at http://www.mediaresearch.org/Profiles/jennings/welcome.asp [7/2005].

[104] Congressman Dick Gephardt (D-Iowa), 'Congressional reaction to Iraq resolution is mixed', CNN.com, 19 September 2002, at http://www.cnn.com/2002/ALLPOLITICS/09/19/bush.congress.iraq/ [6/2005].

[105] Senator Dianne Feinstein (D-California), 'The right course on Iraq', speech to the Senate, 10 October 2002, at http://www.senate.gov/~feinstein/Releases02/r-iraq10.htm [7/2005].

show that they understood the 'common sense' of the situation. Senator Carl Levin declared that 'We begin with the common belief that Saddam Hussein is a tyrant and a threat to the peace and stability of the region. He has ignored the mandates of the United Nations and is building weapons of mass destruction and the means of delivering them.'[106] Senator John D. Rockefeller said:

There is unmistakable evidence that Saddam Hussein is working aggressively to develop nuclear weapons and will likely have nuclear weapons within the next five years. And that may happen sooner if he can obtain access to enriched uranium from foreign sources – something that is not that difficult in the current world. We also should remember we have always underestimated the progress Saddam has made in development of weapons of mass destruction.[107]

In the House, Congressman Henry A. Waxman argued:

Whether one agrees or disagrees with the administration's policy towards Iraq, I don't think there can be any question about Saddam's conduct. He has systematically violated, over the course of the past 11 years, every significant UN resolution that has demanded that he disarm and destroy his chemical and biological weapons, and any nuclear capacity . . . He lies and cheats; he snubs the mandate and authority of international weapons inspectors; and he games the system to keep buying time against enforcement of the just and legitimate demands of the United Nations, the Security Council, the United States and our allies. Those are simply the facts.[108]

Senator Hillary Rodham Clinton agreed:

In the four years since the inspectors left, intelligence reports show that Saddam Hussein has worked to rebuild his chemical and biological weapons stock, his missile delivery capability, and his nuclear program. He has also given aid, comfort, and sanctuary to terrorists, including Al-Qaeda members

106 Senator Carl Levin (D-Michigan), speech to the Senate, 19 September 2002, at http://levin.senate.gov/floor/091902cs1.htm [10/2002].

107 Senator John D. Rockefeller IV (D-West Virginia), speech to the Senate 10 October 2002, at http://rockefeller.senate.gov/2002/flrstmt10102002.html [10/2002].

108 Congressman Henry A. Waxman (D-California), 'Statement regarding the possible war with Iraq', 10 October 2002, at http://www.waxman.house.gov/news_files/news_statements_res_iraq_10_10_02.htm [10/2002].

. . . if left unchecked, Saddam Hussein will continue to increase his capacity to wage biological and chemical warfare, and will keep trying to develop nuclear weapons . . . Now this much is undisputed.[109]

Democrats agreed with the perception being constructed that Iraq was a threat to the United States, and that this threat had to be met with the use of American force.

Those who were to be entrusted with responsibility for the Democrats' presidential campaign also endorsed the 'war on terror' discourse. Senator John Kerry, for example, worked hard to show that he knew where the 'common sense' lay.

[W]ithout question, we need to disarm Saddam Hussein. He is a brutal, murderous dictator, leading an oppressive regime. We all know the litany of his offenses. He presents a particularly grievous threat because he is so consistently prone to miscalculation. He miscalculated an eight-year war with Iran. He miscalculated the invasion of Kuwait. He miscalculated America's response to that act of naked aggression. He miscalculated the result of setting oil rigs on fire. He miscalculated the impact of sending scuds into Israel and trying to assassinate an American President. He miscalculated his own military strength. He miscalculated the Arab world's response to his misconduct. And now he is miscalculating America's response to his continued deceit and his consistent grasp for weapons of mass destruction . . . So the threat of Saddam Hussein with weapons of mass destruction is real . . .[110]

Kerry's words were powerful: Iraq was constructed as an enemy, and a threatening and irrational one at that. The world community recognised this. And the threat was immediate. Kerry's future running mate, Senator John Edwards, echoed these themes:

Saddam Hussein's regime represents a grave threat to America and our allies, including our vital ally, Israel. For more than two decades, Saddam Hussein has sought weapons of mass destruction through every available means. We know that he has chemical and biological weapons. He has already used them against his neighbors and his own people, and is trying

109 Senator Hillary Rodham Clinton (D-New York), speech on the floor of the Senate, 10 October 2002, at http://clinton.senate.gov/speeches/iraq_101002.html [7/2005].

110 Senator John Kerry (D-Massachusetts), 'Statement', 23 January 2003, at http://www.johnkerry.com/site/PageServer?pagename=spc_2003_0123 [2/2003].

to build more. We know that he is doing everything he can to build nuclear weapons, and we know that each day he gets closer to achieving that goal.[111]

Some Democrats were even happy to connect Iraq and terrorism, just as in the statements of its administration. Consider, for example, the words of Senator Joseph Lieberman:

As we survey the landscape of threats to our security in the years ahead, the greatest are terrorists like Al Qaeda and rogue regimes like Saddam Hussein's. Saddam hates America and Americans and is working furiously to accumulate deadly weapons of mass destruction . . . We need not stretch to imagine nightmare scenarios in which Saddam makes common cause with the terrorists who want to kill us Americans and destroy our way of life.[112]

None of these were the sentiments of those on the streets demonstrating against the approaching war in Iraq.

This is not to say that there was unanimity between the White House and the Democrats. The candidate who presented himself as offering the Democrats a radical alternative for the presidential nomination, Governor Howard Dean, was on board with the key elements of the discourse.

There's no question that Saddam Hussein is a threat to the United States and to our allies. The question is, is he an immediate threat? The president has not yet made the case for that. I think it may very well be . . . that we are going to end up in Iraq . . . It really is important to involve our allies, to bring other people into the coalition, to get a decent resolution out of the UN Security Council.[113]

Democrats who were looking for alternatives wanted to conduct the 'war on terror' more efficiently; essentially the issue was to have international support for the attack on Iraq. As Al Gore put it:

To begin with, I believe we should focus our efforts first and foremost against those who attacked us on September 11th and have thus far gotten away

111 Senator John Edwards (D-North Carolina), speech to the Senate, 10 October 2002, at http://edwards.senate.gov/statements/20021010_iraq.html [10/2002].

112 Senator Joseph Lieberman (D-Connecticut), speech to the Senate, 13 September 2002, at http://www.senate.gov/~lieberman/speeches/02/09/2002913614.html [10/2002].

113 Howard Dean, interviewed by Bob Scheffer on 'Face the nation', *CBS News*, 29 September 2002, at http://www.cbsnews.com/stories/2002/09/30/ftn/main523726.shtml [7/2005].

with it. The vast majority of those who sponsored, planned and implemented the cold blooded murder of more than 3,000 Americans are still at large, still neither located nor apprehended, much less punished and neutralized. I do not believe that we should allow ourselves to be distracted from this urgent task simply because it is proving to be more difficult and lengthy than predicted. Great nations persevere and then prevail. They do not jump from one unfinished task to another. We are perfectly capable of staying the course in our war against Osama Bin Laden and his terrorist network, while simultaneously taking those steps necessary to build an international coalition to join us in taking on Saddam Hussein in a timely fashion.[114]

This is worth some focus. Gore was arguing for an intensification of the use of force in Afghanistan, and presumably the northern parts of Pakistan, to destroy the Taliban and al-Qaeda resistance, and then, a move on to 'taking on Saddam Hussein'. This is hardly a challenge to the 'war on terror' discourse. Rather, as with Dean's comments, it was a call to implement the policy programme contained in the 'war on terror' more efficiently. Engaging enemies sequentially was a prescription not that far from a conventional neoconservative's war book.

This appeal to 'efficiency' was a hallmark of the Democrat's response. For example, Governor Gary Locke, in the Democrat's response to the 2003 State of the Union speech, declared:

We need allies today in 2003, just as much as we needed them in Desert Storm and just as we needed them on D-Day in 1944, when American soldiers – including my father – fought to vanquish the Nazi threat. We must convince the world that Saddam Hussein is not America's problem alone – he's the world's problem. And we urge President Bush to stay this course for we are far stronger when we stand with other nations than when we stand alone.[115]

Democrat politicians wanted to argue for an amendment in the policy programme – the involvement of the United Nations – not an alternative to it. Of course, politically it would have made a difference had the war in Iraq been conducted with a 'second' United Nations resolution in February 2003. But this was not a radical change in the discourse,

114 Cited in 'Text of Gore speech', 23 September 2002, *USA Today*, at http://www.usatoday.com/news/nation/2002-09-23-gore-text_x.htm [7/2005].

115 Governor Gary Locke (D-Washington), 'Democratic response to President Bush's "State of the Union" address', 28 January 2003, at http://usembassy-australia.state.gov/hyper/2003/0129/epf303.htm [7/2005].

in which the more dangerous world that had been evidenced by the second American 9/11 had to be addressed by overthrowing the government of Iraq. In short, Democrats were still speaking the language of the 'war on terror', not that of the 'no war for oil' discourse. As Bill Maher put it on the opening night of his new series, *Real Time*, broadcast on HBO on 21 February 2003, 'No more whining about the French. At least they're standing up to the Bush administration, which is more than I can say for the Democrats!'[116]

If the Democrats were responsible for at least the reproduction of the 'war on terror' discourse – albeit with a proposed amendment to the policy programme – that discourse was strengthened by 'experts'. The 'expert' voice – that giving authority to those who claim particular knowledge – was important in legitimising particular perspectives. In the United States, 'expertise' lies not only in academia, but also in a variety of think tanks and non-governmental organisations. Some academics called for war. Michael Scott Doran, from Princeton University, writing in *Foreign Affairs* (both key signifiers of 'expertise') argued that 'Unless America is prepared to abandon its position and pull back from the region, as the British did three and a half decades ago, it must carry its struggle against al Qaeda and Saddam to the finish, putting an end to all doubt regarding its resolve.'[117] Think tanks such as the Heritage Foundation published articles that gave the administration's case greater credibility. Iraq 'is a state sponsor of terrorism that is building and obtaining weapons of mass destruction, which could find their way into the hands of terrorists', wrote Baker Spring and Jack Spencer in September 2002.[118] Michael Ledeen of the American Enterprise Institute spoke of

> the 'terror masters': Iran, Iraq, Syria and Saudi Arabia. Without the support of those regimes, the terrorists would be gravely weakened and would become easy prey. The Middle East phase of the war against terrorism must focus on these regimes and, while each country requires a different strategy,

116 Bill Maher, *Real Time*, on HBO, 21 February 2003, cited at http://www.mrc.org/cyberalerts/2003/cyb20030224.asp#3 [7/2005].

117 Michael Scott Doran, 'Palestine, Iraq and American Strategy', *Foreign Affairs*, January/February2003, at http://www.foreignaffairs.org/20030101faessay 10219/michael-scott-doran/palestine-iraq-and-american-strategy.html [7/20 05].

118 Baker Spring and Jack Spencer, 'In post-war Iraq, use military forces to secure vital US interests, not for nation-building', Backgrounder #1589, Heritage Foundation, 25 September 2002, at http://www.heritage.org/Research/MiddleEast/bg1589.cfm [7/2005].

our most lethal weapon will be the people who suffer under the four tyrants.[119]

Perhaps the most important of these institutions during this period was the Project for the New American Century, or PNAC, an organisation founded in 1997 by William Kristol and Robert Kagan. Prior to the election of George W. Bush as President, Dick Cheney, Donald Rumsfeld, Paul Wolfowitz and Richard Armitage were all members, and of course all became important figures in the Bush administration. In *Rebuilding America's Defenses*, published in September 2000, PNAC had argued that 'the need for a substantial American force in the Gulf transcends the issue of the regime of Saddam Hussein', and had spoken of the challenge of Iran, Iraq and North Korea (although without using the phrase 'axis of evil').[120] PNAC had thus seemed to foreshadow some of the policies that the Bush administration would follow after the second American 9/11, and had involved some of the personnel who had created those policies. The key organ of neoconservatism, the *Weekly Standard*, published articles that spoke to the PNAC agenda in a very direct way. Those against the war formed an 'axis of appeasement', while the administration had developed 'the idea of a morally grounded foreign policy that seeks aggressively and unapologetically to advance American principles around the world'.[121] In October 2002, Reuel Marc Grecht wrote an article entitled 'A necessary war' in which he condemned critics of the approaching war with Iraq, instead arguing that 'A war against Iraq will reinforce, not weaken, whatever collective spirit has developed among intelligence and security agencies working against Islamic radicals.'[122]

Think tanks, academics and other organisations therefore reproduced and legitimised the policy programme, and indeed co-produced

[119] Michael Ledeen, 'The real foe is Middle Eastern tyranny', American Enterprise Institute, 24 September 2002, at http://www.aei.org/publications/pubID.14297,filter.all/pub_detail.asp [7/2005].

[120] Project for the New American Century, *Rebuilding America's Defenses*, September 2000, pp. 26, 16, 54 and 87, at http://www.newamericancentury.org/RebuildingAmericasDefenses.pdf [7/2005].

[121] William Kristol, 'The axis of appeasement', *Weekly Standard*, 16 August 2002, pp. 7–8, at http://www.newamericancentury.org/iraq-081602.pdf [7/2005].

[122] Reuel Marc Grecht, 'A necessary war', *Weekly Standard*, 21 October 2002, p. 19, at http://www.newamericancentury.org/iraq-101502.pdf [10/2004].

it. They also delegitimised views critical of the 'war on terror' discourse. Critics could be condemned and their employers called upon to take action against them, as in the attack on the opinions of a number of academic staff at Columbia University in the early part of 2003.[123] The University of California at Berkeley was criticised by Accuracy in Academia for a lack of patriotism in commemorating the second American 9/11.[124] Another organisation, Campus Watch, 'reviews and critiques Middle East studies in North America, with an aim to improving them. The project mainly addresses five problems: analytical failures, the mixing of politics with scholarship, intolerance of alternative views, apologetics, and the abuse of power over students.'[125] Daniel Pipes, a key figure in the organisation, asked in November 2002 'Why do so many professors hate America?' He argued that common sense dictated that Iraq was a danger, and the only question revolved around the role of the United Nations. 'Visit an American university, however, and you'll often enter a topsy-turvy world in which professors consider the United States (not Iraq) the problem and oil (not nukes) the issue.'[126] In such ways, the 'no war for oil' discourse was further undermined.

A final institution in which the 'war on terror' discourse penetrated was that of the church. Care must be taken here: much church opinion was against the war in Iraq. The World Council of Churches passed a resolution against the impending war in February 2003, a resolution shared by three American churches.[127] And even amongst the evangelical community, support amongst church leaders for war was muted.[128]

[123] See Daniel Pipes and Jonathan Calt Harris, 'Columbia versus America', a letter published in the *New York Post*, 1 April 2003, at http://www.campus-watch.org/article/id/619 [7/2005].

[124] Sara Russo, 'Berkeley rejects patriotism on 9/11', Accuracy in Academia, October 2002, at http://www.academia.org/campus_reports/2002/october_2002_1.html [7/2005].

[125] Campus Watch, mission statement at http://www.campus-watch.org/about.php [7/2005].

[126] Daniel Pipes, 'Why do so many professors hate America?' published in the *New York Post* and the *Jerusalem Post*, 18 November 2002, at http://hnn.us/articles/1013.html [7/2005].

[127] See 'Church leaders united against war in Iraq', World Council of Churches, 5 February 2003, at http://www.ploughshares.ca/CONTENT/BUILD%20PEACE/WCCPressReleaseFeb5.html [7/2005].

[128] See Bill Broadway, 'Evangelicals' voices speak softly about Iraq', *Washington Post*, 25 January 2003.

Yet at the popular level, high-profile evangelicals supported the case for war in discursively powerful ways. The television evangelist Jerry Falwell labelled the Prophet Mohammed (PBUH) a 'terrorist' on the national CBS television *60 Minutes* programme.[129] Much of the evangelical community sees a close relationship between America and Israel as a religious duty. For premillennialists, the Second Coming is a reality that may occur at any moment, and it will be Israel that will play a critical role, for Israel has not been 'replaced' by the church in God's plans. An excellent example of this is the organisation Stand for Israel, which has as its purpose 'To mobilize Christians and other people of faith to support the State of Israel, to encourage prayer among all Americans for peace in Jerusalem, and to educate the public about the facts regarding the Middle East and the security of Israel.'[130] There were political manifestations of this premillennialist support for Israel. In April 2002, President Bush urged the Israelis to withdraw from the Palestinian city of Jenin. Fearing that the President was damaging Israeli interests – and thus evangelical *Christian* interests – a rally was held in Washington which, with only one week's notice, drew a crowd of perhaps over 50,000.[131] The President was subjected to around 100,000 email protests from evangelical Christians.[132]

This evangelical commitment to Israel shaped particular views of Islam. Some of these were well expressed by General William Boykin, later to be involved in the prison abuse scandal in Iraq after the war, from his position as deputy undersecretary of defense for intelligence. Preaching in a church in Oregon in June 2002, Boykin told the congregation: 'Why do they hate us? Why do they hate us so much? Ladies and gentlemen, the answer to that is because we're a Christian nation, because our foundation and our roots are Judeo-Christian. Did I say Judeo-Christian? Yes. Judeo-Christian. That means we've got a commitment to Israel. That means it's a commitment we're never going to

129 Cited in, for example, Richard N. Ostling 'Falwell calls Muhammed "terrorist"', 3 October 2002, referring to the CBS programme to be shown on 10 October, at http://www.beliefnet.com/story/114/story_11456_1.html [6/2005].

130 The mission statement is at http://www.standforisrael.org/ [7/2005].

131 See Steve Twomey, 'Thousands rallied on mall to support Israel', *Washington Post*, 15 April 2002.

132 See, for example, Donald Wagner, 'The Evangelical Jewish alliance', *The Christian Century*, 28 June 2003, pp. 20–4, at http://www.religion-online.org/showarticle.asp?title=2717 [7/2005].

abandon.'[133] In January 2004, preaching to the congregation in Daytona, Florida, Boykin recalled his service in Somalia, and how his unit had failed to apprehend Osman Atto, who was held to be financing much of the violence in Mogadishu. Atto was interviewed on CNN and, according to Boykin, said: 'They'll never get me because Allah will protect me.' Boykin continued:

> Well, you know what I knew that my God was bigger than his. I knew that my God was a real God, and his was an idol. But I prayed, Lord let us get that man. Three days later we went after him again, and this time we got him. Not a mark on him. We got him. We brought him back into our base there . . . I walked in with no one in there but the guard, and I looked at him and said, 'Are you Osman Atto?' And he said, 'Yes.' And I said, 'Mr. Atto, you underestimated our God.'[134]

Calls to God to justify war abounded. Charles Colson – the former Nixon aide who, after serving a prison term, became a committed evangelical preacher – concluded an article in favour of the war in *Christianity Today* with the line: 'Out of love of neighbor, then, Christians can and should support a preemptive strike, if ordered by the appropriate magistrate to prevent an imminent attack.'[135] Colson and a number of other evangelical leaders wrote an open letter to the President, dated 3 October 2002, outlining the case for a legitimate war, drawing on the principles of the just war tradition. Under the requirement of proportionality, they wrote 'How different and how much safer would the history of the twentieth century have been had the allies confronted Hitler when he illegally reoccupied the Rhineland in 1936 in clear violation of Germany's treaty agreements?'[136] The discursive connection between Saddam Hussein and Adolf Hitler was designed to ensure that the reader did not mistake the seriousness

133 The text is at http://www.homestead.com/prosites-prs/generalboykin.html [7/2005]. The original comments were reported by NBC news, but there is now no transcript available – some care should therefore be taken with the source provided here. For a review of Boykin's comments, see 'And he is head of Intelligence?', *Newsweek*, 27 October 2003, at http://webserve.govst.edu/users/ghrank/Political/Cause%20Groups/boykin.htm [7/2005].

134 As note 133.

135 Charles Colson, 'Just war in Iraq: sometimes going to war is the charitable thing to do', *Christianity Today*, 12 October 2002, at http://www.christianitytoday.com/ct/2002/013/41.72.html [7/July 2005].

136 The text of the letter is at http://www.gutlesspacifist.com/evangelicalsonbush.htm [7/2005].

of the stakes. In early 2003, 'when the National Association of Evangelicals declared . . . that "most evangelicals regard Saddam Hussein's regime – by allegedly aiding and harboring terrorists – as already having attacked the United States," it was putting just war precepts at the service of what was in fact a preventative war'.[137]

For others, though, the justification of the war would come straight from the word of the Lord. Roy A. Reinhold wrote of his conversation with God on the issue of the war with Iraq on the evangelical website Prophecy Truths. Although the idea of such a conversation, and the terminology, might seem odd to many outside the evangelical community, it is a format that does speak powerfully to those within that community, as long as the minister himself has credibility. Reinhold certainly does not sit in the centre of the popular representation of that community, but his words illustrate the logic of the thinking:

> If He said go to war, then that is my opinion, and if He said to not go to war then that would be my opinion in the matter.
>
> The Lord said, 'What if I said, do not go to war with Iraq?' I said, 'Then I would be against going to war even though I know that there is evidence that Iraq is directly involved with terrorism.'
>
> Then the Lord said, 'What if I said to go to war with Iraq?' I said, 'Then I would be completely for the war with Iraq.'
>
> The Father then said, 'I am saying to go to war with Iraq.'[138]

Note, of course, not only the divine sanction for the war, but also that God does not demur when He is reminded of the key discursive link between Saddam Hussein and the terrorists behind the second American 9/11.

Perhaps inevitably, therefore, the support for the war in Iraq was strongest amongst evangelical Christians. In October 2002, 69 per cent of evangelical Christians were said to be in favour of the war, significantly ahead of the national average, at that time below 60 per cent.[139] By March 2003, a survey reported that 57 per cent of those attending

137 Bacevich, *The New American Militarism*, p. 145.

138 Roy A. Reinhold, 'Should we go to war with Iraq?', Prophecy Truths, 5 February 2003, at http://ad2004.com/prophecytruths/Articles/Iraqprophecy.html [7/2005].

139 See Jim Lobe, 'Conservative Christians biggest backers of Iraq war', Inter Press Service, 10 October 2002, at http://www.commondreams.org/headlines02/1010-02.htm [7/2005].

evangelical churches had heard a sermon on the approaching war.[140] By the time that the war had begun, in April 2003, 77 per cent of evangelicals reported a negative view of Islam, 70 per cent believed that 'Islam is a religion of violence', while over 80 per cent believed in evangelising Muslims both in the United States and abroad.[141] The use of Christian imagery – for example, the national days of prayer called for September 2002 to mark the anniversary of the attacks of the second American 9/11 – was a powerful discursive connection to all those of Christian faith in the United States.[142]

America's core institutions – the government, the news media, the political opposition, the think tanks and the evangelical churches – were deeply imbued by the 'war on terror' discourse. In each, people were involved not only in the reproduction of that discourse, but also in a process of co-production. However, the 'war on terror' was felt yet more widely in American society.

The 'war on terror' in popular culture

Powerful as all of the above institutions were in solidifying the 'war on terror' discourse, its penetration through all levels of society needed other, more readily accessible, sources. In times of crisis, people would listen to their political leaders, read their newspapers, and understand the power of 'expertise'. Once a week – or perhaps more – they would go to church, and hear a particular belief system that might be explicit about the 'war on terror', but would quite often leave messages implicit. But on a daily basis, it was the organs of popular culture that reproduced the 'war on terror' as common sense, as the way that life had to be lived. In novels, popular music, humour, television and film, the 'war on terror' was marked, and its messages reproduced.

[140] See 'Different faiths, different messages', 19 March 2003, at http://people-press.org/reports/display.php3?ReportID=176; 'Silent evangelical support of Bush's proposed war against Iraq', 26 February 2003, at http://www.npr.org/programs/morning/transcripts/2003/feb/030226.hagerty.html [both 7/2005].

[141] The survey was conducted by the Ethics and Public Policy Center and Belief.Net, 7 April 2003. See http://www.beliefnet.com/story/124/story_12447_1.html [7/2005].

[142] On the national day of prayer, see 'The Proclamation', 31 August 2002, at http://www.whitehouse.gov/news/releases/2002/08/20020831–2.html and the celebration of it by the Traditional Values Coalition, at http://www.traditionalvalues.org/modules.php?sid=418 [both 7/2005].

Popular fiction is a demanding market; authors need particular hooks with which to engage publishers, and then the reading public. Inevitably, the 'war on terror' provided just such a hook. One example of this genre was published in the summer of 2002. Robert Ludlum's *The Paris Option* was written by Gayle Lynds, since Ludlum himself had died a year earlier. A DNA computer is designed and apparently bombed by terrorists in Paris; a US President faces major pan-Islamic terror; and Iraq is a weapons proliferator. Fred Klein, the intelligence chief, tells the US President that a ship 'is carrying tens of tons' of chemicals, 'used in blister weapons and nerve weapons. The freighter was loaded in Shanghai, is already at sea, and is destined for Iraq. Both chemicals have legitimate agricultural uses of course, but not in such large quantities for a nation the size of Iraq.'[143] Key messages reinforced were the power of Islamic terror, the complicity of states, the specific role of Iraq, all underpinned with objective, scientific, 'expert' language. A further example was *The Last Jihad* by Joel C. Rosenberg.[144] Published in November 2002, Rosenberg wrote of President MacPherson's determination, a few years into the future, to win the 'war on terror'. MacPherson is a popular and decisive president; Osama bin Laden has been killed; terrorists strike in the United States, as well as in Paris and London; the President is wounded; and behind all of this, Saddam Hussein is plotting against the West. And there, in a novel of some 350 pages, are all the key narratives of the 'war on terror' discourse. The American President as world leader facing up to absolute challenges, he is successful, in that bin Laden is dead; he is heroic in facing the challenges of Saddam, with Iraq linked easily into the counter-terrorist language. The book reaches its climax with the threat of nuclear terrorism, bringing to bear the last part of the 'war on terror' discursive reality of 2002. The book was incredibly successful. Bill Berkowitz reported in January 2003 that 'During the past month or so, *The Last Jihad* has crashed the best seller lists of the New York Times, USA Today, Amazon.com and Barnes&Noble.com. Its publisher . . . has already ordered a fifth printing.'[145] And a third

143 Robert Ludlum and Gayle Lynds, *The Paris Option* (New York: St Martin's Griffin, 2002), pp. 497–8.

144 Joel C. Rosenberg, *The Last Jihad: A Novel* (New York: Forge, 2002).

145 Bill Berkowitz, 'The Last Jihad is coming to your town', Working for Change, 21 January 2003, at http://www.workingforchange.com/printitem.cfm?itemid=14391 [7/2005].

example, published in early 2003, is James Huston's *Secret Justice: A Novel*.[146] In this book, the hero who flies in to confront a wanted terrorist buying arms in Sudan, captures him after 'interrogating' a suspect so brutally that he dies. Inter-agency fighting in Washington leads to the hero being placed on trial, at the same time as the wanted terrorist. But all the time radioactive cores are being secured in Georgia, and there is a race against time to prevent a dirty bomb from being constructed. The narrative here also contains the fear that America is preventing itself from winning the 'war on terror' – or at least making it more difficult – not recognising that, with such ultimate enemies, the means justify the ends.

Novels allow space for a series of narratives to be developed; those examples above all play on aspects of the 'war on terror' discourse. In popular music, the opportunity to explore themes in detail is clearly less. The art focuses on the music at least as much as the lyric; and the songs themselves are, by convention, relatively short. But the 'war on terror' was a theme here too, and unlike novels, the playing of popular music on radio allows a wider spread and more immediate discursive impact. One of the areas of music most affected by the 'war on terror' discourse was country, and a key example from 2002 was Toby Keith's 'Courtesy of the Red, White and Blue (an angry American)'. This very popular track emphasised many of the key elements of the narrative: an America unjustly attacked; an America of pride and service; an America fighting for justice; an America ultimately victorious, all of which can be found in this excerpt from the lyrics of the song:[147]

> American Girls and American Guys
> We'll always stand up and salute
> We'll always recognize
> When we see Old Glory Flying
> There's a lot of men dead
> So we can sleep in peace at night
> When we lay down our head . . .
>
> This nation that I love
> Has fallen under attack
> A mighty sucker punch came flyin in

[146] James Huston, *Secret Justice: A Novel* (New York: William Morrow, 2003).
[147] Toby Keith, 'Courtesy of the Red, White and Blue (an angry American)', from the album *Unleashed* (DreamWorks, Nashville, 2002).

From somewhere in the back
Soon as we could see clearly
Through our big black eye
Man, we lit up your world
Like the 4th of July

Hey Uncle Sam
Put your name at the top of his list
And the Statue of Liberty
Started shakin her fist
And the eagle will fly
And its gonna be hell
When you hear Momma Freedom
Start ringin her bell
It'll feel like the whole wide world is raining down on you
Ahw [sic] brought to you Courtesy of the Red White and Blue

Justice will be served
And the battle will rage
This big dog will fight
When you rattle his cage
You'll be sorry that you messed with
The U.S. of A.
'Cause we'll PUT a boot in your ass
It's the American way . . .

The *Unleashed* album, from which this track was taken, reached number one in the *Billboard 200* list in the United States, and the *Unleashed* tour, which began in the early autumn of 2002 and finished in March 2003, sold over one million tickets.[148] In a similar vein, Clint Black – another high-profile country music performer – wrote and performed the song 'I Raq and Roll'. Black established a foundation to support the families of fallen soldiers, funded by donations, income from the song, and also funds from the sale of the 'I Raq and Roll' T-shirt. While Keith celebrated unity, Black began the song with a condemnation of those who were not in tune with the policy programme. The song contained the following key passages:[149]

148 See http://music.yahoo.com/ar-253169-news-Toby-Keith [7/2005].
149 http://www.cowboylyrics.com/lyrics/black-clint/i-raq-and-roll-3736.html [7/2005].

You can wave your signs in protest against America takin' stands.
The stands America's takin' are the reason that you can.
If everyone would go for peace
There'd be no need for war
But we can't ignore the devil
He'll keep coming back for more

Some see this in black and white
Others only gray
We're not begging for a fight
No matter what they say
We have a resolution that should put 'em all to shame.
It's a . . . a different kind of deadline when I'm called in the game.

Chorus:
Iraq, I rack 'em up and I roll
I'm back and I'm a high tech GI Joe
I pray for peace, prepare for war
And I never will forget
There's no price too high for freedom
So be careful where you tread

Now this terror isn't man to man
They can be no more than cowards
If they won't show us their weapons
We might have to show them ours
It might be a smart bomb
They find stupid people too
And if you stand with the likes of Saddam
One might just find you . . . .

Others were interested in the issues being raised by the development of the policy programme contained within the 'war on terror' discourse. *Rolling Stone* magazine published a discussion by a panel of 'experts' at the end of 2002, discussing the approach of the war in Iraq for the rock music public.[150] Frances Katz argued that 'in the weeks leading up to the war, MTV's coverage of eleventh-hour diplomacy was extensive and detailed. Even through the first week of the war, MTV continued to provide detailed coverage of events at home and around the

[150] The original is no longer available on the web, but is referred to in the follow up discussion, 'What next', *Rolling Stone*, 16 June 2004, at http://www.rollingstone.com/politics/story/_/id/6185043 [7/2005].

world.'[151] MTV's coverage was in some of its prime-time slots, and reflected the station's calculation that some 60 per cent of its audience supported the war.

The work of MTV in this area leads the discussion on to the role of television and film. The 'war on terror' discourse created a number of opportunities for new programmes. Chief amongst these, perhaps, was Fox's *24*. Set amongst the operatives of the Counter-terrorism Unit, *24* covers dramatic fictional events over the course of a day. The first series was shown in the autumn of 2001. The hero of the piece, Jack Bauer, has to protect an African-American presidential candidate in Los Angeles, while also rescuing his family from 'Serbian' gangsters. Clearly, this was a plotline that had been written before the second American 9/11. The second series, though, has a different flavour. Although no longer on the government payroll, Jack is called back to infiltrate a terrorist organisation that plans to detonate a dirty bomb in Los Angeles. Of course, the storyline played out carefully against the debate over the war in Iraq, given that the series began in October 2002.[152] In some ways a deeper rereading of a series through the 'war on terror' discourse affected *JAG*, the longest-running series of its type in the United States. Examining issues of law and justice in the military, *JAG* began in 1995. By 2002, the eighth series, some of its episodes, too, were constructed through the 'war on terror'. Episode 159 ('Critical condition') in September 2002, for example, concerned foiling a terrorist attack, with one of the key figures injured in Afghanistan. That was the first episode of the new season. Later, episode 175 ('Empty quiver') – shown on 25 February 2003, just a month before the war in Iraq – focused on a missing nuclear missile, and the fear that it might have fallen into terrorist hands. In episode 177 ('Second acts') the identity of one of those killed in the attacks of 11 September 2001 is stolen, and the culprit enters the navy.[153] *JAG* was powerfully able to articulate the new 'reality' for its viewers, having created its characters before the second American

[151] Frances Katz, 'MTV: war coverage with a beat', *Pop Politics*, 17 April 2003, at http://www.poppolitics.com/articles/2003-04-17-mtvcoverage.shtml#frances [7/2005].

[152] See http://www.fox.com/24/ for coverage and for episode guides, see http://www.tv.com/24/show/3866/episode_guide.html&season=2 [both 7/2005].

[153] From observation; see guides at http://www.paramount.com/television/jag/about.htm [7/2005].

9/11, and was able to reaffirm the discourse of the 'war on terror'. The world had changed, and the familiar characters of *JAG* showed just how.

The nature of the penetration of the 'war on terror' discourse in American society can also be illustrated by its reconstruction of American humour. Many of the jokes repeated earlier styles; indeed, some jokes told after the second American 9/11 were restructured to include Iraq. For example, the retelling of the 'Flintstones' joke illustrated earlier in this book: 'What do Saddam Hussein and Fred Flintstone have in common? They both look out their window and see Rubble.'[154] With the resistance to the Bush administration's policies at the United Nations seemingly focused in the arguments of the French and Germans, jokes abounded about Europe.[155] David Letterman quipped: 'A lot of folks are still demanding more evidence before they actually consider Iraq a threat. For example, France wants more evidence. And you know I'm thinking, the last time France wanted more evidence they rolled right through Paris with the German flag.'[156] For Jay Leno, 'Germany is now saying that they won't go along with an invasion of Iraq. However, they did say they would go along if the invasion included Poland, France and Belgium.'[157] However, much of the humour was also at the expense of the administration. Although the 'no war for oil' discourse had not been able to overthrow the 'war on terror', it did have an impact. Jay Leno retold a joke popular amongst the protestors: 'The Bush administration said today there is a lot of support for us to attack Iraq. Exxon, Mobil, Texaco, Chevron, they're all lining up.'[158]

Through these various mechanisms, the 'war on terror' had been powerfully reproduced throughout American society by the power of popular culture, able to reach into the home and the workplace through novels, television, popular music and humour. Although there was a challenge, overwhelmingly Americans thought about their

154 At http://www.laststory.com/Iraq%20Jokes.htm [7/2005].

155 See Felicia R. Lee, 'Americans turn eagerly to jibes at the French', *New York Times*, 15 February 2003.

156 David Letterman, spring 2003, cited in an email by Alastair Mackay-James, 12 March 2003.

157 At http://politicalhumor.about.com/library/blsaddamjokes.htm [6/2005].

158 At http://www.anvari.org/fun/World_Trade_Center/Iraqi_War_Late_Night_Shows_Quotes.html [7/2005].

country and the world, and about their personal and collective security, through the discourse of the 'war on terror'.

Conclusion

From the national unity that had been constructed in the aftermath of the second American 9/11, the move to the war in Iraq – although prefigured as part of the 'war on terror' policy programme – had led to a significant and alternative discourse. That discourse had not been able to overthrow the 'war on terror' due to the depth at which the latter had become a lived experience through the major institutions of American society involved in the co-production of that discourse, and the range of institutions that had been involved in the reproduction of the discourse. It had in many ways not sought to be the mainstream. 'No war for oil' created a foothold in particular parts of the society, notably the music industry, and in the late-night talk shows.

The development of the discourses during 2002 and 2003 can be mapped on to the crisis process that has been under development. The socially constructed origin of the 'war on terror' led to a particular decisive intervention giving particular meaning to those events. Next, a policy programme was developed, drawing explicitly on that decisive intervention, with which the programme was mutually constituted. That in turn produced an institutional restructuring. Then, the discourse became reinforced socially, as a process of stabilisation took place. It was then postulated that the discourse would become exposed by those who identified contradictions, and that the identification of contradictions would lead to a new discursive framework and challenge to the hegemonic position of the 'war on terror'. This clash of discourses would be resolved through a new socially constructed crisis in which a new decisive intervention would create new meaning, new common sense, and thus a new discursive framework.

This is illustrated in the figure 5.1. Throughout 2002, and particularly into early 2003, a new discursive challenge to the 'war on terror' developed, one that created the constructed crisis over the war in Iraq. It sought to challenge the 'war on terror' on fundamentals, and produced widespread 'acts of resistance' to that hegemonic discourse. But it was unable to overthrow that discourse, because of its power in the key institutions of American society and state, and due to the determined marginality of the key actors in the 'no war for oil'

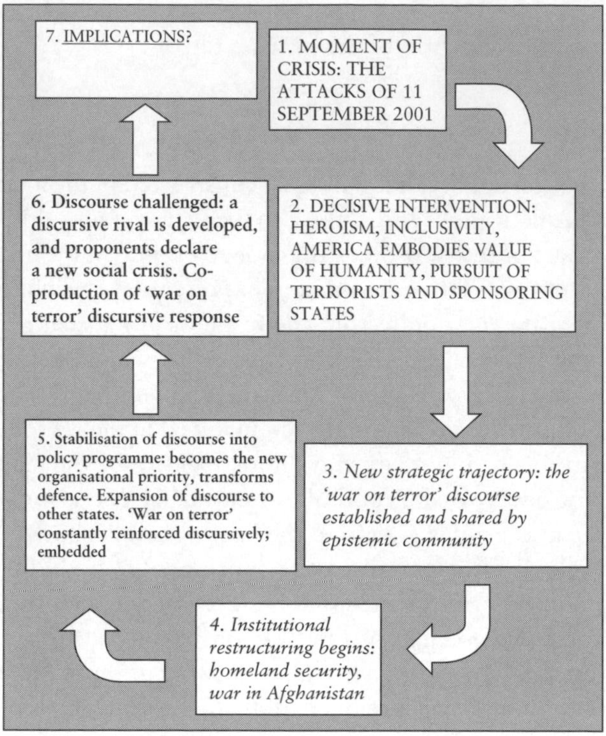

Figure 5.1. The crisis process and policy programme – a newly constructed challenge

discourse. The alternative discourse was kept at the margins, in those institutions that spoke to very particular members of society – such as popular musicians, speaking to some segments of American youth – that were not empowered; or in those institutions that positively revelled in being 'alternative', at being unacceptable to the 'mainstream': that is, those protest institutions who did not seek to be a part of that 'mainstream', and who therefore did not seek to reconstruct that 'mainstream'. Despite the size of the 'acts of resistance', therefore, the discursive challenge to the 'war on terror' was always a marginal one. In contrast, common sense – defined by the hegemonic discourse – was co-produced by government and opposition, by the news media, by evangelical churches and by 'experts', the powerful institutions of the state and society, and was powerfully reproduced through many of the key aspects of popular culture in the

United States. The discursive cards were heavily stacked, and through this process of discursive competition, the 'war on terror' and its policy programme (including the war in Iraq) survived.

The crisis process can now be updated with the analysis of the discursive challenge. Box 1 in figure 5.1 represents the moment of crisis, and box 2 the decisive intervention, as set out in chapter 2. The way in which the decisive intervention created a new strategic trajectory is set out in box 3, and box 4 examines the institutional restructuring that followed. These were the subject matter of chapter 3. The development of stabilisation into a policy programme, box 5, is the subject matter of chapter 4. Box 6 summarises the focus of this chapter, in which the dominant discourse came under pressure from contradictions and alternatives. The discursive challenge to the 'war on terror' was not eliminated through 2003 and 2004, but was kept at the margins, contained, and often ridiculed. Having survived the discursive challenge of 2002–3, the 'war on terror' strengthened throughout 2003–5, and chapter 6 illustrates the increasing power of the discourse of the 'war on terror' in the key institutions of society and state throughout this period, which will comprise the material for box 7.

6 *The discourse strikes back*

Introduction

IN THE LATE SPRING OF 2005, George Lucas released the third of the second trilogy of *Star Wars* films. The *Revenge of the Sith* dealt with a conflict between superbeings in a different galaxy and achieved great popularity at the box office.[1] It also, however, echoed the debates of contemporary America. As Daniel Kutzman noted:

> 'You're either with me, or you're my enemy,' Anakin Skywalker tells Obi-Wan Kenobi before he turns into Darth Vader, in a none-too-subtle echo of President Bush's infamous 'you're either with us or against us' mantra. At another point in the film, as the galactic Senate cheers dictator-in-waiting Palpatine, Padme Amidala says, 'This is how liberty dies – to thunderous applause.'[2]

The message – that abandoning rights in favour of a bigger struggle, in which the stakes are raised to the highest, leads to the total abandonment of the values supposedly being protected – is epitomised by Anakin's descent into becoming Darth Vader. And picking up on the theme, cartoonists enjoyed representing George Bush as Vader.[3] George Lucas had himself made a connection between the film and the Iraq War, even though he had written the original storyline some thirty-five years earlier: 'In terms of evil, one of the original concepts was how does a democracy turn itself into a dictatorship . . . The parallels between what we did in Vietnam and what we're doing in Iraq now are

[1] *USA Today* reported the film grossed $377.3 million. Scott Bowles, 'Grading the summer films', *USA Today*, 7 August 2005.

[2] Daniel Kutzman, 'Star Wars and politics', 18 May 2005, at http://politicalhumor.about.com/b/a/170248.htm [7/2005].

[3] See, for example, the images at http://www.nowar-paix.ca/Posters/bushbmdh_resize2.jpg [7/2005].

unbelievable.'[4] *The Revenge of the Sith* as a popular critique of the 'war on terror' discourse? Certainly that was what many commentators – on both the liberal and conservative wings of the debate – believed.[5] George Lucas' frustration – over the defeat of the 'liberal' agenda in the presidential election – had been named in the *Star Wars* series. *The Empire Strikes Back* had focused on the revenge of 'evil' against 'liberty': Lucas, and fellow critics, felt they now had to endure a politics in which *The Discourse Strikes Back*.

The presidential elections of 2004 had seen a strong endorsement for the 'war on terror' discourse: not just in the victory of President Bush, but in the nature of the campaign, which was one conducted within the confines of that discourse, not one between contending discourses. The discourse struck back in so many ways; not only in politics but, as this chapter will argue and illustrate, in the news media and in the think tanks, in popular books and novels, in television and in film, and in and through the churches.

Part of the power of this was shown in the continued memorialisation of the second American 9/11 as the legitimising foundation for the policy programme. On the fourth anniversary of the attacks, New York City Mayor, Michael Bloomberg, claimed that one in four Americans had visited Ground Zero over those previous four years.[6] The President issued medals to the families of the 442 emergency workers who had died, and the fourth anniversary saw emotional public ceremonies in New York and Washington.[7] These were covered widely on television: Fox dedicated the whole of its morning schedule to the commemorations, with some discussion on Hurricane Katrina interspersed.[8] But there were other examples not connected specifically to Patriot Day, as 11 September has become. In 2005, a shortlist of the designs to commemorate Flight 93 was unveiled, as part of the process to raise $30 million to fund the project.[9]

[4] George Lucas, at the Cannes film festival, in Chris Burns, 'Lucas on Iraq, Star Wars', CNN, 16 May 2005, at http://www.cnn.com/2005/SHOWBIZ/Movies/05/16/cannes.starwars/ [7/2005].

[5] For an assessment, see David M. Halbfinger, 'Latest Star Wars movie is quickly politicized', *New York Times*, 19 May 2005.

[6] *Fox News*, 8.30 am Eastern Standard Time, personal observation.

[7] 'President remembers 9/11 heroes', 9 September 2005, at http://www.whitehouse.gov/news/releases/2005/09/20050909-1.html [9/2005].

[8] Personal observation, Fox, 11 September 2005, 8–11 am EST.

[9] See Kimberley Hefling, '9/11 monument design readied', *Washington Times*, 4 September 2005.

Another illustration of this remembrance industry is contained in the development of commemorative coins. In both 2003 and 2004, demand was high from Americans for the coins. The 2004 coin was marketed as having holographic characteristics.[10] However, the US Mint was at pains to make sure that people understood that the coin, although emblematic of the heroism of New York under attack, was not legal tender. It was not designed for everyday use, to be marked and scuffed in the supermarket and in local shops. It was to be kept, to be accorded that special status as an object that helped people remember what the second American 9/11 had been called into existence to mean. Private companies, of course, sought to get in on the act. The 2004 'Freedom Towers' coin – minted with 'silver reclaimed from ground zero' – was not an officially endorsed product.[11] It was, however, illustrative of the demand for such products.[12]

Memorialisation continued to be a powerful backdrop to the development of the policy programme. This is not to say that following the failure of the 'no war for oil' discourse to prevent war and occupation, there was no opposition, because of course there was. One year after the war in Iraq began, hundreds of thousands demonstrated in the streets of some 60 countries, and in some 200 cities. Perhaps in total there were over 1 million people expressing their support for the ideas contained within the 'no war for oil' discourse.[13] But as impressive as this was as a mobilisation of popular opinion, it had relatively little impact upon the mainstream: in September 2003, a poll published in the *Washington Post* showed that nearly 70 per cent of Americans still believed that there was a tangible link between the attacks on 11 September 2001 and the regime of Saddam Hussein.[14]

The memorialisation connected with Americans continuing to feel vulnerable to further acts of terror on their home soil. In a *USA Today* poll, some 57 per cent of Americans said that the USA was still

[10] Image observed at eBay, www.ebay.com, in September 2004.

[11] See the US Mint's explanation at http://www.usmint.gov/consumer/index.cfm?action=HotItems [9/2004].

[12] See the image at http://www.nationalcollectorsmint.com/uploaded/CNMI_Freedom_Tower.htm [9/2004].

[13] 'More than one million mark war's anniversary with protests', *MTV News*, 22 March 2004, at http://www.mtv.com/news/articles/1485903/03222004/id_0.jhtml [7/2005].

[14] Dana Milbank and Claudia Dean, 'Hussein link to 9/11 lingers in many minds', *Washington Post*, 6 September 2003.

vulnerable, and had been made more so by the war in Iraq.[15] That poll was published on 9 August 2005. On the same day, *USA Today* published an article on how new electronic passports would enhance security; and the previous day it had published a debate on how ready America was to face a terrorist attack with biological weapons (not very, according to the editors).[16] That is, the newspaper that was publishing a poll showing fears of vulnerability was itself feeding that vulnerability with the coverage that it was publishing. 'Terrorism' seemed to be everywhere in American newspapers. On a religion page, there was an article explaining how terrorism was worse in the eyes of God than gambling.[17] In a film review, Steve Lopez wrote 'As the opening credits for the movie *Dukes of Hazard* rolled past on the big screen, it struck me that "credits" might not be the right word. To use a loose analogy, we don't assign terrorists credit for attacks: we assign them responsibility.'[18] Homeland Security Secretary, Michael Chertoff, told *USA Today* readers in an interview the less-than-encouraging news that 'we have to be ready for everything'.[19]

Previously only concerned with the 11 September 2001 attacks, during 2005 memorialisation grew to include acts commemorating the war in Iraq. A whole series of books on Iraq, from the perspective of the American participant, were published in the autumn of 2005. Jason Christopher Hartley's *Just Another Soldier: A Year on the Ground in Iraq* spoke to the mix of boredom, horror and fear.[20] Hartley's blog – www.justanothersoldier.com – had, according to the army, compromised operational security, and led him to being fined and demoted.[21] Colby Buzzell's *My War: Killing Time in Iraq* is critical of

15 Richard Benedetto, 'Poll shows most Americans feel more vulnerable', *USA Today*, 9 August 2005.

16 Roger Yu, 'Electronic passports set to thwart forgers' and 'Today's debate: homeland security' between the newspaper's editors ('Fight against bioterrorism frozen in bureaucratic time') and William F. Raub ('We've come a long way'), *USA Today*, 9 and 8 August, respectively.

17 Dennis Prager, 'Why God hates terrorists more than gamblers', *Los Angeles Times*, 14 August 2005.

18 Steve Lopez, 'Putting "Dukes" to the teen boy test', *Los Angeles Times*, 14 August 2005.

19 'The Forum', *USA Today*, 10 August 2005.

20 Jason Christopher Hartley, *Just Another Soldier: A Year on the Ground in Iraq* (New York: HarperCollins, 2005).

21 Thomas Claburn, 'Army Chief of Staff calls for more oversight of military bloggers', *Information Week*, 1 September 2005, at http://www.informationweek.com/showArticle.jhtml?articleID=170102708 [9/2005].

his government and the anti-war movement for saying they understand what is going on in Iraq, and was also based on his blog site.[22] Kayla Williams' *Love My Rifle More Than You: Young and Female in the US Army* told of the author's work as an interpreter; of her dissatisfaction with those in power; and of the 'special status' accorded to women in the army.[23] John Crawford's *The Last True Story I'll Ever Tell: An Accidental Soldier's Account of the War in Iraq* is the story of a National Guardsman from Florida who had his tour repeatedly extended, and who expressed very little respect for either his superiors or the Iraqi civilians.[24] Taken together, these books mark deep dissatisfaction with the Iraqi war, but also the need to commemorate the sacrifice and the commitment involved. That dissatisfaction had a public face in the summer of 2005 when Cindy Sheehan, whose son had died in Iraq, camped outside the Bush family residence seeking a meeting with the President. She said to the Veterans For Peace convention 'Then we have this lying b******, George Bush, taking a 5-week vacation in a time of war.' Of going to Crawford she said she would be 'waiting until that jerk comes out and tells me why my son died'.[25]

This chapter examines the power of the 'war on terror' discourse in American politics and society in the period after it was challenged by an alternative discourse in 2003. The development of the 'no war for oil' discourse had prevented an attack on Iraq from being seen as simple common sense. But from the end of that war – its 'operational phase' – into the presidential election season of 2004, and into the second Bush administration in 2005, mainstream politics and the news media were framed by the assumptions of the 'war on terror'. Not only that, the momentum of the discourse was furthered by the influence of 'experts', notably in think tanks, and in the spread of the commonsense view that the 'war on terror' had become in books and novels, television and film, and in evangelical churches. Challenged in 2002–3, the 'war on terror' discourse struck back powerfully in 2003–5.

22 Colby Buzzell, *My War: Killing Time in Iraq* (New York: Putnam Books, 2005). His website is http://cbftw.blogspot.com/

23 Kayla Williams, *Love My Rifle More Than You: Young and Female in the US Army* (New York: W. W. Norton, 2005).

24 John Crawford, *The Last True Story I'll Ever Tell* (New York: Riverhead Books, 2005).

25 Cindy Sheehan, 'Address', 5 August 2005, Veterans for Peace, at http://www.veteransforpeace.org/convention05/sheehan_transcript.htm [9/2005].

The politics of the 'war on terror'

In November 2004, George W. Bush won the presidency of the United States for the second time, defeating his rival, John Kerry, by 51 per cent to 48 per cent, by over 3.5 million votes, 30 states to 21, and by 286 electoral college votes to 252.[26] There were many reasons for Bush's victory, but for the purposes of this book, what was important was the degree to which the campaign was structured around the 'war on terror', and the extent to which that 'war on terror' structured the campaign. As George Lakoff put it, 'The "war on terror" is not about stopping you from being afraid, it's about making you afraid.'[27]

John Kerry's campaign criticised the President for the war on Iraq, in quite particular terms. In a speech in Florida, Kerry said 'Mr President, your management or mismanagement of this war, your diversion from Al-Qaeda and from Usama bin Laden, your shift of the troops to Iraq when there was nothing to do with Al Qaeda, nothing to do with 9/11, has made America less safe, not more secure . . .'[28] Yet the Kerry critique operated from inside the logic of the 'war on terror', although disagreeing on the policy programme in some of its details. That is, Kerry accepted that there was a 'war on terror', and offered voters the prospect that he would prosecute that 'war' more effectively, by refocusing on to the hunt for Osama bin Laden, by securing the support of allies for the military and reconstruction work in Iraq. As Richard Jackson has argued, 'Like Bush, Kerry also locates the current conflict within the meta-narratives of Pearl Harbor and World War II, the cold war, civilisation versus barbarism . . . and like Bush, he also believes that "this is no ordinary time" (it is an historic calling) . . .'[29] Kerry, therefore, wanted to fight the same war as Bush, just better. This was

[26] See 'President makes peace offer to political rivals', *USA Today*, 2 November 2004.

[27] George Lakoff, 'Linguistics professor George Lakoff dissects the "war on terror" and other conservative catchphrases', *UC Berkeley News*, 26 August 2004, at http://www.berkeley.edu/news/media/releases/2004/08/25_lakoff.shtml [7/2005].

[28] In Peter Brownfield, 'War on terror on top of voter issue lists', *Fox News*, 18 October 2004, at http://www.foxnews.com/story/0,2933,135833,00.html [7/2005].

[29] Richard Jackson, *Writing the War on Terrorism* (Manchester: Manchester University Press, 2005), p. 160.

particularly powerfully stated in a speech that Kerry made in August 2004:

> I believe I can fight a more effective, more thoughtful, more strategic, more proactive, more sensitive war on terror that reaches out to other nations and brings them to our side and lives up to American values in history . . . I set out a path to win the peace in Iraq and to get the terrorists, wherever they may be, before they get us.[30]

This was a manifesto concerned with making the policy programme more effective and efficient, not a refutation of the 'war on terror' discourse as in the 'no war for oil' discourse. As Eric Westervelt reported on National Public Radio in September 2004, 'Despite heated campaign rhetoric, proposals on Iraq from the presidential candidates are similar and unlikely to change things soon.'[31] In his speech accepting defeat, Kerry was therefore able to link the 'war on terror' and the war in Iraq with ease: 'Now, more than ever, with our soldiers in harm's way, we must stand together and succeed in Iraq and win the war on terror.'[32] Such a statement would not have been out of place for George W. Bush.

The Bush campaign had placed the 'war on terror' firmly at the core. And the centrepiece of that framing of the election took place at the Republican convention from 30 August to 2 September 2004. The first important element of the frame was the location: the convention was to be held in the city that had suffered most in the second American 9/11, New York City, the first time the Republicans had ever met in that city. The second element was to secure speakers who had authority, and who would mark what the election was about. Rudolph Giuliani, the former Mayor of New York City, made a very powerful speech focused on reminding the audience – both in the hall and more importantly on television – of the foundational myth of '9/11'. He expressed gratitude that Bush was President, and evoked an image of the heroic President in New York on 14 September 2001, staying with

30 Cited in 'Kerry remarks at the UNITY 2004 conference', *Washington Post*, 5 August 2004.

31 Eric Westervelt, 'Candidates debate Iraq, but offer similar plans', NPR, 23 September 2004, at http://www.npr.org/templates/story/story.php?storyId=3932253 [7/2005].

32 John Kerry, 'Address to supporters', 3 November 2004, at http://www.johnkerry.com/pressroom/speeches/spc_2004_1103.html [7/2005].

emergency workers longer than the Secret Service wanted. This was contrasted with John Kerry's changing positions on key policies. Giuliani created a pre-history of terrorism with two examples evoked, both attacks on Jews by Arabs (the 1972 Munich Olympics, and the murder of Leon Klinghofer on the *Achille Lauro*). He mentioned Winston Churchill twice; Israel four times. And he evoked the power of freedom, linking it in biblical terms to duty: 'People who live in freedom always prevail over people who live in oppression. That's the story of the Old Testament. That's the story of World War II and the cold war.'[33]

Giuliani's powerful speech was matched by one given by Senator John McCain, who had been a serious contender for the Republican nomination in 2000, and who had been regarded by many Republicans as being a less-than-full supporter of the Bush White House. McCain also evoked the personal memory of 11 September 2001 amongst the audience; praised the resolute nature of the President; called upon God to bless America's military. He explained the totalising effect of the 'war on terror':

> The awful events of September 11, 2001 declared a war we were vaguely aware of, but hadn't really comprehended how near the threat was, and how terrible were the plans of our enemies. It's a big thing, this war. It's a fight between a just regard for human dignity and a malevolent force that defiles an honorable religion by disputing God's love for every soul on earth. It's a fight between right and wrong, good and evil.[34]

And he justified the war in Iraq in political, security and moral terms: 'Our choice wasn't between a benign status quo and the bloodshed of war. It was between war and a graver threat. Don't let anyone tell you otherwise . . . Whether or not Saddam possessed the terrible weapons he once had and used, freed from international pressure and the threat of military action, he would have acquired them again.'[35] McCain's performance was designed to explain the world in the voice of the expert; the unifier; the need for America to do the right thing ('We're

[33] Rudy Giuliani, 'Speech to the 2004 Republican National Convention', 30 August 2004, at http://www.gwu.edu/~action/2004/repconv04/giuliani083004sp.html [7/2005].

[34] Sen. John McCain (AZ), 'Speech at the 2004 Republican National Convention', 30 August 2004, at http://www.gwu.edu/~action/2004/repconv04/mccain083004sp.html [7/2005].

[35] Ibid

Americans, and we'll never surrender') in these objectively defined realities. These messages were underpinned by a speech by Deena Burnett about the courage of her husband, Tom, who had spoken to her from Flight 93 by telephone before fighting the hijackers with other passengers; this testimony powerfully underlined the heroic and tragic memories of the second American 9/11.

The first night was billed under the need for courage, the second under compassion, but again the 'war on terror' filled the screens. The Governor of California, Arnold Schwarzenegger, issued the rallying cry: 'If you believe this country, not the United Nations, is the best hope of democracy in the world, then you are a Republican! And, ladies and gentlemen, if you believe we must be fierce and relentless and terminate terrorism, then you are a Republican!'[36] In the first line, he drew upon the popular resentment that the United Nations had not supported the war in Iraq; and he did so by creating the dichotomy of either believing in America, or not. In the second, he drew powerfully upon his image as an actor in the film series *The Terminator*, that the destruction of the ultimate terrorist enemy was the only way to free America from threat. That same day the First Lady, Laura Bush, gave a speech in which she listed all the important issues that faced America and Americans. And then she wound up to the key point: 'But we are living in the midst of the most historic struggle my generation has ever known. The stakes are so high. So I want to talk about the issue that I believe is most important for my own daughters, for all our families, and for our future: George's work to protect our country and defeat terror so that all children can grow up in a more peaceful world.'[37] On the third night, Democrat Zell Miller was called upon to speak, and he recalled the moral certainties of the Second World War, and contrasted the Democrats' commitment to fight for values and freedom in the past, with the plans of John Kerry in the current campaign. Miller commented that 'Senator Kerry has made it clear that he would use military force only if

[36] 'Schwarzenegger: no country more welcoming than USA', speech to the 2004 Republican National Convention, 31 August 2004, at http://www.cnn.com/2004/ALLPOLITICS/08/31/gop.schwarzenegger.transcript/index.html [7/2005].

[37] Laura Bush, 2004 National Convention address, 31 August 2004, at http://www.americanrhetoric.com/speeches/convention2004/laurabush2004rnc.htm [7/2005].

approved by the United Nations. Kerry would let Paris decide when America needs defending. I want Bush to decide . . .'[38] He contrasted the two men over the 'war on terror' directly: 'George Bush wants to grab terrorists by the throat and not let them go to get a better grip. From John Kerry, they get a "yes-no-maybe" bowl of mush that can only encourage our enemies and confuse our friends.'[39] Miller's attack was matched later in tone and in the level of personal vitriol in a speech by Vice President Cheney.

The culmination of the event was on the final night, as George W. Bush gave his speech accepting the Republican nomination. The roughness of the speeches by Miller and Cheney the previous night allowed Bush, in contrast, to speak more gently, to appear more as a unifier, a world statesman. Bush's speech began with the constructed memories and narratives of the second American 9/11. To an audience chanting 'U-S-A', he said 'So we have fought the terrorists across the earth – not for pride, not for power, but because the lives of our citizens are at stake.'[40] And he connected the second American 9/11 with the war in Iraq: 'We knew Saddam Hussein's record of aggression and support for terror. We knew his long history of pursuing, even using, weapons of mass destruction. And we know that September the 11th requires our country to think differently: We must, and we will, confront threats to America before it is too late.'[41] And so the story was complete: the second American 9/11 had a particular meaning, it changed the way America behaved fundamentally, and in that context, only one electoral choice remained. It is hard to underestimate the power of the 'war on terror' in shaping public perceptions when it was played as hard, and as skilfully, as it was through the election campaign. It shaped how people thought; what was important; which questions were legitimate, and consequently which illegitimate.

Yet in some ways the power of the administration on the 'war on terror' was still a surprise. On 22 July 2004, the National Commission on Terrorist Attacks Upon the United States (also known as the 9/11 Commission) issued its final report. Five Republicans and five

38 Senator Zell Miller (D-GA), 'Keynote address', 1 September 2004, at http://www.gwu.edu/~action/2004/repconv04/miller090104sp.html [7/2005].
39 Ibid.
40 'President's remarks at the 2004 Republican National Convention', 2 September 2004, at http://www.whitehouse.gov/news/releases/2004/09/20040902-2.html [7/2005].
41 Ibid.

Democrats authored a document which criticised the government for being unprepared. In the preface, they wrote:

> We learned that the institutions charged with protecting our borders, civil aviation and national security did not understand how grave this threat could be, and did not adjust their policies, plans, and practices to deter or defeat it. We learned of fault lines within our government – between foreign and domestic intelligence, and between and within agencies. We learned of the pervasive problems of managing and sharing information across a large and unwieldy government that had been built in a different era to confront different dangers.[42]

The report focused on the intelligence services, demanding reform of the CIA and FBI. It did not condemn the administrations of either Bill Clinton or George Bush (although it had said that both should have been more vigilant). One of the key elements of the decisive intervention had been an avoidance of blame on any within the United States, and this was largely upheld by the report in its downgrading of any blame on political figures. Indeed, many of the elements of the decisive intervention were marked in the *9/11 Report*: the memorialisation of the events of 11 September 2001; the focus on American leadership; the construction of an enemy of civilisation; the link between terrorists and weapons of mass destruction.

The Democrats were therefore unable to make political capital out of the *9/11 Report* as their candidate was as much engaged in the discourse – although not all of the policy programme – as the President. In his acceptance speech for the nomination for presidential candidate at the Democratic convention, Kerry emphasised family, and made connections with the Second World War. As Laura Bush was later to do, he spoke of a moment of great danger: 'My fellow Americans, this is the most important election of our lifetime. The stakes are high. We are a nation at war: a global war on terror against an enemy unlike we've ever known before.' As Rudolph Giuliani was to do at the Republican convention, he reminded the audience of the horrors and the heroism of 11 September 2001, and of the key elements of the decisive intervention: unity and leadership in facing the new total enemy. Unity included the response to the *9/11 Report*: 'The 9/11 commission has given us a path

[42] *The 9/11 Commission Report*, p. xvi, at http://www.9-11commission.gov/report/911Report.pdf [7/2005].

to follow, endorsed by Democrats, Republicans and the 9/11 families. As president, I will not evade or equivocate; I will immediately implement all the recommendations of that commission.' Kerry claimed the mantle of the efficient fighter in the 'war on terror': 'As president, I will fight a smarter, more effective war on terror . . . I know what we have to do in Iraq. We need a president who has the credibility to bring our allies to our side and share the burden, reduce the cost to American taxpayers, reduce the risk to American soldiers.' He mentioned the need to prevent the spread of weapons of mass destruction. And so, taking advantage of his own military record, he claimed: 'As president, I will wage this war with the lessons I learned in war.'[43] For all the furore and clamour of the presidential election campaign, it was constructed by and conformed to the dictates of the discourse known as the 'war on terror'.

In such ways, the alternative discourse was silenced from mainstream public debate. But the counter-campaign continued. 'No war for oil' moved into a campaign to withdraw the troops from Iraq, expressed by, amongst others, Bring Them Home Now.[44] United for Peace and Justice mobilised demonstrations and published pamphlets against the war, the occupation and the use of torture by American forces.[45] Violence in Iraq was monitored during and after the phase of the war against Saddam Hussein's forces by Electronic Iraq.[46] The costs of the war were monitored by organisations such as the National Priorities Project and Iraqometer.[47] Another aspect of the campaign was to target those companies and corporations working for profit in Iraq, overseen by organisations such as US Labor Against the War and the Institute for Southern Studies.[48] And some Christian organisations, such as Sojourners, carried a number of these messages.[49] This enormous explosion of internet activism connected those hostile to the 'war on terror' across the United States and, in many cases, with those who held similar views across the world. But internet activism was also important to these groups, inasmuch as

43 From John Kerry's acceptance speech at the Democratic national convention, Boston, 29 July 2004, *Washington Post*, at http://www.washingtonpost.com/wp-dyn/articles/A25678-2004Jul29.html [7/2005].

44 See http://www.bringthemhomenow.org/ [7/2005].

45 See http://www.unitedforpeace.org/article.php?id=359 [7/2005].

46 See http://www.electroniciraq.net/news/index.shtml [7/2005].

47 See http://www.costofwar.com/ and http://www.iraqometer.com/ [both 7/2005].

48 See http://www.uslaboragainstwar.org/#1002 and http://www.southernstudies.org/ [both 7/2005].

49 At http://www.sojo.net/ [7/2005].

they found it hard to access the American news media to express their views.

The news media in the 'war on terror'

In the mainstream news media, the 'war on terror' was powerfully reproduced in terms of a war on and by an organisation motivated by ideology against the United States. America's own terrorists did not fit too easily into this template. After all, Timothy McVeigh had been responsible for the most deadly terror attack in the United States when he had bombed Oklahoma City in 1995. McVeigh, executed in 2001, had killed 168 people but was, according to the FBI, a 'lone wolf'. The FBI's five-year strategy declared that 'The most significant domestic terrorism threat over the next five years will be the lone actor, or "lone wolf" terrorist.'[50] But McVeigh was closely associated with white supremacist groups, as was Eric Rudolph, who had planted bombs at the Atlanta Olympics, and as were the 'Sons of Gestapo', who bombed the Sunset Limited train in Arizona in 1995, killing one and injuring over 100.[51] White supremacism was also apparently the source of support for William Krar, arrested in April 2003 in Texas with enough cyanide to produce a gas fatal to large numbers if released inside a shop or a mall.[52] Krar also had, according to the FBI, a very large cache of weapons and 'more than five false identification documents, including a North Dakota birth certificate, a Social Security card, a Vermont birth certificate, a Defense Intelligence Agency Identification card, and a United Nations Multinational Force Identification card'.[53] The identity cards were discovered when they were delivered to the wrong

[50] Federal Bureau of Investigation, *Strategic Plan 2004–9*, at http://www.fbi.gov/publications/strategicplan/stategicplantext.htm#ct [7/2005].

[51] See Robert Burke, *Counter Terrorism for Emergency Responders* (Boca Raton, FL: Lewis Publishers, 2000), p. 29.

[52] See Mike German, 'Behind the lone terrorist, a pack mentality', *Washington Post*, 5 June 2005; 'Cyanide, arsenal sparks domestic terror fear', CNN, 30 January 2004, at http://www.cnn.com/2004/US/Southwest/01/30/cyanide.probe.ap/; Kris Axtman, 'The terror threat at home, often overlooked', *Christian Science Monitor*, 29 December 2003; and 'Terror plot in Texas?', *CBS Evening News*, 7 January 2004, at http://www.cbsnews.com/stories/2004/01/07/eveningnews/main592012.shtml [all 7/2005].

[53] 'Smith County man admits possessing chemical weapons', *Department of Justice Press Release, Eastern Texas District*, 13 November 2003, at http://www.fbi.gov/dojpressrel/pressrel03/texas111303.htm [9/2005].

address – with a note which said 'We would hate to have this fall into the wrong hands' – instead of to a 'member of a self-styled militia in New Jersey'.[54] The New Jersey Militia argues that democracy 'is the pernicious doctrine that three wolves and a sheep should take a majority vote on what's for supper'.[55] They say 'To add insult upon all Americans, nearly all Ten Planks of the Communist Manifesto have been incorporated into our system, and peaceable Americans are considered fair game at places like Ruby Ridge and Waco.'[56] Yet that Krar might represent some real domestic terrorist threat seemed not to be a story in the United States. Richard Bottoms' research showed that

> the major news magazines – *Time, Newsweek* and *U.S. News & World Report* – have never reported on Krar. Neither has *ABC World News Tonight*, *NBC Nightly News* or *PBS's NewsHour*. The *CBS Evening News* (1/7/04) did one story on the sentencing of Krar and his wife. The nation's major papers also shied away from the story. The *Washington Post* and *USA Today* had no coverage, while the *New York Times* never reported on it, but ran an op-ed by Daniel Levitas about it (12/13/03) – arguing, ironically, that such stories should get more coverage. The *Los Angeles Times* did run a front-page story on the plot (1/7/04), but that was the only time they approached it. The all-news cable channels, despite their 24 hours of time to fill daily, hardly reported on the Krar story either. The story appears twice in CNN's Nexis transcripts (*NewsNight With Aaron Brown*, 12/11/03; *American Morning*, 12/30/03), only once in Fox News Channel's (*The Big Story With John Gibson*, 12/29/03) and not at all in MSNBC's.[57]

Jim Kessler pointed out in the spring of 2004 that 'Since his appointment as attorney general, John Ashcroft's Washington office has issued 2,295 news releases. Not one of them has mentioned the name William Joseph Krar.'[58] In such ways, attitudes and opinions are formed and

[54] Scott Gold, 'Possible domestic terror plot foiled', for the *Los Angeles Times*, reproduced in the *Seattle Times*, 9 January 2004.

[55] 'What is democracy?', *New Jersey Militia Newsletter*, 6:7 (January 2001), at http://www.njmilitia.org/Jan01.html [9/2005].

[56] *New Jersey Militia Newsletter*, 1:1 (July 1995), at http://www.njmilitia.org/jul95.htm [9/2005].

[57] Richard Bottoms, 'Homegrown terrorists: WMD found in Texas, so media yawn', *Fairness and Accuracy in Reporting* (March/April 2004), at http://www.fair.org/index.php?page=1175 [7/2005].

[58] Jim Kessler, 'Outside view: who is William Krar?', *United Press International*, 14 March 2004, at http://www.upi.com/view.cfm?StoryID=20040311-030156-8181r [9/2005].

underlined. And yet the militias are very interested in guns, and believe that the Patriot Act might be used against them. An article entitled 'Are you a terrorist?' says:

> 'The US government now has the power to prosecute any public expression of dissent as an act of 'domestic terrorism', thanks to the super-duper USA PATRIOT ACT . . . under the new law, you are a 'domestic terrorist subject to 25 years in prison', if you engage in acts intended to 'influence the policy of the government by intimidation or coercion'. Which is, of course, the very definition of public protest . . .[59]

The lack of interest in Krar, and any links to the militias, seems surprising. Two months following the bomb attack in Oklahoma City, *Presidential Decision Directives 39* of 21 June 1995 declared that 'It is the policy of the United States to deter, defeat and respond vigorously to all terrorist attacks on our territory and against our citizens, or facilities, whether they occur domestically, in international waters or airspace or on foreign territory.'[60] An *Interagency Domestic Terrorism Concept of Operations Plan* was published in January 2001.[61] Yet the focus on the militias from the FBI declined. In 2005, the FBI reported that 'Violent animal rights extremists and eco-terrorists now pose one of the most serious terrorism threats to the nation . . .', not any threat from white supremacists.[62] The US Marshals' Service chief inspector Geoff Shank put this rather pithily: 'Not a lot of attention is being paid to this, because everybody is concerned about the guy in a turban. But there are still plenty of angry, Midwestern white guys out there . . .'[63]

The lack of official and media interest in supremacist domestic terrorism was offset by saturation coverage of the global 'war on terror'. William Krar did not fit the template of the discourse: Saddam Hussein did. But in reporting the global 'war on terror', 'facts' were not always to the fore. In the late summer of 2003, 20 per cent of Americans

[59] *New Jersey Militia Newsletter*, 7:8 (February 2002), at http://www.njmilitia.org/Feb02.htm [9/2005].
[60] *PDD 39* is at http://www.fas.org/irp/offdocs/pdd39.htm [9/2005].
[61] See http://www.fas.org/irp/threat/conplan.html [9/2005].
[62] Tony Frieden, 'FBI, ATF address domestic terrorism', CNN, 19 May 2005, at http://www.cnn.com/2005/US/05/19/domestic.terrorism/ [9/2005].
[63] In Larry Copeland, 'Domestic terrorism: new trouble at home', *USA Today*, 14 November 2004.

Table 6.1 Frequency of misperceptions: evidence of al-Qaeda links, WMD found, world public opinion favourable

News source	Respondents with one or more misperceptions (per cent)
Fox	80
CBS	71
ABC	61
NBC	55
CNN	55
Print media	47
PBS – NPR	23

Source: Kull, 'Misperceptions'.

thought Saddam had used chemical weapons in the Iraq war of that year, 22 per cent thought that Iraqi weapons of mass destruction had been found, 25 per cent believed that the view of the world was in favour of the American attack on Iraq, 32 per cent believed that it was very likely that Saddam Hussein was personally involved in the attacks of 11 September 2001, and 48 per cent believed that evidence of a link between Iraq and al-Qaeda had been found.[64] These misperceptions did not float freely; they were constructed by (in part) and through (in larger part) the mass news media. Calculating misperceptions of this sort, and mapping them on to the sources that respondents declared that they had for news produced a very interesting pattern as shown in table 6.1. Perhaps predictably, Fox came out top – the worst – but the gap between Fox and mainstream channels such as CBS is actually not that great. And note that CNN did as well as, or better than, the three mainstream channels; although a 55 per cent misperception rate is not that impressive. The best source, though, through this survey was public service television and radio. From this survey it seems that not only Fox, but the mainstream news media, too, were fully a part of the 'war on terror'.

Certain elements of the news media sought to use the 'war on terror' explicitly in order to support the Bush election campaign. The *New York*

[64] See Steven Kull, 'Misperceptions, the media and the Iraq War', *Programme on International Policy Attitudes*, 2 October 2003, at http://www.pipa.org/OnlineReports/Iraq/Media_10_02_03_Report.pdf [7/2005].

Post responded to the release of a video by Osama bin Laden with a headline saying that he 'Urges Bush Defeat'; to help the reader further, Adam Bronsky explained that 'A vote for Kerry is a vote for European anti-Semitism. And terrorists. In Iraq . . . and Israel. It's a vote for Hamas and Hezbollah, Syria and Iran.'[65] On *Fox News*, when a discussant objected to the view that bin Laden was endorsing Kerry, 'saying, "I don't think he's going to have a Kerry–Edwards sticker in the cave," host Neil Cavuto retorted: "He's all but doing that. I thought I saw a button." '[66]

The election coverage in the media also affected how people thought about the future. *USA Today* covered the Republican convention under the title banner 'Praise and protests greet GOP' and, in the reporting, produced an opinion poll asking 'Thinking about the Sept. 11 terrorist attacks, do you think the country will ever completely return to normal?' Just 4 per cent said yes; 28 per cent expressed the hope that it would, one day; and a massive 64 per cent said it would never return to normal. That demonstrated the power of the discourse: because now all but 4 per cent (in a survey) believed that the country had been fundamentally changed.[67] And that, of course, was why the Kerry campaign was fought on conducting the 'war on terror' more efficiently, rather than in terms of thinking about the issues in discursively different frames.

Perhaps emblematic of the impact of the 'war on terror' on the mainstream media, and that media's role in producing and reproducing that discourse, in 2005 the *New York Times* reviewed and decided to change the nature of its coverage. The newspaper's Credibility Committee argued that 'We need to listen carefully to colleagues who are at home in realms that are not familiar to most of us . . .' and that 'We should seek talented journalists who happen to have military experience, who know rural America first hand, who are at home in different faiths.'[68] This was widely seen to be code for an attempt to soften the newspaper's liberal image which, on a number of subjects – including, very powerfully, the 'war on terror' – had been heavily

[65] In Eric Alterman, 'Pin the terrorist on the donkey', *The Nation*, 29 November 2004, at http://www.thenation.com/doc.mhtml%3Fi=20041129&s=altertman [7/2005].

[66] In 'Murdoch exploits 9/11 for Kerry smear', '*Fairness and Accuracy in Reporting*, 1 November 2004, at http://www.fair.org/index.php?page=1997 [7/2005].

[67] Bill Nichols, 'Praise and protests greet GOP', *USA Today*, 30 August 2004; the poll was conducted by *USA Today*, CNN and Gallup.

[68] 'Preserving our readers' trust', *New York Times*, May 2005, at http://www.nytco.com/pdf/siegal-report050205.pdf [7/2005].

criticised by conservatives.[69] The *New York Times*, its Credibility Committee was arguing in effect, needed to situate itself more obviously in the mainstream of the 'war on terror' discourse *because* of its liberal identity.[70] Nor was this the only example of a media outlet examining its market in the light of the 'war on terror'. An advertisement featuring Cindy Sheehan asking why her son had died in Iraq was banned by KTVX-TV Channel 4 in Utah, for being 'incompatible with the marketplace'.[71] The channel is owned by Clear Channel Communications; other stations – including the Fox affiliate – did show the advert in Utah. The *Washington Post*, WTOP Radio, 630 WMAL, WJLA television and news-based Channel 8 all agreed to sponsor the *Freedom Walk*, a Defense Department event in Washington on 11 September 2005 to commemorate 9/11: the event concluded with a performance from Clint Black, who had written 'I Raq and Roll'.[72] Media outlets, in different ways, were conforming to the logic of the 'war on terror'.

Hence, by the time of the London bombs in July 2005, the template of the 'war on terror' was firmly established to explain events, and to put them into their commonsense framework. President Bush constructed the narrative very speedily:

> We don't know who committed the attacks in London, but we do know that terrorists celebrate the suffering of the innocent . . . murder in the name of a totalitarian ideology that hates freedom, rejects tolerance and despises all dissent. Their aim . . . is to remake the Middle East in their own grim image of tyranny and oppression by toppling governments, by exporting terror, by forcing free nations to retreat and withdraw. To achieve these aims, they attacked our country on September the 11th, 2001. They've continued to kill

69 See criticisms at http://www.timeswatch.org/topicindex/T/terrorism/welcome.asp [7/2005].

70 Daniel Okrent, the Public Editor of the *New York Times* – the readers' representative – wrote 'Is the *New York Times* a liberal newspaper?' and answered: 'Of course it is.' See 'Week in review', *New York Times*, 25 July 2004.

71 'KTVX-TV Channel 4, refused to accept the ads. Station executive Jemina Keller claimed that it is an "inappropriate commercial advertisement for Salt Lake City . . . incompatible with our marketplace"'. 'Gold Star Families for Peace TV spot will follow Bush to Salt Lake City', Gold Star Families for Peace, 19 August 2005 at http://www.gsfp.org/article.php?id=92 [9/2005].

72 The *Post* subsequently dropped its support – see David Montgomery, 'Post drops plan to promote Pentagon event', *Washington Post*, 16 August 2005. The *Freedom Walk* website is http://www.asyfreedomwalk.com/from where the list of supporters is drawn.

– in Bali, in Casablanca, Riyadh, Jakarta, Istanbul, Madrid and elsewhere . . . In the face of such adversaries there is only one course of action: We will continue to take the fight to the enemy, and we will fight until this enemy is defeated.[73]

Notice that although 'we don't know who committed the attacks', blame is clearly placed at the door of al-Qaeda, to whom a series of attacks are attributed, along with intention. The primacy of the 'war on terror' was reasserted. Even more quickly, however, on the day of the first bombs, 7 July 2005, discussion on *Fox and Friends* between host Brian Kilmeade and substitute presenter Stuart Varney ran as follows:

KILMEADE: . . . at the G8 summit, where their topic Number 1 – believe it or not – was global warming, the second was African aid. And that was the first time since 9-11 when they should know, and they do know now, that terrorism should be Number 1. But it's important for them all to be together. I think that works to our advantage, in the western world's advantage, for people to experience something like this together, just 500 miles from where the attacks have happened.

VARNEY: It puts the Number 1 issue right back on the front burner right at the point where all these world leaders are meeting. It takes global warming off the front burner. It takes African aid off the front burner. It sticks terrorism and the fight on the war on terror, right up front all over again.[74]

Here is an example of the co-production of meaning – here by the President, and by Fox News – in which an event is understood in a particular way through a particular discourse, and the pre-eminence of the policy programme can therefore be reasserted.

The immediate imposition of the 'war on terror' template on to the London bombings was seen throughout the American media. As Paul Gough noted, 'The Big Three networks hastily scrapped their morning-show plans as they scrambled to react to the bombings . . . The saturation coverage on NBC's *Today*, ABC's *Good Morning, America* and CBS's *The Early Show* set the stage for a day of near wall

[73] George W. Bush, 'President discusses war on terror at FBI academy', 11 July 2005, at http://www.whitehouse.gov/news/releases/2005/07/20050711-1.html [7/2005].

[74] Cited on *Media Matters for America*, 7 July 2005, at http://mediamatters.org/items/200507070005 [7/2005].

to wall coverage on the major broadcast and cable news channels.'[75] The nature of the coverage – including of course factual reporting – also brought the focus from London to America. Between 10.30 and midday (EST) ABC, CNN, Fox and MSNBC had all begun to speculate about what the London bombs meant for America. A little later, Homeland Security Secretary, Michael Chertoff, announced that the national alert status for the United States would be raised from code yellow to code orange.[76] As Mark Jurkowitz put it, 'It is barely lunchtime, and the London bombing has already come home to roost.'[77]

The news media had operated within, and had sometimes extended, the 'war on terror' discursive framework. On many occasions they drew upon the input of experts, and this category forms the third element of the 'war on terror' striking back.

Experts and think tanks fighting the 'war on terror'

One of the most powerful bastions in developing the 'war on terror' discourse has been the 'experts', those that can be called upon to adjudicate between differing opinions. But of course 'expert' opinion is not neutral; it, too, not only constructs discourse but is constructed by it. Indeed, in the 'expert' community – often housed in think tanks – one task is to expand that which is discursively possible, rather like those in the mass media who speak, for example, through Fox. One powerful source of such discursive development has been *The Weekly Standard*, a magazine edited by William Kristol, and consequently much associated with the development of neoconservative thought. Through and after the Iraq War of 2003, there was increasing frustration with America's European allies. *The Weekly Standard* gave full access to the intellectualising of that frustration, which had begun with

[75] Paul J. Gough, 'US media rush to cover London bombings', Reuters, 8 July 2005, at http://politics.yahoo.com/s/nm/20050708/tv_nm/london_dc/nc:1293 [7/2005].

[76] Transcript from Secretary Michael Chertoff, 'Press briefing on the London bombings', 7 July 2005, at http://www.dhs.gov/dhspublic/interapp/press_release/press_release_0700.xml [7/2005].

[77] Mark Jurkowitz, 'Terror diary: from cable news and the pundit shows to the dailies . . .', *Boston Phoenix*, 15 July 2005, at http://www.bostonphoenix.com/boston/news_features/dont_quote_me/multi-page/documents/04823485.asp [7/2005].

the description of the French as 'cheese-eating surrender monkeys' in popular debate, and had moved on to the renaming of French fries as 'freedom fries'.[78] In May 2005, Joseph Bottum – a contributing editor at both the religious journal *First Things* and *The Weekly Standard* – condemned 'Europe' in the following terms:

> A failing civilization can't be argued out of its failing . . . when a culture is tumbling downward, all its truths and facts – indeed, the whole idea of truth and fact and argument – are exactly what its people increasing disbelieve. Does anyone doubt that western Europe is tumbling downward? It cannot summon the will to reproduce itself. It has aborted and contracepted its birthrate down toward demographic disaster . . . it has proved supine in the face of those [Islamic] immigrants' anti-Semitism, anti-Christianism, and even anti-Europeanism.[79]

The discursive format is revealing. In creating a narrative of the 'fall' ('tumbling downwards'), in criticising Europe's 'aborting' and 'contracepting' choices, and in its acceptance of Islam's 'anti-Semitism' and 'anti-Christianism', Bottum illustrates the evangelical roots from which much of this ideology arises, as will be argued later in this chapter.

Bottum wrote as an 'expert'. Other 'experts' legitimise policy and meaning in other ways. For example, Peter Bergen – author of *Holy War Inc.* and CNN 'expert' – gave authoritative statements on the new threat after the Madrid bombings; Michael Scheuer, an ex-CIA operative and author (as 'Anonymous') of *Imperial Hubris: Why the West is Losing the War on Terror* gave sound bites on the nature of the war after the London bombings; some 'experts' enter government – for example, Robert L. Hutchings, former assistant dean at the Woodrow Wilson Centre at Princeton, to chair the CIA's National Intelligence Council. [80] 'Experts' are created by the authoritative positions they hold

[78] 'Cheese-eating surrender monkeys' is derived from *The Simpsons*, and was made popular before the Iraq War by commentators such as Jonah Goldberg. See his 'Inscrutably racism', *The National Review*, 6 April 2001, at http://www.nationalreview.com/goldberg/goldbergprint040601.html [7/2005]. 'Freedom fries' was a term of the Iraq War. 'French' was replaced before 'fries' and 'toast' in the House of Representatives cafeteria in March 2003. 'US Congress opts for "freedom fries"', *BBC News*, 12 March 2003, at http://news.bbc.co.uk/1/hi/world/americas/2842493.stm [7/2005].

[79] Joseph Bottum, 'The last European pope?', *The Weekly Standard*, 2 May 2005.

[80] On Bergen, see Kelli Arena, 'Experts: war on terror could spawn new enemies', CNN.com, 6 May 2004, at http://www.cnn.com/2004/WORLD/meast/03/15/

or have held, and they are able to powerfully co-produce and reproduce discourse. One early example was that of Ebrahim Moosa, Professor of Islamic Studies at Duke University, who wrote in October 2001, 'While many respectable Muslim organizations the world over have condemned the reprehensible carnage at the World Trade Center on Sept. 11, there is a growing number of groups and individuals who equivocate in their rebuke of violence. In doing so, they become apologists for violence and terror.'[81] From there – a discursive move that silences discussion, requiring all to rehearse the mantra of the 'war on terror' regardless of subject matter – it is a relatively small step to the views of Matthew A. Levitt, who said in January 2003, 'We can hardly expect the support of the Arab masses in the war on terror when their most respected journalists and intellectuals are apologists for terrorism.'[82] As James Petras put it in a highly critical analysis of the role of 'experts' in the 'war on terror', 'The Terrorist Experts are the "set-up" people, the motivators.'[83] In his view, the role of the 'expert' is to mouth the views of the establishment, and to silence alternative perspectives.

'Experts' are above all to be found in and through the think tanks. Those organisations are the repositories of self-defined knowledge in particular sectors, and that knowledge is framed by particular political and thereby discursive practices. The role of those think tanks in the United States that have been active in the 'war on terror' has largely been to reproduce that discourse through the power of 'expert' testimony, but some have also been involved in co-producing that discourse. The Project for the New American Century has been central to this. PNAC had campaigned aggressively for George Bush in the presidential elections: in a note entitled 'John Kerry doesn't know his

alqaeda.splinter/; on Scheuer, see 'Experts fear "endless" terror war', MSNBC, 9 July 2005 at http://www.msnbc.msn.com/id/8524679/ [both7/2005]; on Hutchings, see Dana Priest, 'Iraq new terror breeding ground', *Washington Post*, 14 January 2005. Peter Bergen's *Holy War Inc.* (New York: Free Press, 2002) was one of the first studies of Osama bin Laden.

81 Ebrahim Moosa, 'Muslims must not be apologists for terror', *Faculty Viewpoints*, 8 October 2001, at http://www.duke.edu/web/forums/moosa.html [7/2005].

82 Matthew A. Levitt, 'The state of denial', *National Review Online*, 28 January 2003, at http://www.nationalreview.com/comment/comment-levitt012803.asp [7/2005].

83 James Petras, 'The anatomy of "terror experts" ', *Counter Punch*, 7/8 August 2004, at http://counterpunch.org/petras08072004.html [7/2005].

own mind', William Kristol had opened: 'The problem with being an opportunist is that you can easily forget what you've recently said.'[84] But more at the core of its operation, in briefings and discussions with those in the administration – many of whom were formerly members of PNAC – and powerfully through its 'Memorandum To: Opinion Leaders' letters, PNAC has sought to move policy onwards. In March 2004, as the American military in Iraq seemed to be facing increasing resistance, many felt that the doctrine of pre-emption was no longer relevant. The task of PNAC was to resist this, and to make pre-emption simply common sense. In the *Los Angeles Times*, Gary Schmitt wrote 'well before Bush became president, preemption was a necessary policy option. And it will remain one long after he leaves the White House for a simple reason: The world is what it is, and no responsible chief executive can afford to think otherwise.'[85] Not all of this is necessarily supportive of the administration, and that is the point of co-production – sources can lie outside the government. In 2005, PNAC argued for a greater US troop commitment to Iraq. A significant number of PNAC members and others wrote to Senator Frist, Senator Reid, Speaker Hastert and Representative Pelosi in January 2005 as follows:

> The United States military is too small for the responsibilities we are asking it to assume. Those responsibilities are real and important. They are not going away. The United States will not and should not become less engaged in the world in the years to come. But our national security, global peace and stability, and the defense and promotion of freedom in the post-9/11 world require a larger military force than we have today. The administration has unfortunately resisted increasing our ground forces to the size needed to meet today's (and tomorrow's) missions and challenges. So we write to ask you and your colleagues in the legislative branch to take the steps necessary to increase substantially the size of the active duty Army and Marine Corps.[86]

The message was clear: the administration was wavering in the 'war on terror' and needed Congress to bolster it. PNAC would provide the intellectual ammunition for that bolstering. As William Kristol and Gary Schmitt

[84] William Kristol, 'Subject: John Kerry doesn't know his own mind', 19 August 2004, at http://www.newamericancentury.org/defense-20040819.htm [7/2005].

[85] Gary Schmitt, 'Shooting first', *Los Angeles Times*, 30 May 2004.

[86] 'Letter to Congress on increasing US ground forces', PNAC, 28 January 2005, at http://www.newamericancentury.org/defense-20050128.htm [7/2005].

put it in a 'Memorandum to: Opinion leaders' letter, 'Secretary Rumsfeld is putting the President's strategic vision at risk, while those soldiering in Iraq are trying to save a policy in the face of inadequate resources.'[87]

Another key think tank in the provision of 'expertise' was the American Enterprise Institute. AEI provided a forum of independence and legitimacy for the 'war on terror' to be refined. In a speech at a conference on the Patriot Act at the AEI, John Ashcroft said:

> Two years separate us from the day when our nation's stock of consecrated ground grew tragically larger. That day, a familiar list of monuments to American freedom . . . places like Bunker Hill, Antietam, the Argonne, Iwo Jima, and Normandy Beach . . . grew longer by three:
> 16 acres in lower Manhattan.
> The Pentagon.
> A field in Shanksville, Pennsylvania.
> For the dead, the hallowed spaces of freedom are memorials, testaments to their sacrifice. For the living, they are a warning. They are a reminder that the first responsibility of government is to provide the security that preserves the lives and liberty of the people.[88]

The fight for liberty across time, which now included the 'war on terror': this was poignant imagery. The location gave the speech added value: it was not a government press briefing, but rather a conference, to 'share ideas'. The AEI would also seek ways of accelerating the policy programme. In the book *An End to Evil: How to Win the War on Terror* (the Christian motif of 'evil' again) the authors – David Frum and Richard Perle – comment that 'This world is an unsafe place for Americans – and the US government remains unready to defend its people.'[89] They proceed to explain what more needs to be done. In May 2005, Michael Ledeen criticised the loss of momentum in the administration, and called for greater focus.[90] AEI, rather like PNAC, aimed at keeping the momentum in the 'war on terror' going.

87 William Kristol and Gary Schmitt, 'Subject: bring the troops home?' 12 July 2005, at http://www.newamericancentury.org/troops-20050713.htm [7/2005].

88 John Ashcroft, 'Securing our liberty: how America is winning the war on terror', *AEI*, 19 August 2005, at http://www.aei.org/publications/pubID.19040,filter.all/pub_detail.asp [7/2005].

89 From the book blurb: David Frum and Richard Perle, *An End to Evil, AEI*, November 2003, at http://www.aei.org/books/bookID.650,filter.all/book_detail.asp [7/2005].

90 Michael A. Ledeen, 'Drifting', *AEI,* 31 May 2005, at http://www.aei.org/publications/pubID.22598,filter.all/pub_detail.asp [7/2005].

The third think tank to be briefly examined here in terms of its role in the 'war on terror' is the Heritage Foundation. Like both PNAC and the AEI, Heritage sought to keep the momentum going, and to encourage the development of the policy programme. Its series of research papers included a significant number on homeland security and the 'war on terror'. This was all designed to support the administration; Heritage was concerned with reproducing the discourse with the discursive power of the approval of the 'expert'. Ariel Cohen's commentary on President Bush's speech at Fort Bragg in 2005 was: 'In all, President Bush presented a broad and honest strategy to the American people. Iraq is an important part of the long war on terror, and no matter how long it takes, we must prevail there.'[91] In commenting on the Defense Department's *Strategy for Homeland Defense and Civil Support*, James Jay Carafano wrote 'It is just a paper, but if it is put into action it will help make all Americans safer.'[92] But as with the other two think tanks, Heritage was also concerned with moving the policy programme forward, for example, in improving the management of data security, or in terms of making the Department of Homeland Security more efficient.[93]

Think tanks and 'experts' have thereby played powerful roles in legitimising the 'war on terror' discourse, and in delegitimising other discourses; in reproducing the hegemonic discourse; in maintaining momentum in policy development; and in furthering, in co-producing, the policy programme. The above-mentioned think tanks – and of course many others – operated in the midst of what has been termed a 'culture war' in the United States, in which particular markers of identity (essentially 'liberal' or 'conservative') have carried forward a discourse which defines support for, and opposition towards, particular

[91] Ariel Cohen, 'Bush at Fort Bragg', Heritage Foundation web memo 780, 29 June 2005, at http://www.heritage.org/Research/NationalSecurity/wm780.cfm [7/2005].

[92] James Jay Carafano 'Defense Department's serious thinking about homeland security', Heritage Foundation web memo 790, 8 July 2005 at http://www.heritage.org/Research/HomelandDefense/wm790.cfm [7/2005].

[93] On the former, see Paul Rosenzweig and Alane Kochems, 'Data protection: safeguarding privacy in a new age of technology', Heritage Foundation legal memorandum 16, 23 March 2005, at http://www.heritage.org/Research/HomelandDefense/lm16.cfm; on the latter, see Heritage Foundation, 'Reforming the Department of Homeland Security: the Heritage Foundation's research', web memo 706, 30 March 2005, at http://www.heritage.org/Research/HomelandDefense/wm706.cfm [both 7/2005].

policies. As argued earlier, this mapping does not work well for the 'war on terror', as 'liberal' as well as 'conservative' have articulated the 'war on terror' discourse. But when turning from 'expert' opinion to that expressed in popular literature, these distinctions are quite crucial.

The 'war on terror' in books and novels

America's 'culture wars' are a powerful part of everyday debate and life. Stanford University's website includes a section on *Culture Wars 101*, with a variety of helpful definitions and readings.[94] As James Davison Hunter put it in 1991, 'America is in the midst of a culture war that has had and will continue to have reverberations not only within public policy but within the lives of ordinary Americans everywhere . . . *At stake is how we as Americans will order our lives together*.'[95] That America has been undergoing this 'culture war' gives some understanding to the titles of books that might otherwise seem bizarre: Michael Savage's *Liberalism is a Mental Disorder*; Al Franken's *Lies and the Lying Liars Who Tell Them*; and Ann Coulter's *How to Talk to a Liberal (If You Must)*.[96] These are not books about the 'war on terror', but each needs to express a view on that discourse. Thus, Savage explains that 'Real homeland security begins when we arrest, interrogate, jail, or deport known operatives within our own borders . . .'[97] For Savage, the threat is so great that concerns with civil liberties are simply liberal weaknesses, as we see when he says: 'The 9/11 attack on America by the Islamofascists . . . may eventually be seen as the turning point where America breaks free of the chains of socialist oppression . . .'[98] Thus, the threat of 'Islamic' terror can be utilised to break liberal constraints on America. Al Franken, from the 'liberal' side of the 'war' condemns George Bush for 'p***ing off the world'. After the attacks of

94 See http://sepwww.stanford.edu/sep/josman/culture/#cw, although by July 2005, the site was no longer live.

95 James Davison Hunter, *Culture Wars: The Struggle to Define America* (New York: Basic Books, 1991), p. 34. Italics in the original.

96 Michael Savage, *Liberalism is a Mental Disorder* (Nashville, TN: Nelson Current, 2005); Al Franken, *Lies and the Lying Liars Who Tell Them* (New York: Dutton Adult, 2003); Ann Coulter, *How to Talk to a Liberal (If You Must)* (New York: Crown Forum, 2004).

97 Cited in 'Michael Savage diagnoses "the mental disorder of liberalism" . . . , National Review Bookservice, at http://nrbookservice.com/products/bookpage.asp?prod_cd=c6621 [7/2005].

98 Ibid.

9/11, 'we got the world back on our side . . . Then he p****d them all off again.'[99] The administration thereby failed to unite the world against terror, despite that being a key part of the decisive intervention. Coulter, back on the 'conservative' side of the 'war' criticises liberal presentations of the 'war on terror' and the claim that Islam is a religion of peace. 'The [*New York*] *Times* was rushing to assure its readers that "prominent Islamic scholars and theologians in the West say unequivocally that nothing in Islam countenances the Sept. 11 actions." That's if you set aside Muhammad's many specific instructions to kill nonbelievers whenever possible.'[100] On the inside flap of the book, Coulter is quoted as follows, under the heading 'Her 9/11 comments': 'I am often asked if I still think we should invade their countries, kill their leaders, and convert them to Christianity. The answer is: Now more than ever!'[101]

The 'war on terror' is therefore a marker in America's culture wars. The 'conservatives' worried that America had been made intellectually weak by the 'liberals'. As Larry Schweikart and Michael Patrick Allen put it in *A Patriot's History of the United States: From Columbus's Great Discovery to the War on Terror* there had been 'more emphasis placed on Harriet Tubman than George Washington; more about the internment of Japanese Americans during World War II than about D-Day or Iwo Jima; more on the dangers of Joseph McCarthy than we faced from Joseph Stalin'.[102] Jeanne Kirkpatrick felt moved to write a piece intriguingly entitled 'Neoconservatism as a response to the counter culture'.[103] Peter Schweizer's culturally conservative tract is called *Do As I Say (Not As I Do): Profiles in Liberal Hypocrisy*.[104] And in books which were aimed at being populist while examining key

[99] Franken, *Lies*, p. 347.

[100] In 'Ann Coulter: uncensored and uncut', National Review Bookservice, at http://nrbookservice.com/products/bookpage.asp?prod_cd=c6550 [7/2005]

[101] It is possible to purchase a T-shirt with this message at http://www.thoseshirts.com/coulter.html [9/2005].

[102] Larry Schweikart and Michael Patrick Allen, *A Patriot's History of the United States: From Columbus's Great Discovery to the War on Terror* (New York: Sentinel, 2004), frontispiece.

[103] Jeanne Kirkpatrick, 'Neoconservatism as a response to the counter culture', in I. Stelzer, *The NeoCon Reader* (London: Atlantic Books, 2004).

[104] Peter Schweizer, *Do As I Say (Not As I Do): Profiles in Liberal Hypocrisy* (New York: Doubleday, 2005).

political issues, 'culture wars' and the 'war on terror' were frequently intermingled. Sean Hannity's *Deliver us from Evil* (the Christian motif of 'evil' again) tied these themes together explicitly: the subtitle of the book is *Defeating Terrorism, Despotism and Liberalism.*[105] Hannity, one of the leading news anchors for *Fox News*, lays out the problem at the beginning of the book:

> Evil exists. It is real, and it means to harm us . . . When you work in the news business, you deal with the ugly side of life. Every day across your desk comes story after story of man's inhumanity to man, from mass murderers to child molesters to mothers who drown their children to husbands who murder their pregnant wives . . . Still, isolated events like these pale beside the pure evil of September 11. How could anyone witness the horrors of that day, or the mass graves discovered in Iraq after the fall of Saddam Hussein, and dismiss the idea of evil? And yet many people do – most of them political liberals.[106]

Hannity tied together the themes in just over one paragraph. 'Evil' is an objective reality, all around us. In America, it leads to tragic crime. Internationally, it leads to the murder of Americans and of innocent Iraqis. Evil must be confronted, and yet the 'liberals' just do not understand.

These themes are explored in the work of Michael D. Evans, whose writing can be found in American bookstores in the 'Bible and current affairs' sections. In *The American Prophecies: Ancient Scriptures Reveal Our Nation's Future*, Evans commented: 'Liberal politicians and special interest groups continue to propagate a myth that Islam is a peaceful religion.'[107] Later he asserts that 'As for America, Islamic extremists hate everything about us; but their greatest hatred is our Christian majority and biblical principles by which we live our lives . . .'[108] In *Beyond Iraq: The Next Move – Ancient Prophecy and Modern Day Conspiracy Collide*, Evans produces a reading of the war in Iraq through the lens of the Bible, calls for greater support for Israel,

105 Sean Hannity, *Deliver Us from Evil: Defeating Terrorism. Despotism and Liberalism* (New York: Regan Books, 2005).
106 Ibid., p. 2. Hannity describes himself as a Catholic.
107 Michael D. Evans *The American Prophecies: Ancient Scriptures Reveal Our Nation's Future* (New York: Warner Faith, 2004), p. 8.
108 Ibid., p. 24.

and identifies the threats to America posed by Islam, declaring – in the tone of a mainstream neoconservative – 'Iraq will not be the end.'[109]

Many of these 'conservative' writers were pushing the discursive framework of the 'war on terror' in important ways; 'liberals' in general, and the Democrats in particular, were to be denied the right to access patriotism, honour and duty. In that way, 'liberals' were denied access to being part of the value system; they were part of the problem. One author who made this case through comparing the track record of Presidents Clinton and Bush was Richard Miniter. In *Losing Bin Laden: How Bill Clinton's Failures Unleashed Global Terror*, Miniter declared that he will not be producing an even-handed account, but rather an assessment of liberal failure.[110] To underscore the partisan point, he then published *Shadow War: The Untold Story of How Bush is Winning the War on Terror*, and again, the thesis is clear from the title.[111]

The pressure from America's culture wars on the 'war on terror' is clear: it has expanded that which is discursively necessary. In the establishment of the decisive intervention, unity and an absence of blame were central. This began to break down in 2002, and had, by 2005, broken down pretty fully in those issues that were subject to a different template – that of the culture wars. Mapping the war on terror on to the culture wars' divisions cut across the unity that had been part of the decisive intervention. The discourse had to evolve.

Yet attacks on the administration for being weak in the pursuit of the policy programme were also a powerful element in the literary turn after those events. It was not simply the culture wars, with cultural conservatives rallying around the administration. There were those who deemed the policy programme to be too *liberal*. Michelle Malkin, for example, was a strong critic of American vulnerability. In *Invasion*, published in 2002, she wrote 'One year after the attacks, the avenues for death and destruction remain virtually unobstructed.'[112] The subtitle of the book gave a full flavour: *How America Still Welcomes Terrorists, Criminals*

[109] Michael D. Evans *Beyond Iraq: The Next Move – Ancient Prophecy and Modern Day Conspiracy Collide* (Tulsa, OK: Harrison House, 2003), p. 19.

[110] Richard Miniter, *Losing Bin Laden: How Bill Clinton's Failures Unleashed Global Terror* (Washington, DC: Regnery, 2003).

[111] Richard Miniter, *Shadow War: The Untold Story of How Bush is Winning the War on Terror* (Washington, DC: Regnery, 2004).

[112] Michelle Malkin, *Invasion: How America Still Welcomes Terrorists, Criminals and Other Foreign Menaces to Our Shores* (Washington, DC: Regnery, 2002), p. 3.

and Other Foreign Menaces to Our Shores. Malkin's opening chapter was entitled 'What would Mohammed do?' This apparently referred to Mohammed Atta, the ringleader of the attacks on 11 September 2001, but to many Americans this could be read differently. 'What would Jesus do?' was a popular notice on many working desks (including that of the former Vice President, Al Gore). 'Mohammed', in this reading, was the Prophet (PBUH), and stood for values diametrically opposed to those ascribed to Jesus. Malkin followed the success of this book with her 2004 book *In Defense of Internment: The Case for 'Racial Profiling' in the Second World War and the War on Terror*.[113]

Another of the powerful critiques of the policy programme for being too weak was made by Stephen Flynn. In *America the Vulnerable* he wrote that 'If September 11, 2001, was a wake-up call, clearly America has fallen back asleep. Our return to complacency could not be more foolhardy . . . we are sailing into a national security version of the Perfect Storm.'[114] Flynn wanted a major investment in all aspects of American life, from container security to a focus on the security of the food chain. The policy programme, in short, needed to be ramped up: 'This is not a time for timidity . . .'[115] As a Senior Fellow at the Council on Foreign Relations, his words carried the weight of an 'expert'.

If the 'war on terror' was a key part of those books that sought to engage in popular political debate, that discourse had also penetrated the popular novel. Authors worked hard to churn out pot boilers with a terror theme. Patrick Robinson was one author inspired by this war. In *Barracuda 945*, America came under threat from terrorists in a submarine firing missiles at infrastructure, with one of the American protagonists declaring: 'Gentlemen, we have been the victims of terrorism of the worst type since 9/11. Less death, but severe damage to our country.'[116] In *Scimitar SL-2*, terrorists – with links to Russia, China and North Korea – threaten to trigger a massive tsunami with a nuclear weapon, and America's response is undermined by a liberal President who lacks the courage to face the crisis.[117] His third offering, *Hunter*

113 Michelle Malkin, *In Defense of Internment: The Case for 'Racial Profiling' in the Second World War and the War on Terror* (Washington DC: Regnery, 2004).

114 Stephen Flynn, *America the Vulnerable: How Our Government is Failing to Protect us from Terrorism* (New York: HarperCollins, 2004), p. 1.

115 Ibid., p. 155.

116 Patrick Robinson, *Barracuda 945* (New York: Harper Torch, 2004), p. 446.

117 Patrick Robinson, *Scimitar SL-2* (New York: Harper Torch, 2004).

Killer, sees the American hero trying to prevent the Saudi royal family from being overthrown by terrorists with French help.[118] Hostility to France is an added bonus for Robinson in this book. Others take more direct aim at Paris. Michael Chesnoff had entitled his book *The Arrogance of the French: Why They Can't Stand Us – and Why the Feeling is Mutual*.[119]

Other authors followed the formula. Christopher Reich's *The Devil's Banker* sees a terrorist being killed in a Paris explosion linked to a massive terrorist threat, which has to be prevented through following the terrorists' money trail.[120] In *Force Protection*, Islamic terrorism is blamed for an attack on a US naval ship in Africa, though the investigators find that it is more complex.[121] Stephen Coonts and Jim DeFelice's *Deep Black Dark Zone* sees a secret American counter-terrorist organisation struggling against the threats of the use of plutonium weapons against the Eiffel Tower and the Channel Tunnel (or Chunnel, as Coonts continually refers to it).[122] Other authors examine the internal dynamics of the 'war on terror'. W. E. B. Griffin sets the scene around the infighting amongst America's counter-terrorism agencies.[123] Jeffrey Anderson – *Dr* Anderson, playing up the theme of the 'expert' – focuses on the role of 'sleepers' in waging terror attacks on the United States. As the terrorists' warning explains, 'The epidemic in Los Angeles is Allah's warning of the coming plague. He will unleash the nanodeath on the infidels. His nanomachines cannot be stopped until they have destroyed every American man, woman and child.'[124] Jim DeFelice constructs his story around the North Korean development of the e-bomb (which destroys electrical systems), that falls into terrorist hands, who also have sarin gas.[125] The book begins with the death and destruction which follows from a (simulated) collapse of electrical systems in New York. John Weisman's *SOAR – A Black Ops Mission* has a special American team racing a Chinese team to find ter-

118 Patrick Robinson, *Hunter Killer* (New York: Harper Torch, 2005).
119 Michael Chesnoff, *The Arrogance of the French: Why They Can't Stand Us – and Why the Feeling is Mutual* (New York: Sentinel, 2005).
120 Christopher Reich, *The Devil's Banker* (New York: Dell, 2003).
121 Gordon Kent, *Force Protection* (New York: Delacorte, 2004).
122 Stephen Coonts and Jim DeFelice, *Deep Black Dark Zone* (New York: St Martin's Press, 2004).
123 W. E. B. Griffin, *By Order of the President* (New York: Putnam, 2004).
124 Jeffrey Anderson, *Sleeper Cell* (New York: Berkley, 2005), p. 64.
125 Jim DeFelice, *Threat Level Black* (New York: Pocket Books, 2005).

rorists who have captured both hostages and a nuclear weapon that is armed, and ready to fire.[126]

In *Memorial Day*, Vince Flynn tells the story of a CIA agent who has to thwart a terrorist nuclear attack. The terrorists might have a nuclear bomb in Washington, and it threatens to kill the President, other senior figures and foreign leaders. When puzzling what to do – whether to evacuate or not – one figure says that if the President is moved out of the city, and so:

'. . . if they know they can't get him, they'll just kill as many people as they can.'

'And if they manage to get this thing into Washington and end up killing the leaders of America, Great Britain and Russia?'

Rapp shrugged. 'At least there won't be any more ambivalence about the war on terror.'[127]

Christopher Whitcomb sells his books partly by his expertise: he is ex-FBI. In *Black* four subplots fill the book until, at the end, they come together in a story of counter-intelligence and technological challenge.[128] In the sequel, *White*, terrorists are fought in Indonesia and in America, where there seems to be a coalition between Christian and Islamic fundamentalists.[129] David Zeman's *The Pinocchio Syndrome* is a bizarre story of a nuclear attack on an American cruise ship followed by a sinister plague, all of which leads to a political struggle in Washington about how to fight terrorism.[130] Michael Cuningham's *Specimen Days* has a number of stories, the second of which – 'The Children's Crusade' – is set against a series of random terrorist attacks.[131] And there is yet more. Dale Brown's *Act of War* runs the usual gamut in this genre: there is a nuclear attack; the hero has to hunt the terrorists; there is betrayal in Washington; America itself is at risk.[132] And so it is clear that the 'war on terror' has become a key motif in contemporary American fiction. In Nelson DeMille's *Night Fall*, which concerns an investigation into the loss of flight TWA 800 five years after the event (and therefore in the year 2001), we find a couple of jokes:

126 John Weisman, *SOAR – A Black Ops Mission* (New York: Avon, 2003).
127 Vince Flynn, *Memorial Day* (New York: Atria, 2004), p. 319.
128 Christopher Whitcomb, *Black* (New York: Little, Brown & Co., 2004).
129 Christopher Whitcomb, *White* (New York: Little, Brown & Co., 2005).
130 David Zeman, *The Pinocchio Syndrome* (New York: Doubleday, 2003).
131 Michael Cunningham, *Specimen Days* (New York: Farrar, Straus & Giroux, 2005).
132 Dale Brown, *Act of War* (New York: Atari, 2005).

I said to him, 'Harry, what's the definition of a moderate Arab?'

He looked up at me. 'What?'

'A guy who ran out of ammunition.'

He chuckled and said, 'You told me that one.' He advised me, 'You got to watch what you say. What's the difference between an Arab terrorist and a woman with PMS?'

'What?'

'You can reason with an Arab terrorist.'[133]

As with much humour, it tells us something about acceptable attitudes.

Humour is used in a very different way in Art Spiegelman's *In the Shadow of No Towers*.[134] Spiegelman's use of the cartoon to relay political and historical messages achieved international acclaim in *Maus*, as discussed earlier in this book. *In the Shadow of No Towers* is a personal account of the events of 11 September 2001 (Spiegelman and his family lived right by the Twin Towers), punctuated with political observation. We see a family of three, asleep in front of the television, dated 10 September. Then the family on the sofa sitting forward, eyes wide open, hair on end, dated 11 September. And now? The family asleep on the sofa in front of the television, but with hair on end, with the Stars and Stripes where the calendar used to be.[135]

That fiction can have a powerful effect on political debate was illustrated by Richard Clarke's decision to write a novel. Clarke, a former senior intelligence officer, wrote a high-profile book – *Against All Enemies* – about his short time in the Bush administration, criticising the President for ignoring al-Qaeda before the second American 9/11, and for distorting it afterwards.[136] Instead of following this up with another analytical book, Clarke chose to write a novel. 'Fiction can often tell the truth better than nonfiction; characters and plot can drive

[133] DeMille feels bad about this. His next full paragraph reads: 'The Arab and Muslim community in New York, I should point out, is probably ninety eight per cent upstanding and loyal citizens . . .' Nelson DeMille, *Night Fall* (New York: Warner, 2004), p. 177.

[134] Art Spiegelman, *In the Shadow of No Towers* (New York: Pantheon, 2004).

[135] The image is at http://www.randomhouse.com/pantheon/graphicnovels/towersShoe.html [7/2005].

[136] Richard A. Clarke, *Against All Enemies: Inside America's War on Terror* (New York: Free Press, 2004).

home that truth to the reader more effectively than cold facts and analysis.'[137]

The 'war on terror' discourse had become deeply embedded in American writing, and was represented in a variety of literary genres. Much the same could be said for its impact on the music, television and film industries.

Music, television, film and terror

By the end of 2004 and in 2005, with the war in Iraq continuing, though in a different form, there were still acts of memorialisation of the second American 9/11. This was particularly important in terms of reminding Americans why they were doing what they were doing – reminding them of the power of the decisive intervention when it had happened. A very popular example of this in 2004 was the publication of *Brotherhood*, commemorating the 343 New York firefighters who died in the Twin Towers.[138] In 2005, Jim Dwyer and Kevin Flynn published *102 Minutes: The Untold Story of the Fight to Survive Inside the Twin Towers*, the time between the first flight hitting the Towers and the second Tower falling.[139] Based on extensive interviews with the 12,000 people who survived, as well as on media coverage, the authors argued that many others could have survived if communication between the police and fire services had been better, and if building codes had not been based on the idea of keeping people inside in an emergency. In the summer of 2005, some 12,000 pages of transcripts of conversations and oral histories of the September 11th attacks were released, amid much interest from the press and public.[140] The phenomenon of the *Chicken Soup* book series was well entrenched before the second American 9/11. This popular series of books related

[137] Clarke is quoted in 'Richard A. Clarke to write thriller novel', *The Write News*, 15 October 2004, at http://www.writenews.com/2004/101504_richard_clarke_thriller.htm [7/2005].

[138] Frank McCourt, Rudy Giuliani and Thomas Von Essen, *Brotherhood* (New York: American Express Publications, 2004).

[139] Jim Dwyer and Kevin Flynn, *102 Minutes: The Untold Story of the Fight to Survive Inside the Twin Towers* (New York: Times Books, 2005).

[140] See, for example, 'New York releases Sept. 11 tapes, oral histories', NPR, 12 August 2005, at http://www.npr.org/templates/story/story.php?storyId=4797889 [9/2005].

stories to make the reader 'feel good' in a variety of different areas. *Chicken Soup for the Soul of America: Stories to Heal the Heart of Our Nation*, published in 2002, concerned the events of 11 September 2001 and human reaction to it, and contained key elements of the decisive intervention – the call to unity, to global leadership, and so on.[141] Marking the return to memorialisation, 2005's offerings included *Chicken Soup for the Soul Salutes America's Heroes: Stories Honoring Police Officers, Firefighters and Other Emergency Rescue Workers*, which included stories of terrorism amongst others, reminding readers of the heroism narrative in the decisive intervention; and *Chicken Soup for the Military Wife's Soul: Stories to Touch the Heart and Rekindle the Spirit*, with some twenty references to the 'war on terror' in different forms.[142] Congress passed a bill to allow the production of a commemorative coin for 2005, the funds raised from which would be channelled into the cost of a 'Pentagon 9/11 memorial' in Arlington.[143]

In the world of popular music, one of the web-based hits of 2005 was Denis Madalone's rock song 'America We Stand as One'. Madalone sings 'USA . . . America, we stand as one, And you must carry on.'[144] Over 40,000 people logged on to the website in the first five or six days, after which the phenomenon grew much further. But the key imagery here is not in the lyrics, but in the video.[145] Too much for many more cynical commentators, Madalone seeks to speak for those Americans killed on 11 September 2001, in Afghanistan and Iraq and elsewhere in the 'war on terror'. At the beginning of the video, he is entered by spirits on the beach, which presumably means he is speaking for the fallen. We see firefighters and police officers walking in a

[141] Jack Canfield, Mark Victor Hansen and Matthew Adams, *Chicken Soup for the Soul of America: Stories to Heal the Heart of Our Nation* (Dayton, FL: HCI, 2002).

[142] Jack Canfield, Mark Victor Hansen, Rick Canfield and Joseph Woodall, *Chicken Soup for the Soul Salutes America's Heroes: Stories Honoring Police Officers, Firefighters and Other Emergency Rescue Workers*; Jack Canfield, Mark Victor Hansen, Charles Preston and Cindy Pedersen, *Chicken Soup for the Military Wife's Soul: Stories to Touch the Heart and Rekindle the Spirit* (both Dayton, FL: HCI, 2005).

[143] This was the 'Pentagon 9/11 Memorial Commemorative Coin Act of 2005', which can be seen at http://www.theorator.com/bills109/hr1047.html [8/2005].

[144] The video is at http://www.americawestandasone.com/video.html [7/2005].

[145] See 'America stands as one: the exclusive interview', *Orkut*, 20 April 2005, at http://media.orkut.com/articles/0171.html [7/2005].

cloud in the sky, an enormous amount of angel imagery, of course the Statue of Liberty, and a mother and baby by a gravestone, mourning the lost hero. 'I had to go but its ok, you see I'm with you in a different way', sings Madalone. At a point when some felt – or feared – that the power of the 9/11 imagery carried less weight, Madalone proved something different.

Continued acts of remembrance were also influential in the world of television. The fourth anniversary of the second American 9/11 was marked by a special investigative series on the National Geographic Channel. This four hour mini-series, *Inside 9/11*, told the story of the attacks from the origins of al-Qaeda through to the attack itself, and expressed fears for the future.[146] In the field of entertainment, *Rescue Me* was set in the New York Fire Department, and the key narrative of the series concerned the psychological scars felt by the Department's members inflicted by the second American 9/11.[147] The series began in the summer of 2004, and in the first episode, 'Guts', the viewer is introduced to Tommy Gavin, the central figure amongst the firefighters, who cannot escape the pain of 11 September 2001. The next episode centres around claims that several firefighters who died in the second American 9/11 were gay, a claim the key figures set out to refute. In episode 12, 'Leaving', a goodwill tribute to the dead firefighters was the central plot device. Gavin hears the voices of the dead, can't accept that new recruits are worthy of the uniform . . . and so on. The series powerfully reproduced key elements of the decisive intervention in peoples' homes throughout the country for twenty five episodes through 2004 and 2005, when it was commissioned for a third series.

Perhaps the key television series influenced by the 'war on terror' was the very popular Fox-produced *24*. Series three, which was shown from 28 October 2003 to 25 May 2004, began with the series' hero returning from a successful operation to bring drug dealers to justice.[148] But at the same time, a dead body is left in a Los Angeles hospital, killed by a 'weaponised' virus. The agents have to save Los Angeles from attack, while working through the criminal-terrorist

[146] See http://www.nationalgeographic.com/channel/inside911/[9/2005]; also personal observation.

[147] Episode outlines are at http://www.tv.com/rescue-me/show/24321/episode_guide.html [8/2005]. Also personal observation.

[148] For episode dates, see http://www.tv.com/24/show/3866/episode_guide.html&season=3 [8/2005].

link.[149] On the DVD version of series three there are a number of extra features, and as Tony Whitt put it in *Now Playing*, 'The "Biothreat: Beyond the Series" documentary is downright scary . . .'[150] Violence abounds in this series, as in the others, as Bill Keveney mapped out in an article for *USA Today*.[151] In season four, which ran from 9 January 2005 to 23 May 2005, there are a series of terrorist threats from Islamic terrorists, including the bombing of trains, kidnaps and threats to nuclear power stations, and the key protagonists are a family of 'sleepers'. Fox aired two public service broadcasts portraying Muslims in a more positive light. One of the sharpest themes was the increased use of torture on all sides to acquire information.[152] Clearly, the writers were reflecting upon the Abu Ghraib scandal, and clearly the tactic worked: viewing figures rose by over a third.[153] It created debate, and legitimised the space for torture. As Matt Feeney put it, 'Then there is the torture, which occurs with astonishing regularity. On *24*, torture is less an unfortunate last resort than an epistemology.'[154] Drawing on *24* explicitly, Frank Sennett wrote 'If US agents employ torture to obtain information they need to stop an imminent attack – after exhausting all other avenues of investigation – that's justifiable.'[155] Sennett wrote this for the lifestyle section of a magazine based in Spokane, a town in Washington State, which shows just how deeply ideas and issues transmitted in fiction can penetrate through society. *Ethics Scoreboard* made the obvious connection: 'if Americans regarded torture with the revulsion that the nation's values and principles, not to mention its international treaties, would seem to demand, there is

149 The 'events' of the 24 hours of series three are laid out on the Fox website at http://www.fox.com/24/season3/episodes/guide.html [8/2005]. Also personal observation.

150 Tony Whitt, '24: season three', *Now Playing*, 20 December 2004, at http://www.nowplayingmag.com/content/view/434/47/ [8/2005].

151 Bill Keveney, '24: Chaos around the clock', *USA Today*, 13 March 2005.

152 For episodes, see http://www.tv.com/24/show/3866/episode_guide.html& season=4, for the Fox review, see http://www.fox.com/24/ [both 8/2005].

153 Bill Keveney, 'Fictional, "24" brings real issue of torture home', *USA Today*, 14 March 2005.

154 Matt Feeney, 'Torture chamber', *Slate*, 6 January 2004, at http://slate.msn.com/id/2093269/ [7/2005].

155 Frank Sennett, ' "24", agent Bauer makes the only case for torture', *Spokesman Review*, 3 April 2005, at http://www.spokane7.com/lifestyle/story.asp?ID= 57143 [8/2005].

no way *24* would be a popular show'.[156] All the series of *24* have been incredibly popular, rising into the top ten most watched programmes on television list, and have impacted upon the popular consciousness in the United States, and this has been reflected in the awards that the show has won. Kiefer Sutherland, the key actor in the series, won a Golden Globe for his work in *24* in both 2001 and 2003, while he received a nomination in 2002, and also a nomination from the Screen Actors' Guild; and the 2005 series received eleven Emmy nominations.[157]

Yet if *24* is perhaps the central aspect of the 'war on terror' on television screens, it has by no means been the only example. ABC also produced a long-running series, *Alias*, dealing with the world of espionage and counter-terrorism. The series began in September 2001, and by 2005 was in its fourth season, with eighty-eight episodes complete. *24*'s power is that the threat is at home, in America; by contrast, much of *Alias* takes place abroad and amongst other stories, it included the threat of bioterror. Then there was the ABC series *Threat Matrix*, named after the daily briefing given at 8 am to the President on live threats to the United States.[158] In the series, an elite team battles against these threats. Episode 3, shown on 2 October 2003, was based on an Iraqi biological weapons scientist escaping and posing a threat to the United States; based very clearly on particular readings of the Iraqi war that were entirely consistent with the 'war on terror' discourse, the episode was titled 'Doctor Germ', which was the name given by the media to the actual person in Iraq responsible for work in this area.[159] Other series also worked with the theme of remembering the second American 9/11, and with the 'war on terror' discourse. For example, in *Without a Trace*, a series about missing people, episodes 22 and 23,

156 'The real Abu Ghraib whitewash: "24" and public acceptance of torture', *Ethics Scoreboard*, 11 May 2005, at http://www.ethicsscoreboard.com/list/24.html [8/2005].

157 On Sutherland, see http://movies2.nytimes.com/gst/movies/filmography.html?p_id=69200&mod=awards, on *24*'s nominations, see http://www.fox.com/specials/emmy2005/ [7/2005].

158 Series website at http://abc.go.com/primetime/threatmatrix/ [7 and 8/2005]. Also personal observation.

159 See http://www.tv.com/threat-matrix/doctor-germ/episode/265947/summary.html. On Iraq's 'real' Dr Germ, see 'US military holding "Dr Germ" "Mrs Anthrax"', CNN.com, 21 September 2004, at http://www.cnn.com/2004/WORLD/meast/09/21/iraq.women/ [8/2005].

shown in August 2003 – with which the first series ended – concerned a story in which a man who lost his wife in the second American 9/11, and loses his job soon afterwards, strikes out and takes hostages.[160] The plot is based on the events of 11 September 2001, and the dialogue throughout turns on the psychological damage done to those involved. Of the eighteen staff who had worked in the company, fifteen had died on 11 September 2001: those who survived constantly wonder why they did, and why the others did not. Another example was the remake of *Battlestar Galactica*, described in *TV Guide* as 'a dark and dramatic series that speaks to our own real-life anxieties about war, terrorism, sleeper agents and WMDs'.[161] And in 2005, the war in Iraq came to America's screens in the form of FX's series, *Over There*. The most popular issues and fears in the occupation are portrayed in the series: firefights; house-to-house searches; Americans torturing Iraqi suspects; soldiers accused of killing civilians; Iraqis with bombs; journalists kidnapped by terrorists.[162] This was clearly unpalatable: viewing figures dropped by over 40 per cent over the course of the first five episodes.[163]

Taken together, all of these televisual series and events came to underpin the sense of memorialisation, they also supported the notion that the 'war on terror' was common sense, and that there were no alternatives to the policy programme. The 2005–6 television and film season was replete with offerings on the second American 9/11. Discovery Channel produced a documentary drama on Flight 93, entitled *The Flight That Fought Back*. That was shown on 11 September 2005.[164] A&E took a similar line, its *Flight 93* (a working title) was based on recordings made at the time.[165] Universal Pictures committed $15 million to produce *Flight 93*, a feature film that was to recreate the

[160] The plot is at http://www.tv.com/without-a-trace/show/7449/episode_guide.html [8/2005]. Also personal observation.

[161] Ken Fox and Maitland McDonagh, 'DVD: our picks of the week', *TV Guide*, 25 September to 1 October 2005, p. 25.

[162] Episode guides at http://www.fxnetworks.com/shows/originals/overthere/main.html [9/2005].

[163] See Tom Dorsey, 'Low ratings indicate "Over There" may be too realistic', *Courier Journal* [Louisville, KY], 24 August 2005, at http://www.courier-journal.com/apps/pbcs.dll/article?AID=/20050824/COLUMNISTS15/ 508240357/1011/SCENE [9/2005].

[164] See http://dsc.discovery.com/convergence/flight/flight.html [9/2005].

[165] See John Lippman, 'Four years later, studios tackle 9/11', *Wall Street Journal*, 12 August 2005.

flight in 'real' time.[166] Oliver Stone began making a film featuring Nicholas Cage as a Port Authority officer who, after the attack, is trapped under the rubble of the Twin Towers.[167] And ABC began producing a six-hour mini series on an anti-terror expert in the South Tower of the World Trade Center.[168]

The way in which the 'war on terror' was powerfully reproduced on television made this whole policy programme real. Yet it was not only aimed at adults. American media have developed a major market in selling products to children. But this is not only at the level of toys and videos; it is also about selling ideas. One example is Elissa Grodin and Victor Jahasz's *D is for Democracy*, a book aimed at the 9- to 12-year-olds that teaches about democratic structures and American government.[169] Another was Nickelodeon's 'Kids vote for President' feature on their website, and their encouragement to children to take an interest in the 2004 presidential election. In between cartoons, Nickelodeon would show a cartoon figure playing a guitar shaped like the United States singing about the virtues of democracy, in contrast to 'bad' forms of government – 'monarchy, theocracy, military dictatorship' – and summed up in the key lines of the song: 'In the USA we are living large, 'Cos when you vote it means you're in charge.'[170] And then there was the *Left Behind* kids series – in which children's stories are told in the context of the narrative of the best-selling adult series about the Rapture and the 'end of times'. This 'kids'' version had sold over 10 million copies by 2005.[171] And the *Left Behind* theme was made into a film by Cloud Ten pictures, released in the autumn of 2005, to be shown in churches, not 'movie theaters'.[172] Given this, it is inevitable that the 'war on terror' discourse would be shared with children. The second American 9/11 is taught in schools; and books were

166 See Reuters, 'Hollywood hatches plans for third 9/11 film', MSNBC, 16 August 2005 at http://www.msnbc.msn.com/id/8976443/ [9/2005].

167 See Rebecca Murray, 'Oliver Stone set to direct a movie about the events of 9/11', *About*, 8 July 2005 at http://movies.about.com/od/cagenicholas/a/911movie070805.htm [9/2005].

168 See Scott Bowles, '9/11 drama head for big, small screens', *USA Today*, 17 August 2005.

169 Elissa Grodin and Victor Jahasz, *D is for Democracy: A Citizen's Alphabet* (Michigan: Sleeping Bear Press, 2004).

170 Personal observation, Nickelodeon channel, USA, August and September 2004.

171 See at http://www.leftbehind.com/channelkids.asp [7 and 8/2005].

172 See http://www.cloudtenpictures.com/ [8/2005].

written for children on the subject.[173] *September Roses* tells the tale of two South African sisters in New York at the time of the attacks, who witness the loss and heroism of the city, in a book aimed at children '7 and up'.[174] Geoffrey Campbell explained to grades 6–9 the dilemmas of civil liberties, and the ways in which America was vulnerable as, in a separate book, did Laurel Corona.[175] Lynn Peppas' book, *Terrorism Alert!* was aimed at 9- to 12-year-olds.[176] In 2004, BrainPop – which produces educational films for children – created a programme entitled *Terrorism*, which 'suggests ways in which children and families can be prepared by staying on top of the news, and working together to develop a family plan and a ready kit'.[177]

More generally, the American movie industry was also affected by the 'war on terror' discourse. Even a film such as *The Day After Tomorrow*, which was widely seen as an attack on the Bush administration's environmental policy, had a 'war on terror' dimension. Sudden and largely unforeseen climatic change leads to widespread destruction, in which the key image is the freezing of New York; but the destruction of New York (a key image after the second American 9/11) was presaged by the destruction of Los Angeles. That is, LA was destroyed as a means of heightening the viewers' real focus – New York.[178] *Die Hard 4* went into production in 2005, with a 'war on terror' theme. *Team America* sought to offend both sides of America's culture wars, with its portrayal of Americans as brutal and ignorant, but it still emphasised key 'war on terror' themes (whether enthusiastically or not). As Phil Villareal notes, 'in case any of this is too subtle, the lyrics "Pearl Harbor sucks" repeat in one of the tunes. It's

173 For an example of the online production of teaching materials in this area, see *Teaching 9-11*, at http://www.teaching9-11.org/ [8/2005].

174 Jeanette Winter, *September Roses* (New York: Farrar, Straus and Giroux, 2004).

175 Geoffrey Campbell, *A Vulnerable America: An Overview of National Security* (New York: Lucent Books, 2003); Laurel Corona, *Hunting Down the Terrorists: Declaring War and Policing Global Violations* (New York: Lucent Books, 2003).

176 Lynn Peppas, *Terrorism Alert!* (New York: Crabtree, 2005).

177 From BrainPop's material at http://www.brainpop.com/aboutus/pressroom/terrorism.weml [8/2005].

178 *The Day After Tomorrow* directed and written by Roland Emmerich, 2004. See 'Disaster movie used to highlight environment', *Fox News*, 26 May 2004, at http://www.foxnews.com/story/0,2933,120931,00.html [8/2005].

a love song.'[179] And Steven Spielberg directed *Munich*, a film about the Israeli squad that hunted the Palestinian terrorists who had murdered Israeli athletes at the 1972 Munich Olympic Games. Reportedly originally to be titled *Vengeance*, it examines both the value in punishing the perpetrators of violence, and the toll it takes on the punishers.[180] Meanwhile, across the United States, people logged on to their computers to play the game *War on Terror 2*, in which the player is able to shoot terrorists in Afghanistan, the London Underground System, Belfast and Yemen.[181] Or they could buy *Conflict: Global Terror*, a 'squad' game of four 'Gulf War veterans' who were fighting a new enemy in the 'war on terror'.[182] Or perhaps *Terrorist Takedown*, in which the US army attacks a terrorist 'militia' in the Middle East.[183]

In the real 'war on terror', the numbers injured in Afghanistan, and in Iraq in particular, grew over time, and those numbers were shown to the public in major news outlets.[184] To the soldiers, the one binding, justifying narrative was that the occupation of Iraq and the 'war on terror' were contributing directly to American security. At the funeral for Marine Lance Corporal Kevin Joyce, a member of the Navajo Nation, his brother, who also served in the army, said: 'Kevin believed in something. There's a disease over there that might spread to our land.'[185]

The major outlets of contemporary American culture – music, television, film, the internet – were all engaged in the process of producing the 'war on terror' discourse throughout 2003 to 2005, even while disillusionment with the occupation of Iraq grew. This is not to underestimate the level of disillusionment. 'Doubts grow, but war support

179 Phil Villareal, 'Team America hangs together', *Arizona Daily Star*, at http://www.azstarnet.com/sn/ent_movies/43041.php [8/2005].

180 'Spielberg's Munich production begins', *Dark Horizons*, 6 July 2005, at http://www.darkhorizons.com/news05/050706c.php and 'Spielberg terrorism film now called Munich', *Libertas*, 26 July 2005, at http://www.libertyfilmfestival.com/libertas/index.php?p=648 [both 8/2005].

181 The game can be found and played at http://www.2flashgames.com/f/f-23.htm [8/2005].

182 SCI Games – see http://www.sci.co.uk/games/basic.asp?version_id=91 [8/2005].

183 See the review at http://www.rottentomatoes.com/g/pc_games/terrorist_takedown/about.php [9/2005].

184 *USA Today*, for example, keeps a running total on its website at www.soldiers.usatoday.com which tells of how each soldier came to be injured or killed.

185 Quoted in Marley Shebala, 'Mourners reflect on ultimate sacrifice', *Navajo Times*, 15 August 2005, at http://www.navajotimes.com/ [9/2005].

stable' was the headline following a Pew survey in July 2005, in which support for keeping troops in Iraq remained over 50 per cent, but 45 per cent said that the war had increased the chances of an attack in the United States, a figure that had grown by 9 per cent over nine months.[186] Popular magazines, such as *Rolling Stone*, became fascinated by 'soldiers who go wrong' and committed acts of violence when back in the US: was it their fault, or were they driven to it by what they had experienced in Iraq?[187] And the world of high art also began to focus on the 'war on terror' in its domestic aspects. Chang-Jin Lee's public art work *Homeland Security Garden* went on display by the site of Ground Zero. She engaged with members of the public to find which items made them feel safe, and then constructed 200 boxes to show those items. The work 'investigates the multivalent and complex issues of safety, security and personal freedom in the post-9/11 world by asking the public to deeply consider their thoughts and feelings regarding these paramount issues'.[188] On the other coast of America, Michael Mizerany's dance performance *Kruel Summer* was set in the near future, where the Patriot Act is used to inflict Abu Ghraib-style torture on America's gay community.[189] *Kruel Summer* was not going to appeal to the evangelical community – and it was in that community that the occupation of Iraq had particular resonance.

Evangelical Christianity and the 'war on terror'

By the summer of 2005, between seven and fifteen new evangelical churches had been established in Baghdad.[190] Although some evangelical leaders in America had been concerned with how the war was to

[186] 'More say Iraq war hurts fight against terrorism', Pew Research Center, 21 July 2005, at http://people-press.org/reports/display.php3?ReportID=251 [9/2005].

[187] See Jeff Tietz, 'Marine gone mad', *Rolling Stone*, 28 July 2005, at http://www.rollingstone.com/politics/story/_/id/7504249?pageid=rs.Politics&pageregion=single1&rnd=1126163304265&has-player=true&version=6.0.12.1212 [9/2005].

[188] See 'Visual arts: Homeland Security Garden, a public art project by Chang-Jin Lee', Events, World Financial Center, at http://www.worldfinancialcenter.com/calendar/ [9/2005].

[189] See Lewis Segal, 'Dance review: "Kruel" proves to be punishing', *Los Angeles Times*, 20 August 2005.

[190] Caryle Murphy, 'Evangelicals building a base in Baghdad', *Washington Post*, 23 June 2005, says seven; 'Evangelical churches growing in Iraq, says Christian Mission Organisation', *Christian Today*, 18 July 2005, says fifteen.

take place, in general there had been strong support amongst many congregations for the war in Iraq, and that support continued afterwards. Christian Broadcasting Network editorialised on a report that support for the war had declined in the autumn of 2004: 'Half of Americans now think going invading Iraq was the right thing to do. Those numbers could possibly be higher, if dramatic scenes of war and violence were not the only ones grabbing headlines.'[191] It was, therefore, the fault of the mainstream media for faulty reporting that many Americans were losing confidence.

Many in the evangelical movement believe in the literal truth of the Bible: that is, it is literally the word of God. In the words of Liberty Baptist Church, Greenville, Michigan, 'The Bible is to be taken literally, unless it clearly tells you that it is giving symbolism in some form, and then it will tell you what the symbolism means.'[192] It is for this reason that so much focus is placed on the teaching of Darwinian evolution. The Kansas State Board of Education held hearings in May 2005 about the relative merits of evolution and 'intelligent design', or ID.[193] It is the conviction that the Bible has to be read literally that allows evangelicals to give such emphasis to prophecy, and to the Endtimes. Leon Bates' *Bible Map* draws from the Scriptures and identifies the contemporary world as sitting just before the Rapture and the seven-year Tribulation.[194] William MacDonald, in *Armageddon Soon?*, wrote: 'There does not have to be any doubt, confusion, or misunderstanding about what lies ahead. The Bible gives a clear and accurate panorama of the future.'[195] In this, Antichrist plays a crucial role. Discovery Series Bible Study explains that 'When the Antichrist is revealed, the stage will be set for the terrible events of the tribulation. After this satanically empowered leader rises to prominence, the stage will be set for the most distressing period of all history. For 3 and a half years he

191 John Jessup, 'Poll shows Americans split 50:50 on support for the Iraq War', *CBN News*, 18 August 2004, at http://www.cbn.com/cbnnews/news/040818b.asp [8/2005].

192 At http://www.libertygospeltracts.com/question/prequest/literal.htm [8/2005].

193 See 'Kansas educators debate evolution', *CBS News*, 6 May 2005, at http://www.cbsnews.com/stories/2005/05/06/national/main693397.shtml [8/2005].

194 Leon Bates, *A Bible Map* (Sherman, TX: Bible Believers Evangelistic Association, undated).

195 William MacDonald, *Armageddon Soon?* (Kansas City: Walterick Publishers, 1991), p. 7.

will conduct a reign of terror . . .'[196] Terror is therefore to be expected; and many evangelicals look to world affairs through prophecy. That America faces a 'war on terror' fits into a wider understanding of the world and the future. At Favor Minded Ministries the link between world affairs and the Bible is clear:

> Terrorism Around The World, The War in *Iraq*, The attack on our Sovereignty of 911, and *so much more* that is seen happening around us and around the world everyday – Is it detailed in Bible Prophecy? Is the future foretold in the Bible? Have we seen for the first time ever, simultaneous occurrences of these prophecies like never before in history? The Answer is a *bold*, Resounding, *yes*![197]

And in response to the bombings in Egypt in July 2005, Dr Creflo A. Dollar told his flock:

> If you or someone you know has been personally affected by the tragedy in Egypt, please be assured that Jesus is waiting to intercede on your behalf . . . It is easy, during times like these, to allow the spirit of worry to keep you in a state of fear and panic. Satan tries to get you off course by attacking your mind and making you think that you have been abandoned by God . . . But Jesus wants you to continue to be strong in your faith so that you can spread the Good News, particularly during these times of terror and despair when people need it most.[198]

It is therefore not only that there is a ready understanding of the 'war on terror' from those who are concerned with the Endtimes; they are able to identify events in the world as contributing towards the move towards those Endtimes.

The connection between biblical prophecy and the 'war on terror' came in part due to the interest that those concerned about the Rapture and the Endtimes had over how that 'war' might be part of those biblical readings. In October 2004, Sky Angel Television Vice President of Programming, Kathy Johnson, had said, in the context of the forth-

[196] Discovery Series Bible Study, *What Can We Know About the Endtimes?* (Grand Rapids, MI: Discovery House, 2002), p. 17.

[197] 'Are you ready to go?', Favor Minded Ministries, at http://www.favorminded.com/pray/prophplus.html [8/2005]. Emphasis in original.

[198] Dr Creflo A. Dollar, 'Beyond fear', Creflo Ministries, July 2005, at http://www.creflodollarministries.com/home/egypt.html [8/2005]. Creflo Ministries speaks to the African-American community.

coming presidential elections, 'This is an especially critical election, so it's imperative that Christians be as informed as possible by fellow people of faith about issues such as stem cell research, abortion and the war on terror . . .'[199] The 'war on terror' was a *Christian* issue. In September 2005, a film entitled *Day of Miracles* was released, about the events of 11 September 2001. The producer, Leslie McRay, had said that 'We did not want to show the horrors or the political nature of the 9/11 event but rather how God intervened under the most terrible conditions.'[200] As the promotional material put it, the film was 'neither about the terrorists nor getting even but about the miracle events that occurred on and around that unforgettable time in history'.[201] The second American 9/11 was itself to be read as a Christian event – and therefore an attack on Christianity, in which God helps the victims – further marking the 'war on terror' as an element in the end of the world, and the move towards the Tribulation.

The 'war on terror' discourse, then, interconnected with evangelical beliefs concerning the Endtimes, and was reflected in Christian broadcasting and media outlets. Throughout the Midwest, such values were also shown on car bumper stickers, in the shape of ribbons. Common stickers included: 'God Bless the USA'; 'Freedom isn't Free'; 'Pray for Your Troops'; 'POW-MIA: Not Forgotten'; 'God Answers Prayers'.[202] Values as identity markers, expressing connections between the 'war on terror' and the Endtimes.

This intersection of discourses was important and influential. President Bush had said in his 2001 Inaugural Address, 'And I can pledge our nation to a goal: When we see that wounded traveler on the road to Jericho, we will not pass to the other side.'[203] The imagery of

199 In 'As Christians gear up to go to the polls, Sky Angel keeps them informed', Sky Angel TV, 27 October 2004, at http://www.skyangel.com/About/MediaArchive.asp?IdS=000906-FB30440&Id=71 [8/2005].

200 'Day of Miracles will be telecast to billions on 9/11/05', Find Law, 27 June 2005, at http://news.corporate.findlaw.com/prnewswire/20050627/27jun20050833.html [8/2005].

201 'Day of Miracles: True Miraculous Stories of 9/11', *Miracle Films*, at http://www.miraclefilms.com/dayofmiracles.shtml [8/2005].

202 Personal observation, Kansas, Missouri, Nebraska and Iowa, May 2005. See one of the manufacturers' websites at http://www.toyd.com/tshallofyofa.html [8/2005].

203 President George W. Bush, 'Inaugural Address', 20 January 2001, at http://www.whitehouse.gov/news/inaugural-address.html [8/2005].

being involved and committed in the world was directly biblical. David Frum, the former presidential speechwriter, wrote of discovering how important Christianity was in the functioning of the White House in his first meeting. He wrote 'The news that this was a White House where attendance at Bible study was, if not compulsory, not quite *uncompulsory*, either, was disconcerting to a non-Christian like me.'[204] One very popular book in 2004 was a collection of George Bush's speeches, entitled *On God and Country*, with a quote from Charles Wesley – the eighteenth-century evangelist – on the inside front cover.[205] The editor, Thomas M. Freiling, opened the book with the line: 'Not since Abraham Lincoln has a sitting President addressed spiritual issues as frequently as President George W. Bush.'[206]

A number of evangelical leaders claim to have regular conversations with President Bush.[207] Others are consulted on policy: Richard Land, Director of the Southern Baptist Convention, reported that 'In this administration, they call us, and they say, "What is your take on this? How does your group feel about this?" '[208] Some evangelical groups have had special briefings in the White House. In March 2004, for example, one group was addressed by James Wilkinson, Deputy Assistant to the President and Deputy National Security Advisor for Communications, who ran through the key elements of the decisive intervention:

> President Bush, Wilkinson stated, views the current conflicts in Afghanistan and Iraq as war. Wilkinson stressed that the nation must understand that this is a difficult and different kind of war with tremendous challenges, quite unlike previous world wars and even the cold war with the Soviet Union . . . Furthermore, the enemy is cowardly and tends to hide behind the innocent. In spite of the difficulties of this war, two-thirds of Al Qaeda's leadership has been captured or killed. Wilkinson stressed that partisanship should be taken out of the debate . . . Al Qaeda and the enemies of the United States probably rejoice over this partisanship.[209]

204 David Frum, *The Right Man* (London: Weidenfeld & Nicolson, 2003), pp. 3–4. Italics in original.

205 Thomas M. Freiling (ed.), *George W. Bush On God and Country* (Fairfax, VA: Allegiance Press, 2004). 206 Ibid., p. 9.

207 For example, Pastor Robert Upton, Billy Graham and Richard Land.

208 Cited in 'Interview with Richard Land', 'The Jesus Factor', PBS, 29 April 2004, at http://www.pbs.org/wgbh/pages/frontline/shows/jesus/interviews/land.html [8/2005].

209 Robert W. Martin, 'Apostolic leaders given exclusive White House briefing', Ninety and Nine, 12 April 2004, at http://www.ninetyandnine.com/Archives/20040412/cover_wh.htm [8/2005].

But the key part of the interaction was over the Middle East. The ministers objected to a Palestinian state, and feared that an Israeli withdrawal from Gaza might facilitate exactly that. Until Old Testament Israel is intact, and Solomon's Temple rebuilt, there would be no Endtimes and so, no Second Coming. National Security Council Near East and North African Affairs director, Elliott Abrams, sought to reassure the delegation on theological grounds, focusing on the biblical significance of Gaza.[210] The previous spring, religious opposition to the White House supporting the Middle East Road Map had been mobilised. Pastor Robert Upton, one of the organisers of both that and the 2004 White House visit, said of the 2003 protest: 'Within a two-week period, getting 50,000 postcards saying the exact same thing from places all over the country, that resonated with the White House. That really caused [President Bush] to backpedal on the Road Map.'[211]

Attorney General John Ashcroft, a member of the Assembly of God Church, had himself anointed each time he took public office. He said in a speech at Bob Jones University in 2001, 'It is not accidental that America has been the home of the brave and the land of the free, the place where mankind has had the greatest of all opportunities, to approach the potential that God has placed within us. It has been because we knew that we were endowed not by the king, but by the Creator, with certain unalienable rights.'[212] Condoleezza Rice said, 'When I'm concerned about something, I figure out a plan of action, and then I give it to God.'[213] She also connected faith with the second American 9/11: 'This campaign [against terror] has put a certain moral clarity back in international politics . . . [The aim is] to leave the world not just safer . . . but better.'[214]

High-profile evangelical views impact upon a wider sense of the role of religion in America's culture wars, connecting the state and evangclism. During the Vietnam War, the military had reached out to the evangelical community, by presenting Billy Graham with the Sylvanus Thayer award

[210] Rick Perlstein, 'The Jesus Launching Pad', *Village Voice*, 18 May 2004, based on a leaked email from Pastor Upton, at http://www.villagevoice.com/news/0420,perlstein,53582,1.html [8/2005]. [211] Ibid.

[212] John Ashcroft's speech at Bob Jones University, *The Ethical Spectator*, February 2001, at http://www.spectacle.org/0201/ashcroft.html [8/2005].

[213] Cited in B. Denise Hawkins, 'Condoleezza Rice's secret weapon', *Today's Christian*, September/October 2002, at http://www.christianitytoday.com/tc/2002/005/1.18.html [8/2005]. [214] Ibid.

in 1972 for example.[215] The contemporary Air Force Academy is so overrun with evangelical proselytising that it is something its superintendent, Lt General John Rosa Jr, said kept him 'awake at nights'.[216] In 2004–5, a new 'religious respect and awareness' course was established, to be attended by all 9,000 staff and cadets.[217] Cadets must go to class: but if the lecture is on the 'evolution' of airpower, many will sit with their arms conspicuously folded, refusing to engage with any aspect of 'evolution'.[218] Todd Strandbery, who is responsible for the Rapture Ready website, is a sergeant in the US air force at Offutt Air Force Base in Omaha.[219] When Scott McKenzie, an army reservist, was cleared by the Army Review Board of mistreating Iraqi prisons, the 40-year-old Presbyterian deacon said: 'When I got the call, first thing I did was I thanked God . . . I figured that if God leads you to it, God will lead you through it.'[220]

It is, then, perhaps unsurprising that the 'war on terror' connects so clearly with the evangelical discourse about the Endtimes. When there is a war about the future of civilisation, in which all have to choose which side they are on, when the enemy is evil – all of which are elements of the 'war on terror' discourse – the war speaks powerfully to those who are looking for signs of the Tribulation. The evangelical website Gogindex sees that 'The Endtimes are near!' and explained in 2005 that 'The War in Afghanistan has waned, but terrorist cells now regroup. The War on Iraq too has nearly ended. But, dangers still remain. There have been numerous threats of biological, chemical, and even nuclear strikes against Israel and or the US over the past two years. Further concerns include Iran's threat of eliminating Israel with one nuclear strike . . .'[221] Jack Kinsella at the Omega Letter website

[215] Bacevich, *The New American Militarism*, pp. 140–2. The Thayer award was 'conferred annually on a citizen who exemplifies the [US Military] academy's ideals of duty, honor and country', p. 140.

[216] In editorial, 'Zealots at the Air Force Academy', *New York Times*, 11 June 2005.

[217] Matthew Wells, ' "Religious bullying" at US academy', *BBC News*, 27 June 2005.

[218] Personal correspondence. I am grateful to Richard Lock-Pullan for this insight.

[219] Paul Tough, 'That's the news and I'm outta here', *Mother Jones*, September/October 1998, at http://www.motherjones.com/news/qa/1998/09/tough.html [5/2005].

[220] Quoted in Associated Press, 'Army clears 2 reservists discharged on abuse allegations', *Los Angeles Times*, 20 August 2005.

[221] Home page at Gogindex, http://www.gogindex.org/ [8/2005].

reasoned that scientific advance made the destruction of the world increasingly likely in the next twenty years; and human nature being what it is, world peace was unlikely.

> Now we return to the central question of the timing of the Rapture. I don't know the day or the hour, but I know the odds that we will achieve world peace, keep weapons of mass destruction out of the hands of terrorists and avoid total war with the Islamic world in the next twenty years. And, unless we do all that, if the Rapture hasn't already happened, there will be nobody left to Rapture.[222]

We assume from this that the 'war on terror' is the last war before the Tribulation, and that all of this will happen in the next twenty years. At Light for the Last Days they tell us that 'There can be no doubt that the world changed on September 11th. The results of this act of terror, watched by people all over the world on TV, will continue to have profound effects on all nations in a way which must bring us closer to the final events of this age prophesied in the scriptures.'[223]

The 'war on terror' spoke to a significant number of Americans through its connection with evangelical discourses, and wider Christian debates. After all, some two-thirds of Americans said that they believe that humans were directly created by God, in a poll carried out in 2005.[224]

Conclusion

The 'war on terror' discourse, so challenged by the social crisis of the Iraq War and the generation of an alternative discourse – 'no war for oil' – was heard even more loudly throughout the autumn of 2003, through the presidential elections in 2004, and throughout 2005. That discourse had penetrated into the key political and news media structures, into the evangelical community, and into the main outlets of

222 Jack Kinsella, 'Commentary on the news', Omega Letter, September 2004, at http://www.christianmusictv.com/_title_end_times_concluding_remarks_title_.htm [8/2005].

223 'War on terrorism: moving to the End Times', Light for the Last Days, at http://www.lightforthelastdays.co.uk/docs/oneworld_system/war_on_terrorism.html [8/2005].

224 'Nearly two-thirds of US adults believe human beings were created by God', *The Harris Poll*, 6 July 2005, at http://www.harrisinteractive.com/harris_poll/index.asp?PID=581 [8/2005].

popular culture – novels and books, film and television, and music. Indeed, some of those institutions were not only reproducing the dominant discourse; some in the news media, and in the think tanks, were involved in acts of co-production with the administration.

None of this is to say that the opposition was eliminated, for 'no war for oil' continued to be heard, and as the occupation of Iraq became more bloody, support for that element of the 'war on terror' began to decline in American public opinion. But in the main institutions of state and society, no radical alternatives to the 'war on terror' were being articulated; no fundamental challenges to the decisive intervention, and the policy programme that followed, were in sight.

The development of the discourse of the 'war on terror' that has been traced throughout this book from 2001 to 2005 itself constructs a social crisis process. That process, and conclusions about the 'war on terror' itself, comprise the final part of this book.

7 *Conclusion*

Meaning from chaos

On 11 September 2001, as the Twin Towers smouldered, there was confusion everywhere. In his blog, written on the day of the attack in New York, Jeffrey Zeldman wrote, 'The news is running loops of the impact, loops of the implosions. Like everyone else, I watch, hoping to see or hear something that makes sense. But all I learn is that thousands of New Yorkers can die in an instant.'[1] In her contemporary blog, Grace wrote, 'I kept thinking, "This is just like Armageddon." And I didn't even see that movie.'[2] Barbara Clark, in Florida, was one of many who, when she turned on the television, 'couldn't believe what I saw. I thought at first that it was just a movie, but it wasn't.'[3] Adam Oestrich, who had got out of the World Trade Center from the twenty-fourth floor, wrote that as he was walking away, 'we heard this sound that can only be described as a "thundering crack." That is the best I can do. I then saw what I thought was just a chunk of the WTC but it was actually the whole tower. I said it wasn't . . . I couldn't believe it . . .'[4] At 11.39 that morning, Declan McCullagh in Washington sent an email in which he said 'NSA and CIA – their complexes are miles outside of Washington DC proper – have been evacuated. From an NSAer: "I want to know as a member of the intelligence community how the f*** we didn't see this happening."'[5] In her blog, an entry in the early afternoon, the author of saranwarp.com wrote 'i [sic] am sort of numb to the rest of it, isolated

1 Jeffrey Zeldman, '11 September', at http://www.zeldman.com/glamorous/54.shtml [9/2005].

2 'World Trade Center', at http://grace.filsa.net/WTC.html#journal [9/2005].

3 Barbara Clark, 'Stories of September 11', *Digital Archive*, at http://www.911digitalarchive.org/stories/details/11273 [9/2005].

4 At http://www.netwert.com/ideapad/sep11_adam.html [9/2005].

5 *First Hand Reports*, at http://lists.elistx.com/archives/interesting-people/200109/msg00080.html [9/2005].

in brooklyn, and trained by american action films to take things like planes flying into buildings, mass explosions, and the destruction of major buildings for granted.'[6] In the evening, CNN were struggling to create meaning. Joey Chan, the anchor, spoke with Brian Jenkins, a 'terrorism expert'. Chan asked 'I'm wondering if you can give us any of your perspective. Obviously you don't have a crystal ball to look at these things. But should we – regard this – as all being done at this point? It has been silent for much of the rest of this day since this morning.' Jenkins, the expert in obvious confusion, replied: 'One has to be very careful, er, in looking at a multiple co-ordinated attack like this to, to, say exactly. When it was, when it's over – I mean it was, er, thirty-one years ago almost to the day that in a single day three airliners were hijacked . . .'[7]

Shock, horror and, above all for the purposes of this book, incomprehension. There was no template readily to hand to comprehend what had happened in New York and Washington, DC, to those four hijacked aircraft on 11 September 2001. Americans – whether those witnessing the attacks or escaping from the ruins, journalists, experts or government officials – struggled to comprehend what had happened. Meaning had to be ascribed, and that was the task of the decisive intervention. But that meaning did not come 'out of the blue': it had its own genealogy.

'Terrorism' had been a major theme in government and in popular culture before the second American 9/11. Many of the elements of the 'war on terror' had been spoken of by a previous President. In his 1998 'State of the Union' speech, President Clinton had said: 'We must combat an unholy axis of new threats from terrorists, international criminals, and drug traffickers.'[8] Such a statement – including the use of the phrase 'unholy axis' – would not be out of place in the rhetoric of the 'war on terror'. After attacking bases in Afghanistan and Sudan, Clinton had said:

> I want you to understand, I want the world to understand that our actions today were not aimed against Islam, the faith of hundreds of millions of

[6] At http://saranwarp.com/archives/2001_09.php#000550 [9/2005].

[7] CNN live, 11 September 2001, transcript of Andrew Hoskins, University of Swansea.

[8] President William J. Clinton, 'State of the Union', 27 January 1998, at http://www.presidency.ucsb.edu/ws/index.php?pid=56280 [9/2005].

good, peace-loving people all around the world, including the United States . . . My fellow Americans, our battle against terrorism did not begin with the bombing of our embassies in Africa, nor will it end with today's strike. It will require strength, courage and endurance. We will not yield to this threat. We will meet it no matter how long it may take. This will be a long, ongoing struggle between freedom and fanaticism, between the rule of law and terrorism. We must be prepared to do all that we can for as long as we must. America is and will remain a target of terrorists precisely because we are leaders; because we act to advance peace, democracy and basic human values; because we're the most open society on earth . . .

These were the classic elements of the decisive intervention: the need to reassure Islamic peoples and countries; to be resolute towards ultimate victory; America as the target of terrorism not for what it did, but for what it was. All that was missing were the claims of heroism and national unity. But these were big missing items. And although Clinton spoke of the threat of the 'bin Laden network', there was no real construction of the ultimate enemy. This all had to wait for a decisive intervention. At the United Nations in September 1998, the President had spoken 'about why all nations must put the fight against terrorism at the top of our agenda'.[9] That is, a claim to global leadership. The 1999 'State of the Union' speech included seven references to 'terror' or 'terrorists'. The President spoke of the link between terrorists and state sponsors of terror: 'As we work for peace, we must also meet threats to our Nation's security, including increased dangers from outlaw nations and terrorism.'[10] And he focused on Iraq: 'For nearly a decade, Iraq has defied its obligations to destroy its weapons of terror and the missiles to deliver them. America will continue to contain Saddam, and we will work for the day when Iraq has a Government worthy of its people.'[11] The US Commission on National Security / 21st Century worked from 1998 until the publication of its final report in February 2001. In that latter report, the commission stated bluntly that 'The combination of unconventional weapons proliferation with the persistence of international terrorism will end the relative invulnerability of

[9] President William J. Clinton, 'Remarks to the Opening Session of the 53rd United Nations General Assembly', 21 September 1998, at http://www.presidency.ucsb.edu/ws/index.php?pid=54944&st=&st1= [9/2005].

[10] President William J. Clinton, 'State of the Union', 19 January 1999, at http://www.presidency.ucsb.edu/ws/index.php?pid=57577 [9/2005].

[11] Ibid.

the US homeland to catastrophic attack. A direct attack against American citizens on American soil is likely over the next quarter century.'[12] Such an attack occurred in a little more than a quarter of a year, never mind a quarter of a century. The commissioners worried that 'These attacks may involve weapons of mass destruction and weapons of mass disruption.'[13] Indeed, the phrase 'weapons of mass destruction' is used sixteeen times in the document. The report recommended the establishment of a National Homeland Security Agency: in all, 'homeland security' is mentioned 102 times in the 123-page report. The threat was so great that the report recommended the reorganisation and re-equipping of the National Guard, and its dedication to the defence of the homeland. The report also spoke to the need to reorganise the Pentagon, State Department and National Security Council. In many ways, the commission went even further than the administration when it came to reorganising structures after the decisive intervention. But this pre-history was also to be found in the media. In December 1998, the *New York Daily News* declared 'A terror warning for NY and DC' in its headline, reporting that 'Terror kingpin Osama Bin Laden may be preparing to bomb New York or Washington to avenge the US attack on his secret bases in Afghanistan, according to a new report.'[14]

It is into this web of narratives prior to the second American 9/11 that neoconservatism should be fed. The neoconservative critique of the Clinton administration was that it was too weak: as William Kristol put it in 1998 in the *Weekly Standard*, 'As for President Clinton's new "war" on terrorism, it is becoming less and less clear that . . . the Administration really has the stomach for such a "war".'[15] That was evidenced in policy towards Iraq. Again, in the *Weekly Standard*, the call for action was clear. A November 1998 editorial declared: 'There is a way to deal with Saddam that can work, and

[12] US Commission on National Security /21st Century, *Roadmap for National Security: Imperative for Change*, February 2001, p. viii, at http://www.au.af.mil/au/awc/awcgate/nssg/phaseIIIfr.pdf [9/2005]. [13] Ibid., p. 27.

[14] Owen Moritz, 'A terror warning for NY and DC', *New York Daily News*, 14 December 1998, at http://pqasb.pqarchiver.com/nydailynews/37115912.html?did=37115912&FMT=ABS&FMTS=FT&date=Dec+14%2C+1998&author=OWEN+MORITZ&pub=New+York+Daily+News&desc=A+TERROR+WARNING+FOR+N.Y.+AND+D.C. [2/2006, pay site].

[15] Editorial, *Weekly Standard*, 7 September 1998, at http://www.newamericancentury.org/RepubFuture-Sept%207,%2098.pdf [9/2005].

we've outlined it in these pages over the past year: It is to complete the unfinished business of the 1991 Gulf War and get rid of Saddam.'[16] That was not at all surprising. In February of that year, a number of neoconservatives had written an open letter to the President, demanding the overthrow of the Iraqi President. Signatories included William Kristol, Robert Kagan and Michael Ledeen, and also those who were later to be members of the Bush administration, such as Donald Rumsfeld, the Secretary of Defense and his Deputy, Paul Wolfowitz, and John Bolton (later Ambassador to the United Nations).[17] The neoconservatives wanted to build their own 'new world order', based on an informal American empire. As Jonathan Last put it in the *Weekly Standard* when reflecting upon the *Star Wars* film *The Attack of the Clones*, 'The deep lesson of Star Wars is that the Empire is good.'[18] For Last, the Republic is over-bloated government at its worst, and a sort of bureaucratic United Nations unable to act. Its key supporters, the Jedi, are not democratic warriors but a 'Swiss Guard' (you have to inherit abilities to use the Force). Palpatine, the new Emperor, is, at heart, 'an esoteric Straussian'. And so on. The point is not to take this too seriously, but to recognise the pull to empire if it is in the cause of freedom – and that the two might not be in contradiction.

Last's rereading of *Star Wars* – although written after the second American 9/11 – draws the focus on to popular culture. Again, there is a genealogy of the 'war on terror' here as well. Most notably, Tom Clancy published *The Sum of All Fears* well before 11 September 2001, a story about a terrorist attack by 'Arabs' in the United States, with weapons of mass destruction.[19] The terrorist plan is to use a nuclear weapon to try to rekindle East–West hostility, and to prevent peace between the Israelis and Palestinians. A Middle Eastern terrorist group builds a nuclear bomb, to be detonated in Denver at the Super Bowl. Clancy – one of the most popular novelists in the United States – did much to focus thought on the terrorist threat to the United States, with

16 Editorial, *Weekly Standard*, 16 November 1998, at http://www.newamericancentury.org/AttackIraq-Nov16,98.pdf [9/2005].

17 At http://www.iraqwatch.org/perspectives/rumsfeld-openletter.htm [9/2005].

18 Jonathan V. Last, 'The case for the Empire', *Weekly Standard*, 26 December 2002, at http://www.weeklystandard.com/Content/Public/Articles/000/000/001/248ipzbt.asp [9/2005].

19 Tom Clancy, *The Sum of All Fears* (New York: Berkley, 2002; first published 1991).

weapons of mass destruction. In October 1998, Attorney General Janet Reno and 200 law enforcement officials considered how they would respond to a variety of terrorist threats, including one using chemical weapons at a Washington Redskins game.[20]

There were other examples as well. Mark Burnell's *The Rhythm Section*, published in 2000, was about a woman's struggle to discover the terrorists who destroyed the plane her family were in.[21] In America's movie theatres, the terrorism theme had been a strong one. The *Die Hard* series had involved Bruce Willis defeating successive sets of terrorists in three films – *Die Hard* (1988), *Die Harder* (1990) and *Die Hard: With a Vengeance* (1995). *Die Hard*'s terrorist was a business man; those in *Die Harder* seek to free a drug dealer; in *Die Hard: With a Vengeance* the bad guy is an Eastern European. Yet despite the attack on the World Trade Center in 1993, 'Arab' terrorists did not fit the bill. Those three films grossed over $298 million in the United States.[22] *True Lies* grossed nearly half that total itself and began to develop the new terrorist template. Made in 1994, it concerned a domestic plot (husband is involved in counter-terrorism, wife doesn't know . . .) that pivots around a group of 'Islamic' terrorists – the Crimson Jihad – who are in the process of acquiring a nuclear weapon with which to threaten America. Through these films, the identity of the archytypal terrorist changes, from business extremist in the 1980s, through the drug dealer and the traditional European bad guys, into the new trope: the Islamic/Arab fanatic. On television, the cartoon series *Batman of the Future* had an episode, 'Plague', in which 'Batman teams up with Stalker, now employed by the US Government, to track down a villain named False Face who has stolen a deadly virus for a terrorist organization called KOBRA.'[23] Through all is the danger to the homeland, most particularly expressed when the terrorists have weapons of mass destruction.

Concern with terrorism in government, demands from some to invade Iraq, a theme in popular culture that America could be attacked with weapons of mass destruction, all of this predated 11 September 2001. Central elements of the decisive intervention were articulated by

20 Douglas Waller, 'Inside the hunt for Osama', *Time*, 21 December 1998.
21 Mark Burnell, *The Rhythm Section* (New York: HarperCollins, 2000).
22 'Box office history for terrorism movies', *The Numbers*, 9 September 2005, at http://www.the-numbers.com/movies/series/Terrorism.php [9/2005].
23 At http://wf.toonzone.net/WF/beyond/episodes/Plague/ [9/2005].

an American President; key elements were reproduced in popular culture, in think tanks, and in the media. But the issues were not crystallised into a new discourse, because they needed a crisis that would be constructed intersubjectively, and given a particular meaning. Hence, although the 'war on terror' was new, once it was inaugurated by the decisive intervention, it had not come 'out of the blue'. This has not been in any sense a full genealogy, but it does indicate the pre-history of the discourse. That pre-history can now be fed into the crisis process that has been developed throughout this book.

The crisis cycle

From starting with a process of a socially constructed crisis that was cyclical in nature, thinking through the second American 9/11 has produced something that is cyclic in a more complex fashion. Above all, it seems important to consider the impact of crises that do not lead to new decisive interventions; situations in which, although challenged, a discourse prevails, and adapts.

Before examining in detail the new crisis process that has been developed throughout this book, there is one particular argument that needs to be (re)established. It is commonly held that a discourse is produced by government, reproduced and amplified by social institutions. Thus, the 'war on terror' has not been and is not being produced by Fox News and PNAC, their role is, rather, one of cheerleader.[24] In a strictly narrow sense, this must be right: foreign and security policy can only be declared and enacted by government. Yet this does not get to the heart of the creation and development of a discourse. Ideas are generated and developed in a variety of places, not just in government; political momentum behind them is generated in a variety of social institutions, not just in government. That is, the community that generates the discourse is one that goes beyond government: given how many administration officials that were in PNAC, for example, it is hard to see how that could be otherwise. And pressure for developing one strand in the discourse is not limited purely to arguments in the administration or, indeed, in Congress. That is generated in a whole variety of social institutions, including the media, aspects of popular

[24] This is argued by Richard Jackson in *Writing the War on Terrorism* (Manchester: Manchester University Press, 2005); see, for example, p. 174.

culture, and the churches. There is, then, an elite responsible for a decisive intervention, and for the development and redevelopment of a discourse; and that elite exists not only in government, but across key elements in American society.

The new crisis process proposed here and illustrated in figure 7.1 therefore has the following steps. First, an event is of such magnitude that it requires (re)examination; meaning has to be ascribed. That event comes to the attention of a wider public, as well as of the policy-making community: that is, the event demands *public* understanding. There is therefore a contestation of different explanations, each of which is drawn from pre-existing narratives which may or may not have already found forms in which they can be clearly expressed. A crisis cannot be understood through an infinite number of explanations; it can only be

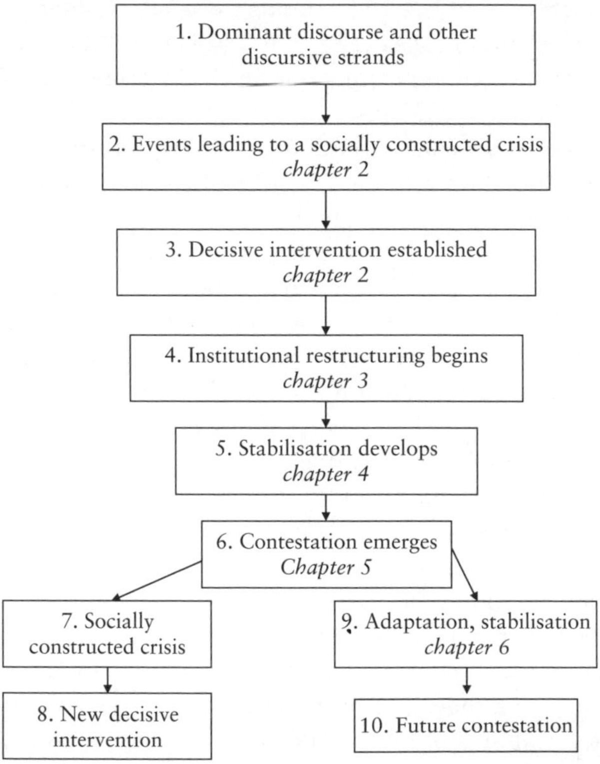

Figure 7.1. The social crisis process as a series of cycles, with application to the 'war on terror'

given meaning by those that have elements that *pre-exist*. The crisis comes to be understood through the decisive intervention that defines it, but that decisive intervention itself has a pre-history, a genealogy that allowed one set of ideas to have discursive power over others. This is shown in figure 7.1 as box 1.

In the case of the second American 9/11, alternatives to the decisive intervention – those that, for example, would have focused on Saudi guilt, or would have criminalised the acts – had little weight. From the complete confusion of the morning of 11 September 2001, the nature of the decisive intervention came to be developed from the evening of the same day. This is one of the most noteworthy features, and perhaps in part comes from the nature of contemporary America. Media power is such that explanation is immediately demanded: although it did take some days and indeed weeks for the decisive intervention to be fully articulated, it could not conceivably have taken years.

The crisis process therefore begins with an event that is understood to be a challenge to the existing way of thinking about a policy area. That is box 2 in figure 7.1. A decisive intervention successfully gives meaning to that event, and begins to create a new common sense through which all alternative narratives are seen to be 'weak', 'foolish' or 'theoretical'. This is illustrated in figure 7.1 as box 3.

That decisive intervention, in the next step, sets a new strategic direction. From explaining what has happened, those elements of the discourse that indicate what is to be done are emphasised. At the same time, those in the epistemic community of that field come largely to share the new understanding. There may be some that hold out: but they become 'mavericks' or 'old thinkers'. The epistemic community itself is defined by the parameters of the decisive intervention in that field.

In box 4, the implications of this setting of a new strategic direction are put into policy. An institutional restructuring begins which leads to particular organisations being (re)formed, practices being updated, laws being introduced or amended. That which exists is seen to be out of date, in need of remodelling. This affects in some ways all aspects of policy and of policy practice. At the same time, the institutional restructuring affects those outside of the policy world as well: in terms of the second American 9/11, it includes non-governmental organisations, academia, the media, popular culture and the churches.

Following this outreach, the discourse becomes stabilised into the policy programme. Richard Holbrooke described this phenomenon:

'Since Sept. 11, this phrase [the global war on terror] . . . has entered the English language, popularized by journalists and administration officials. It is the way our highest national priority is described by almost everyone.'[25] As Richard Jackson puts it, 'a discourse can be considered successful when its words, language, assumptions and viewpoints are adopted and employed uncritically in political discourse by opposition politicians, the media, social institutions (like churches, schools, universities, associations, pressure groups) and ordinary citizens'.[26] As has been shown in the photographs reproduced in chapter 2, in addition, understandings are reproduced in the places of everyday life and work: on the sandwich shop, by the freeway, on the walls of houses, on fences and on school buildings. This is illustrated at box 5.

Stabilisation, however, inevitably has a limited shelf-life: it will be met at some point by contestation. This is where contradictions within the discourse become evident; where the policy programme becomes contested by alternatives. In the 'war on terror', it was the claims made about the need to expand that war into Iraq that, to many, showed that the discourse was fraught with contradictions. Was Iraq part of the 'war on terror'? Was the 'war on terror' really about freedom, or about appropriating oil riches? Did the claim to be on the side of civilisation, against terrorist barbarism, really square with an invasion? Of course, some had argued previously that there were contradictions in the discourse – notably between 'freedom' and the USA Patriot Act – but it was over Iraq that these 'contradictions' came together into an alternative discourse, that of 'no war for oil'.

Contestation is at box 6, and it marks the return of crisis. But it is one that can be resolved in different ways. That crisis might be such that it can only be given meaning by a new decisive intervention, in which case debate moves to box 7, which, in terms of content, is the same as box 2. If this is so, then box 6 has the characteristics of box 1. And box 7 will be followed by a decisive intervention, as at box 8, which, in terms of content, is the same as box 3. But of course that is not inevitable immediately. A particular narrative might be able to survive discursive challenge. If there is a form of crisis, that narrative will not survive unchanged: it will have to adapt in part to that discursive challenge, and this possibility is shown at box 9. Adaptation

[25] Richard Holbrooke, 'Our enemy's face', *The Washington Post*, 9 September 2005. [26] Jackson, *Writing*, p. 159.

leads to stabilisation, which in terms of the 'war on terror' has been the period in which the 'discourse strikes back', the subject matter of chapter 6. However, stabilisation will decay into contestation, and that is at box 10, which, in terms of content, is the same as box 6.

This new, complex, social crisis process is therefore a series of cycles, as shown in figure 7.1, which also maps on to it the case of the 'war on terror' demonstrated throughout this book.

The 'war on terror'

The 'war on terror' 'began for America on September 11, 2001 . . .'[27] On the fourth anniversary of the second American 9/11, the President told his citizens that 'America answered history's call to bring justice to our enemies and to ensure the survival and success of liberty. And that mission continues today.'[28] 'History's call' – or rather, the discourse constructed from the decisive intervention, and the policy programme that followed – created a template that could be applied to America's interaction with others, whether they be foreign nationals, or American 'traitors', such as John Walker Lindh, the so-called American Taliban.[29] It was a template to be called upon in times of national crisis. Hurricane Katrina's devastation of New Orleans and the Gulf coast, and the lacklustre response of government at various levels, had led to much criticism of the President by that fourth anniversary. He responded by making a link between the hurricane and the American response on 11 September 2001. In both there had been sorrow and misery; government investment and a determination to succeed, to 'win'; an outpouring of international compassion; and a call for national togetherness.[30]

Those unhappy with the policy programme – above all, over the war in, and occupation of, Iraq – struggled to find alternative narratives. Most often, an old template came to hand: that of Vietnam. In the

[27] President George W. Bush, 'President proclaims national days of prayer and remembrance', 9 September 2005, at http://www.whitehouse.gov/news/releases/2005/09/20050909-10.html [9/2005].

[28] President George W. Bush, 'President's radio address', 10 September 2005, at http://www.whitehouse.gov/news/releases/2005/09/20050910.html [9/2005].

[29] See Dave Lindorff, 'John Walker Lindh, revisited', *Counterpunch*, 5/6 June 2004, at http://counterpunch.org/lindorff06052004.html [9/2005].

[30] For example, 'President's radio address', 10 September 2005, cited in note 28.

summer of 2005, those supporting 'Camp Casey' – Cindy Sheehan's camp outside the President's residence in Crawford, Texas – were boosted by the support of Jeff Rogers whose father, William P. Rogers, had been Secretary of State for President Nixon. Rogers explained that his father had come to see that the Vietnam War was a mistake, while in office. The parallel with Iraq was made clear.[31] As Josh Getlin and Elizabeth Mehren put it in the *Los Angeles Times*, the Vietnam War offered many an analogy to the Iraq occupation 'because the underlying argument for that conflict – the need for the United States to fight communist expansion – gradually gave way to a belief that the war was bogged down in a quagmire that was killing thousands of Americans a year'.[32] And so the question – 'Is Iraq the new Vietnam?' – was a crucial one in terms of creating a contradiction within the discourse.[33]

In facing this apparent contradiction, the 'war on terror' narrative required continued links to be made between al-Qaeda and Iraq. For example, on 22 August 2005, the President said, in a speech to the Veterans of Foreign Wars:

> Iraq is a central front in the war on terror. It is a vital part of our mission. Terrorists like bin Laden and his ally, Zarqawi, are trying to turn Iraq into what Afghanistan was under the Taliban . . . Terrorists are trying to block the rise of democracy in Iraq, because they know a free Iraq will deal a decisive blow to their strategy to achieve absolute power.[34]

The occupation of Iraq would help prevent a third American 9/11. It had that vital purpose and, thereby, formed a narrative at least as powerful as the 'new Vietnam' narrative. But in this discursive contest, there was no third way; and, unwilling to support the President for domestic political reasons, and unwilling to take on the establishment

[31] Warren Vieth, 'Bush defends war amid Texas protests', *Los Angeles Times*, 21 August 2005.

[32] Josh Getlin and Elizabeth Mehren, 'War could pivot on US hearts and minds', *Los Angeles Times*, 21 August 2001.

[33] For example, Seymour Hersh, 'Moving targets: will the counter insurgency plan in Iraq repeat the mistakes of Vietnam?', *The New Yorker*, 15 December 2003, at http://www.newyorker.com/fact/content/?031215fa_fact; Jeff Jacoby, 'Iraq is no Vietnam', *Boston Globe*, 25 August 2005, at http://www.boston.com/news/globe/editorial_opinion/oped/articles/2005/08/25/iraq_is_no_vietnam/ [both 9/2005].

[34] George W. Bush, 'President honors veterans of foreign wars', 22 August 2005, at http://www.whitehouse.gov/news/releases/2005/08/20050822-1.html [8/2005].

by pressing for a recognition of the implications of the Vietnam analogy, the Democrats were politically paralysed in the period after the presidential election of 2004. They simply had no alternative narrative with which to engage the 'war on terror' and, thus, nothing to say on the subject.[35]

The power of the 'war on terror' trapped the Democrats – and many other political and social institutions – within, silencing other interpretations and policy programmes. In the summer of 2005, New Mexico Governor, Bill Richardson, declared a state of emergency, as the total numbers of immigrants apprehended in three border counties exceeded 40,000 in the year.[36] Yet this was not an urgent problem, apparently, in the 'war on terror'. And neither was the growth in the threat from domestic terrorism: since the bombing in Oklahoma City, the Southern Poverty Law Center has traced sixty actual, planned or thwarted terrorist attacks from white supremacists and militias in the United States.[37] Yet neither migration nor far-right violence seemed to fit the 'war on terror' template.

The 'war on terror', then, was in large part concerned with a battle of narratives. This can perhaps be further illustrated by looking at three alternate readings. The first suggests that the discourse of the 'war on terror' has helped increase the power of its opponents. The second shows how the discourse creates 'extreme' fears, and then constructs those fears into 'realities'. The third argues that within the 'war on terror' discourse there are rhetorical devices and elements of a policy programme concerned with infringing those human rights explicitly supported by the 'war on terror'.

Could it be that the 'war on terror' has actually increased the popularity and power of those ranged against America and its interests? On first reading, this seems ludicrous. The military power of al-Qaeda and its Taliban ally was heavily destroyed in the war in Afghanistan. Significant numbers of al-Qaeda leaders and operatives have been arrested around

[35] Ronald Brownstein, 'Political leaders silence on Iraq War is a dereliction of duty', *Los Angeles Times*, 22 August 2005.

[36] Ralph Blumentham, 'For one family, front row seats to border crisis', *New York Times*, 23 August 2005.

[37] See Andrew Blejwas, Anthony Griggs and Mark Potok, 'Terror from the right', *Southern Poverty Law Center* (Summer 2005), at http://www.splcenter.org/intel/intelreport/article.jsp?aid=549 [9/2005].

the world. Terrorist operations have been thwarted. And whatever view is taken of the war in Iraq, at least the possibility of new weapons of mass destruction being developed in that country has been halted. Thus, the capabilities of al-Qaeda have been massively degraded.

Although all of this may be so, it does not follow that capabilities have actually been undermined. The occupation of Iraq has provided plenty of opportunities for training in terrorism, for recruitment, and for securing weapons. And since the second American 9/11, recruitment has developed in parts of the world that were new to the bin Laden enterprise: the attacks on London in 2005 were carried out by British nationals. Capabilities have therefore changed.

Yet what of intentions? What if it is not the case that the terrorist campaign against America and its allies is motivated by a hatred of western values? What if it is motivated by a hatred of American *actions*? That message was clear in Osama bin Laden's video speech released just before the 2004 presidential elections. He said:

> I say to you that security is an indispensable pillar of human life and that free men do not forfeit their security, contrary to Bush's claim that we hate freedom . . . we fight because we are free men who don't sleep under oppression. We want to restore freedom to our nation, just as you lay waste to our nation. So shall we lay waste to yours . . . I say to you, Allah knows that it had never occurred to us to strike the towers. But after it became unbearable and we witnessed the oppression and tyranny of the American/Israeli coalition against our people in Palestine and Lebanon, it came to my mind.[38]

There then followed a clear narrative. In 1982, America allowed Israel to invade Lebanon. The US Sixth Fleet bombarded the coast. Many people – women and children included – were killed and maimed. This oppression of Muslims continued: in the mass slaughter of children in Iraq in the sanctions; in the indiscriminate killing of Muslims in Iraq in the 2003 war. Terrorism is therefore about changing American policy, about defending Muslims and Islamic lands, fundamentally, about justice.

One can argue of course with the logic of this position; but it is important to see it as a narrative if it is to be fully engaged. Where are the contradictions in this discourse? How might alternative narratives

[38] 'Full transcript of bin Laden's speech', *Al-Jazeera*, 1 November 2004, at http://english.aljazeera.net/NR/exeres/79C6AF22-98FB-4A1C-B21F-2BC36E87F61F.htm [9/2005].

be constructed? Osama bin Laden took very great care in the construction of his story. In his 2004 video, he outlined those interviews that he had given that comprise the text of the narrative. He had thought about the genealogy of his struggle. Saudi Arabia was betrayed when the kingdom was created in 1932, by a family who spoke about Islam, but acted solely in their own interests. Then, that same family humiliated Muslims by inviting Americans into the country in 1990, despoiling the holiest sites of Islam. But it was the Americans who were fundamentally guilty.[39] As in 1982, and in the sanctions after the Gulf War, it was American *actions* that were at fault. In an interview in 1997 with Peter Arnett of CNN, bin Laden put this quite clearly:

> We declared jihad against the US government, because the US government is unjust, criminal and tyrannical. It has committed acts that are extremely unjust, hideous and criminal whether directly or through its support of the Israeli occupation of the Prophet's Night Travel Land [Palestine]. And we believe the US is directly responsible for those who were killed in Palestine, Lebanon and Iraq.[40]

And again, in an interview with ABC's John Miller, in 1998:

> The call to wage war against America was made because America has spearheaded the crusade against the Islamic nation, sending tens of thousands of its troops to the land of the two Holy Mosques over and above its meddling in its affairs and its politics, and its support of the oppressive, corrupt and tyrannical regime that is in control. These are the reasons behind the singling out of America as a target . . . Their presence has no meaning save one and that is to offer support to the Jews in Palestine who are in need of their Christian brothers to achieve full control over the Arab Peninsula which they intend to make an important part of the so called Greater Israel.[41]

And again: in an interview in *Time* in 1999, bin Laden said: 'The Americans should expect reactions from the Muslim world that are proportionate to the injustice they inflict.'[42]

[39] Interview between bin Laden and Robert Fisk for *The Independent* in 1996, at http://www.robert-fisk.com/fisk_interview3.htm [9/2005].

[40] 'Transcript of Osama Bin Laden interview by Peter Arnett', at http://www.anusha.com/osamaint.htm [9/2005].

[41] 'Interview: Osama bin Laden', *Frontline ABC*, May 1998, at http://www.pbs.org/wgbh/pages/frontline/shows/binladen/who/interview.html [9/2005].

[42] 'Wrath of God', *Time Asia*, 153:1, 11 January 1999, at http://www.time.com/time/asia/asia/magazine/1999/990111/osama1.html [9/2005].

In all of this, bin Laden's focus was on American actions, not on American values. Michael Scheuer, the former CIA agent who was the 'head of the CIA's bin Laden unit', put this very clearly.[43] 'Is it possible . . . that US actions could easily be viewed by Muslims as attacks on Islam, its people, and its lands? That is, is it possible that Muslims perceive US actions in the Islamic world in a manner like that with which they perceived Soviet actions in Afghanistan? Unfortunately, the objective answer must be yes . . .'[44] One can argue with the use of the term 'objective' here, but the point is clear: American actions, not values, are the target. And it was related to a point made by Sir Michael Jay, Britain's top foreign policy official: war in Iraq would 'fuel extremism' in the British Muslim community, he predicted, over twelve months ahead of the bombs in London in July 2005.[45]

Therefore, greater involvement in the Islamic world – occupations in Iraq and Afghanistan, support for and pressure on governments such as those in Egypt and Saudi Arabia, perceived pro-Israeli policies – all of these will give validity to Osama bin Laden's narrative. Now there may be good reasons for all of these American policies: but they have consequences. And to the extent that all of these have been part of the discourse of the 'war on terror', that discourse has supported the very narrative that it seeks to undermine.

A second alternative reading of the 'war on terror' suggests that it creates fears, and then looks to see them realised. From the end of 2001 and into 2002, fears were raised that America would be subjected to terrorist attacks by Americans against iconic targets. Men arrested in Detroit for planning a variety of terrorist attacks – including Disneyland in California – were found guilty; only to be released when the prosecution's evidence was found to be flawed.[46] A US District

[43] From 'Inside 9/11', *National Geographic*, shown in August 2005. Available on the website http://channel.nationalgeographic.com/channel/inside911/ [/2005].

[44] Michael Scheuer (Anonymous), *Imperial Hubris: How the West is Losing the War on Terror* (Washington, DC: Brassey's, 2004), pp. 10–11.

[45] Sir Michael Jay, Permanent Secretary at the Foreign and Commonwealth Office, in a note dated May 2004 to Foreign Secretary Jack Straw, reported in 'Straw plays down Iraq war warning', BBC, 20 August 2005, at http://news.bbc.co.uk/1/hi/uk_politics/4196440.stm [9/2005].

[46] See Bennett L. Gershman, 'How juries get it wrong – anatomy of the Detroit terror case', *Washburn Law Journal*, 44 (2005), at http://washburnlaw.edu/wlj/44-2/articles/gers.pdf [9/2005].

Judge held: 'In its best light, the record would show that the prosecution committed a pattern of mistakes and oversights that deprived the defendants of discoverable evidence (including impeachment material) and created a record filled with misleading inferences that such material did not exist . . .'[47] Perhaps it was unsurprising that the prosecutors went beyond their brief: the Attorney General, John Ashcroft, was sanctioned by the courts for his comments on the guilt of the men before trial.[48] Then there were fears that those attacks would involve weapons of mass destruction. Jose Padilla seemed to illustrate this combination of threats perfectly. But there has been no evidence that Padilla actually had any such weapons: the plot was, in the words of FBI Director, John Mueller, in the 'discussion stage'.[49] It took three and a half years for Padilla to be charged, and then it was with conspiracy to murder, and membership of a terrorist support cell.[50]

Such instances were repeated at lower levels throughout America. One woman listened to a conversation between three Muslim-American men in a Georgia diner. She told police that they were making jokes about the destruction of the Twin Towers, and that she thought they were making plans for a new attack. On her evidence, and her recording of the vehicle number plate, the three men were held by police in Florida for seventeen hours while searched and interrogated. Nothing was found, and they were released. The three were medical students about to attend a course in Miami, from which they were barred, for their 'notoriety' would get in the way of 'patient care'. In this case, Brendan Miniter wrote in the *Wall Street Journal*, 'the justice system worked'.[51] Army captain James Yee was accused of espionage, passing messages to and from al Qaeda to those held in Guantanamo

[47] District Judge Gerald Rosen quoted in 'Judge tosses Detroit terror case', *CBS News*, 2 September 2004, at http://www.cbsnews.com/stories/2004/08/31/terror/main639871.shtml [9/2005].

[48] David Shepardson, 'Ashcroft sanctioned for violating gag order in Detroit terror trial', *Detroit News*, 16 December 2003, at http://www.detnews.com/2003/metro/0312/16/metro-10844.htm [9/2005].

[49] See 'US authorities capture "dirty bomb" suspect', CNN, 10 June 2002, at http://archives.cnn.com/2002/US/06/10/dirty.bomb.suspect/ [9/2005].

[50] 'Terror suspect Padilla charged', CNN, 22 November 2005, at http://www.cnn.com/2005/LAW/11/22/padilla.case/ [12/2005].

[51] Brendan Miniter, 'Arresting developments', *Wall Street Journal,* opinion page, 17 September 2002, at http://www.opinionjournal.com/columnists/bminiter/?id=110002276 [9/2005].

Bay. Yee, an army Muslim 'chaplain', was widely vilified: he spent seventy-six days in solitary confinement. And yet, less than a year later, all charges were dropped, and he was reinstated to continue his army career without even a reprimand on his record.[52]

The process of naming terrors – the enemy within, with or without weapons of mass destruction – and then identifying those who fit the constructed bill continues. The fear in California is of a combination of Islamicist terrorists and Los Angeles gangs. 'Los Angeles Police Chief William Bratton said he has long believed prisons are fertile ground for terrorists.'[53] The *Los Angeles Times* ran a series of articles on the link, following some arrests, that seemed to illustrate its reality.[54]

American society, then, has become sensitised to the threats that it faces: those in society are encouraged to think the worst. This was well summed up in an opinion piece by Peggy Noonan in the *Wall Street Journal*. Writing about the 'mistake' of closing military bases, she wrote: 'The federal government is doing something right now that is exactly the opposite of what it should be doing. It is forgetting to think dark. It is forgetting to imagine the unimaginable.'[55] The focus was on the threats of foreign terrorists, inspired by Osama bin Laden's narrative, trained abroad who seek revenge on the United States, such as Mohammed Atta and the other eighteen hijackers; Richard Reid, the shoe bomber; and Ahmed Ressam, arrested at the Canadian border in 1999, apparently determined on bombing Los Angeles International Airport. In addition, Americans have become fearful of ghosts within the country, and this is directly attributable to the 'war on terror' discourse. Peter Bergen argued that 'since 9/11 there has been no evidence of sleepers . . . operating in the United States. Either these sleeper cells are so asleep they are effectively dead, or they simply don't exist.

[52] Laura Parker, 'The ordeal of Chaplain Yee', *USA Today*, 16 May 2004. The campaign to secure an official apology to Yee is at http://www.captainyee.org/

[53] In Matt Krasnowski, 'Probe fans fears of prison terror plots', *San Diego Union Tribune*, 22 August 2005, at http://www.signonsandiego.com/news/nation/terror/20050822-9999-1n22prison.html [9/2005].

[54] See, for example (all in the *Los Angeles Times*), Greg Krikorian, 'Arrest made in possible terror plot', 16 August 2005; Greg Krikorian and Jenifer Warren, 'Terror probe targets a Folsom prison', 17 August 2005; Solomon Moore, 'Radical Islam an issue in prisons', 20 August 2005.

[55] Peggy Noonan, 'Think dark', *Wall Street Journal*, opinion page, 25 August 2005, at http://www.opinionjournal.com/columnists/pnoonan/?id=110007154 [9/2005].

The onset of the Iraq War and the presidential election both offered perfect occasions for the supposed cells to strike, but nothing happened.'[56] The 'war on terror' encourages all to think about that which over ten years before the second American 9/11 Tom Clancy had called 'the sum of all fears'.

A third aspect of an alternative reading of the impact of the 'war on terror' discourse examines the implications for those named as terrorists. As shown above, to be accused of terrorist acts can lead to imprisonment without trial, even if the accused is an American. And even if the accusation is false, it can lead to the destruction of careers, and undoubtedly, of personal relationships. But it has led to worse, and that is because of the nature of the stakes.

In the 'war on terror', the terrorists are the ultimate enemies: they are barbarians, who seek to destroy civilisation itself. And so all means of defeating that enemy are in some ways legitimised. When a group of National Guardsmen were charged with using a stun gun on a captured Iraqi, who was handcuffed and blindfolded, their potential courts-martial were referred to by Lieutenant Colonel Cliff Kent as being for 'suspected terrorist abuse'.[57] The designation of the term 'terrorist' came before any trial; and of course was also being used to indicate that a different standard of treatment was acceptable.

That different standard of treatment was fully part of the policy programme of the 'war on terror'. In a memorandum to the President in January 2002, White House Counsel Alberto Gonzalez wrote that in his opinion and that of the Department of Justice, the Geneva Convention III on the Treatment of Prisoners of War did not apply to those captured al-Qaeda and Taliban fighters.[58] As Donald Rumsfeld put it:

> The al-Qaeda is not a country. They did not behave as an army. They did not wear uniforms. They did not have insignia. They did not carry their weapons openly. They are a terrorist network. It would be a total misunderstanding of the Geneva Convention if one considers al-Qaeda, a terrorist network, to

[56] Peter Bergen, 'Beware the Holy War', *The Nation*, 20 June 2005, at http://www.thenation.com/doc/20050620/bergen/7 [7/2005].

[57] In 'Guardsmen in Fullerton Unit face courts-martial', *Los Angeles Times*, 23 August 2005.

[58] Original at http://msnbc.com/modules/newsweek/pdf/gonzales_memo.pdf [9/2005].

be an army . . . the Taliban also did not wear uniforms, they did not have insignia, they did not carry their weapons openly, and they were tied tightly at the waist to al-Qaeda . . . there isn't any question in my mind but that they are not, they would not rise to the standard of a prisoner of war.[59]

Thus, those prisoners held in Guantanamo Bay would not have formal, internationally recognised rights. They would not have American rights either, according to the administration, for the sovereignty of the base ultimately lay with Cuba, not the United States. By the end of 2004, the International Committee of the Red Cross issued a report in which it said that the treatment of prisoners at Guantanamo Bay was 'cruel, inhumane and degrading . . .'[60]

In August 2002, Gonzalez wrote in a confidential memorandum for the President in which torture was redefined to be that which must 'inflict pain that is difficult to endure'.[61] At the time that this legal work was underway, Americans were torturing and murdering prisoners at Bagram Collection Point detention centre in Afghanistan, according to a 2,000-page official army investigation that lead to several charges.[62] One of the deaths was of a man held to be innocent of any wrong doing; he was simply in the wrong place, at the wrong time. Later, in Iraq in 2004, a scandal emerged at Abu Ghraib. Seymour Hersh's article in the *New Yorker* was just the beginning: unlike Bagram, there were many photographs showing an extraordinary range of abuse of prisoners.[63] *Newsweek* argued that 'as a means of pre-empting a repeat of 9/11, Bush, along with Defense Secretary Rumsfeld and Attorney General John Ashcroft, signed off on a secret system of detention and interrogation that opened the door to such methods'.[64] By the summer

59 In 'Secretary Rumsfeld media availability en route to Camp X-Ray', *Dodd News*, 27 January 2005, at http://www.dod.mil/transcripts/2002/t01282002_t0127sd2.html [9/2005].

60 Josh White and John Mints, 'Red Cross cites "inhumane" treatment at Guantanamo', *Washington Post*, 1 December 2004.

61 'Memorandum for the President re: Standards of conduct for interrogation', 1 August 2002, at http://www.washingtonpost.com/wp-srv/nation/documents/dojinterrogationmemo20020801.pdf [9/2005].

62 See Tim Golden, 'In US report, brutal details of 2 Afghan inmates' deaths', *New York Times*, 20 May 2005.

63 Seymour Hersh, 'Torture at Abu Ghraib', *The New Yorker*, 10 May 2004, at http://www.newyorker.com/fact/content/?040510fa_fact [5/2005].

64 John Barry, Michael Hirsh and Michael Isikoff, 'The roots of torture', *Newsweek*, 24 May 2005, at http://msnbc.msn.com/id/4989481/ [9/2005].

of 2004, at least eight separate official enquiries were underway into allegations of serial abuse by the US military.[65]

It was Abu Ghraib in particular that focused concerns on how the 'war on terror' was being conducted. President Bush gave interviews with *al-Arabiya* and *Alhurra* in May 2004 to try to manage the crisis. He said that he viewed 'the Abu Ghraib prison abuses as abhorrent'. And he was cited as saying that 'What took place at Abu Ghraib does not represent America, which is a compassionate country that believes in freedom.'[66] The contradiction in the policy programme was clear for all to see. Yet despite all the revulsion at the acts and the evidence of the abuse, as Elizabeth Holtzman argued, 'it has prompted no investigative commission (in the manner of the 9/11 commission) with a mandate to find the whole truth, or full-scale bipartisan Congressional hearings, as occurred during Watergate. Indeed, it is as though the Watergate investigations ended with the prosecution of only the burglars . . .'[67]

The pattern is fairly clear: the enemies in the 'war on terror' are so appalling that it has been 'common sense' to change the rules of war and detention so that those enemies might be 'encouraged' to provide vital information. Constructing an ultimate enemy contains the seeds of dehumanisation, and it is that which has become part of the policy programme. Needless to say, the treatment of prisoners by some Americans in the 'war on terror', and the changing legal guarantees of rights, was taken as evidence by those who argued from within the 'no war for oil' discourse that they had been right all along. Not In Our Name declared: 'The true nature of the American occupation has been revealed to the world. It is an occupation of abuse and torture that is dehumanizing and denying all human rights to the Iraqi people.'[68]

Misreading the nature of the 'enemy', and thereby giving discursive resources to that enemy; being consumed with conjuring up fears, and

[65] See 'US military prisoner abuse inquiries', *Canadian Broadcasting Corporation*, 23 August 2004, at http://www.cbc.ca/news/background/iraq/prisonabuse_inquiries.html [9/2005]

[66] The President's remarks in 'Global message', 6 May 2004, at http://www.whitehouse.gov/news/releases/2004/05/20040506-1.html [9/2005].

[67] Elizabeth Holtzman, 'Torture and accountability', *The Nation*, 18 July 2005, at http://www.thenation.com/docprint.mhtml?i=20050718&s=holtzman [9/2005].

[68] See the statement at http://www.notinourname.net/war/statement-prison-10may04.htm [9/2005].

then constructing evidence of them; and dehumanising the enemy, leading to acts damaging to the strategic direction of the 'war on terror: all had been part of the record of post-second 9/11 America. But above all, the power of the discourse rested in the way in which it affected everyday life. The nation's key icons have been affected. Visitors were unable to visit Liberty Island after the attacks; over four years later, access was still only to the pedestal. Certain vehicles were no longer allowed to cross the Hoover Dam. Vehicles were no longer permitted to stop on the Golden Gate Bridge, due to security restrictions.[69] The 'war on terror' has been reflected to Americans through the television news and the newspapers; in books and novels; on television and in the cinema; and in a multitude of images on sandwich shops, by freeways, in the street and on school buildings. As Marc Siegel put it in *USA Today*, 'Terrorism is everywhere. Only it isn't.'[70] Terrorism is not a more common event than deaths through cancer or traffic accidents, through homicides or drug taking. But it *feels* different. That is the power of a discourse.

[69] On the Statue of Liberty, see http://www.nps.gov/stli/prod02.htm. On the Hoover Dam, see http://www.usbr.gov/lc/hooverdam/crossingguide.pdf.

[70] Marc Siegel, 'Terrorism is everywhere. Only it isn't', *USA Today*, 9 August 2005.

Select bibliography

Alexander, Bevin, *How America Got It Right*, New York: Dutton, 2005

Anderson, Jeffrey, *Sleeper Cell*, New York: Berkley, 2005

Bacevich, Andrew J., *American Empire*, Cambridge, MA: Harvard University Press, 2002

The New American Militarism, New York: Oxford University Press, 2005

Bergen, Peter, *Holy War Inc.*, New York: Free Press, 2002

Brown, Dale, *Act of War*, New York: Atari, 2005

Brown, Michael E. (ed.), *Grave New World*, Washington, DC: Georgetown University Press, 2003

Burke, Robert, *Counter Terrorism for Emergency Responders*, Boca Raton, FL: Lewis Publishers, 2000

Buzzell, Colby, *My War: Killing Time in Iraq*, New York: Putnam Books, 2005

Calhoun, Craig, Price, Paul and Timmer, Ashley (eds.), *Understanding September 11*, New York: New Press, 2002

Chesnoff, Michael, *The Arrogance of the French: Why They Can't Stand Us – and Why the Feeling is Mutual*, New York: Sentinel, 2005

Clancy, Tom, *The Teeth of the Tiger*, New York: G. P. Putnam, 2003

Clarke, Richard, *Against All Enemies: Inside America's War on Terror*, New York: Free Press, 2004

Coulter, Ann, *How to Talk to a Liberal (If You Must)*, New York: Crown Forum, 2004

Crawford, John, *The Last True Story I'll Ever Tell*, New York: Riverhead Books, 2005

Crouch, Paul, *The Shadow of the Apocalypse*, New York: Berkley, 2004

Cunningham, Michael, *Specimen Days*, New York: Farrar, Straus & Giroux, 2005

DeFelice, Jim, *Threat Level Black*, New York: Pocket Books, 2005

DeMille, Nelson, *Night Fall*, New York, Warner, 2004

Dickson, Paul, *Sputnik: The Shock of the Century*, New York: Walker & Co., 2001

Dixon, Wheeler Winston (ed.), *Film and Television after 9/11*, Carbondale, IL: Southern Illinois University Press, 2004

Dwyer, Jim and Flynn, Kevin, *102 Minutes: The Untold Story of the Fight to Survive Inside the Twin Towers*, New York: Times Books, 2005

Eagleton, Terry, *After Theory*, London: Penguin, 2003

Edkins, Jenny, *Trauma and the Memory of Politics*, Cambridge: Cambridge University Press, 2003

Evans, Michael D., *Beyond Iraq: The Next Move – Ancient Prophecy and Modern Day Conspiracy Collide*, Tulsa, OK: Harrison House, 2003

The American Prophecies: Ancient Scriptures Reveal Our Nation's Future, New York: Warner Faith, 2004

Flynn, Stephen, *America the Vulnerable: How Our Government is Failing to Protect us from Terrorism*, New York: HarperCollins, 2004

Franken, Al, *Lies and the Lying Liars Who Tell Them*, New York: Dutton Adult, 2003

Freiling, Thomas M. (ed.), *George W. Bush On God and Country*, Fairfax, VA: Allegiance Press, 2004

Frum, David, *The Right Man*, London: Weidenfeld & Nicolson, 2003

Gaddis, John Lewis, *Surprise, Security and the American Experience*, Cambridge, MA: Harvard University Press, 2004

Griffin, W. E. B., *By Order of the President*, New York: Putnam, 2004

Hannity, Sean, *Deliver us from Evil: Defeating Terrorism, Despotism and Liberalism*, New York: Regan Books, 2005

Hartley, Jason Christopher, *Just Another Soldier*, New York: HarperCollins, 2005

Hay, Colin, *The Political Economy of New Labour*, Manchester: Manchester University Press, 1999

Huntington, Samuel, *Who Are We? America's Great Debate*, London: Simon & Schuster, 2004

Jackson, Richard, *Writing the War on Terrorism*, Manchester: Manchester University Press, 2005

Jeffrey, Grant, *War on Terror: Unfolding Bible Prophecy*, New York: Water Brook Press, 2002

Kagan, Robert, *Paradise and Power: America and Europe in the New World Order*, New York: Random House, 2003

Kent, Gordon, *Force Protection*, New York: Delacorte, 2004

Krugman, Paul, *The Great Unraveling*, New York: W. W. Norton, 2004

Ledeen, Michael, *The War Against the Terror Masters*, New York: St Martin's Press, 2002

Ludlum, Robert and Lynds, Gayle, *Robert Ludlam's The Paris Option*, New York: St Martin's Griffin, July 2002

MacDonald, William, *Armageddon Soon?*, Kansas City: Walterick Publishers, 1991

Malkin, Michelle, *Invasion: How America Still Welcomes Terrorists, Criminals and Other Foreign Menaces to Our Shores*, Washington, DC: Regnery, 2002

In Defense of Internment: The Case for 'Racial Profiling' in World War Two and the War on Terror, Washington, DC: Regnery, 2004

Marsh, David, Buller, Jim, Hay, Colin, Johnston, Jim, Kerr, Peter, McAnulla, Stuart and Watson, Mathew, *Postwar British Politics in Perspective*, Cambridge: Polity Press, 1999

McCourt, Frank, Giuliani, Rudy and Von Essen, Thomas, *Brotherhood*, New York: American Express Publications, 2004

Miniter, Richard, *Losing Bin Laden: How Bill Clinton's Failures Unleashed Global Terror*, Washington, DC: Regnery, 2003

Shadow War: The Untold Story of How Bush is Winning the War on Terror, Washington, DC: Regnery, 2004

Munslow, Alun, *The New History*, Harlow: Pearson, 2003

Rampton, Sheldon and Stauber, John, *Weapons of Mass Deception*, New York: Jeremy P. Tarcher, 2003

Reich, Christopher, *The Devil's Banker*, New York: Dell, 2003

Robinson, Patrick, *Barracuda 945*, New York: Harper Torch, 2004

Rosenberg, Joel C., *The Last Jihad: A Novel*, New York: Forge, 2002

Savage, Michael, *Liberalism is a Mental Disorder*, Nashville, TN: Nelson Current, 2005

Schmidt, Vivien, *The Futures of European Capitalism*, Oxford: Oxford University Press, 2002

Schweikart, Larry and Allen, Michael Patrick, *A Patriot's History of the United States*, New York: Sentinel, 2004

Silberstein, Sandra, *War of Words*, London: Routledge, 2002

Spiegelman, Art, *In the Shadow of No Towers*, New York: Pantheon, 2004

Stelzer, Irwin M., *The NeoCon Reader*, London: Atlantic Books, 2004

Todd, Emmanuel, *After the Empire*, New York: Columbia University Press, 2003

Weigl, George, *The Cube and the Cathedral*, New York: Basic Books, 2005

Weisman, John, *SOAR*, New York: Avon, 2003

Whitcomb, Christopher, *White*, New York: Little, Brown & Co., 2005

Woodward, Bob, *Plan of Attack*, New York: Simon & Schuster, 2004

Zeman, David, *The Pinocchio Syndrome*, New York: Doubleday, 2003

Index